No Finish Line

Discovering the World's Secrets
One Bird at a Time

Bernard F. Master

LITTLE WHITE DOG PRESS

PUBLISHED BY LITTLE WHITE DOG PRESS

Little
White
Dog
Press

ISBN-10: 0989158977
ISBN-13: 978-0-9891589-7-8
Full Color Edition

Dedicated to those who love me
and to those whom I love:

Grandpop Joseph Majeski, Grandmom Sophie
Master, Gilbert and Leona, Julie, Susan, Ken and
Chris, Dana and Rene, Eric and Tara, Sarah, Alex,
Emmett, Astrid, Luke, and Wyatt.

The Quest for the Holy Rail
By Jui Ling Roark

Like a mediaeval monk, he rises alone
in the darkness and stillness that come before dawn.
His purpose is pure, aesthetic, ascetic...
(while others lie warm in their beds. How pathetic!)

He searches the skies, from its depth to its height
Prayerful and watchful for a glimpse, for the sigh,
For a sign of God's gift, the mystery of flight
made manifest to any and all with insight.

Communing with nature, his eyes pierce the gloom,
in search of winged creatures, his vision's on "zoom".
From the shores of Lake Erie to the plains of Khartoum.

His mission undaunted, his faith is rewarded.
It must be the most any man has recorded...
He's counted each one in a way quite religious
and the sum of his prayers is a number prodigious.

But they're birds and not angels, on a wing and a prayer,
that he's counted and named with such consummate care.
So the point of this poem is the man with the quest
Is our neighborhood ornithologist!

ANNOTATED TABLE OF CONTENTS

COVER PHOTOS

*All photos taken by Bernard F. Master
(from top to bottom)*

Lilac-breasted Roller, Serengeti, Tanzania

Rueppell's Griffon, Waza, Cameroon

Rufous Hummingbird, Apple Creek, Ohio

Short-tailed Frogmouth, taken at night, Mount Kerinci, Sumatra, Indonesia

Mount Chimborazo, taken from Papallacta Pass, Ecuador

A portion of the proceeds from this book will be donated to global conservation efforts so that future generations can enjoy the splendor of birding and the outdoors.

FOREWORD

Foreword by Bill Thompson III, owner and publisher of Bird Watcher's Digest, *a master birder, author of ten birding books, popular master of ceremonies at national birding events and peerless raconteur.*

The tall, impeccably groomed, mustachioed man behind the steering wheel suddenly turned over his right shoulder and sternly said: "Cut the crap! This is serious business! I don't want to spend the next twenty-four hours listening to you two guys razz each other! Enough! We've got birds to see!"

This was my first meeting with Dr. Bernard Master. Four of us were in his luxury SUV, twenty minutes into an Ohio Big Day birding record attempt. A Big Day is when you try to see as many birds as possible in a set geographic area within a single twenty-four-hour period. Our mutual friend and fellow avid birder, Jim McCormac, had invited me along as a member of the team. As we drove up Ohio Route 23 north, headed for Lake Erie and a midnight start, Jim and I began needling each other, as we always do. It went on for only a few minutes before Bernie put a stop to it. This was my first clue that Dr. Bernie Master took things seriously. It was embarrassing to be reprimanded like a misbehaving schoolboy, but before long Bernie—as if nothing had ever happened—began asking me about music, my work at *Bird Watcher's Digest*, and where I'd traveled as a birder. We had a fantastic, if tiring, day—getting along well to the very end, and finishing with 186 species. I recall Bernie being chagrined that we'd missed the record—a seemingly impossible total of 206 set years earlier. His intensity as a strategist and competitor seemed at odds with his affability.

There are some human beings who seem to live on a different plane of existence. You can spot them a mile away—they're the ones whose personalities electrify a room when they enter. They move and speak with a confidence that stands out. They always seem to know people wherever they go, and this is because they meet new friends so easily. People are naturally drawn to them, as if there were some actual magnetic quality to their presence. That's because there is.

In the movie *Forrest Gump*, fate and fortune place the lead character at the center of some of history's (and pop culture's) most remarkable moments. Reading the stories contained in the book you now hold, you'll note a similar right-place, right-time theme. Connect the dots of Bernie Master's life and you'll note that he is one of those magical souls. His life is awhirl with fame, fortune, warfare, disease, invitations from European royalty and the highest levels of American politics, courtroom drama, social and economic change, world travel, intrigue, kidnapping, show business, and the back-stabbing, friend-losing, drunk-with-greed realm of corporate America. Oh and he's a birder who has seen a few thousand birds here and there.

Bernie Master has spent his life in a determined, tireless pursuit of several things: success as a family man, success as a doctor, success as a businessman, success as a birder—all of which he achieved. What's most impressive to me is not Bernie's incredible record of success in the business world—where his business acumen has taken him to the top. One gets the sense in reading about his life, that he has an ability to focus very, very intensely. He is passionate about success. And his success has given him the opportunity to do many good things. Chief among them is his support of bird conservation causes all over the world. I feel certain that the satisfaction that Bernie felt in successfully taking his own company public pales in comparison to the feelings derived from making a difference in the world of bird conservation.

He's the epitome of doing well by doing good.

Bernie Master is a world birder. To be a world birder—someone who tries to see as many of the world's 10,000-plus bird species in their lifetime as possible—typically requires a lot of money and a lot of time. It's not cheap to fly to Madagascar or Malaysia to seek endemic birds in remote habitats. I've run into world birders in many places in my years of birding travel. They are typically middle-aged men, very wealthy, with a lot of ego tied up in ratcheting up their world bird list as fast as possible. It's an imposing challenge to see some of the truly rare birds of the world. Once, on a trek in the Philippines, on the island of Mindanao, I was with a small group trying to see the Philippine Eagle, one of the largest and rarest raptors in the world. After a morning-long, very challenging hike up a rough trail through the jungle, we emerged on a small clearing, and our guides pointed across a mist shrouded valley at one of the few known nest sites for this, the national bird of the Philippines. I had just gotten my spotting scope on the nest, which contained a single, nearly grown nestling when a pair of sweaty American men—both birders—burst into the clearing. The larger of the two walked directly over to me, elbowed me off my own scope, and took a three-second look at the young eaglet. "Yep! Got it! Okay, what's next?" And off they went up the trail, in search of the next "tick" or check mark on their life list. This was callously rude to the point of being repulsive. But that's how many world listers are.

Bernie's take on a getting a giant world list is a little different. On his travels with his wife Susan, he makes a point of not missing local points of cultural and historical significance—even if it means missing a few new birds. After decades of successful world birding, he realized there were a few bird families for which he'd never seen a representative species. So, naturally, he chose to try to see at least one member of every bird family on the planet. This is a fascinating, but no less challenging goal, especially given the constant changes in bird taxonomy wrought by DNA analysis and the resulting splitting of existing species into new species and even new families!

His worldwide pursuit of birds is epic. There are many challenges along the way: gout on Attu, cranky fellow travelers, bandits, altitude illness, nearly impassable hiking trails, and many, many hard-to-find birds.

No Finish Line contains what every good autobiography should. It has moments of joy and wonder, adventure, multiple dramas in real life, frustrations, soul searching, victories and defeats, dreams and goals, small-world moments and kismet, friendships made and friendships broken, love and loss, and an unquenchable passion for living. The best part is, it's told in Bernie's own voice. This is no ghostwritten puff piece. It's Bernie Master in his own words—his Master's voice, if you will. And he's a tell-it-like-it-is, calls-'em-as-he-sees-'em kind of guy.

If you don't know this man, I hope you get to. These following pages offer a great sense of who and what he is. I feel lucky to know this remarkable human being.

As we were discussing this manuscript, Bernie asked me if he thought the material was actually enough for two books. And I realized that, of course, he was right. His life, larger than most, certainly couldn't be contained in a single book. Further proof that, for Dr. Bernard Master, there is *No Finish Line*. I'm watching for the sequel.

—Bill Thompson, III

Whipple, Ohio
November 2014

INTRODUCTION

After years of urging by friends and family to write about my world birding adventures, I finally sat down at my computer and "hunt and pecked" this autobiography. I quickly saw the connection between my business ventures and my birding exploits. Birding was my pressure release from my building a $100,000,000 business from the germ of an idea. My business and my birding were integrally intertwined. In the 1980s I made the leap from birding to conservation. *No Finish Line* is about world birding, business, conservation, and medicine. I have selected my most exciting adventures from the 105 countries and six continents in which I have birded. The reader can follow American and world bird totals after each chapter. I am the first American to have seen a representative of all 229 bird families in the world. I even have a bird named after me! *Vireo masteri*, in Colombia.

My business chapters include a blueprint for building a vertically integrated health care company and a "how to" chapter on "going public." These chapters include the ways I have found to innovatively overcome the many obstacles every business person faces.

My conservation stories are interspersed throughout. They give an insider's look at the largest (but not necessarily the most effective) conservation organizations in the world.

My medical career includes a year in Vietnam as a battalion surgeon in a combat unit; a year as post surgeon for the U.S. Army's Military Intelligence School; and thirty-five years of primary care practice in the inner-city of Columbus, Ohio. As an entrepreneur, I developed a highly effective health care system for the State of Ohio.

The four elements of my story are meshed in chronological order—with birding as the common thread. My varied experiences include meaningful conversations with President Bill Clinton on national health care; Queen Noor of Jordan and Prince Bernhard of the Netherlands about world bird conservation; the Rev. Jesse Jackson on health care for the underserved; and Wilt Chamberlain about some controversial passages in his book.

The title, *No Finish Line,* comes from my observations of the unending skein of accomplishments by my friends and family members, their lives spent learning for the joy of learning, and their unselfish contributions to the betterment of our world. My own life has been one amazing adventure after another with no finish line in sight.

CHAPTER ONE
The Beginning: My Early life in Philadelphia, Pennsylvania

The longest journey begins with a single step.
—Lao-tzu

It all began for me in 1946. My father, Gilbert Master, was a doctor in Philadelphia. For his relaxation, he would go bird watching. I would always tag along with him. I was four years old when I recorded my first list of nine birds in Morris Park, a small patch of green in the Overbrook section of West Philadelphia. This paper and pencil list with place, date, time, weather conditions, and species was carefully laid in a shoe box with the hundreds more that would follow until sometime in the 1980s. That's when I painstakingly entered them all into a "new" computer program called BirdBase.

The date was February 18, 1946. The weather was clear and cool. I saw and identified—with the help of my father—my first Downy Woodpecker, Crow, Carolina Chickadee, Tufted Titmouse, Starling, Cardinal, Goldfinch, Slate-colored Junco, and Song Sparrow. When I look at that first tiny list, a flood of memories follows. This was the beginning of a hobby, and later a passion that would last a lifetime. Today that list has grown to nearly eight thousand species from 105 countries.

1945

Figure 1-1. Me (age four) in front of our Lansdowne Ave. house in Overbrook, Philadelphia.

Figure 1-2. Me (left, age seven); family friend Doris Rogers (middle); sister Julie (right, age four). Lansdowne Ave., Overbrook, Philadelphia.

West Philadelphia was a concrete jungle of row houses with postage stamp sized-lawns and a few plane trees, sycamore look-alikes, planted in the 1930s.

The only neighborhood birds we saw at that time were House Sparrows, Eurasian Starlings, and Rock Pigeons, all introduced from Europe in the nineteenth century, not very exciting. By the time I was twelve, I had my first bicycle, a fire engine red Schwinn, which gave me a freedom that I had never experienced before! I was riding everywhere on the weekends—to small corners of Overbrook to see and record birds. My early tools were a three power pair of opera glasses and my dad's 1946 *Peterson's Field Guide to North American Birds, 3rd edition*. I moved up to a six power pair of mid-quality German Army field binoculars that my mother's brother, Uncle Vince Majeski, had brought back from World War II. Nearly every Sunday my parents, younger sister Julie, and I would take long family rides in my dad's first car, a new 1949 Plymouth coupe, to places of natural history importance such as Cape May and Parvin State Park in New Jersey, as well as to Tyler Arboretum and the the embryonic Hawk Mountain Sanctuary in Pennsylvania. We also took many short jaunts to various parts of Philadelphia's sprawling Fairmount Park, the second largest city park in the United States, where we would take long bird walks. On one of these walks, we spotted a Yellow-bellied Sapsucker, a life bird for me. We hopped a fence and began stalking this bird. We did not see a jackbooted Philadelphia motorcycle cop approach us. Suddenly we heard a commanding gruff voice demand, "What are you doing here?" We were so startled by his presence that my father barely replied in a soft voice, "We are looking at a Yellow-bellied Sapsucker." The police officer stared at us incredulously for what seemed like an eternity, weighed the "sapsucker" answer, looked us up and down, nodded ever so slightly and finally said "m-huh." He pointed to a grand house on the property saying, "This is the Commissioner's house. Now scram."

In 1943, my Grandfather Joseph Majeski purchased a vacation house, built in 1885, in North Wildwood, New Jersey. This became our summer residence and still is to this day. When I became aware of my surroundings at around age twelve, I discovered that we were only nine miles away from the tip of Cape May, the mecca of American birding for decades and the site of the largest fall bird migration in Eastern North America. Every fall my father and I would bear witness to the migration spectacle—so amazing and filled with such adventure and surprises that it formed a lasting impression on me. I now own that house and we are in our fifth generation of enjoying the magnificent natural splendor of the area.

Figure 1-3. Our family vacation home, North Wildwood, New Jersey.

There is a difference in meaning among the words "birdwatching," "birding," and "ornithology." Birdwatchers are those who enjoy looking at wild birds whether it is in gardens, bird feeders, or in casual outdoor settings. They are some of the seventy-five million people in America who love the beauty of birds and enjoy watching the habits displayed by these feathered creatures. Birdwatching is the second most popular American hobby—second only to gardening. Birders, on the other hand, are those who go into the field, keep notes, make lists, and may belong to bird clubs and bird-oriented organizations such as the National Audubon Society. Many of these birders claim they do not keep lists. Everyone keeps lists! Their lists may not be written down or entered into computer programs, but these people keep their bird lists in their memory bank. They know what bird they saw, where they saw it, and the particulars of the sighting. Many birders' conversations revolve around birds, no matter whom they are talking to. Some birders suffer from what Gabryelle Rowland, the non-birding wife of noted bird tour leader, Forrest Rowland, calls B.A.D.D.—Birders Attention Deficit Disorder. These folks are always birding. Someone afflicted with B.A.D.D. cannot finish a normal sentence if he or she sees or hears a bird. For example, while riding down the road in the middle of discussing the deepest of subjects, say, the meaning of life, a birder will suddenly blurt out, "Stop the car! Pull over! What the hell! I just saw a Painted Bunting! What is that doing in Ohio?" There is no cure for this malady, and it is contagious! Finally, there are ornithologists. These are professionals who study birds scientifically.

By the time I was fourteen I was fully into birding. My father and I often drove to Tinicum National Wildlife Reserve, which became John Heinz National Wildlife Reserve in 1972. It is a 1,200-acre freshwater tidal wetland located in Southwest Philadelphia, only a mile from the Philadelphia International Airport. This was our favorite spot because it was close to our home, boasted an extensive bird list including many hard to find species, and best of all had a wonderful naturalist named Jim who showed us birds. Jim was a middle-aged African-American. I never knew his last name. I did know he was a great birder, filled with bird knowledge that he was happy to share with us. Whenever we visited, Jim always had an unusual bird or two that he found to show us. Now, when I reflect on conversations with him, I realize that *he* was the rarest of birds. Over the years—with all of my hours in the field and serving on many conservation boards—I can recall meeting only six or seven African-

American birders. Jim showed me my first Glaucous Gull and my first Iceland Gull, named every duck before it hit the water, and identified a dozen or more species of shorebirds, egrets, and herons using no field guide. He was always right.

Once you are aware of birds, they pop up everywhere. One cold spring morning we found an emaciated, recently dead Clapper Rail on our West Philadelphia house steps. No notes, no clues left behind. Clapper Rails are birds of the salt marshes—their closest habitat is more than one hundred miles away from our home. Was this an act of divine providence? A prank by one of our birding friends? Or one of those billion-to-one chances that a migrating rail just died in front of our door on its passage north? I always suspected it was a practical joke, but no one ever came clean. I know these jokes are too funny to keep to oneself for long and they eventually slip out. We never heard the rail's origin, and I suspect I will never know the answer. On another occasion, my father found the frozen carcass of an Atlantic Puffin on a South Jersey beach in the dead of winter. This is a small fish-eating bird in the alcid family, rare in New Jersey. He brought it home and placed it on our windowsill facing our next-door neighbor's porch. It was so cold that it froze to the windowsill, but it looked alive, just resting. Alarmed, our long-time neighbor, Mamie Donnelly (an older woman living alone) called my father on the telephone to say that a bird has been looking into his window for three straight days, and he better do something about it. He moved it, but I never found out what he did with it.

Our best trips were always to Hawk Mountain in the Blue Ridge Mountains of the Appalachian Mountain chain. This demanded early 5 a.m. starts and long four-hour drives in my father's car, his slow dull-gray, four-door, stick-shift 1951 Plymouth. Today, this trip would take about an hour and a half to go the eighty miles to the 2,600-acre sanctuary in Kempton near Reading, Pennsylvania. We would shorten the time by singing songs and rounds and harmonizing with each other. My mother had a musical ear and taught us how to sing all the harmony parts.

Figure 1-4. My mother, Leona Majeski, 1930s.

Figure 1-5. My father, Gilbert Master, 1930s.

We would play Geography, License Plates, and Trivia to pass the time. Finally, we would arrive at the legendary Hawk Mountain. Our first trip was in 1953, a mere two years after it was fully open to the public. We met Maurice Broun, Hawk Mountain's first warden and then curator, and birded with him learning his method of pinpointing migrating raptors for others to see by calling out their position as they appeared over each numbered separate ridge in the horizon, a method still used today. One humorous story about Hawk Mountain that keeps reappearing and was told to me by a colorful Columbus, Ohio, birder, involves this method and Pete Dunne, formerly the Director of the Cape May (New Jersey) Bird Observatory. Pete was calling out raptor IDs using the Broun method for location. His raptor ID skills were especially sharp, and he could identify bird specks in the far distance by flight pattern, hints of color, and silhouette. "Female Red-tail over number one, male Peregrine over two, male Coop over one." There was a young couple sitting among the group observing all of this. The young man in total frustration blurted out. "I can't even see the damn bird, and he can see its testicles!"

The elevation surprisingly was only a little more than 1,500 feet, but as a thirteen-year-old, I felt as if I were sitting on top of the world. The Commonwealth was promoting the shooting of Northern Goshawks by offering a $5 bounty as late as 1951 when this horrid practice was mercifully banned. I saw my first Northern Goshawk in the fall of 1954 with Mr. Broun. The best part of Hawk Mountain bird trips was the meatloaf sandwiches my mother would prepare. The cool, crisp autumn weather, the hike up to the top and all the excitement gave us a hearty appetite, and mom never failed to provide.

Figure 1-6. Friends Nora and Dr. Bob Katrins (left); my dad, Dr. Gilbert Master (middle); and me, at Hawk Mountain.

I was both a Boy Scout and Explorer Scout. I concentrated on birds and, of course, achieved the Bird Study merit badge. Later, in medical school, I became a Bird Study merit badge counselor and had fun teaching young scouts this hobby of mine. I birded regularly until I was about sixteen, when I discovered girls and sports. Up until then, I thought all boys my age were also birding. Man, was I wrong. My classmates at Overbrook High School didn't have the faintest idea of what I was talking about when I got on the subject of birds. We were all about high school basketball, the Philadelphia Eagles, the Phillies, and the Warriors (later the 76ers). Our hero was Wilt Chamberlain, a senior at Overbrook when I was in the ninth grade at Beeber Junior High. He was a legitimate seven footer, the best high school basketball player in the country and a model citizen, great guy. The Overbrook Hilltoppers lost only one game with him in three years, and that was the City Championship of 1955 against West Catholic High School. He went on to the

University of Kansas, the Harlem Globetrotters, and then continued to dominate the sport with the Philadelphia Warriors, San Francisco Warriors, the Los Angeles Lakers, and the Philadelphia 76ers. In my opinion "Dippy," (our Hilltopper name for him taken from the constellation name—Big Dipper), was the greatest basketball player of all time. I saw Wilt years later at the U.S. Open Tennis Championships in Flushing Meadows. I was sitting in famed French champion Henri Leconte's box in the third tier and I felt this huge presence standing next to me. It was Chamberlain. I said "Hey, Dip!" He knew immediately I went to "the Brook," and we talked for two hours—games, scores, players, and coaches. When we finally got around to his book, which created a lot of controversy and derision about his boast of bedding twenty thousand women, a mathematical and physiological improbability, he told me he rued the day he wrote it. His mother never forgave him for that. He said the idea was foisted on him by his publisher who wanted to sell more books. I took it as an undeclared admission that it was a complete fabrication, but he never actually denied it.

In the late 1950s and early 1960s, I birded in some of my spare time while attending Ursinus College, a small liberal arts school in Collegeville, Pennsylvania. Founded in 1869, Ursinus produced one of the greatest of all modern American writers, "The Catcher" himself, J.D. Salinger, and thousands of physicians, dentists, lawyers, and teachers. Throw in a lot of ministers, scientists, and successful businessmen and businesswomen, and there you have the graduate picture. Ursinus was not only known for its prominent faculty and graduates, it was also a perennial contributor to the Miss America contest in Atlantic City and Liberty Bowl Queens in Philadelphia. The younger brother of the current Dalai Lama, Lobsang, an acquaintance of mine, attended Ursinus for one year until he was called back to help his brother. He died under mysterious circumstances in the 1970s.

My roommate of four years and closest college friend, Jay Bosniak, was a non-birder, but was a talented sketch artist and could draw birds—and just about anything else—beautifully. He is now a prominent orthopedic surgeon in Long Branch, New Jersey, and a noted painter of natural outdoor scenes in the cubist manner. Our other roommate, John Swinton, was a "closet" birder, musician, and poet. He became a Professor of English at Pennsylvania State University and a published writer of poetry. I did not know he was a bird lover until many years later when we corresponded.

At Ursinus I often took walks along the Perkiomen Creek where I spotted Scarlet Tanagers and Baltimore Orioles. Great Crested Flycatchers gave their signature "wheep" calls. Red-tailed Hawks were at the top of the food chain. These hour-long respites relieved the stress of my pre-med studies. My *Peterson Field Guide* was always nearby. I also played basketball and was on the track team for relaxation. Teaching at Ursinus at the time was a young professor, Dr. Robert Stein, who was busy separating the Traill's Flycatcher Complex into two species, Willow Flycatcher and Alder Flycatcher. They are in the genus *Empidonax*, which translates to "gnat killer." There were ten species of these small flycatchers in this genus in the U.S., and they are among the most problematic species to identify for most birders. These two look-alike species are best told apart by their voice. I frequently saw Dr. Stein walking into the field with his recording equipment. I regret to say I didn't have a clue what he was doing. I missed an opportunity to participate in the making of an important ornithological discovery. His contribution remains on the list of American birds, as there are now eleven species of *Empidonax* flycatchers recognized in the U.S. today.

During medical school at the Philadelphia College of Osteopathic Medicine in the mid-1960s, my field trips dwindled to a few a year, mostly in Cape May in the summer and fall. I do remember one frigid February Sunday however, when my father and I dragged along a classmate, Dick Lynch, who had never birded before, to Swarthmore College out on the Main Line. A flock of White-winged Crossbills was being seen in the Swarthmore woods on a regular basis. These would be a new bird for me, a "lifer," as we birders call a new bird to our list. Their bills actually cross over each other as an aid to pry open cones for their seeds. The three of us struggled through a blinding snowstorm for two hours until we discovered the flock of some twenty birds calmly feeding on hemlock cone seeds. The exhilaration I felt on this success quickly warmed my frozen fingers and toes. We celebrated with a thermos full of hot chocolate. Dick thought we were crazy. He never looked at another bird after that. He made a career of medicine in the U.S. Army and was one step away from becoming its Surgeon General.

My summer jobs, ages eighteen through twenty-one, were working as the Nature Counselor at Camp Akiba in Reeders, Pennsylvania, located in the green and then unspoiled Pocono Mountains. This was an ideal job for me—outdoors, great kids from the Philadelphia area, delicious food from Chef Max, nightly basketball games among the counselors, lots of birds to look at, beautiful female counselors, and a healthy salary to help pay for my college education. I couldn't believe my good fortune—interpreting nature and getting paid for it. The camp was owned by "Red" Sherr, a former professional basketball player for the Philadelphia Spas, a team in the country's first professional basketball league. His daughter, Lynn Sherr, a fine athlete in her own right, became a famous news anchorwoman for a national TV syndicate.

Music played a big part of our summers in the Poconos. I formed a doo-wop group with Kenny Goldblatt and the Kornfeld twins. We sang Motown and rock and roll hits in four-part harmony with that special "Philly sound," in the evenings to the delight of the campers and the other counselors. At Overbrook High School I had formed a singing group called The Cashmeres. The other members of the group were Brent Edwards, Harold Saunders, Johnny Gonzales, and Lenny Borisoff (later calling himself Len Barry). Occasionally Jimmy Mealey sang bass and Jerry Gross played piano. Lenny couldn't harmonize to save his life. I tried to teach him, but he just couldn't hear the harmonies.

He would follow me in the Overbrook halls and beg, "Bernie, my man, hit a note."

I would sing a simple middle C, and he would always miss his harmonic note. I made him our lead singer. We were the main act in all the Overbrook talent shows and performed at parties, "hops," and hospitals all around Philadelphia. We even had club dates and made a few bucks. The summer I graduated, Lenny, Jimmy, and Jerry joined two guys from West Philadelphia High School and formed The Dovells, a name taken from the popular Hotel Deauville in Miami. That fall they recorded a number one hit, "The Bristol Stomp," and "went gold" selling over a million records. This led to a world tour with Dianna Ross and The Supremes, Martha and the Vandellas, and the musical genius, Ray Charles, all now in the Rock and Roll Hall of Fame. I went to college that fall. The Dovells went to the Apollo Theater.

Figure 1-7. The Dovells and me (middle), Rock and Roll Reunion, Valleydale, Columbus, Ohio, 1987.

The famed Harlem's Apollo Theater in New York! This was the apex showplace for all rhythm and blues artists. The one and only James Brown and his Famous Flames, The Temptations, and Smokey Robinson and The Miracles had all played the Apollo. Adoring fans would line up for hours to buy tickets to see the best in the business. That night, The Dovells were on the same stage with Little Anthony and The Imperials, Curtis Mayfield and The Impressions, The Cadillacs, and the great comedienne, Jackie "Moms" Mabley, a regular at the Apollo. It was a night filled with superstars. These five handsome white kids from West Philly simply "turned out" all the other acts and tore the place up with Lenny leading the beautiful tight harmonies in their soulful Philly sound coupled with their street-smart inner-city choreography—splits, twirls, and cool coordinated steps. The jam-packed African-American audience couldn't believe their eyes and ears. They had never seen anything like this and went wild with appreciation. They were dancing in the aisles, standing on their seats, and gave a long, standing ovation. They wouldn't let them off the stage and their applause begged for two encores.

Overbrook High School was not only famous for its world-class athletes but also for the star entertainers it produced. The list of singers includes Len Barry and The Dovells; The Orlons (songs "South Street" and "Don't Hang Up") of Lansdowne Avenue; blues singer Solomon Burke; Dee Dee Sharp of "Mashed Potato" fame; and Randy Cain, tenor with the Delfonics ("Didn't I Blow Your Mind This Time?" and "Oh Girl"). Len Barry, as a solo performer hit number one on the pop charts with his song, *"One, Two, Three,"* covered later by many pop singers including The Chairman of The Board, the legendary Frank Sinatra. Dovell bass singer, Jimmy Mealey, wrote "Here Come The Judge." Frankie Smith wrote "Double Dutch Bus" sung by Raven-Symoné from the Cosby show. At the very top of this monument to Overbrook talent sits the world famous mega-movie star, Will Smith. Not to be overshadowed by this list of luminaries is Guion Bluford, the world's first African-American astronaut in space.

After graduation from Ursinus, I married my college sweetheart, Inge Habeck, a beautiful and intelligent young woman of Estonian ancestry. She helped me as we struggled through four years of medical school together. We had our first child, Ken, during my first med school year. I took extra jobs to supplement the monies our parents were giving us to live. Following my first year of college, I applied and was accepted to work for the National Park Service in the Washington, D.C. area as a Park Ranger Naturalist. I took residence in Georgetown at the Sigma Phi fraternity house on K Street during the week, and drove home to Atlantic Highlands, New Jersey to be with Inge and Kenny on the weekends. The rent was only $30 a month. I owned my car outright, and gasoline was relatively cheap then. I made a great salary including mileage for my car, and my expenses were low. I only ate one meal a day to keep my expenses down. All the important and interesting national monuments and museums including the Carter Baron Theater were on National Park grounds and were free to me. I was invited to many picnics as I walked around the parks. My job was great. Every day I drove to a different park and gave interpretive nature demonstrations with my black rat snake, turtles, and insects and led general nature walks for inner-city school kids. They loved it, and I loved it. My office was in Rock Creek Park, another beautiful city park much like Fairmount Park in Philadelphia. Here, my first sighting of a Pileated Woodpecker, the largest woodpecker in North America, stunned me. In 1940 the great cartoonist, Walter Lantz, modeled Woody Woodpecker after this species. I saw and heard my first Northern Parula high in the treetops along the Chesapeake Bay with the bright morning sun showing off its multitude of colors. This little gem is one of the smallest warblers in North America, barely more than four inches long. A little ball of feathers, it migrates all the way to Middle

America and the West Indies in the winter. Its magenta and violet breast bands on top of its yellow chest are set off beautifully against its greenish back. Its song is a signature ascending buzz with the last note flipping over. I currently have them nesting in my home patch. When I hear the resident male sing, I always think of my first one, that beautiful Maryland morning. My most unforgettable bird memory that summer was hearing the ethereal harp tones of the Veery every morning outside my office. It remains my favorite bird song. The *Catharus* thrushes have the best songs. Their syrinx, an organ analogous to our larynx, allows them to harmonize with themselves. Mystic Buddhist monks in Tibet can do this too. The money I made that summer would ease our money problems in the coming year.

Graduation day arrived on June 11, 1966, the same day as the birth of our second child, my beautiful daughter, Dana. I ranked third in my class and received the Obstetrical Prize, the Physical Diagnosis prize, the Dean's Award for best clinical student, and a gold fob for my Lambda Omicron Gamma professional fraternity's highest academic average. I was selected to intern in my profession's best hospital teaching program at Doctors Hospital, Columbus, Ohio. Ten days after Dana's birth, I loaded everybody into our 1956 Chrysler and hit the road for the Buckeye State.

CHAPTER TWO
Vietnam: Combat and Birding

War is too important to be left to the generals.
—Col. Jack Ripper quoting Clemenceau in the movie, *Dr. Strangelove*

PART ONE

My internship at Doctors Hospital in 1966 was a breeze. I was well prepared from my medical school training and moonlighting at various Philadelphia hospitals during my last two years in school. Just about every medical specialty had some appeal to me. I passed the Ohio Medical Board exams with the highest score of any participant that year. Because I could not decide on a specialty, I decided to join a small group of general practitioners in the Linden area of Columbus until I figured out what I wanted to do. There were no family medicine residencies yet established in any hospitals anywhere. In fact, in the State of Ohio you could practice without completing an internship as long as you passed the Ohio Medical Boards. This was a throwback to the early days of medicine when older physicians tutored medical students. At twenty-six years of age, I was the youngest practicing physician in Ohio. Things were really going well for me in the growing practice where I was learning the art of medicine and making a decent living. I became a partner in my second year. For recreation I would bird the famous

Green Lawn Cemetery, south of downtown Columbus, the second oldest cemetery in Ohio. During spring migration, this 328-acre green space would provide food, cover, and water to thousands of birds on their northward movement.

I was rudely awakened from this idyll one day in June 1968, when I received a letter from the Department of Defense informing me that I was drafted into the United States Army. I was in shock. This call-up was part of a special nationwide draft for physicians, 120 in all, with the youngest first, as I would find out later. *There were 550,000 men serving in Vietnam, and LBJ needed me?* I tried to get out of this predicament. There was one physician in my region, Dr. Jack Hutchinson, who—according to rumor—had the power to recommend my deferral. I visited with him. My argument was that I had two young children, and I was practicing in an underserved area. I had a lot of time and money invested there. He listened with a stony face and gave me no counter-argument. The letter I received a week after that meeting told me his decision. I was to report to Fort Sam Houston, Medical Field Service School, San Antonio, Texas, on January 16, 1969.

In December I said goodbye to my family, patients, friends, and colleagues. I drove the 1,500 miles to San Antonio. I arrived on the day of the first Super Bowl to carry the Super Bowl name, Super Bowl III, January 12, 1969 and watched the New York Jets, heavy underdogs, bring its brash quarterback, Joe Namath's prediction of a victory to fruition by defeating the Baltimore Colts, 16-7. I reported to Fort Sam headquarters, went downtown and had an officer's suit made, picked up my captain's bars and caduceus, and started classes the next day. Inge, Kenny, and Dana joined me the next week in a very comfortable townhouse. For fun we would go birding, visit the Alamo, and stroll the San Antonio River Walk. The Tex-Mex food was delicious—a new taste for us.

San Antonio had its birds. We frequently visited Olmos Park. There I saw my lifer Golden-fronted Woodpecker, lifer Long-billed Thrasher, and lifer Lesser Goldfinch. Other birds of interest that we never saw back east were Bewick's Wren, Spotted Towhee, and the noisy Great-tailed Grackle. This last species was then considered one with the Boat-tailed Grackle. They are now split into two species. I believe we were only seeing the Boat-tailed. The Great-tailed Grackles range is farther west. Along deserted highways we watched families of Bay-winged Hawks (now called Harris's Hawks), hunt rabbits and other small prey in coordinated groups. This behavior is rare in birds. It is much more common in some families of canines, felines, and cetaceans. Army ants in the insect world and the Yellow Saddle Goatfish in the fish world also hunt this way. Harris's Hawks' habit of back-stacking—standing on each other's backs when perches were scarce—is unique in the bird world.

The Army's seven-week course was a monumental waste of time. They taught me who to salute and who I was to salute, the size of a company, battalion and brigade, and other useless army stuff. I shot an M14 on the firing range, a rifle that was already antiquated at the time and replaced by the M16 as soon as I got to Nam. We were given map reading and compass instructions that I already knew from my Boy Scout days. On our final day we crawled on our bellies through an obstacle course under barbed wire with machine guns firing way—and I mean *way* over our heads. The only thing I found of practical value was a refresher course on tropical medicine. I used much of this information in the twelve months to follow. After the seventh week, they gave us a final examination on all the army stuff. I thought, *what would they do to me if I purposely tanked it? Send me back home?* No chance. They needed any doctor who could fog a mirror. There was a pediatrician from Haiti in my group through all the field drills. He couldn't hit the broad side of a barn door on the rifle range, got lost until morning on the map reading course, and didn't know a thing about adult medicine. It didn't matter; they took him anyway.

Our orders came on graduation. It was a forgone conclusion we were all going to Vietnam. Maybe, just maybe,

I would be stationed stateside or Europe. I read my orders. I saw "APO San Francisco!" Yes! I was stateside. I was elated. No Nam for me. Maybe the Presidio. My elation was short-lived. I wanted to double check since I really couldn't decipher all the army acronyms and abbreviations on my orders. I saw a soldier with three stripes up and three stripes down on his arm walking by. I remembered in one of my classes that this was a master sergeant, someone very wise and someone not to fool with. Even though you outranked them, they knew how to put you in a world of hurt. So I stopped him and very politely asked him where I was to be stationed.

He looked at my orders for about a nanosecond and said, "Doc, you're goin' to Nam."

I asked him what the "APO San Francisco" meant. He told me that was the post office designation for Vietnam.

A week later I donned my uniform adorned with my shiny captain bars and caduceus. I said a choked farewell to Kenny, Dana and Inge and flew to San Francisco. There I transferred to a commercial airline with a hundred other doctors headed for an uncertain future. The twenty-two-hour flight, with a short refueling stopover in Hawaii, was noisy with voices of the men telling stories and jokes like they were going on some kind of camping trip. Nobody slept. The airline hostesses were cheerful and compliant. The alcohol was flowing, and the din inside the cabin was rising. Unexpectedly, a voice boomed from the intercom rising above the noise level.

"This is the captain speaking. Gentlemen, you have just entered the airspace of the Republic of South Vietnam."

And then silence. I mean total silence. It was so quiet you could hear the intestinal rumblings from the guy sitting in the last row. The sympathetic nervous system was kicking into second gear. I began contemplating my mortality. Would we be shot down, crash and burn before we landed? That's how much I knew about the enemy's lack of missile capabilities.

We arrived at Tan Son Nhut Air Force Base in Saigon without being shot down. The plane door opened, and I stepped out into an alien environment, in one I would spend, hopefully, prayerfully, safely my next twelve months. Forty-five years later I can still feel the intense heat hitting my face, the cloying humidity blanketing my body and the sweat pouring from beneath my useless tailored stateside woolen uniform. I can still smell the noxious odor of a mixture of kerosene and something else hitting my nostrils. That something else, I learned later, was human waste, tons of it, being burned in fifty-gallon diesel cans. I walked down the plane's steps to the steaming tarmac. My first sight, directly in my line of vision, was a sign with an arrow: "Bunker in case of rocket attack." I immediately located the bunker because I expected to be showered with rockets any second. A bus with armed guards and steel barbed wire encased windows took us to the transit billets. I was assigned to an officers' barracks and there I waited for my duty assignment. During the next four days and nights I never left that barracks except for meals. I kept hearing the explosive sounds of artillery. I thought we were under attack. Fortunately, there was another officer there, a captain in the Quartermaster Corps who was on his second tour of duty. He was savvy to the origin of all the ordnance sounds.

I lay awake all night asking him, "Incoming or outgoing?"

He always said, "Outgoing."

Neither of us slept. I had no clue if he were really telling the truth or just trying to assuage my anxiety. I passed those four days reading paperbacks, eating, sleeping, taking multiple showers, and writing letters back home. Finally I was called to meet a lieutenant colonel, Medical Corps, for my duty assignment. Maybe I would luck out and be assigned to a hospital, very safe and very far from the front lines. I learned later there were no front lines. Everything was a target in this war. During the past year I had corresponded with my best friend and classmate, Dr. Norman Ruttenberg. He told me he was in Quang Tri as a radiologist, and it was safe there. I kept the name, Quang Tri, in the front of my memory bank in case I had to use it. I walked into a small, cramped office for my interview. The colonel said that since I was a 3400, which was a GMO (General Medical Officer), I was required to spend at least six months in the field with an infantry unit, and then I would be rotated back to a hospital. Well, that sounded only half bad.

"Where would you like to go?" he politely asked, as if I knew anything about anything.

At first I couldn't believe my good luck. This was beginning to sound like a corporate interview with a prominent Wall Street firm. *But, Master, get real! This is the Army.*

I said, "How about Quang Tri?" holding my breath waiting for his answer.

He had a gleeful look on his face when he heard my response.

"Great!" he said much too quickly for my comfort. He said that there was an opening for a battalion surgeon there. "Would you like to see where it is?"

"Sure," I said with dwindling confidence. I was developing serious reservations about my choice. There was a very long map of South Vietnam high on the wall beside us, almost reaching the ceiling. He got out of his chair, stepped onto the table at which I was sitting, fully extended his arm, and with his index finger pointed to a dot high up on the map. That was Quang Tri. Oh my God—it was the northern-most province in South Vietnam, hugging the DMZ, a stone's throw from North Vietnam and thousands of enemy troops. *Wait until I get a hold of that Ruttenberg!*

I boarded a Lockheed C130 Hercules transport the next morning for the 668-mile flight north. I was sure we would be shot down, and crash and burn before I had treated my first patient. We weren't shot out of the sky, but instead landed safely at Quang Tri Marine Base, sixteen hours flying time in all. I reported to the brigade surgeon, a major in very stiffly pressed immaculate jungle fatigues. I made a mental note that this probably indicated either he never got his candy ass out into the field or there was simply nothing to do. He was a military career orthopedic surgeon. He greeted me politely but reservedly. A few pleasantries were passed, medical schools exchanged, and then he told me that I was assigned as the battalion surgeon to the First Battalion, 61st Infantry, First Brigade, Fifth Mechanized Infantry Division. I was standing in Northern I Corps, one of the four Corps divisions of South Vietnam, and that I would report to him on all medical matters. I had no idea what all that meant. I guess I skipped that class at Fort Sam. I asked him what my duties were, and he said that I would take care of a little sick call in the morning and the rest of the day would be mine. They hadn't had any action up here for a long time, and he reassured me it was very quiet. His orderly telephoned my unit at Landing Zone (LZ) Sharon and told them to pick me up. Looking back, I wondered why his pants didn't immediately catch on fire.

I waited on a bench outside the major's office thinking that things were not adding up: DMZ, LZ, "a little sick call." It was stinking hot and there was no shade. Even though it was 92 degrees Fahrenheit. I was still wearing my idiotic stateside greens. Everything was getting on my nerves. I was shaking my head negatively. I looked up, peering into the distance for my ride. No jeep, but I could see a form of a man, backlit by the glaring tropical sun, striding toward me. When he came into detailed view I thought it was John Wayne in the flesh. He was a marine captain, about six feet two, 185 pounds, extremely fit and tanned with that Moroccan leather look, earned from months in the bush. His hair was cut "high and wide." In a moment he was standing next to me. He was a marine's marine, a real leatherneck. His steely eyed gaze fixated on me as he took me all in, but softened as he sat down next to me. In an instant he had figured me out.

"Hi, Doc. New in country?"

I couldn't imagine how he could tell. Was it my white pasty skin, my overweight 205 pounds with my paunch pushing hard against my jacket, or was it that ridiculous green uniform I was still wearing with only my shiny captain's bars and caduceus that gave me away? Somebody had to be the FNG (fn new guy), and I guess this time it was me. I did wear a lonely single ribbon over my left coat pocket. It was the National Defense Medal that every rookie got when he first entered the Army. A trained eye can read your uniform like a roadmap. I had no shoulder patches because I hadn't been anywhere. I had no ribbons because I hadn't done anything. I was in the Medical Corps, which, to a professional soldier, meant I was the same as a civilian. He asked me where I was going. I told him LZ Sharon. No immediate response.

He finally said, "You'll be okay." He then gave me the sagest advice of the war that ended up taking me through every hardship I encountered in the next year and beyond. "Listen to your first sergeant and you'll be all right."

Oh yes, the "first sergeant" again. He keeps coming up. I asked him how long he had been in country.

He said, "364 days and counting. I'm so short I can walk under a latrine door without opening it!"

A marine's tour of duty was thirteen months. In the army, a tour was only twelve months. My ride was finally approaching. I said goodbye and thanks to that good man. He was one squared-away marine. The driver spotted me right away. Even a private knew I was an FNG.

PART TWO
LZ Sharon

The driver headed southwest over a hot and dusty treeless dirt road. Vietnam has two seasons, hot and dry and hot and wet. My driver carefully drove around a soda can and any seemingly harmless debris in the road. There was a steady stream of military vehicles coming and going, mixed with a few Vietnamese on bicycles, motorbikes, and cyclos. These were small flimsy three-wheeled pedal-driven—and in some cases motorized—modes of transportation for the civilians. They would carry everything from families (of up to five), to livestock, to bundles of wood to make charcoal for their cooking fires. Medically speaking, motorbikes caused the most common and most severe trauma cases. Huey helicopters were fluttering past us. All sorts of fixed-wing aircraft were zooming above us. I received military salutes from unnamed faces all along our way. I could see low, forested hills to the west of us and extensive sandy flat terrain to our east. There were a few villages with their black pajama-clad male inhabitants going about their daily chores. The women wore the traditional *owyays*, white for unmarried girls, black for married or older women. And, as always, kids being kids, played and laughed—mindless of the war. The native population looked calm but emotionless, no waving, no smiles. They appeared immune to the presence of all these foreigners. They basically wanted to be left alone, raise their families, tend to their crops, and enjoy life as any American would. Mostly there were miles and miles of rice fields. Vietnam was known as the rice bowl of Southeast Asia, an exporter of rice feeding all of their Asian neighbors. They were so good at rice farming that they were able to stretch the usual Asian two grow seasons a year to three.

We arrived at LZ Sharon late afternoon. It was a lonely, dusty fire base about fifteen acres in all. Hastily thrown up plywood living quarters called *hootches* with tin corrugated roofs battened down by sandbags were scattered every which way. Each structure was sandbagged. We passed the Battalion Aid Station, another hootch with a gigantic red cross painted on its side, but did not stop. Protocol demanded that I report to my commanding officer first. Large canvas temporary tents were randomly placed. There was a motor pool loaded with half torn down M48 Patton tanks and Armored Personnel

Carriers (APCs). Shirtless grease-covered mechanics were busy trying to get them into working order. We passed guard towers and sandbagged bunkers set in strategic areas around the compound. The entire perimeter was enclosed by concertina wire—steel barbed wire with razor blades set about every six inches. I was thinking this was all good. The driver took me to the command post to report for duty, present my orders, and meet my battalion commander. Lt. Col. John Hartigan was away from the LZ at a brigade meeting, so the introduction had to wait. I was driven down to the Battalion Aid Station (BAS) to get settled in.

Figure 2-1. My hootch (left); Battalion Aid Station (right), LZ Sharon.

As my jeep pulled in, a tall smiling tan crew-cut second lieutenant came out to greet me. This was 2nd Lt. Klemm Ungemach, my MSC (Medical Service Corps) junior officer who would be my bunkmate, bodyguard, administrative assistant, and my eyes and ears for the duration of the war here. When I found out he was from Roseville, Ohio, an hour east of Columbus, an Ohio State University graduate, and a rabid Buckeye football fan, I knew this association would be a fruitful one. I was beginning to relax already. Klemm took my duffle and carried it into the hootch, our living quarters. We talked for an hour about home, the conditions here, and some of the problems. We were in Delta Company, a support company with medics, mechanics, cooks, and a quartermaster. The company's commanding officer was Capt. Jack Langston. He had administrative authority over everyone and everything in D Company except the doctor. I was in charge of all things medical. We both reported to Lt. Col. Hartigan. Klemm took me up to the quartermaster and got me fixed up with all my new duds—everything from head to toe—jungle fatigues, helmet and liner, flak jacket, jungle hat, canteen, mess kit, mosquito repellant, and a .45 caliber sidearm with holster, garrison belt, and ammo. The shirt and pants were loose and allowed the skin to breathe. The boots were the best of all—water repellant, rugged, comfortable, and allowed for good air circulation, which was important to avoid foot fungus. Foot care in an infantry unit is paramount. That evening I met all the medics at the BAS and my acting first sergeant, Sgt. 1st Class Krapse. Most of the medics were out in the line companies, and I would meet them in due course. Among my medics were four Non-Commissioned Officers (NCOs), all sergeants of various grades who had planned on making the army a career. They were older than the other medics and had a lot more experience. They also had stripes on their shoulders and had earned leadership positions through merit or time in service. They were supposed to command the respect of their juniors, but honestly as the days and weeks moved on, I saw only one who fit the bill, Sgt. Darger, a full-blooded Lakota Sioux Indian from South Dakota.

The next day I was called up to report to the "old man"—Lt. Col. Hartigan. I was ushered into his office, gave him the requisite military salute, and was offered a seat. The colonel was an educated man from a midwestern town and an ROTC background, former English major. He was a man in his forties of medium build and height, tan, displayed a serious demeanor, and never smiled. He was soft-spoken and articulate. He explained what the conditions were like here, and what he required from me in the way of paper reports. There were one thousand men and officers divided into three line companies, not surprisingly A, B, and C—Alpha, Bravo, and Charlie—and one support company—Delta—and Headquarters. We were a conglomerate of tanks, APCs, and straight ground pounders, riflemen, also called "grunts." We had an artillery unit, the 1/77, attached to us. That was it. I told him I was not a rookie in medicine, had good training, and had been in general practice for a year and a half before being drafted. Of course I would do my best for him and the men in all situations. I think he knew all of that anyway. I could see my opened file sitting in front of him on his desk. After that very inconsequential first meeting, lasting only about fifteen minutes, he bid me good luck, and I went back to my hootch to get a good night's sleep for a long next day.

Figure 2-2. Sunset, LZ Sharon.

In the morning, I attended my first sick call. Most of the troops were out on the line, so I only saw about twenty men that morning. I carefully went over each case with all the medics observing, eliciting symptoms from the patients while pointing out important diagnostic signs. I instructed them on proper history taking and physical examination, just basics at first. There were no unusual cases that morning, just the usual fungal rashes, URIs, strains, sprains, and anxiety. I reviewed my treatment protocols for these conditions with them. These were later put in writing. I then inspected all of the equipment, instruments, pharmacy, and supplies. I had the men tell me all of their standing operating procedures for things like logging patients in and out and keeping records. I also asked who had the authority to do what. I inspected all the forms for which we were responsible that would be sent up the chain of command. I made a long list of things I would requisition to better take care of our men. We needed a microscope. I did not change anything that first day.

I was told the previous battalion surgeon, a southerner from Louisiana, was competent and well liked. He was not involved in any combat action, though, and tended to stay away from confrontation with the brass. Klemm had been the real leader there for some time. Sgt. 1st Class Krapse, the acting first sergeant, was busy all day "fixing" an old generator out back and was never very visible. Platoon Sgt. "Pop" Wadas was fifty-five years old, a Korean War veteran, and an alcoholic who was busted many times for behavioral problems. Those days were over, and he was just a quiet old man now. The BAS functioned without him, and I never sent him to a line unit. The other eight medics around the BAS were sharp, well trained, reliable and eager to learn more about medicine. I liked them. They all got along with each other and never posed any disciplinary problems. There was a strong bond among them. Every so often I would rotate them to the field units and bring the line guys back to LZ Sharon. During that year, out of a total of one hundred medics who rotated through the 1st/61st, I only found one shirker. He was a real wiseass, a true sociopath, and liar. There was always a problem with the number of morphine syrettes he carried. There were always some missing. I never knew whether he was selling them or using them himself. His number never matched up to the number of cases he said he had treated in the field. He told us he was Jewish so he could get out of the field to go to Da Nang for High Holy Day services. His company commander never complained about him, so I left him in the field.

I reviewed each individual's administrative file. During the 1960s, President Johnson's Secretary of Defense Robert McNamara instituted a program designed to increase the Army's manpower called "McNamara's 100,000." Those who were not previously qualified to enter the armed forces by reason of low mental aptitude or physical impairment were reclassified to meet McNamara's new lower standards. The base IQ was set at eighty. I could tell who they were because their service record and health care jackets carried a big red S on the front page. They also had a prefix 100 on their health care records. We had such a man in our medic platoon. I would keep an eye on him.

That second night I was invited to the officers' mess. There was a buzz of excitement in camp because of the arrival of the "new doctor." Mess would begin with all the officers of the battalion who were in base camp meeting at the bar for drinks and conversation. One by one, I met the staff, the Ex-O, a major who was second in command, Intel, Signal, Ops, Personnel, Chaplain, Artillery, and Quartermaster. They were all captains, a few lieutenants including Klemm, and two warrant officers who had the title of "Mister." There were no company commanders or platoon leaders present that night, as they were all out in the field. I would meet them later. They all had time-honored military nicknames like "Sparky" for the signal officer; "Chappy" or "Padre" for the chaplain; and "Doc" for me. The nickname "Doc," I learned later, was a very special title of endearment reserved only for those surgeons they really liked and respected. Medics were also called "Doc" by the men in their units. If an equal called you "Captain," I'd say you'd better watch out.

Dinner followed, always begun by a prayer of thanks by Chappy with a fervent request for the safety of our men. These dinners were not very common. They were called by our CO only for special occasions like the night I arrived, after battles won, for special guests, and when Brigade or General staff would visit. The rest of the time, we ate in D company's mess hall. Seating was always carefully orchestrated with the colonel, executive officer, and guest of honor in the front table facing the room. The other officers were selectively placed in the other cloth-covered tables around the room. Dinner was served by the enlisted men under the watchful eye of "Cookie," the master sergeant cook. The food was always hot and tasty with some kind of meat, usually steak, powdered mashed potatoes, and canned vegetables. There was homemade cake or pie for dessert. After dinner there was a short talk by the CO on the subject of his choice, some announcements, and usually all would join in singing a patriotic song like "America the Beautiful" or "Home On The Range." There is a long tradition of *a cappela* singing in the military going back thousands of years. We would then say our goodnights and depart for the evening—overall, an impressive and enjoyable night.

Nothing happened of note the next two days. I was still feeling my way around, getting more comfortable with my situation, but there was one troubling fact emerging. Klemm and my NCOs were telling me the morale among the line medics had been low for some time and should be dealt with. What was the problem? The company commanders were using our medics along with the infantry on the defensive perimeter to protect their encampment from attack. This strategy was fraught with problems. The biggest problem was that once under attack the medics could not leave their place in the line to attend the wounded. Another big problem was that the medic tracks were defensive vehicles only with a single 60 mm machine gun and no armor plate protecting the gunner. The infantry tracks had powerful .50 caliber offensive machine guns once used to shoot down enemy aircraft. These were sitting behind a mounted armor plate protecting the gunner. Although the medics had basic skills in infantry tactics and were familiar shooting various weapons, they were considered non-combatants in the articles of war. They were no way near the proficiency of an 11 Bravo rifleman. A medic wielding a weapon forfeited his non-combatant status and could be shot by the enemy. Years of experience in these matters caused the U.S. Army to issue directive after directive banning the use of medics in this way. I felt our commanders were flouting these time-honored rules by placing our medics and fighting men in an untenable dangerous position. All the regulations from our Brigade rules of engagement, I Corps, USARV regulations, and Geneva Convention proscribed this breach of the rules of war.

In the early hours of the fifth day, all of this became moot. I was rudely awakened by my CQ banging on my door and calling my name. "Capt. Master, the colonel wants all the officers to report in full battle dress to the command post now!" I jumped out of bed, hurriedly brushed my teeth, and washed my face. No time to shave. I then put on my jungle fatigues with my nice shiny captain's bars and caduceus, slipped into my boots, and for the first time wore my pith helmet and flak jacket. I placed my garrison belt around my waist, checked my .45 to see that a full clip was loaded and holstered, and attached it to my belt. Sgt. Krapse was already waiting for me in our jeep, motor running. On the way to the CP I wildly speculated about what was so urgent. I had not heard any gunfire that night; in fact it was deadly quiet. When I got to the CP, I saw every officer in the battalion, including all company commanders and platoon leaders who had come in from the field, jammed into the conference room quietly ready for the colonel to speak. I knew then something very, very important was happening. An air of calm expectancy prevailed.

Our colonel began, "Gentlemen, we are moving out this morning at 0600 hours to Con Thien on the DMZ. We will be conducting search and destroy missions against Viet Cong and North Vietnamese enemy forces. The order of march is the following…"

Well, I was only half paying attention because my brigade surgeon said I did not have to go on missions like this.

I heard, "…Charlie company, Signal, Doc…"

'Doc!' I swore I just heard, 'Doc.'

He finished his briefing and then asked if there were any questions. I raised my hand, and in front of the whole officer command, the NFG asked the dumbest question he has ever asked or will ever ask in his life.

"Do I have to go?"

There was a long pause as the battalion commander pondered the meaning of my question and then barked, "OF COURSE YOU HAVE TO GO. YOU ARE OUR DOCTOR!"

I imagined hearing his brain finish his sentence with, *YOU F'N IDIOT!* I tried to avoid the stares of my fellow officers as we were dismissed, and I slunk out of the room. I told Sgt. Krapse to drive me back to the BAS. What happened to that "little sick call" the brigade surgeon was feeding me? I was feeling pretty low at that point, both from humiliating myself in front of my peer group and also from contemplating the horrors awaiting me during the next few days. The only way to overcome that monumental gaffe was to excel in the days to come.

I had no idea how to prepare my track for battle. No worries, Sgt. Krapse said he would handle everything. I told Klemm what was happening, hurriedly wrote a letter to my wife, and then watched as they packed my APC with the equipment and supplies he knew I would need for at least a month. I made mental notes. Maybe I would learn something. Klemm was needed at the BAS in my absence. At 0500 I prepared to join the line of march and hopped inside the track.

I saw Sgt. Krapse standing beside the track shaking his head negatively, lips pursed in paternal disapproval. "No

Doc, get out and sit on top. You'll get blown up if you stay inside and we get hit by an RPG."

I hearkened back to the sage advice of that marine captain I briefly met in Quang Tri. "Listen to your first sergeant." We joined the line of march right behind Signal Corps and headed north on Highway 1 at precisely 0600.

I took my five best medics with me. I chose buck Sgt. Darger as my NCO-in-charge. I left Krapse back to fiddle with his generator. Although extremely quiet, Darger seemed steady and reliable. Every time the line of vehicles would come to a halt, our driver (another medic) would fishtail us in the opposite direction from the vehicle in front of us. This was both a defensive maneuver to cover the vehicle in front of us with fire as well as an offensive maneuver in case we had to move away or jump into the fray. We moved through Quang Tri, Dong Ha, and passed a Montagnard resettlement village. These minority hill people had been living in the central highlands of Vietnam extending all the way north to China for centuries. They were not ethnic Vietnamese and were the subject of derision and torture by the Vietnamese communists. The 40,000 "Yards," composed of six tribes, paid extreme loyalty to the Americans and were valuable allies. They were very short in stature due to their nutritional deficiencies and genetics but were ferocious fighters.

Figure 2-3. Montagnards resettlement village, Quang Tri.

We passed over the Qua Viet River Bridge into a long expanse of low-lying plains. By late afternoon we had reached our destination, Con Thien, Vietnamese for "Hill of Angels," an abandoned Marine Corps firebase laid out with old raggedy sandbagged bunkers and pillbox firing stations facing the "Z." A year before, it was the scene of some of the bloodiest fighting of the war, when during the 1968 Tet offensive the communists tried but failed to capture it. It lies only three kilometers from North Vietnam. Because there were no bunkers or large holes for cover, I set up my BAS in a large canvas tent. We were completely unprotected from enemy fire.

Figure 2-4. Medics and me (first row, center), Con Thien, February 1969.

It wasn't five minutes before the enemy had us spotted and zeroed in. I heard "INCOMING!" and watched everyone hug the ground. It took me about a second to do the same. I did not react to the sound of the rockets at all on my own. I had never heard that sound before. From that moment on the sound of incoming rockets was forever burned into my brain. Seconds later 220mm rockets were accurately raining on our position. I saw massive chunks of hot metal flying through the air over my head only thirty feet from where I was once standing. The noise from the explosion was truly deafening. I lost my hearing and had constant ringing in my ear, called tinnitus in medical terms, for three days. We quickly tended the wounded and called for a Medevac. No problem there. We were only a few miles from the Quang Tri Marine Corps Hospital and a chopper arrived in about fifteen minutes. The rocket barrage stopped. It was just a message from Charlie telling us he knew we were there, and he knew our every move. We threw smoke for the Medevac and loaded our wounded into the chopper. Nightly, for the next week, our line companies sent out platoons on "search and destroy" missions looking for Charlie. The searches yielded nothing. There was no one to destroy. There were no firefights or ambushes. Charlie had disappeared for a while. Later in the war, the Army abandoned this "search and destroy" strategy and switched to "winning hearts and minds." During that week I conducted sick call, treating the usual maladies. We stood down after a week and headed back south on Highway 1 to LZ Sharon.

The problem of the company commanders using my medics on the guard perimeter kept surfacing. It was becoming a real problem. I was determined to deal with it. As our men came back from the field for gear or supplies, they were filling in Klemm on this unceasing dangerous practice. They couldn't refuse an order for fear of court-martial. On the other hand, they felt they could not do their job properly if attacked. They were between the proverbial "rock and a hard place." I had to evaluate the veracity of their stories and the depth of their feelings. This was a tough task ahead of me, but I was resolved to find an equitable solution. The medics were carrying enough responsibility as it was. One problem facing me was I was so new. I had no "street cred." I hadn't "earned my stripes" yet. I had no reputation to fall back on. I hadn't made any valuable alliances. I logically started by going to my colonel and asking his advice. I made a formal appointment to meet with him and explain the problem. It wasn't long before I was sitting in front of his desk, explaining the facts, as I knew them, and giving a solution by removing the medics from the perimeter. I told him this was causing low morale among the medics. These tactics would impair the effectiveness and success of his command. He listened, but without hesitation, said he always allowed his company commanders to do as they saw fit. He had no intention of changing his policy. He also added that my medics performed well during the rocket attack. That was it. Or was it? I did not feel beaten, just stalled. I went back to the BAS to ponder my options.

The next few days I walked around our compound. There were no birds to see to ease the tension, not even an Asian Tree Sparrow, the most common bird in the populated parts of Vietnam. I was thinking about my medics when my colonel unexpectedly sent me a message asking me to fly out to the bush with him and talk directly to the company commanders about their use of medics. Capital idea! I took this as a very positive sign and of course I gladly said yes. Besides, this would be a great opportunity to meet my other medics and see how they were set up. There were six to eight assigned to every company. That afternoon we took the boss's helicopter and flew east to the beach on the Gulf of Tonkin where all of our line units were standing down. I met each company commander. Alpha Company was headed by Captain Starr (that was his real name), a friendly sort, from the Midwest, about my age and a graduate of Officers Candidate School. He politely explained they were undermanned and had to use the medics to fill the gaps. Nothing more to talk about. He later lost his arm to an enemy hand grenade and received the Distinguished Service Cross (DSC), our nation's second highest decoration. We went over to Bravo Company's area and met their commander. Let's call him Captain Butthole. He stared at me with a hostile and unwavering gaze, his eyes squinting as if he were sizing me up for a shot from his M16 while I was explaining the problem. I don't think he heard a word I said. I was an irritating insect who stumbled into his domain that he would shortly squash. I knew I was in trouble when he called me Captain. I never saw his eyes blink during that whole conversation. It felt more like a showdown than a conversation. He was a hard-ass who had come up through the ranks. He was completely unsympathetic to my position, and didn't want to hear about a bunch of crybabies whining about anything. Here was a dangerous man. Later he was assassinated by his own men in a firefight, the last bullet coming from a .45 discharged into his skull at point blank range. The last was Charlie Company, commanded by an older seasoned career officer, Captain Terrific. He listened politely but said they needed every man on the line. I told him it was against regulations and the morale was bad. He said, "Well, so be it. That's the way it is going to stay." Two months later he brilliantly directed the defense of our position at Khe Sanh against overwhelming enemy forces. He was one hell of an officer. Keep in mind these conversations took place with our commander standing right there. They couldn't back down in front of him, at least not to a doctor. I went away with nothing, but I went in with nothing. I wasn't beaten yet. I did get to meet all of our line medics. I think the fact that I made the effort to talk to their commanders and fought for them greatly lifted their spirits. At least that was what I was told many years later.

The next few weeks were slow. I decided to break protocol and visit my brigade medical commander to see if he could bear pressure to help our medics. This was a blunder. I got polite dithering. I then made an appointment to see our brigade infantry commander, a full bird colonel and Lt. Col. Hartigan's boss. This proved to be a monstrous blunder. He asked me if I had talked it over with Hartigan and I said I had. That is why I was there to see him. His answer was the same as Hartigan's. These matters were best left in the hands of the company commanders. I sought out the USARV surgeon, the top medical brass in Vietnam, a brigadier one star. He refused to do anything about it, too, calling it a company matter. I was checkmated and felt terrible. Things got a lot worse for me from there. My activities—going outside the chain of command—drifted down to Hartigan. This form of disloyalty to one's commander was considered worse than deserting, nearly a capital offense. I was called into Hartigan's office. I brought with me my file of copies of all the regulations backing my position. I could find no exceptions. I walked into Hartigan's office. I stood in front of him because I was not invited to sit down. No perfunctory conversation. He started right in by telling me his boss told him of all my various visits. He was pissed! He said he had never seen such a flagrant display of disloyalty in all his years in the army. I handed him my carefully collected papers backing my position. Without even looking at them, he tossed them to the floor. The pages scattered all over his office. He said, "When you are under my command, I own you—body and soul. You are dismissed."

Well the shit had hit the fan. I was in hot water, had no position of strength, and nobody in my corner. At least I spoke out for my men. For the next month I was *persona non grata* around the battalion. There were no invitations to the officer's mess and no communication with the other officers, especially the infantry. Word had gotten around that I had tangled with the boss and lost.

The next day Capt. Jack Langston, D company commander, came down to the medic area and tried to hassle me about some minor issues about my medics. It was all pure nonsense. They were piling on. I would have none of it. A shouting match ensued, and I told him to leave the medical facility. This was my domain, and I used a phrase that would get any commander's attention: "You are impairing the health of the battalion's command!"

Outwitted by the doc, he left in a huff. Obstructing the work of the surgeon was a serious charge, and Jack Langston was not going to elevate our skirmish to a full-fledged battle with the Medical Corps. He was an old-line soldier and was too savvy for that. I told Klemm I was done jousting with windmills. I was gaining a lot of weight. Because of all the stress, I was eating a lot of comfort food—fats and carbs. I tipped the scales at 240 pounds in April, only two months after coming into the country. I was at my emotional nadir. I decided I needed to talk to my best friend, Dr. Norm Ruttenberg. He had been in Nam for ten months and had a lot more experience with the brass than I had. He had a great sense of humor, and I needed a good laugh. He also had a fiery temperament, and I needed some of that, too. I knew from his last letter that he was stationed at the 18th Surgical Hospital in Da Nang as a radiologist. I made arrangements with the doc of our sister battalion, the 1/11, to cover me, had orders cut to send me to the Da Nang Surgical Hospital for the weekend, and headed down Highway 1 with Krapse at the wheel. After 3-1/2 hours and 116 miles, I found the surgical hospital and Norm's hootch. I burst into his room without knocking. He was lying on his cot asleep. I shook his foot. He awoke slowly but couldn't make out my backlit face right away. When he finally recognized me, he leaped from his bed and gave me a big bear hug. We talked into the early morning hours. He explained the facts of life in the military in Viet Nam. Rule Number One: The military loves its rules and regulations but it uses them selectively to serve its own purposes. In my case, combat overrules everything. Rule Number Two: The most important officers in the unit are the commander and the doctor. Without the commander, everything falls apart until the next in command takes over, but without the doctor there is no one to take his place. Men die. Men get frightened. Who will take care of them? The morale plummets in free-fall. Rule Number Three: Unless the doctor commits egregious high crimes, no one touches him. There is nothing anyone can do to him. They can't bust him in rank, take his pay, or banish him to North Vietnam. Maybe he gets lucky and they send him home like Br'er Rabbit's "don't throw me in the briar patch" in *Tales of the South*. Norm's message to me was basically, tell them "to kiss you where the sun don't shine." You are practically immune from punishment. Rule Number Four: You are the only doctor. Nobody knows what you know. Run your medical unit the way you see fit.

Reenergized and inspired, and with newfound confidence, I took Norm's Rules back to LZ Sharon. The next ten months were dramatically different.

Deus ex machina. At the end of April I received a late evening summons to headquarters. Once more the room was filled with every officer in the battalion. I could sense the gravity of the situation. The officers seemed edgy. It seemed much more serious than our earlier mid-February briefing. The colonel arose to face the room. His poker-faced expression showed no tell lest he tip his hand at what he was about to say. He paused a long time for emphasis. He began, "Gentlemen, tomorrow at 0600 our entire battalion will go to Khe Sanh. We will meet elements of the 325th NVA Regiment in battle under the personal command of Gen. Giap." We all knew his name, Vo Nguyen Giap, a famous warrior, defeater of the French at the climactic battle of Dien Bien Phu in 1954. "Many of you will not come back. I wish you Godspeed and good luck. Are there any questions?" I knew to keep my mouth shut. After a pause, "Dismissed." As I suspected, this was a lot more serious than before. The North Vietnamese Army was not a ragtag, undisciplined, unmotivated band of ruffians. They were uniformed, well armed, and well trained. Their leaders, some going back to the French occupation and even the Japanese occupation of WWII, were professionals experienced in tactics and well indoctrinated in their cause. Once again, Sgt. Krapse prepared my track.

Figure 2-5. (Left to right) Me, unknown medic, Medic Carlson, Sgt. Darger, Medic Ezekial Campbell.

We traveled straight up that familiar Highway 1 until we made a sharp left turn above the Qua Viet River and headed east. This was a new route for us. The terrain changed from flatland to fairly good-sized hills, every curve and turn an ambush waiting to happen. The city of Khe Sanh and its airstrip, where the marines valiantly and victoriously fought their seventy-seven-day war a year before, was just a pile of rubble.

Figure 2-6. Khe Sanh, April 1969.

That was during the Vietnamese holiday, Tet '68, when the whole country exploded with NVA and VC troops attacking the South, and we knew what the results were. The South almost capitulated to the North. Now it was Tet a year later, and we were all on high alert. We arrived at our destination around noon. The engineers had preceded us and bulldozed flat several hills for our arrival and encampment.

Figure 2-7. Khe Sanh; Laos in background, April 1969.

Figure 2-8. Me at BAS, Khe Sanh, April 1969.

We were three kilometers from Laos and the Ho Chi Minh Trail. The engineers dug out a deep hole for us to set up our aid station below ground surface. It was the end of the dry season, and no rain was in the forecast to flood us. We were in the headquarters command section with the three line companies set strategically around us. Concertina wire was rolled in place and foxholes were dug. Machine gun nests were sandbagged and ready for firing. Claymore mines were set in place. All equipment was tested and ready to go. The line medics were fully supplied. The command post was established. There was a feeling of tension in the air like before a big game. The men were serious in their demeanor, no joking but confident and ready to get it on. I didn't know what their private thoughts were. They all had on their game faces. This would be my first battle actually facing the enemy, and I said a little prayer. There are no atheists in a foxhole.

We were getting negative reports from our recon teams about enemy in the area. But it was just a matter of time. We were near their main supply route, the Ho Chi Minh Trail. Earlier intelligence said that communist forces were all over the place. I kept thinking any time now, any time now. It was Ellsworth Bunker, American Ambassador to Vietnam, who famously said, "Vietnam is a boring place interrupted by moments of stark terror." And then it happened! Just before midnight, April 27, I heard one of our machine guns open up, *ak-ak-ak*, and then another, and then more joined in. Our M16s started blasting away on full automatic with no stopping. I had heard them other nights shoot a few rounds and stop. This was different, much different. Then everyone opened up as all hell broke loose. I even made out the sound of our medics' 60-mm machine guns joining the fight. Our tanks were firing at moving squads of enemy soldiers. The noise was deafening. The NVA commanders used whistle commands to direct their troops because the noise of battle obliterated any voice commands. Their mortars were exploding in our compound by the tens like infuriated killer bees stinging that hated honey bear. Our flares were lighting the battlefield. Shadowy helmeted uniformed figures were clambering outside our wire. They were so close I could hear them excitedly shouting to each other. We blew our Claymore mines exacting more unseen casualties. Our medics were attending our wounded. *Too hot to call in a Medevac. Stabilize these guys until morning when we can get them out.* Barrages of AK-47s and RPGs were raking our position.

Figure 2-9. The battle begins, incoming and outgoing tracer rounds, ours are red, NVA are green, early morning, Khe Sanh, April 28, 1969.

Like Army ants, the enemy was streaming through a breach in our wire with a full suicidal frontal attack. Our tanks accommodated them by lowering their canons and firing at point blank range into masses of charging NVA flesh. They breached our wire on our right flank with Bangalore torpedoes—sticks of dynamite wrapped in bamboo poles. They threw their dead comrades over the barbed wire and climbed their backs to reach us. A team of sappers was running amok in our camp tossing dynamite indiscriminately. Chicom grenades were flying everywhere. Sgt. Darger and I jumped into our foxhole. Darger had his M16 locked and loaded. I had my .45 cocked and ready. In the silver light of the flares, I could see a sapper running toward us, hands filled with dynamite. I saw his face. Darger raised his M16 and took aim. At the very last second the attacker veered off to be swallowed up by the darkness. The dogs of war were unleashed from both sides. Pandemonium prevailed. There was no let up. Our perimeter was continually being attacked by fresh troops with RPG and AK fire. There was hand-to-hand fighting. Our flamethrower squad moved out and reduced a whole NVA squad to charcoal. They were swarming all over us. I heard our commander call "Code Broken Arrow" repeatedly, giving our coordinates over the radio. This emergency call sign was only used when your position was about to be lost. Artillery from a distant battery finally began to shower 155-mm howitzer shells outside our position, marching them right up to our perimeter almost on top of our own men. Some of those rounds contained "Willie Pete," white phosphorous that would burn through flesh right down to and through their bones. Two fighter jets from Da Nang arrived about 0400 and rocketed and napalmed the area immediately outside our fighting position. They made pass after pass, immune to the small arms fire from the enemy below. The night was ablaze with burning earth and bodies. The smell of napalm filled my nostrils. When would this hell end? My medics were performing miracles and tens of wounded were at our aid station. It was still too hot to call in the Medevacs. Finally, as dawn was breaking, Puff the Magic Dragon, a fighter helicopter, flew in, and for good measure, poured sixty rounds a second into any enemy soldier still moving. B52 bombers joined the slaughter and dropped their bomb load on the fleeing enemy soldiers. It was over. It had turned into a rout, a massacre—a complete victory for us, a blood bath for them. During the battle, three of my medics in Alpha Company formed a defensive position in a B52 bomb crater on our left flank, dragged their patients out of harm's way into the crater, and defended them against wave after wave of NVA attackers. One of those medics carried a wounded man under each arm out of harm's way to the crater despite heavy enemy fire. He was my "McNamara's 100,000." I kept an eye on him, all right. I watched him get the Silver Star that night for his bravery, the highest honor of any medic in our platoon. His name was Billy Scarborough. The other two, Specialists Doug Haney and Chris White, were awarded the Bronze Star with Valor.

The sunrise of early morning April 28, allowed me to view the carnage on the entire battlefield. Enemy bodies were strewn in all directions, thirty-five in all. We reckoned another 350 were wounded. Going through their pockets, we found bags of marijuana along with a few personal effects, pictures of family. I judged the average age to be around nineteen. Entire elements of the 325th NVA Regiment were wiped out. There were two bodies tangled on the concertina wire. They were hammered with machine gun fire before they made it through. Brains and other body parts were indiscriminately scattered over the killing field.

Figure 2-10. NVA soldier KIA, Khe Sanh, April 28, 1969.

Hordes of flies were arriving. All the bodies were checked for signs of life. There were none. Shockingly there were tourniquets on all of their arms and legs. I had never heard of this tactic before. They were so committed to their task they would not allow a wound to their arms or legs deter them. I found only one charred sneaker where our flamethrowers were operating. Nothing else. Blood trails were seen going down the hill. We followed them and found empty shallow graves at the bottom, apparently dug before their attack. We estimated they began crawling up our hill under the cover of darkness for about three hours before midnight. Once in place they launched their assault with all the venom and hatred they could muster. We lost seven riflemen and one officer, Lt. Vann. Lt. Vann had the great misfortune of stopping at our position the afternoon before on his way to Quang Tri to go home. His tour of duty was up. He had a serious fungal infection that I treated. That night he joined one of our line companies. An RPG killed him when the track he was fighting from blew up.

Figure 2-11. Our Armored Personnel Carrier (APC) destroyed by NVA Rocket Propelled Grenade (RPG), Khe Sanh, April 28, 1969.

Coincidentally, another lieutenant, independent of Vann, was also on his way back from the field and stopped in to see me. He had the flu. He was from Columbus, and I knew his father, a famous neurosurgeon from The Ohio State University. He also joined a line unit, fought like hell through the night and made it. The wounded were triaged, and eight men were evacuated to the Quang Tri Marine Corps Hospital, bandaged, sedated, IVs running, and accompanied by our medics.

One of our machine gunners, who in the heat of battle forgot to wear his asbestos gloves while changing the gun's white-hot barrel, suffered from third degree burns, charred right down to his finger bones.

Figure 2-12. Khe Sanh, April 28, 1969, spent casings from a .50 caliber machine gun.

About twenty others were treated for minor injuries and remained. Specialist Doug Haney was choppered in from the field carrying his dead company commander. No amount of supportive words could comfort him. He also had his eardrums blown out from the concussive force of an enemy mortar. We sent him back for treatment despite his protestations. Our dead were placed in body bags and sent to the rear. The enemy dead were given a mass burial. All of their weapons were collected into a bomb crater and blown up with C4.

Figure 2-13. Medic Chris "Sonny" Eing with Bangalore torpedo.

The battle was over, but the pageantry had just begun. Helicopters were dropping out of the sky like blackbirds landing in a cornfield. Generals and colonels from the rear were there to bask in the glory of their planning and training.

Figure 2-14. The "Big Brass" fly in after the battle, Khe Sanh, April 28, 1969.

The man who had directed our battle so successfully was none other than Captain Terrific, the same captain who had refused my pleading to take my medics off his line a couple of months back. He had performed magnificently under the most severe pressure, doubtlessly saving all of our lives with his quick decision-making and calm demeanor. Hearty congratulations were passed around to all of the officers and fighting men. No one said a word to the medics who had gone about their duties heroically and skillfully that night. This was always par for the course. I don't think they took us for granted, but after the fighting, we seemed to become invisible. The infantry soldiers always looked after their own.

My one regret about the war was I was so naïve about the way the Army worked, that I never proposed any of my men for awards of valor, medals they had earned with their guts and devotion to their men. I believed our work was our reward. (Many years later, I got that chance.)

I had never seen an impact command ceremony before. Our commander lined up a group of our men all standing at rigid attention. The commanding general of I Corps went down the line, one by one, pinning bronze and silver stars on their chests. The adrenaline was still flowing, and the exhilaration of victory and survival filled the air. I swore I heard "The Battle Hymn of the Republic" playing in the background. Damn, what a sight!

As we were heading back to our area, I heard what sounded like bees whining over our heads. It wasn't quite over yet. The boys in green had left snipers on the next hill to pick off some careless soldiers. A radio call with their coordinates to our artillery battery finished them off.

Figure 2-15. In the distance, U.S. artillery eradicating enemy snipers, Khe Sanh, April 28, 1969.

Finally it was over.

After a few more days, we headed back home to LZ Sharon. The rains had started to come and they came in buckets. The Khe Sanh roads became practically impassable with their slick, slippery clay soil. I had a new inexperienced track driver, McNamara. He had never driven an APC in Nam. The roads were narrow, on one side steep vertical walls, on the other side a sheer drop into deep canyons. The slightest miscalculation and we were in serious trouble. It was also a perfect set up for an ambush. We would be sitting ducks with nowhere to escape, no cover and no maneuverability. The "pucker factor" was ten on a scale of ten! For hours, McNamara guided our track up and down the treacherous terrain with great skill and courage despite his inexperience and got us down and back to Highway 1 safely.

Figure 2-16. I return from Khe Sanh, early May 1969.

During one long delay, I spied a small bird, a tiny Kingfisher flying repeatedly from its perch snatching flying insects and returning to the same branch. This must be *Ceyx erithaca*, the Black-backed Kingfisher, the smallest kingfisher in the world, a pure lifer for me.

I was looking forward to a long rest at LZ Sharon. This was the most tired I had ever been. We were barely back at Sharon for one day when the colonel's command sergeant major, the highest ranking enlisted man in the battalion, personally came to the BAS and extended me an invitation from the colonel to attend officer's mess that evening. *Okay, let's see what this is all about.* I arrived for the prerequisite drinks and chitchat. The colonel greeted me warmly and directed his conversation toward me. He said he admired the way my medics and I had performed our duties the night of the Khe Sanh battle. He was grateful for so few deaths under such severe conditions, and attributed much of this positive result to the immediate and skillful actions of my men and me. He invited me to sit on his right at the head table. I accepted his words and invitation with thanks and humility. He asked me if I needed anything, and I told him I requisitioned a microscope two months ago but never got it. The next day I had my microscope.

The days at Sharon were getting longer as we moved into summer. I was settling into a mundane routine, sick call, reading books, and writing letters home. For exercise we organized touch football and "jungle rules" volleyball games with our medics.

Figure 2-17. I place a spike in a "jungle rules" volleyball game.

My Combat Medical Badge arrived. We all switched to black cloth "subdued insignia" and removed all shiny brass metal from our uniforms, which had been an easy target for the enemy to locate and kill our leaders. Klemm and I would discuss our battalion's medical issues in the evenings. These conversations would always get around to home. I told him if we ever got out of this, we would have a reunion at the Kahiki, the best restaurant in Columbus. I had time to reflect on my life and my hopes for the future. I was watching young men being killed, vanishing before they even had begun to live, not enjoying the freedoms for which they were fighting. I had been unhappy for a few years in my marriage to Inge because of her infidelity. I tried, but never came to terms with it. One evening I told Klemm that I was going to divorce her when and if I returned home; life was too short.

One morning I saw a young trooper complaining of foot pain at sick call. I knew he was a ground pounder, and foot pain could severely hamper his performance, placing him and his squad in danger. I took his history, nothing remarkable there. Examination of his feet was also unremarkable. I found out his company was going back to the field in a couple of days. I wondered if that was the cause of his foot pain. "Malingering" was a problem in Nam but not a huge problem. I gave him a "profile" for light duty for two days, thinking if he had a strain, a little rest and warm soaks would take care of his problem. A "profile" is a note written to his superiors excusing him from duty for medical reasons. It was inviolable. Two days later he was back with the same complaint. Physical examination including skin color, pulses, and joint mobility were all negative. He had a normal arch—no flat feet. Maybe I was missing something, so I sent him up to Quang Tri hospital for an X-ray of his feet. The next day he returned to the BAS with a profile excusing him from all duty for a week written by the brigade surgeon. The X-rays were negative. I found out that his company had left for the field that same morning. I felt strongly he was a "shammer," a shirker. I was angered on many counts—he had gone above my head and had the orthopedic surgeon write him a profile; he was gaming the system. He was indeed a shammer. The rear echelon brigade surgeon had fallen for his story and superseded my authority; and he was forcing the other guys in his unit to pick up his slack. I ceremoniously tore up his profile in front of him and my medics. They had never seen that before. The soldier was caught off guard. He thought he had gotten one over on the doc. His reaction was violent. He cussed me out in front of my men, lunged in my direction, and threatened to kill me. Klemm, who was there, reacted immediately. He took the safety off his loaded M16, stepped between my assailant and me, and jammed the bore of his rifle hard into the man's chest. My other medics, seeing my danger, grabbed their rifles, switched the safeties off and with fingers ready on their triggers pointed them menacingly. Klemm pushed him backward, and he fell out of the BAS. He kimbled away with his back to us, cussing me the whole time. I told Klemm to contact his first sergeant and start preparing court martial charges. I had just been involved in the bloodiest battle our troops had endured, brave men were dying for their country—and this crud was *pretending* to be disabled so others would put their lives on the line for him. I would have none of it. I took his death threat seriously. I checked my hootch to make sure there were no gaps in the ground sandbags for a hand grenade to roll under my floorboards. This was called "fragging." Fragging was becoming more popular among some crazies, like this man, for even minor slights. That night, I posted sentries outside my sleeping quarters and slept soundly. The following day, surprisingly, the man was back with his first sergeant, hat in hand, meekly asking for a reprieve. I was still mighty pissed. I refused to relent and sent them both away. I kept the sentries posted the next couple of nights. A few days later, I was told that the man's mother died and he was sent home on a mercy leave. That psychopath probably arranged her death, too. I never heard from him again.

At the Quang Tri PX I saw a book entitled *Birds of South Vietnam* by Philip Wildash. It was a first edition published in 1968 by Charles E. Tuttle Company, Inc., of Rutland, Vermont & Tokyo, Japan. It was the only book about Vietnam birds available, because the 1931 four-volume *Les Oiseaux de l'Indochine Francaise* was out of print and difficult to procure. Besides, *Les Oiseaux* was a reference book and not a field guide. There was only one book for sale. Had there been more and other birders snapped them up? I perused a copy before I purchased it. I was going to buy it anyway. The cover flap described the author as a lifetime birder stationed at the British Embassy in Saigon for two years. It described 586 species only of South Vietnam. The geographical distribution was divided into two zones, north of Qui Nhon to the DMZ and south of Qui Nhon to the Mekong Delta. There was a short history of ornithology in Indochina and a map of South Vietnam. Twenty-five colored plates of rather rudimentarily drawn subjects by the author himself were conveniently placed across from the description of those birds. The descriptions were succinctly divided into three sections—habits, distribution, and identification. There was a foreword by Jean Delacour, a French ornithologist, preface, systematic list of birds, bird anatomy lesson, a description of the geography of South Vietnam, and a page of definitions. A short bibliography rounded it out. It wasn't a *Peterson's Field Guide,* but at least it would point me in the right direction. I bought it for $3. The next day I requisitioned a pair of 7 x 35 army-issue binoculars from the quartermaster.

I never birded in Vietmam—I mean truly birded, looking for new species and keeping field notes. I was too busy and too cautious to leave my compound. All the birds I saw in Nam were incidental to my job.

The following is a list of species with their common names at the time and today's names. I kept the list from February 12, 1969 to February 11, 1970:

Original Names	Modern Names
Common Cormorant, *Phalacrocorax carbo*	Great Cormorant
Little Egret, *Egretta garzetta*	
Osprey, *Pandion haliaetus*	
Barred Bustard Quail, *Turnix suscitator*	Barred Buttonquail
Little Ringed Plover, *Charadrius dubius*	
Wood Sandpiper, *Tringa glareola*	
Little Tern, *Sterna albifrons*	
Orange Breasted Green Pigeon, *Treron viduata*	Orange-breasted Green Pigeon
Blue-throated Bee-Eater, *Merops viridis*	Blue-throated Bee-eater
House Swift, *Apus affinis*	Fork-tailed swift, *Apus pacificus* ID corrected
Schach's Shrike, *Lanius schach*	Long-tailed Shrike
Lesser Skylark, *Alauda gulgula*	Oriental Skylark
Barn Swallow, *Hirundo rustica*	
Richard's Pipit, *Anthus novaeseelandiae*	Oriental or Paddyfield Pipit, *Anthus rufulus*
Bronzed Tree Pie, *Crypserina temia*	Racket-tailed Treepie
Tree Sparrow, *Passer montanus*	Eurasian Tree Sparrow
Common Myna, *Sturnus tristus*	*Acridotheres tristis*
Chestnut-back Shrike, *Lanius collurioides*	Burmese Shrike
Roseate Minivet, *Pericrocotus roseus*	Rosy Minivet
Jack Snipe, *Lymnocryptes minima*	*Lymnocryptes minimus*
Gray Heron, *Ardea cinerea*	
Yellow-bellied Wren-Warbler, *Prinia flaviventris*	Yellow-bellied Prinia
Red Turtle Dove, *Streptopelia tranquebarica*	Red-collared Dove
Unlisted Dwarf Kingfisher	Black-backed Kingfisher, *Ceyx erithaca*

The summer months were upon us, hot and hotter with heavy downpours and strong winds called the monsoon. One quiet afternoon my CQ ran to get me. A radio message came in that two of our men in the field had been seriously injured by a Claymore mine. They were sending a chopper to pick me up and fly me to the men. This sounded peculiar because Claymores were our defensive mines detonated only by our own men, the old version of today's IEDs (Improvised Explosive Devices). Why were there no medics there already? A Huey helicopter landed in front of the BAS. I called for Sgt. Darger, grabbed a medic's emergency pack, and was airborne in seconds. I had been in helicopters many times before and was used to the extreme banking upon takeoffs and landings. You might expect to fall out of the doorless helicopter any second, but you don't because the centripetal force and gravity plant you to the craft's floor. I had learned from my first sergeant the safest seat was the rear left passenger seat. If the chopper was hit and went down, the clockwise motion of the rotary blade would kill the right rear seat passenger first. One had a minutely slightly better chance to survive in the other seat. Upon arrival I saw a bloody mess with two men on the ground, riflemen standing helplessly over them. No medics were there because these two were away from camp setting up a distant listening post. One of the men, Abraham who had been acting strangely recently, apparently went berserk and blew the Claymores. The other soldier, Byrd had the supreme misfortune to be standing next to him. Haney, just a week before had seen Abraham talking to himself and visually hallucinating. He reported Abraham's bizarre behavior to his CO with a recommendation to send him to the rear for psychiatric evaluation. The company commander told Haney that if he sent everyone who complained of mental problems to the rear, he would be left with no fighting men. So the warning signs were already there, but the CO failed to act.

Rapid assessment: both alive, Byrd unconscious and unresponsive, Abraham alert but in great pain; despite lower mandible missing, no appreciable bleeding. Byrd's airway open with shallow respiration and weak rapid thready pulse, chest clear and abdomen negative; spurting arterial blood from right arm and left leg, face mangled, in shock. I worked on Byrd, the more seriously wounded of the two, Darger on Abraham. Tourniquets were applied to Byrd and IVs started above the tourniquets, two in Byrd. Morphine given; loaded in the Huey. This was not one of our regular rescue helicopters. There were no hooks to hang the IVs. Darger held one, and I handed the other to Abraham who was sitting up with a blank stare.

I yelled to the young army warrant officer pilot, "Fly as high and fast as you can to the 3rd Marine Hospital."

Altitude for safety, speed for necessity. Abraham had an iron constitution and was remarkably stable. He and Darger watched as I worked feverishly on Byrd, clamping off arterial pumpers, rotating tourniquets and opening the saline IVs to full throttle. He was in hemorrhagic shock from massive blood loss. I couldn't possibly overload his nineteen-year-old heart. And then, damn this war, he stopped breathing and had no pulse. I had no idea how far we were from the Quang Tri Marine Corps Hospital. I immediately administered artificial respiration as was taught in that era, chest pump and mouth-to-mouth breathing, alternating with Darger on the top.

I kept calling to him, "Don't go, don't go," over and over again. "Come back, come back."

And then an almost imperceptible pulse and slow labored respirations began.

"Keep it up, Byrd, keep it up." After what seemed like an eternity, we landed in the yard of the hospital. Their corpsmen were waiting for us, and they run-carried the men on gurneys into the ER. I gave a quick synopsis of their history and treatment to the naval surgeon in charge as they were working on both men. There was nothing more for me to do. The navy corpsmen at the Marine Corps Hospital were some of the best in Nam. I left feeling completely emotionally and physically spent and flew back to Sharon. I believed Byrd would die from irreversible shock and blood loss. I wasn't worried about Abraham. There was never any follow-up communication between the hospitals and the battalion surgeons in the field. I guess they didn't have the time. I often wondered about the outcomes of the many wounded I sent to the rear treatment facilities. I did not find out Byrd's and Abraham's fates until 2008, nearly forty years later.

Fast forward to 2008. I received a call from Dana, my daughter, who was visiting our South Jersey shore summer home. She said that she had picked up a message left on our telephone voicemail from a Doug Haney a week ago but forgot to call me. He said he was one of my medics in Vietnam. It was urgent that I called him, and he left a contact number. I could not recall who he was, and I wondered if I should call him. What could he possibly want so long after the war? I called Klemm, with whom I had stayed in close contact, and asked him if he remembered Haney. There were so many men and medics that year, he couldn't remember him either. What if he were an imposter, a "wannabe," looking for some favors? There were lots of "wannabes" around, Navy Seals, Green Berets and medic imposters, many falsely trading on the reputations of the men who had in fact served honorably in combat. I decided I had nothing to lose, and called the number. He answered the phone on the second ring. "Hello," a voice said hesitantly.

"This is Dr. Master. Were you trying to reach me?"

There was a long pause and then, "Dr. Master, thank you so much for calling. I have been trying to reach you for years," he said excitedly.

Before I let the conversation go any further, I said that after so many years, I truthfully could not place his name, and I wanted to ask a few questions. I had already mentally prepared a few knockout questions.

"In what company did you serve?"

"Alpha."

"Who was your company commander?"

"Captain Starr," he said without hesitation.

"Name some of the other medics you served with."

He mentioned names with which I was familiar. "Okay, Doug, what can I do for you?"

"Well, sir, do you remember the night of April 28 at Khe Sanh?"

"Yes, who could forget?"

"Well, sir, I was supposed to get a Bronze Star with 'V' device, and I have never received it."

I thought about that. "Okay, why do you want it now?"

"For my family, sir."

He passed the identity quiz, and I thought his reason was plenty good. I told him I had not filled out any of these medal forms for many years. If he would fill them out and send them to me, I would read them carefully. If they rang true, I would sign and return them. It was then his responsibility to walk them through channels at the Pentagon. He agreed, and after many "thank yous" we hung up. A few days later I received his packet of forms in triplicate. They were filled out to the minutest detail describing his role in our now famous Khe Sanh battle of April 28, 1969. He wrote factually about his and two other medics' forming a defensive position in a B52 bomb crater protecting their wounded men against the repeated onslaught of enemy soldiers. I signed it and mailed it back.

I completely forgot about this whole episode. Two years later, I received a call from Haney.

"Sir, I got it."

"What do you mean, you got it?"

"I received my Bronze Star with 'V.' There will be an award ceremony this Memorial Day at the Sacramento, California, State House Vietnam War Memorial. As my commanding officer, I want to give you the honor of pinning it on my chest."

It was unbelievable. He had doggedly maneuvered his request through the red tape and the Washington bureaucracy over a two-year period, a testament to his patience and character. "Of course I will be there. It will be an honor and a pleasure." I immediately cancelled my Maine birding plans with my birding buddy, Dr. Tim Fitzpatrick, a traditional yearly excursion to his Lubec, Maine, home. I always looked forward to this. Tim easily understood what this meant to me and to Doug Haney. We can always go birding. This, however, was a once in a lifetime experience. Thinking back, there were a lot of "what ifs." What if Dana had completely forgotten to relay Doug's message? More importantly, I was only a month away from removing the landline from that home, since we all use cell phones now. What if Doug had tried to reach me after that? My home phone was unlisted. What if I did not call him back? Was this fate, luck, or providence at work?

I flew to Sacramento the day before the ceremony. I had already boned up on the conduction of the actual medal ceremony with my long-time friend, Tom Manion, a two-tour Vietnam First Recon marine. He was up on all the protocols, having remained engaged in corps activity throughout his post-corps life, if there is such a thing. I wanted it to be as professional as it could be for Doug Haney. I checked in at the Hyatt, which faced the State House green. I called Doug and set up a meeting with him for that evening. I walked over to the Vietnam Memorial to check things out. It was amazing. The "Wall" was a replica of the Washington, D.C., Wall except it only carried the names of the California dead. There were bronzes expertly and artfully cast surrounding the Wall. It was dignified and stirring. That night I greeted Doug for the first time in almost forty years. He brought his entire family, wife, son, grandchildren, and best friends; I recognized him right away. The following morning I strolled over to the Wall. I was wearing a civilian suit with my army decorations over my left breast pocket as prescribed. My Bronze Star lapel pin in place for a little extra emphasis. The crowd was filing in, and a somber and respectful mood filled the air. There were about three hundred in all, many from the Sacramento Vietnam Veterans of America Chapter 500. Most of the guys were dressed in jungle fatigues and bush hats, medals and unit citation ribbons in place. Facial hair predominated. These were the guys who had seen it all. I imagined there were enough PTSD cases in the audience to keep a mental health facility busy for a lifetime. They were still living their war. Many had their families with them. There was a sprinkle of local and state politicians. A large contingency of ethnic Vietnamese veterans were there. The flag of South Vietnam flew below the Stars and Stripes. I was given a seat of honor and a program. I looked over the program to see when I would present Doug his Bronze Star.

"12:00 noon, Guest Speaker, Dr. Bernard Master; 12:30, Medal Ceremony."

What? Guest speaker? A half hour?

I didn't know about this! I was unprepared to talk for thirty minutes to three hundred plus strangers. This felt like one of those nightmarish dreams I used to have being unprepared for Dean Pettit's Organic Chemistry exam and receiving a failing grade. I surveyed the audience and knew what my address would contain. When I was called to the podium at noon, I began talking about Khe Sanh, April 28, 1969, in vivid detail. Every man out in that crowd had their own April 28. I added ten minutes about PTSD for the wives and families of these injured men. There were knowing nods as I mentioned temper outbursts, hyper-alertness, self-absorption, and recurrent nightmares and the necessity of treatment. I was on their wavelength and everybody knew it. I extolled the virtues of Doug Haney, all my medics, and all the fighting men that night and every night. I rocked the place. There was no fidgeting, no talking. The audience and I were one. Afterward, I smartly carried out the medal ceremony and sat.

Figure 2-18. Me placing the Bronze Star with Valor device on my former medic, Doug Haney, for his actions at Khe Sanh (1969), Memorial Day, Sacramento, CA, 2008.

There were a few remarks from politicos, and then it was over. I received the good wishes of many of the men, Chapter 500 Commander, an army nurse and Doug. He thanked me profusely and then said, "I have a present for you," as he motioned to someone in the crowd. I watched as an older, graying African-American man limped slowly toward me. He came very close so that I could see every feature of his leathery face.

He spoke saying, "Do you know who I am?"

"I am sorry but I do not."

"I am Sherrell Byrd. You saved my life on the battlefield."

Disbelief was followed by a wave of exaltation flowing through my body as I realized it was true. Standing in front of me was the greatest present anyone had ever given me.

"I thought you died."

"Well, here I am," he said, smiling.

He handed me two paintings, gifts he had made for this occasion, both scenes from our time in Vietnam. We all walked slowly away talking about his final days in Nam. I asked him if he wanted to recount to me his long road to recovery. He readily told me his story. He had emergency surgery at the Quang Tri Hospital immediately after we carried him in. After one week post-op, he was still in critical condition. His prognosis was poor. The doctors did not think he would live, but he was nineteen years old; he was strong and had great determination and faith. He made slow progress over the following few weeks. When he was strong enough, they flew him to the hospital ship, *USS Sanctuary*, in the Gulf of Tonkin for more treatment and recovery. He had lost his right arm, left leg, and right eye but his will was not gone. After three weeks they flew him to an Army hospital in Japan. He spent eight months there getting stronger and stronger. They fit him with a new arm, new leg, and prosthetic eye. He learned to use these prosthetics as well as his natural limbs. Physical therapy continued until he was well enough to return to the States. He landed in San Francisco where he ran into Doug Haney and, of all people, Abraham, his old nemesis whose insane act had changed his life forever. He was discharged from the Army because of his wounds. He returned to St. Louis and got a job at General Motors and married. Seven years later he went to college on the G.I. Bill and became an art teacher. He taught art in high school in Belleville, Illinois, for thirty years. His three children, nine grandchildren, and one great-grandchild are all good, productive citizens and a credit to their parents. Sherrell was a great soldier and is a great American. Byrd's story can be seen on a three-hour video in the Library of Congress. There is no finish line for him. Abraham died of natural causes several years before the ceremony. He never acclimated to civilian life.

Figure 2-19. Former comrades-in-arms, Doug Haney (left), me, Alan Bush, and Sherrell Byrd (right).

Between April and October, our battalion was involved in three more major operations, two at the "Z" and one in October back at Khe Sanh. Ellsworth Bunker's words were prescient. In between these operations the days dragged on with little to do. I held sick calls daily.

Figure 2-20. Fire Base Alpha 4, DMZ, 1969.

There was always malaria. After any contact with the enemy, cases of malaria would pop up two to three weeks later. I learned that malaria was endemic to the Vietnamese who were chronic carriers. The lifetime of an adult Anopheles mosquito, the insect host of the potentially deadly *Plasmodium falciparum*, the causative agent, was about a month. Their range during their entire lifetime was no more than a football field. During enemy contact, the female mosquito would bite an infected Vietnamese soldier and buzz over to bite one of our men, transferring the parasite. I diagnosed many a case of malaria and even dengue fever. After eight months of sick calls, pitched battles, firefights, ambushes, mines, snipers, malingerers, threats, and malaria I felt mentally fatigued and suffered from burn out.

Figure 2-21. Tiger killed by Claymore mine outside sister battalion 1/11 camp.

I was becoming irritable, impatient, and short-tempered. I was not sleeping well—always listening for incoming or the sound of my name to come for some medical emergency. I had earned my Combat Medical Badge, the same as my medics, an award that only a few doctors were privileged to wear. I also had a Bronze Star from the first six months of action. I was down from a massive 240 pounds in April to my low of 185 pounds in October from the heat, loss of appetite, dysentery, anxiety, exercise, and poor eating habits. Letters from home were a balm but not enough. I did not do drugs and only drank alcohol sparingly. I always wanted to be clear headed and ready for action. I felt a strong sense of loyalty to my men and medics, and I sensed it was being returned. I didn't think I was bored, but I did need a change of scenery badly. The USARV rules called for a rotation of doctors every six months out of the field to an army hospital. My transfer was overdue by two months. I called Saigon to find out when I would be transferred. I reached someone in the medical transfer section and gave my name. I told him I was two months past the regulation limit and I wanted a transfer to a hospital. The voice said I must have a replacement before I could leave. I asked him where my replacement was. He had to put me on hold to find out.

After about fifteen minutes, he came back to the phone and said in a serious tone, "Captain Master, your replacement is still in medical school."

During one of the operations on the DMZ, word was sent to me that my close friend, First Lt. Brian Heath, was killed in a rocket attack back at Quang Tri. Ironically, he had been in all the heavy action against the NVA back in October 1968, and never received a scratch. He was a platoon leader of uncommon skill and bravery. He was extremely intelligent and had a smile that would light up the room. As a boyishly handsome and fun loving Irishman, no doubt he was popular with the ladies back in Florida. He, Klemm, and I spent a lot of our down time talking about home, sports, and history. He was a real American history buff. He loved astronomy. I had a cardboard star identifier, and we would try to sort out the constellations at night. There was no ambient light in Nam, and the coal black starry night was awesome. The human eye can count two thousand individual stars in the blackest sky, and Brian wanted to know the name of every one of them.

While he was supervising loading of supplies to send to us at the Z, a rocket attack covered the airstrip. Instead of hitting the ground immediately, he tried to run across the airstrip to a bunker. Shrapnel hit him in his head and heart, and, still running, fell dead into the bunker. The irony of his being in the rear and dying and my being at the front unscathed never escaped me. I never got a chance to say goodbye to my good friend.

Figure 2-22. First Lt. Brian Heath (left), me, First Lt. Klemm Ungemach (right), LZ Sharon, 1969.

Col. Hartigan had left in September with full regalia and a huge party in the officer's mess. We all said something we thought no one else knew about him, mostly humorous. He, in turn, addressed each officer individually. When he came to me, it was obvious he had buried the hatchet four campaigns ago. He said I was the finest battalion surgeon he had ever seen, a comment I cherish to this day. We were all in good spirits but saddened to see him leave. You never know what the next commander will be like. He was Lt. Col. John Swaringen, a West Pointer. I briefed him on the health of his new command. He explained what reports he wanted from me. No problem there. I had been well schooled by Hartigan who had edited my early reports and even marked them up with red pencil like some schoolmarm. Swaringen was on his way to becoming a general. He went by the book, no nonsense, but was fair and even-handed. Nothing really changed, and it was a seamless transition.

It was at this time that Secretary McNamara switched our military tactics from "Search and Destroy" to the "Win the Hearts and Minds" policy. I was told that I would be sent to un-pacified villages filled with VC and VC sympathizers to render medical care. *Okay, this will be interesting.* I was pretty much aware of the tropical diseases extant in the native population like plague, malaria, dengue, hookworm, and tuberculosis, but I had never actually seen plague, small pox, or the really exotic diseases, let alone diagnosed and treated them. Our troops simply never got them. The drill was to helicopter to the outskirts of the village. Vietnamese Popular Forces (PFs) and some of our men would reconnoiter for enemy soldiers in the vicinity, and then I, with a couple of medics and an interpreter, would go in and do my thing.

Figure 2-23. MEDCAP, somewhere in Northern I Corps.

Sometimes a firefight would break out as our guys would find and kill some VC hiding in the village. So much for "winning hearts and minds." We would enter, set up a small aid station, and begin treating the *hofs* and *dows*, coughs and pain.

Figure 2-24. MEDCAP, somewhere in Northern I Corps. Interpreter Kong (left), KIA later.

The line of patients was long with usually only the elderly and children. It is a universal truth that all mothers want their children cared for.

The Vietnamese also had great respect for their elderly. I suspected a lot of TB and dispensed medications for long-term use. Headache was a common complaint. Hookworm was endemic in the rural areas because of fields filled with "nightsoil." These were fields used by the locals in which to defecate.

Public health programs were absent throughout Vietnam. Hookworm was endemic in Vietnam. Rural Vietnamese would defecate in the fields, using their feces for fertilizer. Their feces contain hookworm, which, when walked on, would enter through the barefoot skin of the next person using the field, keeping the cycle of infection and reinfection going. The symptoms of hookworm are stomach pain and signs of anemia. I roughly judged the status of their red blood cell content by the color of their conjunctiva and the pallor of their skin. I didn't have lab capabilities to make definitive diagnoses so I relied on history and physical alone. Here is where the adage of the great Hopkins physician, Sir William Osler, was born in mind, "Never leave the bedside without a diagnosis." This was like practicing in the nineteenth century. Anti-helminthics worked wonders. I used cough syrups and decongestants for their URIs, aspirin for pain and Darvon Compound for severe pain. Once in a great while I would Medevac someone with a surgical abdomen or an overwhelming bacterial infection with sepsis. I saw my first cases of small pox and plague in all of its forms during these MEDCAPS (Medical Civilian Action Programs). Vietnam had the dubious distinction of having the most cases of plague of any country in the entire world. The rat population exploded during the war, and all efforts of eradication of this carrier were woefully inadequate. Over the weeks that followed, certain intelligence was picked up by our men in the field that altered my mode of treatment radically. Medications I was dispensing were being found on captured VC. The treated villagers were also trading meds, one bottle of blue syrup for two bottles of red syrup. Darvon Compound capsules, with their beautiful red and gray colors, commanded an especially high premium. I switched strategies—I used no pills except aspirin; no syrups, URIs would self-resolve; and injectable long-acting penicillin for bacterial infections. This solved the diversion problem. I was also up against long-existing cult practices, moxibustion, cupping, and shamanism. The practice of covering a newborn's umbilical stump with fresh water buffalo dung was commonplace. This practice caused dangerous infections, even sepsis in the newborn.

PART THREE
Saigon

"Captain Master, your transfer orders have arrived."

This message arrived at Sharon in late October. I had given up any hope for a transfer and resigned myself to a full tour with the $1^{st}/61^{st}$. My orders read to report to Tan Son Nhut AFB, Saigon. I knew there was a hospital for wounded North Vietnamese and Viet Cong there. This could be interesting duty. I was interested in new medical experiences. I said my farewells to the officers and men of the battalion, making sure I personally saw every one of them. I bade special goodbyes to my medics. Klemm and I said, "Until we meet again, friend," and I was off to Saigon.

At Tan Son Nhut, I was housed in the officer's billet until I received my final assignment. So it wasn't the prison hospital after all. That evening I went to the officers' shower to wash off the travel grime. While I was shaving, I happened to see in the mirror a man behind me with the nametag "Masters" with a caduceus and captain's bars on his shirt. My name does not have an "s" on the end but my father's older brother's did. My father always insisted his own spelling was correct. I turned and said I was a "Master" also and a physician. Could we be related?

He said in Yiddish, "Are you Jewish?"

I understood a little Yiddish and replied that my father was. He said then we probably are related. We went to the officers' club and talked for hours about our families. He was Frank Masters, MD, a psychiatrist on his way home to St. Louis after a full tour of duty at a hospital. We compared family trees as far back as we knew. There might have been a common ancestor five generations back. We called each other cousins anyway. We still stay in touch.

The next day my orders arrived. I was on my way to the highly vaunted 3rd Field Hospital in Saigon. Its reputation for excellence in the Southeast Asian theater preceded itself. Its doctors and nurses were some of the best in the entire uniformed services. They counted on their roles—neurosurgeons, hand surgeons, and thoracic surgeons to name just a few. I was very excited about the opportunities awaiting me here.

Figure 2-25. Third Field Hospital, Saigon.

There were medical lectures, a medical library and journal clubs, social hours with other medical staff, good hot freshly prepared food, and it was relatively safe tucked in downtown Saigon. I reported to a bird colonel lifer medical doctor. After snapping him my best infantry salute, I handed him my personnel file and was invited to sit down. I didn't realize how bad a shape I was in. I sported a shaggy handlebar moustache and needed my head shorn of my much too long hippy-looking hair. My tired, gaunt facial expression told him all. My fatigues were old and dusty. My Australian bush hat was tilted cockily to one side. My dog tags were hanging from my neck, and in infantry mode, on one boot. He didn't need to look at my file. I would have been the prototype for Elliot Gould in the movie, *MASH*.

He said, "I want you to do nothing for a while. Rest and renew yourself. I will call you when we need you."

What a wise man, the physician in him emerging and recognizing the signs of battle fatigue. I was housed in a downtown hotel with a nice spacious western-style room complete with a flush toilet and hot shower in my private bath. What luxury! A real flush toilet. The hotel had a maid come in daily to straighten my room, do my laundry, and polish my boots. I was left on my own to explore downtown Saigon, once "The Pearl of the Orient." Still a model of French colonial architecture, Saigon transported me to the 1930s. On its bustling streets I saw automobiles for the first time in nine months, Citroens, Mercedes, and Peugeots. Real taxicabs were mixed in with the thousands of bicycles and cyclos. The citizenry were actively going about their business in their traditional dress; however, I began seeing a few Vietnamese dressed in Western clothes for the first time. I saw my first fat Vietnamese, either a high ranking government worker, or a successful businessman I supposed. On Tudo Street there were the infamous "Tea Bars" loaded with prostitutes catering to the GI trade. I found out later that American soldiers, NCOs, who would re-up, owned some of these establishments. There were many legitimate bars and restaurants offering five-star French and Vietnamese cuisine for inexpensive prices. I was still too gun shy to enter these places on my own and had most of my meals at the hospital. I saw an open-air black market running for blocks and blocks offering everything from live chickens to army issue jeeps. Black market goods like Chivas Regal Scotch and Marlboro cigarettes were displayed openly with impunity. The mood in the Saigon streets was cold and business-like, no hostility, no sense of dread. Things moved along as if there were no war going on, no fear of a Khe Sanh here.

The colonel finally called me to his office.

"I have a very nice quiet spot for you, Phu Lam in Cholon."

Cholon was the Chinese district of Saigon. Phu Lam Signal Battalion housed all the heavy equipment and switch lines for all the communications in South Vietnam. The hotline between the White House and Generals Westmoreland and his successor Creighton Abrams was also there. One can imagine the security level at this installation was the highest. I arrived at Phu Lam the beginning of the dry season. There was heavy security at the gate with heavily armed MPs checking everyone's ID against a "permission to enter" list.

Figure 2-26. Phu Lam Signal Battalion, Cholon, Saigon.

I met my new commander, and that night at the officers' club, met all of the other officers, a mixture of captains, first lieutenants, and an executive-officer major, all Signal Corps. There wasn't a crossed rifle among them. They were happy to have a doctor who had been up North with a fighting group. They asked lots of questions about everything I had seen and done. I was billeted in an officer's barracks with my own private room and bath. It had a real bed, shower and flush toilet, writing desk and chair, closet and telephone. All the rooms shared a hootch girl who did the wash, cleaning, and boot shining. The compound was sprawling over several acres, fenced in with high chain link and barbed wire. The perimeter was heavily guarded by MPs with M16s and .50

caliber machine guns. Gigantic signal antennas were everywhere. I was taken to the dispensary, which would be my office for the next three months.

Figure 2-27. Phu Lam Dispensary; Sgt. Pridgeon (left),
Nurse Ba Trinh (right).

There I was introduced to my medical staff, three medics, all specialists and one NCO, my first sergeant, Sgt. 1st Class Pridgeon. There was also a Vietnamese nurse, Ba Trinh. I was replacing a doctor who had replaced a doctor killed a year ago. During that doctor's last week in Nam, he left the compound to go out to the countryside to take souvenir pictures, got out of his jeep, and stepped on a mine. There were about seven doctors killed in the war. One, James Sosnowski, DO, a friend of mine from my Columbus hospital, was blown up while he was in surgery. He had unselfishly draped his body over his patient to protect him from exploding mortar shells.

Over the next few days I went through my medics' personnel files, reviewed the SOPs, and inspected our equipment and pharmacy. I made few changes. The daily routine was sick call in the morning for about eight to ten patients, half GIs and the other half civilians working at Phu Lam. Everything was routine. One patient in particular presented an interesting challenge. He happened to be an American in his fifties, head of all construction in Saigon—a big job. The army contracted out all of its building construction to private American corporations. He was a very brittle insulin-dependent diabetic. He had a nasty looking diabetic ulcer on his lower leg that just wouldn't heal. He had been to the Third Field Hospital specialists with poor results. He lived in Saigon, and out of desperation was trying the Phu Lam Dispensary. During my year and a half in private practice, I had some success with these indolent diabetic ulcers. The first thing I addressed was his diet and exercise. He had been enjoying the good life in Saigon, eating and drinking without care and was taking no physical exercise. His blood sugars were out of whack. I impressed on him a well-balanced diabetic diet, cut down his alcohol, and asked him to stop smoking. My father, a foot surgeon in Philadelphia, taught me a trick to heal these things. After each careful and repeated debridement, use a powdered antibiotic on the wound, not a cream or ointment that many docs were using. The powder acts as a nidus for fresh tissue to cling, and upon which new healthy tissue could grow. Add daily walking exercise, increasing the distance every day to tolerance. Magically, I had this chronic ulcer healed in a month. There were a few perks to my job. My grateful patient was so happy with the result that he invited me to dinner at his beautiful French colonial villa. It was a wonderful meal expertly prepared by his Vietnamese cook and exquisitely finished with a one-hundred-year-old Napoleon Brandy.

The Phu Lam compound held a very well-appointed officers' club, Olympic-sized pool, a full basketball court, a library, a PX, and a mess hall. I was taken aback at all this luxury and felt some resentment that the fighting men up North had none of these. After sick call I would join the other officers in a basketball game at noon, the hottest part of the day. After the game we would do calisthenics together. At

185 pounds, I was in the best physical shape of my life. I learned to play Bridge and spent many evenings passing the time with this fascinating game. I never left the compound. No souvenir picture taking for me. I had seen all of Vietnam I ever wanted to. I was counting down the last ninety days, and in military parlance I was "short"—meaning I only had a short time left before I DEROSed (Date of Return from Over Seas). I was taking no chances.

Sgt. Pridgeon was a squinty-eyed career soldier. He was finishing his second tour of duty in Nam. I found out later he owned a bar downtown and was protecting his asset. He was a master scrounger and could procure anything the dispensary needed. His brother was also an NCO in Saigon, posted at the docks where the transport ships would come in. Our guys always had steaks or lobsters for our weekly cookouts. I never asked where they came from. Ba Trinh was a quiet comely woman in her forties, very kind in her manner, efficient in her duties, and respectful to me. Reputedly she was a Hmong tribeswoman, one of the minorities of Vietnam, ill-treated by the ethnic Vietnamese. The medics had never been in a line unit but were well trained and eager to learn.

There was one bad apple in the bunch, a lazy drug-using shirker. I had Sgt. Pridgeon keep an eye on him, and gave him no duties of responsibility. I was not a shrink and was not ready to assume those duties. I sent him to psychiatry in Saigon. The drug of choice in Nam in 1969 and 1970 was marijuana with some LSD slipping in with returnees from R&R in Hawaii. Marijuana was present among the men but not rampant, and I did not consider it a big problem. THC, the active ingredient in marijuana, was four- to five-times more potent in Nam than the grass being smoked back in the U.S. I was told it really carried a wallop. It was cheap and readily available. Heroin and amphetamines were not considered a problem then, but later, toward the end of the war, became epidemic. Alcohol consumption was huge among the men, but also not a big problem. Beer was free to the men in the field and considered one of the perks of the job. Officers, NCOs, and enlisted men's clubs were on every base, and alcohol with top shelf-brands was always available for little money. The best scotch was only twenty-five cents a shot. In my opinion, the tension and pressures of the war, the natural camaraderie among men sharing similar tough experiences, the macho culture and military traditions of meeting clubs, toasting and the like, fostered this drinking culture. There was no doubt that at least a few career officers and NCOs were functioning alcoholics.

The days crawled by. During the last three weeks, I left my room only for sick call, a game of basketball, and meals. I had acute "short-timer's" syndrome. I was not able to depart Vietnam until I had a replacement. The rules were clear on that. There was still a shortage of general medical officers in Vietnam. Finally, a week before my expected date of return to the States, my orders arrived. Now I had to wait for my replacement, the NFG. Word arrived five days later that my replacement was at the Third Field Hospital. I donned my stateside green woolen suit with the shiny captain's bars, caduceus, new division patches, Combat Medical Badge, and a few new ribbons. I was tan, lean, and in prime fighting condition, never felt better. I said my farewells to all the medics, fellow officers, and teary-eyed nurse Ba Trinh. (I always wondered what happened to Mrs. Trinh after the fall of Saigon.) Sgt. Pridgeon drove me to Tan Son Nhut AFB. I boarded a commercial 727 and, in what seemed like a flash, was deplaning in San Francisco.

Figure 2-28. The plane that brought me home, February 11, 1970.

When I finally stood on American soil again, I said a little prayer and literally kissed the ground. I met Inge, Kenny, and Dana in Newark, New Jersey, for a tearful reunion. Kenny, six, looked at me for a long, hard time. Dana, three, knew me right away. It was February in Atlantic Highlands, New Jersey, where my family was staying with my in-laws while I was in Nam. Three things I remember the most—first, loads of fat Americans everywhere, all ages and both sexes. Second, I could never get warm. I walked around the house for a month with my coat on. Third, the sounds of helicopters coming out of Fort Monmouth would make me pull over to the side of the road until I realized where I was. I must say that when I returned home, I received no disrespect for my service like so many other brother veterans. I did not realize it at the time, but know it now, that, for us, the war is never over.

CHAPTER THREE
Post Surgeon: Fort Holabird, Dundalk, Maryland

*Peace is that one glorious moment in history
when everybody stands around reloading.*
—Attributed to Thomas Jefferson

My orders came from Fort Monmouth, New Jersey, posting me to Fort Holabird, Maryland. I had a month to settle back into family life and rediscover all the things I missed about America. I decided to drive to Dundalk, Maryland, to have a look around. The town was in the outskirts of Baltimore, pretty run down, old and sooty. It was a few miles from the Chesapeake Bay, and I was happy that I was back on the East coast. I discovered that Fort Holabird was the home of the Military Intelligence School for the U.S. Army. This would be interesting. The MI guys travel all over the world and are a suspicious sort, but they are very interesting to talk to when they decide they want to talk to you. What rare diseases from all over the world would challenge me? I drove a short distance south and checked out some possible rental homes I had circled in the Baltimore Sun newspaper. I settled on a cozy ranch style home in Severna Park, Maryland, next to the Severn River. It sat on a large wooded lot with a big backyard for the kids and our Bullmastiff, Impala, to play. It was only walking distance to Ken's elementary school. And, it was about a half hour from the fort and eight miles from

Annapolis and the Naval Academy. After settling in, I reported to Fort Meade, Virginia, the administrative authority of the many army forts in the Maryland-Virginia-Washington triangle. The following Monday morning, I reported to my new assignment. The first thing to hit me was that the parking lot for the doctors seemed like miles away from the dispensary. We were jammed in the lot with hundreds of other cars belonging to students and all sorts of army and civilian personnel. This simply would not do. The dispensary was housed in a building that showed its age with storm-warped wooden windowsills and blackened stones from the Dundalk soot. It was a white elephant from a bygone era. It needed a serious facelift, if not a complete makeover. The long wooden corridors and whitewashed halls were dimly lit from its old yellowish light bulbs hanging down from ten-foot ceilings. Notwithstanding these flaws, it had a certain old-fashioned charm about it. I presented myself, shiny captain's bars, caduceus, Combat Medical Badge, and all my Vietnam Campaign ribbons to the post surgeon. I immediately read his uniform. He hadn't been anywhere or done anything. He had never left the states. He only held a captain's rank, which was a big disadvantage for the medics in a fort this size heavy with all of its brass. He was a pediatric neurologist, Hopkins trained, and was nearing the end of his two-year military obligation. He appeared somewhat disconnected from his job, probably counting the days when he would enter civilian life again. I really couldn't blame him. He went over my duties with me, daily sick call, shared night call, and weekend call, which required being physically present at the base on a rotating basis with the other docs. *This will never do. Weekends at the fort? Who made up these rules?* All of our specialist consultations went to Fort Meade or Walter Reed Hospital, depending on the type and seriousness of the case. I met our first sergeant, Sgt. 1st Class Roberts, two RNs who had been there forever, and four medics, all with favorable first impressions. Next I was introduced to our civilian radiologist who had a back office and a poor attitude.

He had a high ranking civilian GS rating, which made him equivalent to a lieutenant colonel, yet he had no authority over any of us military doctors. He was a graduate of the University of Maryland, but he thought he had graduated from Harvard. I told him I was a graduate of the Philadelphia College of Osteopathic Medicine. *A DO?* He could not believe the army was allowing Doctors of osteopathic medicine to serve as medical officers. It was a little-known fact that before DOs were first inducted into the armed forces, the AMA extracted a promise from the army that a DO would never outrank an MD. This covenant was shattered forever when the military brass saw how competent and well trained the osteopathic physicians were, and how well they performed under fire. That agreement became forgotten history and Ronald Blank, DO, became the U.S. Army's first surgeon general graduate from an osteopathic medical school. This radiologist's animosity toward me and DOs was immediate and glaring. Over the next few months his unprofessional behavior steadily worsened. I tried to deal with him with professionalism and politeness. This just fanned his fire. The only way to treat a bully is to punch him hard—right in the mouth. He and people like him are their own worst enemy. They are so caught up in their irrational hostility that they are easily brought down, and the best part is they never see it coming.

I was shown my office, a rather small space with an examining table, chair, gooseneck lamp, and writing desk—something out of an old B war movie. I checked the equipment, lab and pharmacy, and got a list of all the tests that could be performed on site and a list of their drugs. The drug list and tests available were up to date. There was no pharmacist. The medics did all of the dispensing. Over the next two days I went to work seeing patients and treating common illnesses. There was one major difference between Vietnam and Fort Holabird—there were female patients here, lots of them. My stint in private practice helped me tremendously in knowing how to diagnose and treat gynecological problems, perform Pap smears, and, sadly, perform medical legal examinations for rape victims. I was gradually introduced to the other doctors as the first week wore on. Neal Kolsky, MD, and Frank Palmisano, MD, turned out to be outstanding physicians. The third doc, over the next few months, showed himself to be a loser and a shirker. He was hardly ever at the dispensary so I did not have much contact with him. The post surgeon just endured him. We could carry his load easily because the patient counts were low. I thought the dispensary was overstaffed with doctors anyway. The third day I was called by one of my colleagues to examine a Marine Corps gunny sergeant with a 105-degree fever. He suspected a tropical disease but had no experience in that area. Because I was the only Vietnam veteran among us, he thought I could make the diagnosis. He was right. Gunny had just returned from a tour of duty in Nam. He "smelled" like malaria to me. I had seen so many cases. I looked at his history, felt an enlarged spleen and liver, and immediately shipped him to Walter Reed Hospital with a presumptive diagnosis of malaria. Bingo, path slides were positive for *Falciparum* malaria.

By the end of the month, the post surgeon's contract with the Army was up. He rode into the sunset, most likely into a lucrative Hopkins' group practice. Because I was the oldest doctor at the fort and had more time in service than any of the other doctors, the Fort Meade medical commander asked me to assume the duties of post surgeon. That was fine with me. There were a million things I wanted to change. Our previous leader was passive, did not like confrontation, and had kept the status quo for two years at the dispensary. There were no new programs initiated and no new equipment or medical procedures introduced. I had some distinct advantages over my predecessor, and I would use them for the good of the doctors and the patients. Serving with an infantry unit for nine months had toughened me, and I knew exactly how the Army worked. Use your first sergeant. The doctor was untouchable. Run the medical facility like you know how. "Norm's Rules" were in play now. I moved into the more expansive and impressive post surgeon's consultation room. I insisted that I, as post surgeon, would extend the courtesy of my medical care to all the foreign military intelligence officers and their families. This diplomatic move went a long way with the foreign officers and their families who were used to white glove treatment in their own countries. I had the first sergeant requisition paint and signs. The doctors were no longer going to walk "miles" in all kinds of weather to get to their offices. First sergeant painted four parking spaces immediately in front of the dispensary with the sign, "Parking for Surgeons only." No one complained.

One Friday afternoon, while standing in the fort commissary reading bulletin board messages, I heard a voice behind me brusquely ask, "Captain, do you work at the dispensary?"

"Yes," I answered not having a clue what was going to follow.

"I want you to get a haircut and have all the other doctors get a haircut," said this MI lieutenant colonel, whom I had never seen before.

I was flabbergasted. Colonels Hartigan and Swaringen, my former battalion commanders in Nam, had never disrespected me this way. I was offended and mightily pissed! I forgot about it for the time being, finished my duties at the dispensary, and went home for the weekend. Well, he didn't forget about it. First thing Monday morning my office phone rang.

"This is Col. Jock Itch. Did you get a haircut?"

I was incredulous that I was receiving this ridiculous phone call to start my week. I quickly collected myself. I was a thirty-year-old doctor just back from Nam, and I had this butthole colonel—not in the line of my command—giving me some chicken shit orders about practically nothing.

He went on, "Did your men get haircuts?"

"No," I said getting more irritated by the second.

"Why not?" he demanded.

"We are too damn busy taking care of your men!" I barked and slammed the phone down.

A few minutes later the phone rang again.

"What?"

His voice was in a controlled rage. "We were disconnected."

"No, colonel," I said, and that famous line by Warden Strother Martin delivered to convict Paul Newman in the movie, *Cool Hand Luke,* popped into my mouth. "'What we have here is a failure to communicate.' Now, I have to get back to my patients," and I hung up on him again.

"First sergeant!" I fairly screamed down the hall.

Within seconds Sergeant Roberts appeared. "Sir?"

"Take a contingency of medics and go over to Colonel Jock Itch's area and shut him down! I mean everything, swimming pool, mess hall, heads. Massive E. coli contamination!" The battle had begun and I had all the big guns.

"Yes, Sir."

Sergeant Roberts was off in a flash. A couple of hours later he returned with a big grin.

"Done, Sir, and they weren't very happy about it."

A strain of Escherichia coli causes a bacterial disease, Traveler's Diarrhea, completely debilitating the patients for about a week and potentially closing down the fort, bringing all of its activities to a standstill. Everything has to be scrubbed with disinfectant and then retested before it could function again. I had lots more in store for this moron—and all by Army regulation. Later that afternoon my phone rang. It was the big boss, General Good Guy, Fort Holabird's commander. I was surprised it took him this long.

"Doc, what's going on between you and Col. Jock Itch?"

"Well Sir, we found a massive contamination of E. coli, you know, fecal matter, throughout his area and well, we had to shut him down until he repaired the problem. You know

Sir, HE WAS IMPAIRING THE HEALTH OF YOUR COMMAND."

Those magical words I learned in Nam. This phrase translates to, *YOU WILL NEVER BE PROMOTED AGAIN*, to all savvy commanders. Even worse, all kinds of public health agencies would be swarming over the fort, likely even bringing some bad press.

"Okay, Doc. Carry On."

The one-day "Haircut War" was over. I never heard another word about haircuts.

The next week, my Fort Meade medical commander came over to see me. He told me I had been promoted to major and presented me with a second Bronze Star for my last six months in Nam. Those shiny captain's bars were replaced with major subdued gold oak leaves, and the captain's hat with a field grade officer's hat with the "scrambled eggs" golden brocade on its bill. With this elevation, I felt emboldened to improve the dispensary's condition and status even more. I recommended, and they received, a pay increase for my two RNs who hadn't had a raise in years. I recommended, and Sergeant Roberts received, another stripe, making him an E-8 master sergeant. Because the sick calls were so light, we did not need four doctors on duty at all times. I changed the duty roster to a four-day week for the docs with four doctors on duty Mondays, our busiest day, and three doctors the other days. And now that hated rule of being physically present on the weekends. Since my first day, there were never any cases serious enough for a doctor's attention on the weekends. I thought it was a waste of time and resources to have the docs sleep over Friday through Monday. Besides, I had a family and I wanted my weekends with them. The medics would rotate evenings and weekends and triage the cases, calling the doctors into the dispensary for cases they couldn't handle. This was done without fanfare and not a negative word was heard. I only had to come in once that year. I was asked to accompany an officer to the home of a family in the middle of the night to deliver the horrible news that the husband and father of two was killed in Nam.

In keeping with my mission of improving the health care of the men at Fort Holabird, I established a dermatology clinic one afternoon a week. I was getting pretty good at diagnosing and treating skin conditions. I had a couple of years under my belt seeing various kinds of rashes, weird ones in Nam and common ones in Columbus, Ohio. This clinic saved the patients from traveling across town to visit a Fort Meade dermatologist, thereby saving everyone time and expense. The top brass liked it, too. We were seeing lots of "lumps and bumps," growths that could easily be removed by a general practitioner. I had removed a lot in Nam and in my practice in Columbus. I showed Dr. Frank Palmisano how to excise small growths, since he was going directly into private practice after his army hitch and needed that skill. We both manned the newly formed "Minor Surgery Clinic" one afternoon a week. We were keeping ourselves busy by helping our patients.

There was one more bit of unfinished business with Dr. Butthole, the arrogant radiologist. I figured, give him enough time, and he would screw up. A jerk like that couldn't help himself. He was nasty to the patients and disrespectful to me. I was now a field grade officer and the new post surgeon. Morale was at an all-time high at the dispensary. We didn't need his brand of surliness spoiling our day. Sure enough, he gave me my chance to have him booted. I had a soldier I diagnosed with pneumonia whom I sent back to radiology for a chest X-ray. After a few minutes, I walked back to look at the X-ray. This was an important part of my care of a patient, personally reviewing their X-rays and lab work. The radiologist saw me standing there, turned his back and ignored me. I asked him to show me the X-ray of my patient.

He said, "What for? You don't know what you are looking at anyway."

Au contraire, Butthole, I had great training and I did know what I was looking at. Well, I gave him enough rope and he finally hung himself. I left his room, went directly to my phone, and called the fort commander, Brigadier General Good Guy. I told his clerk it was urgent.

He came to the phone and said, "Hello, Doc. What can I do for you?"

I said I had a serious situation here at the dispensary with the civilian radiologist. He was interfering with the medical treatment of one of his men, a very sick enlisted man with pneumonia.

"Sir, he is impairing the health of your command. I would like you to suspend him from his duties immediately and remove him permanently from the dispensary. This is not the first time I have had trouble from him."

The next day he was gone forever.

Weekends were filled with family excursions to Washington to see our nation's riches. We loved the Smithsonian and the Lincoln Memorial. We paid our respects to the Tomb of the Unknown Soldier, JFK's gravesite and the Iwo Jima Memorial. The changing of the guard ceremony at the Tomb was thrilling. Trips afield took us to State and National Parks, Maryland's historic town, St. Michaels, Teddy Roosevelt Island, Fort McHenry and Civil War battlefields. We picked fossil shark's teeth and millennial old shells from the beach at Calvert Cliffs, Maryland. We explored the city of Baltimore and learned about Edgar Allen Poe. The restaurants were great with fish and crab fresh from the Chesapeake Bay. Of course, there was birding. One outing to David Hall Park, Maryland, with the Virginia Audubon Society produced a list of seventy species on April 18, 1970.

We visited Glen Echo, on the shores of the Potomac. It was here that a prominent role was played in the famous Alger Hiss–Whitaker Chambers spy affair. A Prothonotary Warbler starred as the "key witness." Alger Hiss, once a high-ranking member of the State Department was accused of being a Soviet spy. His accuser was Whitaker Chambers, a former communist whom Hiss claimed he never met before and did not know. To prove to the House Un-American

Affairs Committee (HUAC) that Chambers knew Hiss well, Chambers related that Hiss had told him he had seen the rare Prothonotary Warbler at Glen Echo, a small park along the Potomac. Later at a break in the proceedings, and not an official part of the record, Richard Nixon (before he became President), asked Hiss if he had ever seen a Prothonotary Warbler at Glen Echo Park. Hiss admitted that, yes, indeed he had seen that rare bird along the Potomac. The Committee took this little off-the-record fact as confirmation that Hiss and Chambers did know each other and Hiss was lying about it. Hiss later admitted knowing Chambers but not by that name, rather by Chamber's pseudonym, Carl. Hiss was convicted of perjury and sentenced to five years in prison. I believe that Hiss was innocent and agree with President Harry Truman's assessment that the charges were trumped up. Remember that this was the Joseph McCarthy era. McCarthy, a headline seeker, made the outrageous claim that the State Department was filled with communists. In Hiss's defense, The HUAC members, all non-birders, didn't realize that birders, having seen a rare bird, would excitedly tell everybody of their find. Hiss's Prothonotary Warbler discovery could have reached Chambers from any number of sources.

Over the next few months, I had a couple of very interesting patients. What began as a routine examination of a soldier with dysentery turned into the most fascinating case of my professional career. A twenty-eight-year-old Green Beret staff sergeant came to see me with the chief complaint of persistent diarrhea for a year! He was suffering from fatigue and weight loss. He had been taking over-the-counter meds for his diarrhea, but they were no help. I asked him his past traveling history, but he said he was prohibited from telling me because it was classified. These MI types were always very guarded with their information. His secrecy made the diagnosis more difficult, but I was determined to figure out the cause of his problem. His physical exam showed a thin, white male in no acute distress. He looked chronically ill with pallor and had an enlarged liver and spleen. Everything else was non-contributory. I started my testing with the obvious—stool analysis and culture, complete blood count, urinalysis, and blood liver screen. I asked him to come back in a week to receive the results. In a week, I received the data from Fort Meade and reviewed it expectantly. His blood count was all out of whack with severe anemia, a high white blood cell count, and a pronounced eosinophilia indicative of a parasitic infestation. And then the payoff. The stool sample showed *Leischmania donovani*, a protozoa causing severe debilitation, and if untreated, leading to death. This trooper had *Kala-Azar, Visceral Leischmaniasis*, rarely seen in the States. The visceral form of this disease was not very common anywhere although its skin form, *Cutaneous Leischmaniasis*, was common in tropical countries, especially Africa, Central and South America. Even though he would not reveal where he had been in the last five years, at this point of his treatment it was moot because we had identified the offending organism in his stool. Later I learned what a lucky find this was, because *L. donovani* is rarely found this way, tissue biopsy being the gold standard. I referred him to Walter Reed Hospital for treatment. About six weeks later he returned to the dispensary for a follow-up visit. He reported they had given him some powerful heavy metal treatment with success. He was gaining weight, and his energy was returning. He was extremely grateful for my involvement in his case. Over the course of the next few months during check-ups, he revealed his story to me. He was part of the hit squad chasing Che Guevara in Bolivia. Che was a radicalized Argentine working for Fidel Castro fomenting Marxist style revolution throughout South America. The hit-squad—composed of Bolivian army personnel, CIA agents and our MI sergeant—caught up to Che in early October, 1967, in Vallegrande, and by order of the Bolivian President, was assassinated a couple of days later, shot point blank in the head. The official press release stated that Che was killed by South American Indians.

Interesting to me was the Bolivians' rejection of Che's Cuban style of Marxism and their continuation to reject it to this day.

The commandant of Fort Holabird had a debilitating chronic sinus infection and complained of severe headaches and difficulty breathing from stopped up nasal passages. I ordered X-rays, blood count, and allergy testing. I began treating him with, among other things, a series of silver nitrate packs to his nasal mucous membranes and heat lamps to his sinus cavities with great results. This was a remedy taught to me by an old-timer ENT specialist. At last he was able to breathe, and his headaches abated. On each visit we would learn a little bit more about each other. During the Vietnam War he was a staff member to General William Westmoreland. He was present at the Hawaii Conference in 1968 where he briefed President Lyndon Johnson on the current state of the war. It was widely held that Westmoreland lied to the President by creating a rosier picture of American success than really existed. I asked the colonel about this. Did Westmoreland lie? The colonel said no, that Westmoreland was using the intelligence afforded him from the commanders in the field who did in fact create a more positive picture of pacification than actually existed to make themselves look better. Body counts, a McNamara metric, do lie, and they were puffed up. General Westmoreland was also of the old-school tradition, which went all the way back to the Revolutionary War days, of, *I'll try harder, Sir.* This meant Westmoreland could win the war with the number of soldiers he had in the field at the time—a woeful underestimation as it turned out. From the information LBJ received at this meeting, he elected to continue the war, keeping the status quo in the South, and escalating it in the North with carpet-bombing. The war dragged on for seven more years with thousands more of our men killed and wounded.

The rest of my year in Maryland proceeded smoothly, and I was contemplating my options for the future. I could enlist for another four years. I could return to my former general practice in Columbus. I could look for a residency somewhere. The army option presented too many rules and regulations. The residency option meant I was starting over at the bottom of the ladder and using up another three valuable earning years. Returning to my old practice had the most appeal, and in the spring of 1971, I rejoined my two partners, Drs. Arnold Allenius and Richard Leedy back in Columbus.

At this time, I began creating a personal bird list. At the end of subsequent chapters I have included my world list and American Bird Association list tallies for various points in my life.

WORLD 689 • ABA 619

CHAPTER FOUR
The MEDCenters: Full Service Primary Care Centers

Our greatest glory is not in never failing, but in rising every time we fail.
—Confucius

The demographics of my practice had changed considerably during the two years I was in the Army. The Linden neighborhood was in a state of flux. The largely white working and middle-class patients were moving north to the outer rim of Columbus, and in their place came poor and lower-income whites and African Americans. The elderly, having no means to move, stayed put. Lyndon Johnson's "Great Society" gave us not only the Civil Rights Act of 1964, but also Medicaid and Medicare in 1965. The payor class of our patients went from high-paying company insurance and cash to low imbursements from these federal programs. Do we move north to follow our patients or do we stay in Linden and treat whoever walks through our doors? We decided to stick it out in Linden. Our practice was growing rapidly with this policy. We were the only doctors in the area who would accept Medicaid and Medicare patients. These patients, up until now, were being treated at The Ohio State University hospital clinics or in the emergency rooms. We changed that pattern once it became known that all were welcome in our practice. Twenty to thirty new patients a day were being seen by our four doctors. I was working Monday through Saturday. We rotated call every fourth week. I was making hospital rounds early in the morning and getting to the office by 9 a.m. During lunch or after office hours, I would make house calls. I covered the ER on my call week. I delivered my own OB patients. I went to two nursing homes a week. I would get home around 9 p.m. most days, tuck in the kids, and have dinner. The next day brought the same routine.

I bought my first house in the upper middle class Worthington Hills section of the northwest community of Worthington, an older historic town sixteen miles from downtown Columbus. I was very close to the freeway, and it was almost a straight shot to my office. My unbroken, heavy work pace started to wear on me after a year and a half. I began to take Wednesday afternoons off and worked every other Saturday. I played racquetball and squash at the downtown Salesian Boys and Girls Club with my new friend, Larry Kaufman, a pharmacist. He was from Cleveland, had a heart of gold, and I loved his big city ways. Larry taught me how to play tennis. I loved the sport, a combination of power and elegance. I even took lessons at Donald Dunn's Columbus Indoor Tennis Club on Joyce Avenue. Sundays were reserved for family outings to various places of interest like the Serpent Mound in Adams County, COSI, the Columbus Zoo, or just walks in the nearby Metro Parks.

We went to a lot of AKC dog shows. I had purchased a Bullmastiff for protection before I left for Vietnam, a beautiful female named Impala. Her actual name was "Ntala," but over the phone the breeder's voice in British Columbia sounded like she was saying "Impala." She was a fine specimen of the breed, a big red, with black muzzle, dark eyes and ears, square face, straight top line, and well angled hocks. She had a beautiful disposition, but at twenty-four inches at the withers and weighing 120 pounds, she looked very imposing. On weekends my wife, Inge, would show Impala at AKC events. Impala finished her conformation championship before she was two years old. She was lovely and we wanted her pups. We bred her to "Red Steve," the dominant winning Bullmastiff in the country, owned by Virgil and Adele Millet from Long Island. After a couple of tries over a period of two years, we gave up. Later she turned out to be sterile from endometriosis, a very painful gynecological condition.

For relaxation, I was birding again, mostly in Green Lawn Cemetery and Franklin County Metro Parks. My practice was growing rapidly. Hypertension, diabetes mellitus type II, and heart disease were rampant in this new population. Having been an asthmatic since age seven, I took a special interest in this disease. One thing I included in my treatment regimen of these patients was a home visit to inspect for allergens. Why do so many asthmatics have dogs or cats in their homes?

Dr. Arnold Allenius, our senior partner, a veteran doctor and smart businessman, decided we should expand our building. The empty lot next to us was available, and he purchased it for $250,000. Our expansion housed twelve more treatment rooms, and space for a pharmacy, podiatrist, psychologist, lab, optometrist, and a private office only for Dr. Allenius. He was beginning to separate himself from us. It was a beautiful building designed by the creator of the Kahiki and Top restaurants, architect Coburn Morgan. The building floor plan and the rent structure became the model for my later buildings, ten in all. We added five more doctors at one time to handle the deluge of patients. In 1971, we hired the first physician's assistant ever to work in Columbus. Joe was a good practitioner but was misguided and tried to unionize our office. He did not succeed.

This one-stop health care shopping was the first of its kind anywhere. Under one roof was all the medical care the average patient would need. It saved travel time and expense for the patients and was lucrative for our practitioners. We practically emptied the OSU clinics. Our staff was highly trained and completely subservient to the needs of our sick patients. We learned what to do by doing the opposite of OSU's surly, indifferent, and unfriendly staff. If the patient needed forms filled out, no problem. If they needed off-work notes or handicapped parking forms filled out, we did it. We never worked by appointments because our clientele never kept them—it was first come, first serve only. Our halls were immaculate, gleaming, and spacious with no obstruction to eye contact between doctors and nurses. We invented a color-coded system of flags on each room. Each practitioner was assigned a color, which meant a patient wishing to see a particular doctor would have that doctor's flag outside their room. All of the nurses had one color. In 1974 we opened a new medical clinic in Victorian Village, a medically underserved area half way between OSU campus and the center of downtown Columbus.

I was selected to work there and build the practice at Dennison Avenue Medical Center (DAMC). It was another Coburn Morgan architectural masterpiece, beautiful yet functional. All of the allied health care professionals from Linden followed us and opened up their second offices. I handpicked my staff from the original office. I chose Sheryl Cardwell, an African-American single mother, whom I had lured from the hospital six years before, to be my office manager. One of nine children of a West Virginia coal miner and his wife, Sheryl knew the meaning of hard work. She was intelligent and a quick learner, never shying away from any duty no matter how large or difficult. She turned out to be a great choice, and we worked together for the next twenty-three years. I had complete confidence in her abilities and character.

Toward the end of 1973, I was catching the drift that the other six doctors in the original Linden practice were disgruntled with the way the profits were being divided up. Allenius was raking 12.5 percent off the top from the practice to begin with and keeping all of the rents on top of that. The remainder was split eight ways including Allenius getting an equal share on top of his already whopping 12.5 percent. He even stopped seeing patients and hid out in his private office. He wasn't contributing a penny to the bottom line. It became apparent that we were all working for him. He basically was hogging all the money. We all met clandestinely to discuss our demands. Our plan was to give him a chance to rectify the problem by creating a more equitable split, something based along the lines of production, or we would leave to start another practice to compete with him. We thought if we opened an office nearby, the patients would follow us. The meeting with Allenius did not go well. He wouldn't budge on any points. He thought his value was in the management of the practice and demanded special favor as its founder. He was a former drill instructor in the Marines, and he was treating us like raw recruits. He wanted us to bend to his will. We would have none of that. We started planning our move *en masse*. I went out and found us a suitable medical building just up the street with room for a pharmacy. Larry Kaufman would be our pharmacist. We were ready to leave in December, and we told Allenius the week before.

I received a call the next day after our announcement. Allenius said he urgently needed to see me that day. After office hours, he came to my office and we sat down to talk. He looked a mess, hair unkempt, eyes bloodshot, and a worried look on his face. He started by paternalistically saying that he could not understand our bad attitude with everything he had done for us. Nevertheless, he had two big investments in both buildings and both practices, and he knew he could not pay the mortgages by working them alone. He wanted to offer me a deal I could not refuse. I owned a small percentage of the DAMC building and practice. He owned the rest. He would trade me my percentage of the building for his percentage of the practice. He would become my landlord, I his tenant. The rent would be $8,000 per month, triple net, for ten years. He knew I was the only one of the group who was capable of generating enough income to pay his rent and cover his mortgage payments. To sweeten the deal, he would also give me all the furniture, equipment, drugs, and supplies on the shelves, and the accounts receivable. I couldn't believe what I was hearing. This was a deal of a lifetime, a no brainer. I knew this practice inside and out. The receivables were about $100,000, which would more than sustain me until I developed my own income stream. I was grossing about $20,000 a month and growing rapidly. I didn't have to ask for another thing. He recognized his financial bind, and I was his solution. I agreed to the terms, and we shook on it. This one move changed the entire direction of my life. The next day I called the other doctors to tell them I was not joining their group nor was I staying with Allenius. I would be staying at DAMC, owning and operating my own practice. The reaction was surprisingly vitriolic and reproachful. One of the docs who had an especially deep hatred for Allenius called me a Benedict Arnold. He predicted I would fail. Two others did not talk to me for twenty years. Dr. Richard Leedy, always the gentleman, cautioned me about making the right decision. Two of the other docs simply left the group and found positions outside of Ohio.

The practice was filled with surprises and challenges. One of my pregnant patients asked me to deliver her at home with natural childbirth, no sedatives, no pain meds. I considered the risks but accepted the challenge. I naively told her that I would deliver her at home, but if there were any problems, she had to promise she would not sue me. I cannot imagine any doctor doing that today. No practitioner in Columbus was doing home deliveries. I found out why later. I agreed to deliver her at home partly out of willingness to please her, partly to experience this new medical adventure, and partly from bravado following my Vietnam experiences. I had confidence in my obstetrical experience, having delivered more than one hundred babies and my RN, Terry Hinderer, had worked in obstetrics at the hospital for several years. She had lots more experience than I did. Terry and I talked over our plan. After the delivery, I would tend the mother and she the infant. We put together the OB pack with everything we thought we would need for delivery day. Then we waited. Early one morning during a blizzard, I got the call that she was in labor. I called Terry, and we met at the patient's house. It was a comfortable two-story in Victorian Village, only a block from the hospital. There was something strange about the scene that I saw when I entered. First of all, the house was filled with all of her girlfriends in a party atmosphere. There was the aroma of burning incense veiling the smell of marijuana. I heard rhythmical chanting and steady drumbeats coming from the back room. *Uh-oh! What did I get myself into?* No time to think about alternatives—the baby was crowning. We hurriedly created as sterile an environment as possible in her bedroom. This was her first birth and she needed an episiotomy, a surgical incision under local anesthesia to allow more room for the baby's exit. No problem there. She delivered swiftly. So far so good. *But damn!* The infant was limp and blue. This was going to take the skill of a doctor and a lot more. I left the mother who was bleeding and immediately attended the baby, suctioned the mouth and manually cleared her airway, rubbed her with a towel to keep her warm and to stimulate her crying. She had a slow heartbeat but was not breathing. I said a little prayer, smacked the bottom of her feet, and flicked her chest.

"Come on girl, you can do it."

After what seemed like an eternity, she sputtered a cry and then a full hearty cry. I was holding a squirming pink beautiful girl. I handed her to my nurse for cord care, and Terry bundled her up. Back to the bleeding mother. I delivered the placenta and repaired the episiotomy. Luckily there were no other complications. Mother and baby were stable. Friends and family surrounded the mother and baby. The mother lit up a joint. I now knew the cause of the baby's initial lack of response—it was stoned! The origin of the chanting and drumming came into the room, her husband, a Sioux Indian from the Dakotas. It was a joyous occasion for everyone, but a freak show for me. I had survived a near catastrophe caused by my own hubris. I gave thanks for the great result, and swore I would never do another home delivery. This is what hospitals are for! Fifteen years later I received a long distance call from South Dakota. It was from the woman I had delivered at home. She had been thinking about me and wanted to thank me for bringing her wonderful daughter into the world. The next voice I heard was from a cheerful healthy fifteen-year-old, Morning Star, wanting to say "Hello." That call made it all worthwhile.

Figure 4-1. Me, standing in front of my flagship Master MEDCenter, Columbus, Ohio, 1984.

By the third year, the practice had tripled in volume. I decided to go home at 6 p.m. every day to have a sit down dinner with my family. I hired the hospital residents to finish up the rest of the patients. I added a physician's assistant (PA). PAs were relatively new in Ohio. The Ohio State Medical Board had not yet promulgated the rules for this group of professionals except that they had to work under the license of a physician, and their duties had to be approved by the Board. The patients thought they were doctors. The doctors in the Columbus community resented their right to practice. To me it was a forgone conclusion that physician extenders like PAs would become necessary and important in the care of patients. There weren't enough physicians in underserved areas or busy practices like mine. My PA, Sam

Hulett, was an exceptional practitioner and had impeccable credentials. He was a former navy corpsman in Vietnam, which immediately endeared him to me, and had trained at Bethesda Naval Hospital. It came time for our appearance in front of the Board for his licensing. I knew this was an especially conservative group of men. They enjoyed the dubious reputation of suspending the licenses of more doctors than any other state medical board in the country. It was 1975, and the peace talks in Paris were dragging on. The Vietnam War was still prominent in everyone's mind. I began by educating the Board on Sam's medical background—PA school, Navy corpsman, and on-the-job training at DAMC. I enumerated all the duties he was qualified by training and experience to perform. When I got to the pelvic exam and Pap smear, a Dr. Ruppersburg spoke up. He was an old venerable Ob-Gyn specialist from Columbus. He strongly objected to any non-physician invading that sacred vault called the vagina. I explained that he was trained at Bethesda Naval Hospital, one of our nation's finest institutions and had abundant experience with this procedure. In my and the Navy's opinion, he was qualified to perform this examination. Ruppersburg persisted with his argument. I could tell by the body language of some of the other members of the Board that he was on his way to convincing them to deny Sam these privileges.

I interrupted Ruppersburg's rant and said, "Doctor, where were you in 1968?"

He said matter-of-factly, "Here in Columbus."

"Well, do you know where Mr. Hulett was? And I looked at the whole Board. "He was on the battlefield in Vietnam saving the lives of your sons and brothers. He has earned his right to practice his profession in Columbus, Ohio."

The vote was 8-0 in favor with one abstention.

The practice continued to grow, and I hired another PA and two more physicians. By the end of 1978 we were nearing $1,000,000 in gross revenues. I didn't know it, but there was a shark circling my business waiting to dine on my success.

One morning I received a call from Bank One telling me my checking account was overdrawn. What? That was impossible because I always kept a five-figure balance to pay all of my bills and meet two payrolls a month. I smelled skullduggery and told the bank to send me copies of every check $2,000 or greater, front and back ASAP. The next day I was reading checks paid to phony companies for phony services. These checks had not been written from my business checking account, but rather from my payroll checking account. The amounts were between $2,000 and $5,000, written over the span of two years and added up to a whopping $100,000. My signature was trace forged. How could this happen? I had specifically hired an accountant to reconcile my checkbook every month to prevent this. I called my accountant, Berry Kessler, and explained to him the facts. He said he had to check on some things and would call me back. I had bills to pay and a payroll due the coming Friday. I wanted answers right away. I called the Columbus Police Department, and a detective came out that day. Berry called me back and said he thought it was Bob Rapp, the junior accountant in his office, the very guy whose duty it was to reconcile my checkbook every month. Instead of protecting me, he was stealing from me.

At his criminal trial, Judge Tommy Thomson found him guilty and pronounced his sentence: "Mr. Rapp, you were in a position of trust. You stole one tenth of a million dollars from Dr. Master."

He could have said, "one hundred thousand dollars," but he chose the word "million" for effect.

"You must go to jail. I sentence you to two years in the Lucasville Penitentiary."

This was a notoriously bad place to be. Only the most hardened and violent criminals were sent there. After the sentencing I walked up to Rapp and asked him why, of all his clients, he only stole from me. He replied that, of all his clients, he thought I was the only one who wouldn't put him in jail. He had mistaken my kindness toward him over the years for weakness. I never thought Berry was behind the embezzlement, but I learned later that Berry's son was involved, and Berry covered up his participation. Kessler's insurance company repaid me the full amount. I always personally reviewed my own checkbook after that episode. After the dust settled, I called Berry to tell him I was moving my business to another accounting firm. He was very angry and hurt, but I did not trust his counsel anymore. He tried to talk me out of my decision. He told me to be careful, which I took as a veiled threat.

He said, "You can always test the mettle of a man when he is under stress."

I said I had to do what any prudent businessman would do in this situation. Upon recommendation of my attorney Alec Wightman, I hired Tom Giusti as my accountant. Tom has honestly and efficiently done my work for more than thirty-five years.

Berry Kessler was a fascinating man. He was a Korean War veteran and former IRS agent. Dr. Allenius had recommended him. He was always very friendly to me, inviting me to his birthday parties and spending a lot of time giving me advice about finances and life in general. He cautioned me to stay out of the spotlight and fly below the radar. I liked him, as well, and gave him a Bullmastiff puppy that I had whelped from one of my prize litters. Berry had a very dark side to him. It was rumored that he had Art Shapiro, a prominent Columbus tax attorney, murdered by a Chicago hit man because Shapiro was going to turn State's evidence about a dirty tax scheme that Berry had allegedly hatched. Those were the days of multiple tax write-offs for "non-recourse financing," and Berry was backdating his client's tax returns to obtain these lucrative deductions. There was never an indictment. He was married, but there was always a girlfriend in the wings. I had always believed if a man cheated on his wife, he would cheat in other things in life like business and friendships. It was also rumored that he was behind the murder of at least two others. His modus operandi was to form a business partnership with someone who needed cash, take out a hefty "key man" insurance policy on his new partner, and then have him bumped off. Berry just couldn't control his inner Mr. Hyde. Many years later, after I had left him as a client, he was convicted of murdering a Florida man for the insurance money and sentenced to death. The irony of this story is that Berry never collected the insurance proceeds because his victim had been pocketing the monthly insurance premium money and never paid the insurance company a penny. Berry sat on death row in a Florida prison for ten years while appeal after appeal was turned down. He was about to make legal history with his appeal to the U.S. Supreme Court that killing an octogenarian was cruel and unusual punishment and therefore unconstitutional when he died in his sleep at age ninety.

Berry did have a good and bright side. In 1974 I wanted to move to Bexley, a city within the City of Columbus, to one of those stately mansions for which the town was known. I found a five-acre property directly across from the Governor's mansion and presented a fair contract to the owner. It was not only rejected, but the owner, Dixie Smith, took the property off the market for reasons unknown. It was later purchased by Leslie Wexner of the Limited Company. I was heartbroken and told Berry about what had happened. He told me not to worry. He had a better home about to come out of probate that he would help me buy. About a week later, he drove me to Medick Estates in Worthington.

As we approached this unbelievably majestic home sitting on top of a wooded ravine he said, "Here it is. What do you think?"

I was dumbstruck. This was my dream house, reminiscent of The Main Line in Philadelphia where the "bluebloods" resided. It was an ivy-covered three-story limestone Scottish manor house set on two manicured acres with a stream meandering through. I had never aspired to a house so grand. It was love at first sight. There were twenty-two rooms in its twelve thousand square feet. The woodwork, marble fireplaces, Italian terrazzo, parquet, and matched and fitted oak floors were breathtaking. I had never seen any finer workmanship anywhere. I couldn't afford it.

Berry, ever the accountant, said, "Yes, you can."

He told me Judge Metcalf of Probate Court was willing to do a quick sale to rid the property from the court's rolls. It had been in probate since 1972. This was the original Medick Mansion built in 1928. The Chase family purchased it in 1960 following the death of its owner, Frank Medick. In 1972 Clifford Chase shot and killed his father, mother, and brother. Ironically, his parents were psychologists. Only his sister survived because she was not there at the time. This fact created a monumental dilemma for me. I loved the house, but how would I shed its tragic reputation? I was thirty-four years old and believed I could accomplish anything, especially after my Vietnam experiences. The purchase price was set by the court at $140,000. I had $40,000 in the bank, but I needed to borrow the rest. First mortgage interest rates were skyrocketing to fourteen percent and beyond. Inflation was soaring. I went to Al McFarland, president of States Savings in Worthington. He agreed to lend me $100,000 at fourteen percent but added a kicker of $40,000 in one-year CDs. *Ouch!* How would I pull this off? My father was good for $10,000. Berry threw in $10,000. He had a client, George Rosenberger, a stranger to me who kindly put up another $10,000. I scraped together the last ten. I closed on the house and took possession in December, 1974.

Figure 4-2. My Worthington, Ohio, home.

In 1977, my wife and I agreed to a dissolution of our fifteen-year marriage. We realized there was no love or respect left in our relationship. It was done quickly and without rancor. We split our net worth down the middle, and I gave her use of a rental home free of rent forever. Two years later she remarried, and I became a single parent because both children elected to stay with me.

I experienced a sense of freedom and renewed energy. It did not hurt that the fourteen percent mortgage served as a tremendous impetus to work as hard as I could. These were the Jimmy Carter days, and inflation was growing unbounded. My revenues were growing, but my expenses were growing faster as inflation was eating my profits. I decided to build a second medical center to create more income. Dr. Charles May had joined my practice earlier. He had all the qualities of a great physician—intelligence, medical knowledge, talent, communication skills, and as a former pharmacist, knew his pharmacology cold. He was also a hard worker, a great asset to me and the practice. With Dr. May minding the store, I was free to build my second clinic. My due diligence in site selection was always to drive through the heavily concentrated low-income and elderly patient neighborhoods. I would find out where the nearest medical facility was located. Invariably my favorite sites were always noticeably underserved. For my second practice I chose the Bottoms, on the near south side of downtown Columbus. My site would be in the shadow of the megalith, Mount Carmel West Hospital. I had discovered that the great Mount Carmel had its family medicine practice located ten miles away on Riverside Drive in order to attract higher-pay patients, not exactly its mission statement to deliver health care to the poor and elderly. This was perfect for me. I went about buying four inexpensive lots including Shroyer's Funeral Parlor. Dick Royder, the realtor helped me with this project as my stalking horse. It needed to be re-zoned for medical usage, which I thought was a slam-dunk being located in the same block as a hospital. *Not so fast!* The great and mighty Mount Carmel was out to stop me. I don't know why. My building, the Town Street Medical Center (TSMC), being right across the street would only increase their referral base. Maybe they did not like Medicaid patients. Maybe they were anti-osteopathic physicians. Maybe they did not like me. I did not really care what their reason was; I was going to get this done. At the time there was only one DO, a neonatal pediatrician, on their staff. Mount Carmel exerted considerable political influence on the zoning commission, and my request for re-zoning was unanimously turned down. They thought it was over and had squashed this interloper like a worm. *Not so fast! Game on!* I needed allies to gain approval in the next and final step, Columbus City Council. I personally lobbied each council member, presenting the architect's beautiful rendering, the number of jobs I would create, the tax base I would expand, and the fact that the nearest general medical facility was ten miles away. Jerry Hammond, president of city council was persuaded by my reasoning. I was not finished. I met with Father Schweitzer, the pastor of Holy Family Parish and the spiritual leader of the Bottoms. I explained my mission and garnered his full support. I remodeled Shroyer's funeral home and used it to start seeing patients right away. It was zoned for multi-use so no zoning problem there. I gathered hundreds of signatures from the patients for a petition to city council to change the rest of the properties zoning to medical. Come the night of the city council meeting, I rented a bus, served coffee and sandwiches, and drove fifty patients to the meeting. My friends, led by the irrepressible John Van Krevel, also came along to see the fireworks. We filled the council hall. When my request for re-zoning came before the council, I spoke on its merits. I showed photos of the ramshackle properties I was replacing with architect Mark Feinknopf's modern and creatively designed new medical center. I presented the petitions, and council members checked the addresses to see if their wards were represented. They looked at the council seats filled with my supporters. It did not hurt that Father Schweitzer's representative spoke forcefully on our behalf. Mount Carmel Hospital did not expect this massive assault against their opposition. They were reeling as the outcome was already apparent. Their once smug representative gave a weak rambling counter argument. No one was listening. Finally, Jerry Hammond added his political weight to our side when he complimented me for tearing down those ugly "Quonset huts" and providing the patients with a bright new medical facility. The vote was 7-0 for us. The crowd erupted from their seats with a rousing standing ovation. The Town Street Medical Center (TSMC) was born. Jerry Hammond and I became lifelong friends. Every year at Christmas, I sent a donation to the Holy Family Church. The Franklinton Businessman's Association and the Ohio Legislature gave me awards for the beauty of the building and our service to the community.

My model of one-stop medical services provided in modern, efficient, and inviting surroundings was working. I added more doctors and PAs to serve the ever-growing demands of increased patient loads. In 1981, I joined with Dr. Elliott Feldman, a long-time friend to build the Bryden

Road Medical Center, located in leased space in the old St. Ann's Hospital. Because I already was managing two other practices, I needed his help to spread the financial and administrative load. After we had set up our practice at St. Ann's and invested quite a bit of capital, our building was about to be sold out from under us in a bid auction. The realtor we dealt with never revealed he was also on the board of St. Anthony's Hospital, a clear undisclosed conflict of interest. Although our bid was the highest in total, we lost to the new St. Anthony's Hospital who wanted to create a nursing home. Never fretting, we purchased a long-vacant theater several blocks away and established the Main Street Medical Center. With the full support of the Main Street Businessman's Association and activist Walter Cates, we had another successful venture. The community paper, the *Call and Post,* wrote a tremendous puff piece in our behalf.

By 1982 we were growing financially by 20-30% a year. My key MEDCenter was still my first, Dennison Avenue Medical Center (DAMC). On one single day in March, during the peak of an especially virulent flu epidemic, four of us treated 350 patients! One of our doctors was on vacation. We went non-stop, no lunch or dinner, working late into the evening, and all returned to our homes exhausted. These heavy patient loads were good problems to have. With all this success I wanted to make sure my lease included a renewal clause. I was two years away from the end of my lease so I decided to re-read it, this time with a more educated and experienced eye. To my shock and dismay, my attorney had not protected me with a renewal clause. I might be in danger of losing the building and the practice with it. It was not too soon to start talking to my landlord, Dr. Allenius. The meeting did not go well for me. Allenius was willing to renew my lease but at the exorbitant and incredible rate of three times what I was paying now! I knew he was a hardliner and inflexible from our previous negotiations, but this was unconscionable. Greed had gotten the best of him. Numerous attempts through meetings and phone conversations to move the number down to a more realistic number failed. It soon became clear to me that if I agreed to his outrageous terms he had a bonanza. If I did not agree to his terms, he had a lucrative practice to take over. He believed he could easily hire doctors to fill our roles. He thought his position was strong and fortified from attack. He was the dumbest smart man I ever knew. He did not count on my resolve. He underestimated my ability to succeed. He mistook my easy manner for weakness. I had to go on the offensive. When you're being run out of town, turn around, march back into town, and pretend you're leading the parade.

The next twelve months found me quietly buying up all the properties around the DAMC building. I had acquired about $200,000 worth of properties with $65,000 and a series of mortgages and notes. My friend Jerry Hammond, president of Columbus City Council, helped me re-zone the properties to allow medical usage. My architect, Mark Feinknopf, prepared a beautiful rendering. I had good banking connections with Al McFarland at State Savings. Dr. May and I were committed to moving our entire practice next door to compete with Allenius and any new doctors he would hire. Now, the advantage swung to me. His $2,000,000 dollar investment was in danger. We had a loyal patient base and a trained staff ready to go next door. I had Dr. May and other great doctors and physician assistants. In our final meeting, I unveiled our plan to Allenius. He appeared in shock. As an ex-Marine he knew he had just lost the battle before the first shot was fired. I gave him one out, a deal he couldn't refuse. For the outrageously small sum of $500,000, I would sell him everything and would not compete with him. His investment would be secure and he could expand his parking. I already had my eye on a better location on one of the most highly trafficked and visible locations in Columbus, ready for sale. He ranted and raved, jumped up and down, but in the end he took my deal.

I bought the historic Winder's Chevrolet property on High Street in the Short North for $240,000, twenty percent down and a mortgage for the balance obtained from my friend, the great Alan McFarland, president of State Savings. It was a two-acre lot with a twenty-five-thousand-square-foot, one-and-a-half story building sitting on one acre and another five-thousand-square-foot building sitting on another acre, giving us the largest parking lot in the Short North neighborhood. I set about rehabilitating the properties to provide the community with the Master-May MEDCenter, another one-stop complete healthcare facility. There was no government money involved as the *Columbus Dispatch* once had erroneously reported. All of my renters from DAMC opened up offices here. The patients followed from DAMC and we were busier than ever. I hired another doctor, Dr. Clayton Royder. There were six of us now. We were seeing two hundred patients a day, more than the combined Ohio State University outpatient practice centers. By 1984 I reckoned I had captured the majority of the Medicaid population in Central Ohio. They were all being treated in my MEDCenters by my doctors.

CHAPTER FIVE
Health Power:
A New Concept of Managed Health Care in Ohio

I don't lose sleep over the potential for falure [sic].
I can't even spell the word.
—Dr. Bernard Master, adapted from Gen. James Mattis

In 1983, the Fee-For-Service (FFS) Medicaid program was costing the State of Ohio $1 billion a year to cover the health care costs of its nearly one million Medicaid recipients. Medicaid was a shared health care program by the States and Federal government for the poor and disabled. I knew Ohio was looking for a way to curb their skyrocketing costs. The present system had to change before it bankrupted the state. Managed care was one way to do this. I began exploring health care delivery systems that would lower the cost of treating the poor and at the same time improve access and quality of care. The HMO Act of 1973 signed into law by President Richard Nixon was based on these principles. I had a large stake in the future of Medicaid because my MEDCenters were heavily dependent on Medicaid revenues. I wanted to be a leader in the solution and not a loser in the system. There was only one small not-for-profit managed care plan for Medicaid in Ohio. It was a Health Maintenance Organization (HMO) model similar to earlier plans in California like Kaiser Permanente. It was limited in scope because all of the enrolled patients had to go to one office and see only their doctors. It had about 8,500 patients, and they could not go outside the plan's panel of physicians. It was located in Cleveland, a city with 250,000 Medicaid recipients. I wondered why it was not serving a much larger patient base. I met with its director to learn about its structure and operations. I thought its single building model and restricted doctor panel were hampering its growth. But growth was not its goal. I learned the not-for-profit operators consciously chose not to be any bigger. It was a nonprofit foundation and had limited goals that it was meeting. I went to many managed care conferences and read all I could get my hands on about health care systems all over the world. I talked to industry leaders and policy makers.

At this time, Democrat Richard Celeste, a former Peace Corps director, was making a run for the Ohio governorship. He was a progressive, whose attention was on support for human services and civil rights. I got to know him and discussed various preventive health care models for Ohio Medicaid recipients. He knew the overburdening costs of the present FFS system and was familiar with the highly successful Harvard HMO plan. He indicated he would be very supportive of my efforts to curb health care costs without sacrificing quality in this population. Richard Celeste became Ohio's sixty-fourth Governor. Armed with my knowledge of health care delivery systems and the new governor's tacit approval of managed care, I set about building a new model HMO for Medicaid in the State of Ohio. I contacted the Pace Group in Dallas, Texas, a highly recommended HMO consultant. They said it would cost $1 million to set up the health care delivery system I envisioned. My idea was a "Network HMO," unique to managed care in Ohio and the country. I would start in Columbus with my four MEDCenters (the fourth, Parson's Avenue MEDCenter, was being completed) as the hub of a giant wheel. I named my new company Health Power, Inc., because I believed without good health one cannot achieve the power that life affords us. Our logo was a shiny red apple. Health Power

(HP) would contract with the State of Ohio for a certain sum per patient per month called "capitation." This was actuarially calculated the beginning of each contract year based on the previous year's health care costs plus a profit to the HMO minus ten to twenty percent savings to the state. In return for this capitation, HP would assume the risk of the entire health care cost of the Medicaid patients as long as they were enrolled in HP. The patient was free to leave the plan at any time. Health Power in turn would capitate the MEDCenters for all primary care, emergency room, pharmacy, and hospital costs, thereby shifting the economic risk to the doctors. There were three risk pools—primary care, pharmacy, and hospital. The idea was to reduce the profit incentives to overtreat patients by overprescribing and over-testing as was often done in the present FFS system. The treating physician's incentive then shifted to keeping the patients healthy by emphasizing preventive care and keeping the patients out of the hospital. Eighty-five percent of the Medicaid health care dollar in Ohio was spent for hospital care. Hospital overstays for numerous reasons were the rule under the present system. Emergency room (ER) care was being used for the most minor ailments. Many patients used the ER as their primary care physician, a very expensive visit for the state to pay. The State of Ohio had a law, the Good Samaritan Law, that ERs could not turn away any patients. This invites chronic abusers like deadbeats and drug seekers, and overloads the capacity of any emergency department. Some used the ER for convenience, some because few physicians would accept them as patients, and some because of generations of ingrained habit. HP would stop these abusive practices by only allowing true emergencies. The "gatekeeper system" provided that referrals to specialists, ERs, and hospital admissions could only be made by the patient's primary care provider, the "gatekeeper." The network of providers would also include some select practices in Columbus besides my own. The advantage to the doctors would be steady cash flow with prepayment the first of every month, a paperless system with no billing, incentive bonuses for proper utilization, and more patients to treat. The disincentives to prevent underutilization were threats of malpractice lawsuits, ejection from the network, and the doctor's own ethics. The marketing arm of HP would enroll FFS patients into our managed care family practice provider network. The advantage to the patients to enroll was a caring qualified family doctor delivering appropriate care, wider access to more doctors, and referrals to specialists who would not turn them away. In addition, we added free transportation to their doctor's appointments. No excuse now not to get your Pap smear or your child's immunizations. As an added incentive to enroll, we included over-the-counter meds like Tylenol® and aspirin, baby thermometers, Band-Aids®, and vaporizers. These low-cost items could help keep patients out of the ERs. The doctor network would be enhanced with psychologists, pharmacies, labs, podiatrists, and optometrists.

How was I going to raise the money to get all of this done? I set out to raise $2,000,000, twice as much as was recommended by the Pace Group. I consulted with Baker and Hostetler attorney, Alec Wightman, who suggested a private capital raise to only qualified investors buying stock in HP, $30,000 for 10,000 shares. I personally called and met with every potential investor, starting with doctors and ancillary health care providers who would participate in the network, and vendors presently rendering services to the MEDCenters. I sold it out in sixty days.

I hired the Pace Group to put all the pieces in place. Our first office was an inexpensive rented space in the north end of Columbus on Morse Road. My first "employee" was an IBM mainframe big enough to fill a small room. Next I hired Barbara Ratti, a very experienced administrative assistant with great office skills. We went on a nationwide search for a CEO with HMO experience and found Glen Sperry from California, the epicenter of HMOs. Sperry then filled in the other key slots of finance, medical, and marketing directors, using the Pace Group as our search firm. With all the players in place, we went about the task of securing a contract with the State of Ohio to enroll Medicaid patients. No big problem there as the state was eager to solve its budget woes. HP, in turn, contracted with the MEDCenters and other family docs on a capitated basis. At first many doctors and patients were hesitant to join a new system, but there were early adapters. Our marketers were taking patients from FFS practices and placing them with our network providers. The howls of complaints of unfair practices were heard all the way to the statehouse. The FFS docs were taken completely by surprise. They had not seen me coming. One group tried to start their own HMO, but they disagreed on everything and it soon fell apart. The FFS camp was in disarray as we picked off their patients in large numbers. By the end of the first year, we had enrolled sixteen thousand patients of the sixty-five thousand available in Franklin County. Outsider physicians seeing our success, swallowed their pride and wanted in. Our biggest problem was getting the first hospital contract. Without a capitated hospital contract or at least a discounted fee schedule, we would not make a profit because the "fat" was in excess hospital days and exorbitant hospital charges. We were going to cut hospital lengths of stay and rebundle unbundled hospital charges to save money. We would look for secondary forms of health insurance that hospitals were overlooking. In return, we would direct our patients to only contracting hospitals. The hospitals agreed to accept payment for disease codes and not per day of stay rates. Every hospital in Columbus contracted with us except the arrogant, high-and-mighty Mount Carmel. If our patients somehow found their way into one of Mount Carmel's hospital beds, we would send an ambulance ASAP and move them to one of the other participating Columbus hospitals. They never did contract with us, and we never cared. In our first operating year, we saved $3.2 million from the previous year state's actual costs. Half of that savings went to the state and half to HP. We were making a dent in the medical excesses, and the FFS establishment felt it. They were crying

119

and whining about "unfair marketing practices," spreading rumors and flat-out lies about HP and managed care in general. They were feeding sensational stories, all untrue, to the TV stations and the newspapers. One Columbus station, Channel 4 Columbus, fell for it and did a weeklong series on HP about the "abuses" they uncovered. They had concocted sensational lies about our company garnered from the FFS side. They never bothered to get the facts by interviewing anyone associated with our company. One ridiculous allegation was that we were enrolling Vietnamese people without an interpreter. Yes, we had enrolled a family of English speaking Vietnamese who did not need an interpreter. I was furious and tried to get an interview with the station to tell the true story, but the reporters refused. They even parked their TV truck outside of my private residence and broadcasted my name and address to the public like I was some common criminal. One of my good neighbors came to my defense and chased them away. All this did was make me redouble my efforts and work harder. To this day, Channel 4 Columbus is banned from viewing by my family for its despicable and unethical reporting.

I added a fifth office with very few Medicaid patients in 1985. I wanted to diversify the MEDCenters' payor base. I bought it from an old timer whom I knew from the hospital staff. The price and terms seemed reasonable. He was grossing $250,000 a year, but had no recent growth since he wanted to retire. It was in Grandview, a very stable community bordering Columbus. I paid him $65,000 over two years and set about improving the physical plant, expanding parking, and adding X-ray and physical therapy. I was pleased with the purchase until I worked there on a day the doctor had off. What a shock! Nearly every patient was a chronic pain patient receiving narcotics and tranquilizers. I had unknowingly bought a drug practice! This doctor's prescribing habits should have been a red flag to the medical and pharmacy boards. I wondered why there had never been an official intervention. Shame on me. I had failed to check the charts as part of my due diligence. I hated this type of practice, playing the roles of doctor and detective, wasting the majority of my time trying to figure out who was drug seeking and who was legitimately ill. This was not my idea of good medicine. I immediately went to work, trading drug abusers for family patients. I wanted to see only the familiar general practice patients in my waiting room—hypertensives, diabetics, heart disease and pulmonary patients, in which a good doctor could make a big difference in the quality of their lives. It took me two years to turn that practice around, and with the improved demographics, came improved revenues, almost doubling the profits.

With managed care taking hold in Columbus, I turned my attention to Dayton, Ohio, which also had a large Medicaid population, about 45,000 recipients. I met Burt Schear, MD, a fabulous character out of a Damon Runyon story. He and his son, Martin, had three general practices in Dayton treating the elderly and low-income population. Burt was a smart businessman and experienced general practitioner. I explained my concept to him and his wonderful wife, Betty, who had an MBA, over dinner one night. He got it right away and wanted to be a part of this new venture; Betty was more cautious. They finally invested $100,000 into HP. His three practices would be the nucleus of the Dayton provider network. Burt's son, Martin Schear, MD, an exceptional and respected family doctor, became HP's medical director. The State of Ohio granted us a license for Health Power of Dayton, and we became the first managed care organization in Montgomery County. Martin wrangled a few more practices into our network, and every hospital in Dayton contracted with us. After seeing our success, many more managed care plans started up in Ohio but HP was first, and by then had dominant market share in both Franklin and Montgomery counties. I thought there was no stopping us. However, the FFS doctors had not given up. They kept carping to their legislators and the newspapers about our "intrusion into their comfortable lifestyles," and late in 1986 the shit hit the fan.

Thanksgiving of 1986 did not bring me a turkey with all the trimmings. In its place, the *Cleveland Plain Dealer* wrote a scurrilous article about my phantom connection to the governor. Their allegation was that HP's managed care Medicaid contract was a "thank you" from the governor for my large political contributions. Nothing could be further from the truth. Managed care's time had come to Ohio. They failed to mention that there were sixteen other identical contracts with various other companies throughout Ohio, all worded the same and all paying the same amounts. My contract was a "sweetheart deal," but were the others legitimate contracts? The article was front page, above the fold, with headlines and photos of me. The *Plain Dealer* went on to say that I was building a Medicaid empire stretching from the Ohio River to Lake Erie. The series ran into the following week. The articles were filled with intrigue and collusion, the product of two *Plain Dealer* reporters, Maryann Sharkey and Jim Webb. Sharkey, once a good reporter, fell in with the fantasist, Webb. Their twisted thinking and wild imagination was boundless. I could not neutralize them with the truth. Their story was already written. The newspaper had reams of paper and ink by the barrels. I was defenseless. I just had to wait it out. After he left the *Plain Dealer*, Webb continued to confabulate the news for other newspapers. He wrote a story for a San Diego paper that the U.S. Government was behind the drug trade in Southern California to raise money for the Nicaraguan Sandinistas. He committed suicide in San Diego a few years later. Sharkey drifted into oblivion.

1987 was the most stressful year of my life. The fallout from the *Plain Dealer* articles finally came. The governor's office was hypersensitive to bad press. They knew the articles were patently false, but they adopted a defensive posture. One of the governor's chief advisors was Jan Allen, an attorney of less than average abilities in my opinion. She advised the governor to have the Department of Human Services (ODHS) audit HP for quality of care and financial stability. ODHS put a freeze on our enrollment until we passed these audits. There were other managed care plans starting up in our areas, and with the freeze, they were rapidly catching up to our enrollment numbers. I was losing about $1 million a month in gross revenues. I calculated that within three months, HP would be bankrupt and out of business. I was responsible for $2 million of investor money. All would be lost. The morale at HP was at its nadir. But we passed all the audits with flying colors. There was no longer any reason to hold us in a deep freeze. Days and weeks went by without a word from the Ohio Department of Human Services (ODHS) announcing the thaw. Nothing came. I had to go to the governor personally and ask for the thaw. One morning I went to the statehouse to see the governor, no appointment. I knew his secretary well; she told me to go right in. There, sitting next to him, was Jan Allen. I began by reciting the events starting with the *Plain Dealer* articles and ending with our passing the audits. I asked him to lift the freeze. It was a dire situation for me. Allen chimed in by saying that an election year was coming up, and this could create more bad press and political fodder for the Republicans. In other words, damn the audits and damn me. Her advice was for the governor to do nothing and keep the freeze on my enrollment until after the election.

I switched to the offense and said, "Governor, I am not asking for any favors, I am telling you this is based purely on merit. We have passed all the audits and jumped over all the hurdles placed in our way by your ODHS, and you must lift the freeze now or I will be out of business."

Allen told him again not to do it.

Dick Celeste, my "friend" said to me, "It will all work out."

I left his office with my mind fully focused on the seriousness of my problem. HP had three months to live. I walked out the north side of the statehouse building, the side facing the tall office buildings on Broad Street. These buildings housed some of Columbus's "white shoe" law firms. My feet took me across the street to the law offices of Victor Goodman, once the personal attorney to four-time Republican Governor Dick Rhoads. Having no appointment, I asked his secretary to see Victor right away because I wanted to retain his services. No problem. Within two minutes, I was seated before this Republican icon. We had never met before, but he said he knew of me. He had read the *Plain Dealer* articles, I imagined, as a Republican, with glee. I told him my problem and asked him to help me. He said he would "check me out" and let me know. The next day, a Thursday, he called me to tell me he would work for me. He told me to write two personal checks to two separate campaign funds. They were not large checks; in fact they were surprisingly small. I delivered them as requested. On Friday the freeze was lifted!

Figure 5-1. Left to right, my "friend," Governor Richard Celeste, his wife Dagmar, my wife Susan, and me.

The year 1987 had more in store for me. The Ohio legislators voted to increase the financial reserves of all HMOs because of recent financial failures in other parts of the country. At the time HP did not meet the financial requirements of the new law. I had to go out and raise another $2 million to save HP. It was a much harder raise now because the Ohio Department of Insurance (ODI) had put HP "on supervision" until we met the new statutory requirements. This meant a state employee from ODI was sitting in our office approving or denying every move we made. Every prospective investor knew we badly needed the money, and everyone knew we were on administrative supervision at least for a while. On top of that, the Federal Medicaid rules required at least twenty-five percent of a plan's membership be non-Medicaid private insurance patients. They mistakenly believed that a seventy-five percent to twenty-five percent mix of Medicaid to non-Medicaid would insure quality to the Medicaid patients. HP was only at eighteen percent non-Medicaid and at a marketing standstill. In the non-Medicaid arena we had very tough competition. We were up against old and respected insurers like the "Blues," Blue Cross and Blue Shield, Nationwide, and a slew of other insurance giants. I went back to my investors and raised an additional $2 million in just two months, a tremendous vote of confidence in me. Okay, HP was now off of supervision but we couldn't add any more Medicaid patients until we reached the twenty-five percent non-Medicaid mark. This was a real catch-22 because with every three new Medicaid patients, we needed another private-pay patient. We were at a standstill again. My biggest assets were my now twenty-five thousand HP Medicaid patients. I made a cold call to the CEO of Grant Medical Hospital, Donald Ayers. I had heard they were having financial difficulties. I had a simple proposition for him. I would make Grant HP's preferred hospital provider with their getting most of our hospitalized patients, outpatient surgeries, and OBs (obstetrics), I would also send Grant my MEDCenters private patients. We had a big OB practice. This meant an additional two hundred deliveries a year to fill their new obstetrical wing. All of that would give them a potential total of $20 million a year boost to Grant's sagging revenues. In addition I would give Grant a five percent minority stock position in HP and a voting seat on the HP Board. In exchange for this I wanted all of the hospital's employees to be enrolled in HP and carry the HP card. In addition, I wanted an interest free $250,000 loan for our operating expenses. That was a deal he could not refuse. All of the Grant doctors were part of our network anyway, so there was no changing of providers for their employees. The addition of their hospital and outpatient centers employees would put HP over the required federal seventy-five to twenty-five mark. He wanted to think about it, but very early the next morning he called me to agree to all the terms as we had discussed with no changes. We were off and running again.

In the midst of this stormy period I received a call on a late Friday afternoon from Dr. Elliott Feldman, my friend and partner in two practices. I could hardly believe what he told me. Glen Sperry, the HP CEO, was a patient at the Parsons Avenue Medical Center. He rattled on to his treating physician about how dissatisfied he was with me and my leadership as Chairman of HP. He was unhappy with his salary. He complained about not having any HP stock. He was planning on leading a walkout of all our senior management! His demented plan was to extort me into giving him stock in HP and a big fat raise. The doctor, who was a shareholder in HP himself, called Elliott after the visit to raise his alarm. Could it be true? Sperry was the picture of professional propriety, neatly groomed, closely cropped hair parted on the side, buttoned down white dress shirts, striped ties with muted colors, conservatively styled suits, and wing-tipped shoes. This delusional man was masquerading as the loyal dutiful servant of HP, but he was a voracious wolf in sheep's clothing. As I learned later, he was afflicted with the *hamartia* in Aristotle's *Poetics*, the "tragic flaw." I immediately called Alec Wightman, our corporate attorney, and told him what I had just learned. I asked him to meet me at the HP offices first thing Monday morning. Alec did not act surprised, and I always wondered about that. I only had one course of action. I arrived early Monday morning with one goal in mind. Alec met me in our conference room since I did not keep a private office there. Early on I had ceded my Chairman's office to Sperry to save precious space. My central office was in my home. When Alec arrived, I called Sperry's secretary to notify her boss I wanted to see him in the conference room. The whole office was in a state of heightened suspense because they all recognized my car in our parking lot when they arrived at work. They knew I only came in for important meetings and special occasions. Sperry walked into the room. He knew something was up when he saw me sitting at the table, not smiling, no greeting and my *consigliore* by my side.

"Sperry," I said, "You're fired. Go clean out your desk. Mr. Wightman, please accompany him to his office and make sure he only takes personal items, and then escort him out to the parking lot."

Sperry never asked why.

Alec took him down the long hall, and I could hear that crazed man yelling to all of our management who had peeked their heads outside of their offices, "Who is coming with me?"

Everyone ducked back into their offices. They wanted no part of the failed coup. There was no severance package, no farewell party, and no gold watch for Sperry. The Sperry era was over. In the days that followed, I had a group employee meeting explaining what had happened and that I would be the interim CEO. I then met with each employee to find out their duties, their problems, and their successes. What I learned was somewhat discomforting and sometimes outrageous. Sperry, a married man, was accused by his private secretary of alleged sexual harassment. She was very attractive, young and had very few secretarial skills as I discovered over the next few weeks. My first secretary, Barbara Ratti, an older woman, who had tremendous office skills, was relegated by Sperry to the secretarial pool probably because of her loyalty to me. Another surprise appeared when I asked Sperry's secretary to arrange a simple luncheon at the office for a couple of visiting businessmen. The luncheon came, and I almost choked on my food. We were eating from the most expensive china and using the most expensive cutlery I had ever seen in an office setting, a Sperry purchase during the time I was begging for investment money. She also told me of Sperry's three-hour, three-martini lunches for which our shareholders were footing the bill. How could I have made such a big mistake of hiring this guy? The Pace Group had recommended him after what I thought was a vigorous vetting process. For my own satisfaction, I called the head of the last company he'd listed on his résumé that he'd worked for. They had not had any trouble from him, but surprise, surprise, he had not been their CEO as he had stated on his résumé. He was VP of Marketing. They said he moved on to another company and became their CEO, but was fired in his second year when he audaciously gave himself a hefty raise without permission from his Board. Aha, the "tragic flaw" had shown itself earlier. Sperry had conveniently left this little episode off of his résumé. His miscalculation of the consequences of his disloyalty and unethical behavior was another case of mistaking my kindness to him for weakness. I lost track of Glen Sperry; however, a few years later I heard he committed suicide in Arizona, Roman style cutting his wrists while lying in a warm bath.

The employee morale was low because of all the regulatory problems and bad press we had gotten that year. The one thing that was jumping out at me during all of these interviews was that many of Sperry's hires, the vice presidents and the middle management department heads were one pay grade above their true capabilities. I had to diplomatically and humanely rectify this. With all of my other ventures, the five MEDCenters, my own family practice, and some outside investments, I was too busy to remain CEO. I hired a search firm to replace Sperry, but did not like any of the candidates they sent me. I wanted someone experienced in the HMO game, but this was a tough order in a fledgling industry. Pat Talley, our VP of Finance, came to talk to me. He felt confident that he could assume the duties of the CEO position on an interim basis until I found a permanent fit. He wanted to be considered for the permanent seat when the time came to select. Pat was a good man, well liked by the employees, knew the company well, and had no glaring faults. He was conservative in his accounting and was of good character. I agreed to try him out with a salary raise, new office and title as interim CEO.

I made all of my personnel changes at one time to minimize damage to the morale of the employees. I learned if you have bad news, let it be known all at once. Don't drag it out. Friday is the best day of the week to do this, so the affected employees won't stew about it all week and sour the attitude of others. I talked to each affected employee individually. Pat Talley was elevated to the interim CEO position. The Medicaid marketing director was let go with severance. The position of executive assistant to the CEO was eliminated, and the young woman who held it was given severance. Barbara Ratti was restored to executive assistant serving all the VPs and got back her deserved respect. One of the VPs was demoted to director and she voluntarily left the company. The VP of marketing, a chum of Sperry's, also voluntarily left. An in-house attorney, another Sperry hire and co-conspirator snake in the grass, also left, firing a mean-spirited parting shot at me in writing. A few other random positions were vacated. When the smoke cleared, we were left with a nucleus of dedicated, hardworking employees. HP was now lean and hungry and poised for the success it would eventually achieve.

The troubles of 1987 were not over—far from it. The worst was yet to come. Attempting to improve the financial department of the MEDCenters, I created a new position,

Director of Finance. I hired a man who had a financial background working for the State of Ohio. He interviewed well and his references checked out. His job was to improve our billing speed and accuracy, develop new profit centers, and find cost savings for the practices. This turned out to be a monumentally poor judgment of character on my part and almost bankrupted the MEDCenters. He proved to be worse than worthless. He was a parasite, slowly draining the life out of our business. Month after month, our cash flow was dwindling to practically nothing. Our accounts receivables were growing at a rapid rate. He had no answers. I discovered the answer. It was simple. He had not billed one insurance company in six months. This dumbbell thought someone else in the company was doing it. I don't know what he did in those few months, maybe strolled around the office admiring his nametag with the words "Director of Finance." I had to borrow money from the banks to meet payrolls and keep our doors open. The Huntington Bank turned me down, and I never worked with them again. Bank One, now Chase, came to my rescue, and I have been always grateful. The one silver lining in this massive dark cloud was that the work had been done and the accounts receivable, once billed, would be massive. It was just a matter of billing it and waiting the usual ninety days before receiving the checks. All of my vendors said they would wait for their payments, so we could continue to have our necessary drugs and supplies delivered. During the time I was rectifying his mistakes, this same idiot came to me and had the effrontery to tell me he could bill it all in a month and save the company, but—and here is the incredible part—he wanted to be my fifty-fifty partner! I literally threw him out of my office into the street. Was this his plan from the beginning? He miscalculated my resolve and overestimated his worth. By underestimating me, he joined the growing long line of losers who mistook my kindness for weakness.

I formulated a plan that would restore the financial stability of the company rapidly. Sheryl Cardwell, my regional manager, was in charge. I didn't have enough data entry people to do the billing rapidly enough. I brought all five managers to one MEDCenter to do the billing. They were all smart and understood the process. We worked twelve hours a day, seven days a week. I paid time and a half for Saturdays and Sundays. We billed the big dollar amounts first. There was also a little bit of luck. My son, Ken, came in on weekends from the University of Cincinnati Medical School, where he was a student, to help me. Ken was handsome and smart, and one of the young female employees developed a crush on him. One Sunday, this young female biller, working side-by-side with Ken, told him that someone was stealing money from the practice. Ken asked who it was and the biller said, "Lisa Bynum," our cashier, a ten-year trusted employee. Ken asked her how she was doing it, and the biller told him her *modus operandi*. I had installed a system to prevent theft. The computer, daybook recording patient payment amounts, cash drawer, and receipt book all had to match at the end of the day. After the close of business, the managers would make the final check. No one could leave until any error was accounted for. The deposit was taken to the bank's night depository every night. We would then look for a bank receipt with the matching dollar amount in the mail later in the week. My system failed when Bynum saw that the manager stopped checking her. Thirty-five thousand dollars and one year later we found the theft. My insurance company paid me quickly, and I had some money to pay bills. Lisa Bynum was put on criminal probation, only because her father agreed to pay back the insurance company. I had seven money handlers in my MEDCenters. I announced that the following day everyone would undergo a lie detector test. The test would cost $500 per examination. The next morning, two cashiers failed to show up. I figured they had something to hide. They were fired. There never was a lie detector test arranged. I just wanted to see who the guilty parties were.

Dr. Charles May and I had been together for ten years. I really admired the guy—excellent physician, good judgment, and a very calm demeanor. His behavior began to change radically in the office. He was short with the patients, yelled at the nurses for minor misdeeds, and seemed angry with me. I thought we needed a heart-to-heart talk. I sat him down and asked him point blank what the matter was. He was being well compensated, in addition to having great benefits and perks. He was a ten percent owner of a building that bore his name, Master-May MEDCenter, which I gifted him in 1984, and a forty-nine percent owner of the practice, which I also gave him with no buy-in. I finally dragged out of him that he wanted to be on his own. I understood immediately. He was producing most of the revenues except for the capitation check we received every month, which was my doing. He was in fact my junior partner but really wanted to be senior in his own practice. This is a natural maturation process for many juniors. I reflected to ten years prior, when Dr. Allenius gave me a chance to be autonomous. I would do the same for Dr. May. I thought it over, and the next day I offered to swap him the thriving Grandview practice, lock, stock, and barrel, in exchange for his ownership of the Short North practice, building, and a little cash. We shook on it and parted amiably, a testament to his character and our mutual respect. Dr. May went on to have an outstanding career in medicine.

About that same time, Dr. Feldman wanted to buy me out of the Parsons Avenue MEDCenter (PAMC). PAMC was my fifth and last center in Columbus, completed in 1984. He had a son who was graduating from medical school and wanted a ready-made practice for him. I understood completely, and we swapped the PAMC building and practice and a little cash for the MSMC building and practice. Feldman and I parted amiably and remain friends today.

From 1988 to 1993, HP enjoyed steady growth. I wanted to take HP to Cincinnati, a city with forty-five thousand Medicaid recipients being served by only a few city-owned public health centers and hospital emergency rooms. The public health centers were under the direction of Dr. Broadnax, who fell afoul of the law that year. They were in administrative disarray. They were easy to market against anyway because their physicians were part-time and had no ownership position, no chips in the game. There were no dominant providers there like the Schears in Dayton or me in Columbus. There were no managed care plans there either. Before I could develop Health Power of Cincinnati I would have to build a MEDCenter. In 1989 I chose the Over-the-Rhine (OTR) neighborhood just north of downtown and south of "pill hill," the section of Cincinnati where six hospitals were located. It was a chronically underserved area because of its Medicaid population, perfect for me. By that time I had great borrowing power. The funds were obtained from a Cincinnati bank with a personal signature, and the design contract was awarded to Denny Riga, a Columbus designer whose office is now the Columbus Foundation building on Broad Street. An interesting side note is that Denny agreed to sell me his building for a new site for my growing HP offices. I fell in love with this gorgeous turn-of-the-century stone mansion, but I declined his reasonable offer because it was much too grand to house a business serving Medicaid patients. Today I make frequent visits to that beautiful edifice on Broad Street as a member of the Columbus Foundation's Green Funds.

Developing the OTR MEDCenter was challenging. I had to quietly put together six adjoining lots including a White Castle with eight individual owners. Whenever I bought properties I used a straw man, a fictitious name. Using my own name would drive up the price. My man on the ground was Bill Loving, a whiz at real estate and a deal maker. Bill diligently went about collecting all the White Castle's owner's signatures who were spread all over the country. As it turned out, they were relieved to get rid of it. In fact the whole neighborhood was happy to see it razed. It had been the focus of drug dealing in the OTR area for a long time. The other five parcels fell into place without a struggle. Riga assigned Harold Baker to do the architectural design work. When finished, it won an award from the City of Cincinnati for the most outstanding design of the year. I hired Arnaldo Roldan, MD, MPH, to be the lead physician at OTR, a great fit because of his expertise in public health as well as medicine. The night before our grand opening, he called to say he had changed his mind and was not going to Cincinnati. I was in shock. What were my options? We were opening tomorrow morning at 8 a.m. I had no physician backups and I had a $2,500,000 investment. I had to go myself. And I did make that two-hour drive down and two-hour drive back every single day for three months. It was grueling, but I had no choice. The first day I treated thirty-five patients, and the practice grew steadily from there. I joined the Deaconess Hospital staff as an attending physician in the family medicine department. I had no intention of attending patients in the hospital, rather, I needed a hospital connection to refer the very sickest patients and get sophisticated testing that I couldn't offer myself. This relationship worked out well, and they made OTR a low-interest startup loan, which I eventually paid back. One innovation at OTR was a series of health posters, handsomely done by a professional artist. The themes were diabetes checkups, blood pressure checks, Pap smears, immunizations, and other basic health care reminders that I hung in the waiting and exam rooms. Why not send these messages to a waiting patient? Maybe it would prompt them to ask for services and improve their health. Bring the patient onto his or her own health care team. They were so effective that I made prints and put them in all the MEDCenters. I also placed TV monitors with continuous health care message (that I received for free from drug companies). These were not popular, and the patients demanded their soap operas be broadcast. I developed a free transportation system for patients to come to my office. I hired a social worker to guide our patients to needed social services such as food pantries and WIC, the federal program for Women, Infants and Children. Physicians began calling me asking for jobs. After the third month, I finally felt confident enough to stay in Columbus.

HP of Cincinnati began soon after as the first managed health care program in Hamilton County. Two more MEDCenters followed, Avondale and North Fairmount.

CHAPTER SIX

Birding Around the World: Select Trips to Florida, Arizona, Hawaii, and Costa Rica

Following the light of the sun, we left the Old World.
—Christopher Columbus

During the chaos of 1987, I reverted to a time-honored family coping mechanism, the same one my father used to find answers to his own overwhelming problems. The tools were basic: nutritious food, exercise, fresh air, a restful night's sleep, your support system—those who love you without reservation, your family. Amazingly, nearly eighty years after my father began using this comprehensive approach to a healthy lifestyle, *Medscape Medical News*, reported on October 3, 2014, the findings of a twenty-five-year study related to Alzheimer's disease. The preliminary research suggested that using these same simple and natural tools as recommended by my father, on a long-term basis, would produce a reversal of memory loss from Alzheimer's disease!

The pressures of 1987 were crushing. There were so many problems coming at me at once. My friend and sweetheart of five years, Susan Jones, was invaluable to me during this time. We took long walks and explored various solutions to all of the year's problems. Not only was Susan beautiful, but also level-headed with an abundance of common sense. At the very least, she was a sounding board for my ideas. One by one, the answers became clear. One by one, I surmounted every obstacle—the *Cleveland Plain Dealer*, Sperry, May, regulators, theft, business failure, and potential bankruptcy. We walked from my home along a beautiful path that followed Tucker Creek until it spilled a half mile later into the Olentangy River. My spirits brightened as we stopped to look at the wonders of nature—flowers, butterflies, and of course, birds. These were not power walks but conversational strolls. I started looking at birds again, and it gave me a familiar, comfortable feeling. I showed Susan the birds, and she instantly became a birdwatcher. I bought us both binoculars and dug out my *Peterson's Field Guide*. As everything was coming together in my business world, I felt stable enough to ask Susan to marry me and gave her an engagement ring. She had a nine-year-old son, Eric, who came with her as a "package." No problem there. I liked him a lot. We birded at Green Lawn Cemetery and Arboretum and Sharon Woods Metro Park mostly. We joined a few organized bird walks but preferred birding together, just the two of us. I kept field notes on all of our sightings. I never thought about keeping a cumulative list because back East such lists were shunned. No one talked about how many birds they had seen or even cared. It was considered gauche. The birds themselves are the beauty of the hobby.

Green Lawn Cemetery (GLCA) is the most famous and most productive birding spot in Central Ohio. It was established in 1848 and is noted for its Civil War cemetery, seven Ohio state champion trees and original Tiffany chapel windows. Famous persons are buried there, including World War I ace Eddie Rickenbacker and author James Thurber. Its 360 acres include a pond, fields, wooded ravines, scrub, a butterfly garden, and mixed woodlands—a mecca for birds and birders alike, especially during spring migration.

GLCA is mentioned in bird reports as far back as the early 1900s. Columbus Audubon bird club had some of its walks here in the 1910s. The announcement of the walks was always published in the *Columbus Citizen-Journal*. A trolley on

High Street brought people to within walking distance to the cemetery. Its list of rarities include American White Pelican, Mississippi Kite, Golden Eagle, Franklin's Gull, Barn Owl, Snowy Owl, Western Kingbird, Bell's Vireo, Clay-colored Sparrow, Harris's Sparrow, both Red and White-winged Crossbills, and Hoary Redpoll. All the eastern warblers including Kirtland's, Swainson's, and the hybrids Brewster's and Lawrence's have been observed there. The cemetery bird list stands at 219 species.

We always started our walk around the central pond, or "pit." It was once a small quarry, the stones of which formed the foundation for the cemetery roads. It was here that Susan and I made a most fruitful association. As we were birding one morning, we noticed a car circling us over and over. The driver was an older man and there was an older woman in the passenger seat. There was no one else around. Being from Philly, I always had my antennae up.

The window came down and the driver spoke, "Do you want to see a Saw-whet?"

Obviously he was a birder—and a good one at that, to find the secretive Northern Saw-whet Owl."

We looked at each other and simultaneously said, "Sure!"

We followed him over to an ancient yew. They hopped out of their car and pointed to a little fluff ball sitting about twelve feet up, blending in beautifully with the surrounding greenery. This was a lifer for us! Over the coming years we annually found a few Saw-whets, always in yews. I calculated the average date of their arrival at GLCA to be March 22. We began chatting with the couple, Cloyd (known as "Todd") and Margaret Dawson. Todd had been an avid birder for years and was a member of the Milt Trautman birding group. They would bird every Saturday, all day long, following different routes covering all the hotspots from Adams County south to Ottawa County north, and from the Indiana border west, to the Pennsylvania and West Virginia border, east. They knew in which part of the state to find different families such as shorebirds, raptors, or passerines—and when to find them. What a valuable resource for us. He invited us to join them some Saturday.

After birding the pond usually twice around, we would walk to the "Bridge," an iron structure built around 1900 spanning a ravine. On the way we would always stop to look for and marvel at the female Great Horned Owl and her three to four owlets present in most years in Section fifty. In the ravine we flushed American Woodcock from the leaf litter in February and March. Yellow-bellied Sapsuckers loved the soft wood to drill their wells, and thrushes were numerous in spring and fall migrations. On April 28, 1985, a Swainson's Warbler was found here by a beginning birder with a *Peterson's Field Guide*. The evergreens attracted winter finches in irruptive years (when the birds don't normally winter in their "own" area). Cooper's Hawks built their nests here. From the bridge we would stroll north along a ridge lined with hardwoods extending to the northern boundary of the cemetery. Bewick's Wrens used to be found along the chain-link fence as late as the 1960s. I always found something exciting here. One year (on May 17, my birthday) we spotted a Connecticut Warbler, a rare Loggerhead Shrike (extirpated from Ohio), Red-headed Woodpeckers whose numbers were declining rapidly and Pileated Woodpeckers in migration, a rare treat. On May 8, 1997 in a three-hour period I observed a massive fallout with 736 individuals representing sixty-nine species.

We would retrace our way back to the entrance and park in the administrative building parking lot. I found a migrating Golden-winged Warbler here. They no longer nested in Ohio. Across the street there is a large campus green that skirts the mausoleum. Killdeer, Eastern Meadowlarks and Eastern Bluebirds were often seen here. The campus green backs up to a brushy area, good for sparrows and especially Fox Sparrows in March and early April. A Clay-colored Sparrow, rare in Ohio, found by Todd Dawson, was recorded singing here by Dr. Donald Borror in 1973. This recording resides in the Cornell Laboratory of Ornithology. A Harris's Sparrow, a bird from the West, was seen here May 1, 1965. Remarkably, one year later a Harris's Sparrow was seen again west of the woods.

FLORIDA

With the troubles of the year behind me, we really needed a fun and relaxing vacation centered on birds. The hardest part of planning a birding trip is picking a route where you can see the most number of new birds in the shortest amount of time. We chose the Florida Keys, the week after Christmas, as our destination. With the warm sun, white sandy beaches, foamy breakers from the Atlantic surf, and plenty of new birds, we decided to just wing it with no reservations and see what life brought us. We flew into Fort Lauderdale, rented a car, and made our way a little bit north to Loxahatchee National Wildlife Refuge, first stop on our birding odyssey. Our only companion was *A Birder's Guide to Florida,* by James A. Lane (revised by Harold R. Holt in 1984). This was an amazing piece of work! James Lane of Massachusetts Audubon had written a series of bird guides, painstakingly documenting where to find birds and directions to them for many of the hotspots in the U.S. before he died in 1987. These guides were the most useful tools for out-of-state birders prior to the internet.

Wes Hetrick of Fairfax, Virginia, wrote a story about Lane published in *Bird Watcher's Digest,* which I will always remember. Jim and Wes were birding Madera Canyon in Southeast Arizona when they bumped into a young birding couple. They shared their bird findings with each other and birded together for a couple of hours, becoming instant friends on a first-name basis. The couple had picked up a copy of Lane's *A Birder's Guide to Southeast Arizona* at the Desert Museum, and because of it, extended their trip another month. Jim never let on that this book was his own. When they finally parted, the young man gave Jim his dog-eared and worn copy to guide them for the rest of their stay. They never knew the tribute they were paying to its author.

At Loxahatchee, we recorded a single Smooth-billed Ani and a Limpkin, both new birds for us. The Limpkin is the only species in its family, Aramidae, therefore in a "monotypic" family. The Limpkin and the Osprey represent the only two monotypic families in the United States. The Limpkin is one of the most far-ranging birds of the Americas, ranging from Florida to Argentina. It is related to rails and cranes. Its name comes from its apparent limping gait. The Osprey can be found in nearly the whole world.

At one point, we thought we were looking at a couple of Black Ducks when the light bulb in my skull went on. These were not Black Ducks, common in our area and rare in Florida, but the very closely related Mottled Ducks, never recorded in Ohio, but common in Florida. Both species have silver underwings, but the Mottled Duck has a buffy throat and head, and paler crown and eye stripe. The adult male Mottled has a bright yellow bill. The male Black Duck has a greenish-black bill and a colder brown throat and head. One field mark for the Mottled Duck, which I learned on this trip but is not noted in all field guides, is that its bill is more spatulate than the Black's. As we were watching the Mottled Ducks, a Purple Gallinule came into view from the dense vegetation and "walked across the water" using its long padded toes. The gallinule was a lifer for us. That's the way it is in birding.

Botanical gardens are a great place to find local birds and migrants, so we headed to Fairchild Tropical Gardens in South Miami. At the Gardens we found the exotic Indian Hill Myna, not countable by the ABA because it had not established itself long enough in the U.S. At that time the American Birding Association (ABA) had set the standard of ten years for exotic parrots and twenty-five years for everything else. These numbers were arbitrary but reasonable considering their experience with exotics. After all, it was only a huge game played on the map of the world as its board. We were hoping for a chance to see the Blue-gray Tanager and Java Sparrow in Miami, but they had already died out.

The Garden had lots of common Florida birds. Flocks of White Ibis (a species only accidental in Ohio and new for us) were so busy searching for crustaceans in the shallow ponds that they never noticed us. Right next to them were the Glossy Ibis, a bird with which we were familiar from New Jersey. When birding in a new locale, it is beneficial to see the common birds. You get a feel for what is around and expected. New species then stand out. There also may be recognizable racial differences in their plumages and calls, different from the same species at home. We spotted a Red-shouldered Hawk, but hold on. Its colors were so washed out. The Red-shouldered Hawk in southern Florida is the subspecies, *alleni*, much paler and with a substantially paler head than the northern subspecies, *lineatus*. Sometimes migrating *lineatus* birds are found in Southern Florida, but they are much darker and usually stick out.

Our next stop was the town of Kendall only a couple of miles away. We were after the Red-whiskered Bulbul, introduced in 1960 from Asia. They had taken hold here, and the Lane Guide said to look near the Kendall Methodist Church. We drove to the church, and on a pole in the church's parking lot we spied our bird right away. *Damn, this guy Lane is good!* On to Redlands Fruit and Spice Park about eight miles away for the White-winged Dove, and another exotic, the Spot-breasted Oriole. Got 'em both. The beautiful black and orange Spot-breasted Oriole was introduced into Miami from Southern Mexico in the 1940s and has hung on with a small breeding population. We decided to head into the Keys and found Highway 1 for our 150-mile journey south. *We'll save the Everglades for another time.*

The weather was great, downright balmy. Visibility was clear. We were happy thinking about all the snow and ice we had left behind in Ohio. Jim Croce's "I've Got a Name" (moving me down the highway) was playing on the radio. We stopped to check many of the mangrove-dotted shallows for shorebirds, terns, and big waders. Our most wanted list included Sandwich Tern, Reddish Egret, Wood Stork, Roseate Spoonbill, and Short-tailed Hawk. We stopped at the National Audubon Research Department in Tavernier and got their detailed booklet, *Birding in The Florida Keys*. This along with our Lane Guide was a tremendous help.

At Upper Matecumbe Key in Islamorada we saw Roseate Terns and our first Reddish Egret—the flamenco dancer of the bird world. The egret was doing its characteristic "umbrellaing," as I call it, creating a canopy by holding its wings spread aloft to produce shadows. The shadows attract small fish and lunch for the egret. In addition, it was stamping its feet and running in the shallow water to stir up more prey. The only thing missing were castanets. Our bird was the reddish form of the species. Now we were hoping for the other less common white form. Checking all the wires for migrant flycatchers, we saw Eurasian Collared Doves but no Scissor-tailed Flycatchers or Western Kingbirds. There were four records of the rare Loggerhead Kingbird here but not for us. The Collared Dove came to Florida in 1982 from the Bahamas. Originally from Asia, it has become one of the world's greatest colonizers invading all the semi-tropical and temperate zones of the globe except Australia.

Moving farther south, we began to see Magnificent Frigatebirds floating lazily in the warm tropical air. They occasionally take a fish from the surface, but they make their living by chasing seabirds, terns and gulls, forcing them to give up their catch to these pirates. At Channel Key we observed a Peregrine Falcon chasing any hapless bird flying by his bridge. Grassy Key gave us the less common white form of the Reddish Egret, just as active as his reddish relative.

We stopped at Marathon for the Burrowing Owls that were known to live on the Marathon golf course. After tramping around for a while with no success, I decided to ask someone where the owls were. Who better to ask than the golf course groundskeeper? He easily pointed out three burrows that we had just blindly walked past. Florida Burrowing Owls typically build their own burrows or take over abandoned gopher tortoise or armadillo burrows. One of the burrows was attended by a pair of owls standing side-by-side in front of their home. It reminded me of Grant Wood's 1930 painting, *American Gothic (House)*. Momma or daughter was at least a third bigger than poppa. This great size difference between genders is the rule throughout the owl world. The theory for the size difference is that the females are larger because they defend the nest, and the males are smaller because they capture smaller prey, so there is always a varied food supply, large and small. Outside their burrow was a small clump of cow dung to regulate the microclimate within and attract insects for a quick snack. This was the Florida subspecies, *floridana*. The other twenty-one subspecies ranged from Canada to Argentina. The couple was very accommodating and allowed close-up portraits, which hang in my summer home to this day. We also spotted a White-crowned Pigeon near a water hazard, which was par for the course.

Figure 6-1. Burrowing Owls, golf course, Marathon, Florida.

Ohio Key produced about two thousand Dunlin. This was the largest flock of this species I had ever seen. There were a few other "peeps," small shorebirds, but no Semipalmated Sandpipers, as they are not in the U.S. this time of year. Key Deer Refuge in Big Pine Key did not disappoint. We saw the smallest deer in North America, the endangered Key Deer. It was the size of a large dog, standing about two feet at the shoulder. This is the smallest subspecies of white-tailed deer. At that time there were no more than three hundred in existence. Road kills accounted for thirty to forty deaths a year. Despite intense searching, we kept missing our big three, the Roseate Spoonbill, Wood Stork, and Short-tailed Hawk. In birder's parlance we were "dipping" on those species. We couldn't find any Mangrove Cuckoos either, but most of those had migrated south by October.

We celebrated New Year's Eve, 1987, quietly at a small but comfortable Key West motel. Luckily, without a reservation, we got the last room available in the town. The next day we became sightseeing tourists and explored the town with its quaint shops and people. It was an odd mixture of successful businessmen, professionals, tourists, fishermen, and down-and-outers. You couldn't tell one from the other. We did go over to Key West Cemetery to check for winter residents but didn't see much. We wandered over to the Ernest Hemingway House, a National Historical Landmark, on Whitehead Street. It was a charming Spanish Colonial hewn from native rock in 1851. Fortunately for us, it was open for touring every day of the year so we popped in for the tour. It was filled with his books, personal photos, antique European furniture and his big game hunter trophies. In 1928, he wrote *A Farewell to Arms* in Key West but not in this house. It wasn't until 1931 that he moved here. A sea captain gave Hemingway a present of a parti-colored black-and-white, six-toed cat whose descendants we saw scurrying around the grounds. Much later in Haddonfield, New Jersey, my son, Ken, inherited a stray cat with six toes. I wonder …

The next day we began our journey back to reality, poking into various birding locations along the way hoping for a sighting of new species. We found nothing new until Tavernier. The Audubon Center earlier had tipped us that a flooded field behind a church held Roseate Spoonbills. We were getting desperate to see one. A birder cannot go to South Florida and not see a spoonbill. We drove over to the Memorial Methodist Church and pulled into the parking lot quietly, so as not to spook any birds. Jackpot! Not only were there six Roseate Spoonbills in a rain pool but also a dozen Wood Storks feeding in the wet field.

Sitting quietly on a fence, almost unobserved except for Susan's sharp eye, was a Short-tailed Hawk. We hit our trifecta, a perfect ending to our self-spun adventure. To this day, the Roseate Spoonbill is Susan's favorite bird. With mission accomplished, we flew home with seventeen lifers indelibly stored forever in our minds.

WORLD 690 • ABA 620

ARIZONA

Hungry for information, I began subscribing to bird magazines, and became a member of the hobby group, the American Birding Association (ABA) in 1987. I saw an ad in an issue of the ABA's birding magazine, *Birding,* about an organized Arizona bird tour led by John Shipley, owner of Goldeneye Nature Tours. Susan and I had never birded on a real tour with perfect strangers led by a professional guide. In fact, we had never birded outside of a few states in the eastern U.S. This sounded like a great adventure—new birds in a new state.

The six-day tour was only $495 per person and offered a potential list of 472 species. That's about a buck a species, not counting airfare. I considered this to be an excellent value. Later I figured out that 472 was the entire State of Arizona's bird list. That was okay because the next six days of birding blew me away—fantastic scenery, interesting Native American culture, and amazing birds. John Shipley knew his birds and where to find them. We birded all the famous bird haunts I had been reading about: Madera Canyon for the Yellow-eyed Junco; Kino Springs for the brilliant Vermilion Flycatcher (a bird that looks like it just flew from the illuminated pages of a medieval manuscript); Patagonia Lake for the rare Neotropic Cormorant; and Sulfur Springs Valley, well known for its raptors and sparrows.

On the next to last day, we visited the magical Chiricahua Mountains, where a century before, Geronimo rode with his band of Apaches. These majestic peaks rose from the Sonoran Desert to almost ten thousand feet. We visited some of the residents' bird feeders in Portal to see hummers and whatever feathered visitors popped in for a snack. About this time, I started to feel ill with fever and jaw pain. By morning I had high fever and could barely open my mouth. I could feel a swelling in my gums next to a molar. It was a tooth abscess. With every beat of my heart, I could feel the pounding pain. I felt really toxic. I was taking Tylenol® with no relief. I asked John to get me to a doctor or dentist, but there were none in these remote areas. John said they had an Emergency Medical Technician (EMT) in this town, and I asked him to get him. The young man arrived, a newly fledged EMT, and I asked him to find a needle and syringe somewhere in town. He had never done an aspiration before. Lying flat on my back, I guided his hand with a diabetic's needle into this bulging mass. I was aided by a mirror and flashlight Susan was holding for me. I enjoyed immediate relief as he aspirated the pus.

"Good job, son!"

He rounded up some penicillin tablets and Darvon® Compound capsules from the neighbors, and I was back looking at Mexican Chickadees the next day. Necessity was the mother of invention that day. I finished the trip with 142 species of birds, including such rarities as Green Kingfisher and Stripe-backed Tanager, ten species of hummingbirds, an incredible seventy-two lifers, and vivid memories of some of the most beautiful scenery in America. Over the years, these first memories of Arizona lured me back again and again.

WORLD 698 • ABA 662

HAWAII

Business continued favorably at the MEDCenters and HP. I was feeling good. It was time to marry Susan. We were married on our front lawn under a majestic Scarlet Oak tree with Susan's father, mother, and our children in attendance. My son, Ken, was my best man and Susan's twin sister, Sandy, was her matron of honor. We were off to Hawaii for our honeymoon. Our wedding reception would wait until we returned. We checked into the Hilton Hotel on the Big Island of Hawaii without my suitcase; it had been lost by the airline. I thought it would arrive at any time, so I bought some cheap walking shorts, T-shirt, and sandals to hold me for a day or two. I wound up wearing the same clothes for a week. The airline didn't have a clue where my bag was. Susan wanted beach and pool; I wanted birds and volcanoes. We compromised. In the mornings we went our separate ways, joining each other for lunch and beach in the afternoon, comparing notes, and enjoying great dining at night.

Birding Hawaii took a great deal of study because practically all the birds would be new. There were seabirds, native birds, shorebirds, and introduced birds. I reasoned that if I concentrated on finding the native birds, everything else would fall into place. This strategy worked, and by the end of a week I had seen twelve endemics and fifty species overall.

Figure 6-2. Rare photo of Little Amakiki taking seed from the
hand (Susan's), Ilikai.

My one big disappointment was dipping on the Nene,
Hawaiian Goose. I mistakenly thought I would see Hawaii's
state bird everywhere. What I did not know was that it was
molting its feathers this time of year and had disappeared
from its golf course and roadside haunts to inaccessible
places for protection.

At the Volcanoes National Park, I scored big with omao
(Hawaiian Thrush), Elepaio, Apapane, and Amakiki in the
fern forest—all endemics and all on the endangered species
list. White-tailed Tropicbirds floated effortlessly in the
volcano caldron. It is here I learned the word, *aa*, for the
basaltic lava with broken rough surfaced blocks called
"clinkers." *Aa* is a great Scrabble word. A park ranger told me
I could find the Iiwi at Kipuka twenty-one and gave me
directions; however, it was on fenced private property. A
kipuka is a patch of forest surrounded by hardened lava flow,
an island of life. When I got there I saw some cattle punching
going on with real Hawaiian cowboys. The kipuka was too far
away to see any birds. The cowboys were on horseback,

rounding up cattle into a big delivery trucks. I walked over to the gate and waited for a truck to exit. About twenty minutes later, one truck did. When the driver got out to open the gate, I asked him if I could go in and look at some birds. He was a short tobacco-chewin', rough-hewn image of Robert Duvall. I didn't know what, if any, response I would get.

He said, "You mean the Iiwi? Sure, go on in. If anybody asks what you're doin', tell 'em Shorty said it was okay."

I was floored that this roughneck new his Hawaiian birds. "Thanks, Shorty," and I made the short walk to the koa forest.

Within minutes I was staring at two very curve-billed and very red Hawaiian Honeyeaters, the Iiwis. Driving back to the hotel, I stopped to look at a light form Io, the Hawaiian Hawk, a symbol of Hawaiian royalty—just the way I was feeling at that moment.

There are twenty-two species of seabirds nesting in Hawaii. Newell's Shearwater is one of those. We were finding them littered on the highways as roadkill. Apparently they are attracted by the island lights, and fly landward into moving vehicles on the roads. There are small boxes placed throughout the island the size of mailboxes to hold injured or dead birds until they are collected by the authorities.

Figure 6-3. Roadkill, Newell's Shearwater

The Hawaiian Petrel was a native bird high on our target bird list. One day we drove to South Point, Ka Lee, the southernmost point of the United States. It is also conjectured to be the landing site of the first Polynesian settlers 1,500 years ago. As we were scanning the Pacific Ocean in front of us, we saw three seabirds flying high above the waves with deeply banked arcs and glides. These were Hawaiian Petrels. We imagined the first Hawaiians seeing this same sight from this same place.

The Hawaiian Stilt had eluded us. It frequents fresh water ponds, but we were only seeing salt and brackish wetlands. This is an elegant black and white wader with long, bubblegum pink legs. We had to find fresh water. I was not going home without seeing this bird. I found a nice sized pond on the map. We found a gravel parking lot and a trail skirting the beach, which I thought would take us right to the pond. We walked for a while looking for the pond but none appeared. We saw a large group of sunbathers on the beach and walked into their midst to ask directions. *Oh my God*—we had walked onto a nude beach! I thought, *Well, I got this far, and I'm not going home without seeing the Stilt.* What a sight we must have looked to the nudists—two tourists, fully dressed with cameras and binoculars around our necks. I walked over to a man on a blanket, who was naked as a jaybird. I didn't care, but Susan was staring at this guy.

I yelled at her, "Don't look, Ethel," but I don't think she heard me because she kept staring.

I asked him if there was a pond here and he pointed (with his hand, I might add) to the pond about twenty feet away, right in front of us. I hustled Susan over to the pond, and there was our prize—six Hawaiian Stilts. As a bonus, we also spotted the Hawaiian Black-crowned Night-Heron, Hawaiian Coot, Hawaiian Moorhen, Northern Shoveler, Blue-winged Teal, and Pied-billed Grebe. We scurried back to our car heads, down, avoiding any eye-to-body contact.

The island is filled with exotic birds, each group of immigrants bringing their favorite birds. The Japanese brought the White-eye; Indians, the Kalij Pheasant and pesky Common Mynas; and the South Americans, the Yellow-billed Cardinal. Hunters brought the Wild Turkey, Gray Francolin, and Japanese Quail. They were all countable, valid "ticks," by ABA standards. As the birders say, "A tick is a tick." However, there are some birders who will not count any "introduced species" on their lists.

Our honeymoon ending, we headed to the airport. There were two young fellows standing outside the hotel waiting for a taxi to take them shopping. I had some extra time so I volunteered to drop them off, but they wanted to go in the opposite direction from the airport. I took them anyway. After dropping them off, I turned back to the airport. I saw a dark crow-like shape flying toward us. I pulled over to the side of the road and put my bins on one of the rarest birds in the world, the Hawaiian Crow, the Alala. It had a BirdLife International conservation designation of "Critically Endangered," the last designation before extinct. (BirdLife International is widely recognized as the world leader in bird conservation.) This means there was a ninety percent chance of its being extinct in ten years. They were being wiped out by predators, disease, and habitat loss. Rats were eating their eggs and young. Avian pox and avian malaria were taking a heavy toll, and mankind was doing its best to clear the Alala's forest habitat. There were only a couple left in the wild and seven in a rehab center. To find one freely flying was an extremely rare occurrence. My good deed was abundantly rewarded.

Figure 6-4. Hawaiian Crow at rehabilitation center.

The airline never found my bag. When I returned home, I made an insurance claim. Six weeks later, the airline sent me a check for about ten cents on the dollar. I had lost all of my good clothes (including my favorite birding T-shirts) and souvenirs of Arizona and Florida. Two weeks after I received the check, the airline called to tell me that they found my bag, and it would be delivered in the morning. The next morning came and went without a bag. That evening, I called the airline to find out where my bag was. They told me it had been sent out the day before. They sounded alarmed. The next morning the airline called to tell me my bag was found on its way to Indiana in the delivery man's car (along with a dozen other customers' bags) after he was pulled over by the Indiana State Patrol on I-70.

When asked why he stole the bags, he replied, "Well, you know me."

I finally got my bag the third day. I called the insurance company, told them the story, and asked them what to do with the insurance money I had received.

"Keep it, and we will come pick up the bag."

"Wouldn't you rather I send the money back?"

"No, it's not ours anymore. We sold it to a middleman, and now they get it."

I wanted to pay them back, but their system would not allow it. This kind of practice was the tip of the iceberg as to why the airlines were losing money. Since they had only paid me ten percent of the true value, I took out all my favorite T-shirts and good clothes and replaced them with other clothes closer to the ten percent value.

WORLD 732 • ABA 662

COSTA RICA

1989 was a year of growth for the MEDCenters and HP. It was time for another New Year's birding trip. This time we would take our seventeen-year-old son, Eric, to broaden his horizons. I was hoping to make a birdwatcher out of him. We wanted to visit a country that was close, friendly, safe, warm, and had great birds. Costa Rica would fit the bill by all accounts I had read. We opted for a Victor Emanuel Nature Tour (VENT). This would be our first venture outside of the U.S. looking for birds. At that time VENT was considered one of the "Big Three" bird tour companies along with WINGS and Field Guides. They all shared an equally fine reputation. This was our first chance to experience the timelessness and beauty of the tropical rain forest. The clock was ticking on this precious resource, and we wanted to feel it and live it before it was too late. The rain forest, with its complex communities of untold numbers of living things, was vanishing at a rapid rate. We wanted to participate in our planet's recovery. This tour was designed to see most of the forest habitats in Costa Rica, from Subtropical and Upper Tropical Rainforest called "cloud forest" to Lower Tropical Zone and Tropical Dry Forest. For this trip I upgraded my binoculars from a cheap Japanese made glass I had used for eighteen years to a top of the line Zeiss 10 x 40. I bought Susan a Zeiss 7 x 35. Wow! What a difference!

Our leaders were David and Mimi Wolf, a husband and wife team from Texas. David was an expert in Neotropical birds and Mimi was a terrific artist. As it turned out, they were very pleasant to be with, too. David unavoidably missed the first three days of the tour due to the death of his father. Mimi took over, and although I discovered her birding skills were not nearly to the level of David's, we only missed a few birds. The first day I counted forty lifers! I had never experienced so many new birds in one day before, and it was overwhelming.

There was a family of four from California with us. They had two daughters, one Eric's age and the other a little younger. The father thought this would be a general nature tour. He did not read all of VENT's material before he signed up. They quickly found out that the tour was about birds. They didn't know anything about birds, and they did not want to learn. The father, John, an OB-Gyn specialist, developed into a nasty and rude tour participant. For some reason, he picked me out of the group of eight as the target for his jibes and spiteful remarks. At first I played him off, thinking it was all in fun. It wasn't fun; his remarks to me—and only me—became more barbed and personal. I tried to ignore him, but he started to insult me right to my face. I was trying to figure him out. Was it the old "town and gown" rivalry, GP versus specialist? Or was it my expertise in birding that was bugging him? I finally came to the conclusion that he was just an asshole. I entertained punching him out, Philly style, so he would leave me alone and let me enjoy the birding. I realized that was not a viable solution. I told Susan I was not enjoying the trip because of his obnoxious behavior. She said to ignore him, but I had already tried that without success. This schmuck was having the time of his life, not from the birds, but from my obvious annoyance. Every chance he got, he would make some stupid remark about me. I was having a terrible time. About mid-trip, the solution struck me like a thunderbolt. If I took away his source of enjoyment—my open irritation from his verbal bullying—the game was over. I developed my "invisibility act," which I only rarely had to call upon on future bird tours with tormenting "black fly" clients. The invisibility act employs a simple device that works perfectly and is actually fun to watch the resulting reaction from the hectoring party. Here is the way it works: The bully becomes invisible to you. You cannot hear or see him. He will come very close to your face to say something to you, and you look right through him without acknowledging his presence, or casually walk away. When he calls your name from the back of the van, ignore him. When he tugs on your shirt to get your attention, walk away. When he tries to sit next to you on the bus, spread out. You never acknowledge his presence for any reason. It worked like kryptonite on Superman. I took away his power. John became morose and sulked the rest of the trip. He completely left me alone. It was checkmate. He was defeated and deflated. There were even days that he never joined the group for birding. My spirits soared to be rid of this parasite. I really got into the birding, and David was a marvelous teacher. It didn't hurt either when monkeys hurled their dung on John and his wife. The rest of the tour was fabulous.

At Cerro del Muerte, I and another participant were the only ones to see the Resplendent Quetzal, the iconic symbol of Costa Rica. I thought we would be seeing them everywhere, but this year they did not show. Resplendent Quetzals are best seen in Panama, I learned later. Everyone was rewarded by scope views of an Ochraceous Pewee, a rarely seen oak forest endemic, and later at Volcano Poas, a Volcano Hummingbird, a tiny relative of our Rufous Hummingbird, showing its rose-red gorget.

La Selva Biological Station is part of the Organization of Tropical Studies (OTS) network, a leader in research, education, and conservation in the tropics. It invites researchers as well as the non-scientist public to share its rich tropical lowland rainforest. Susan, Eric, and I were housed with another guest, a gentleman we did not know. It was a little awkward at first, but he turned out to be a very sensitive and considerate roommate, so there were no problems.

The first morning we all watched a Great Tinamou in the open footpath, and two minutes later spotted a calling Slaty-breasted Tinamou in the underbrush. These are normally two skulking species, difficult to see. The dawn chorus emanating from the forest was alive with new sounds for us. The hoot of a distant Rufous Motmot, the quavering calls of tinamous, and the laughs of the woodcreepers filled our ears with question marks. "David, what was that trill? Mimi, what is that whooping sound?" Insects and frogs sounded like birds, and birds like insects and frogs. Mammal sounds were entirely foreign. David, our leader patiently sorted them out and identified every call and peep for us. Two magnificent King Vultures literally swooped ten feet over our heads to get a better look at us. A pair of seldom seen Semiplumbeous Kites sailed into view, and a black-and-white Hawk-Eagle, another hard to find bird, floated above us. We had fantastic close-up looks at the much-persecuted Crested Guan, hunted for its meat. A Sungrebe, fanning its rainbow tail, was spotted at the La Selva footbridge and nearby a usually secretive Gray–necked Wood-Rail strutted right out into the open. We had fabulous studies of the odd and rarely seen hummingbird, the White-tipped Sicklebill, its bill aptly named. One misty morning a gorgeous pair of Chestnut-colored Woodpeckers came out of the forest to show themselves. A Band-backed Wren appeared, one of fifteen wren species in Costa Rica we saw this trip. No other place in the world has this variety of wrens. Chestnut-sided Warblers, a familiar bird breeding in our Ohio forests, seemed to be everywhere in their drab winter plumages.

Mammals were plentiful with a white-faced capuchin, a large troop of spider monkeys, and a two-toed sloth (the less frequently seen of the sloth species). Deppe's squirrel and the animated miniature Alfaro's pygmy squirrel scurried almost unnoticed through the trees. Agoutis, which are large rodents, and coatimundis, relatives of raccoons were common. Susan and I saw a kinkajou, normally a nocturnal animal, stumbling around during the day. Kinkajous, called "honey bears," are also related to raccoons. This one definitely looked ill with its lifeless eyes, runny nose, and sluggish movements. On New Year's Eve day, three teams of birders participated in the Costa Rica Christmas Bird Count (CBC), an official Audubon bird count. CBCs were originated in the States as a substitute for hunting birds, going all the way back to 1900. Susan's and my team found 113 species. The entire group produced a total of 310 bird species, probably the largest list of any CBC in the Americas that year.

Snakes were scarce. We found one coral snake mimic on the trail. A tour participant found a small boa constrictor coiled up in the laundry room and woke up the whole camp with her screaming. The one animal I was extremely wary of was the Paraponera ant, the "bullet" ant, a large venomous stinging ant. Its sting is said to require morphine to subdue the pain, which lasts twenty-four hours and can lead to death in hypersensitive individuals.

One of my greatest birding moments occurred on this trip. We visited *Los Cusingos*, the plantation home of one of the world's leading ornithologist, Dr. Alexander Skutch. A Baltimorean and trained at Johns Hopkins, Dr. Skutch moved to this remote patch of land in 1941 and lived a simple life off the grid. He wrote forty books and published more than two hundred scientific papers and articles. He made major contributions to ornithology, botany, and philosophy. The field guide we were all using, *A Guide to The Birds of Costa Rica*, was written by him and F. Gary Stiles. He accomplished all of this from his simple home in the rain forest without phones, plumbing, or electricity. He used an ancient 1930s Corona typewriter, under lights provided by a car battery, to produce this mountain of information. In his book, *Birds Asleep*, he maintained that swifts, those perpetual flying machines, actually slept on the wing. I considered the irony of one living off the grid contributing so much to those living on the grid.

Figure 6-5. Me with Dr. Alexander Skutch in his Los Cusingos office.

I encouraged our son, Eric, to engage this great man in conversation. And now, so many years later, this meeting remains indelibly impressed into Eric's memory. Dr. Skutch volunteered a bird walk around his garden. He pointed out the hard-to-see Spot-crowned Euphonia and then a memorable moment occurred. I found myself alone with him as he showed me his very own Turquoise Cotinga, a bird of uncommon beauty, deep violet and intense glossy blue, perched on top of a bare tree. He knew it would be there as he saw it there every day. We watched it together for a lifetime.

Our group broke away from his *finca* (farm) to enter the forest in search of ant swarms. In my opinion, the ant swarm is the most exciting and fascinating phenomenon in the bird world. Ant swarms are made up of army ants, their prey, and birds that follow the swarm. Army ants are in both the Old and New Worlds. They split from a common ancestor one hundred million years ago. There are more than 120 species of army ants in the New World. They are the most ferocious social hunters, and hunt by forming aggressive predatory foraging groups. They do not form nests like other ant species. *Eciton burchelli* is the predominant species in the New World. The workers are blind and sterile females. The queen, of which there is only one to a colony, is also blind with a large belly area called the "gaster" and an elongated extended abdomen. She lays a colossal three to four million eggs a month. The males are winged and resemble wasps. They are large and develop oversized mandibles to protect the colony. Their other function is to mate with the queen. After mating, their wings fall off. *She must be one heck of a gal!* They must travel to feed their enormous population of up to fifteen million individuals. They begin their nomadic wanderings ten days after the queen lays her eggs, and travel for about two weeks taking their eggs with them. They consume an unbelievable five hundred thousand individual prey every day. Their diet consists mostly of insects, spiders and small vertebrates, and sometimes snakes, birds and oily seeds. During this time larvae are produced, and then pupal cases are spun. Then the colony enters its stationary phase, and bivouacs in a tree hollow or burrows underground for about three weeks to allow the pupae to develop. Since there are no larvae to feed during this phase, the queen is fed exclusively. When new eggs hatch, the nomadic phase is resumed. Every three years a new queen is born, and the colony divides.

Our group was lucky to find a raiding swarm. The first thing that struck me was the enormous size of the swarm trail. It was about sixty feet wide and one hundred feet long. The ants were flushing and capturing all sorts of insects, a few earthworms, and even a small snake. The second thing that struck me was the rustling sound of the tens of millions of feet collectively marching over the dry leaf litter. This sound is unique in nature. Last, and most important to us, were the birds that were attracted to this spectacle—the antbirds. There was an amazing scene unfolding in front of us, larger than any Cecil B. Demille epic with a cast of millions.

Antbirds do not eat ants. The Antbirds were feasting on the animals that the ants were flushing. Their terror-stricken prey were running and flying for safety as fast as they could. There were no defenses against the ant horde.

Antbirds belong to a very large family, the *Thamnophilidae*. There are approximately 250 species in this family but only eighteen attend ant swarms. These are called obligate antbirds because they are obliged to follow ants for their sustenance. The inner circle of the arena was composed of a Bicolored Antbird, the only obligate, hopping at our feet, and a Dot-winged Antwren. A little farther out were a Black-hooded Antshrike and Chestnut-backed Antwren. A White-throated Robin, which seemed out of place, sneaked into the party but kept on the fringe. Some of the antbirds were giving high-pitched harsh whistles, which penetrated the loose understory of the forest, announcing to other birds that there was food here. There was a Plain Xenops and Tawny-winged Woodcreeper low on the trees lying in ambush to eat the bugs that were scurrying up the trunks to escape the ants. Every bird was eating something. A Gray-headed Tanager, a fruit eater, watched the show from a safe distant perch. Outside of this circle of mayhem was a Sharp-shinned Hawk waiting for his opportunity to snatch any unwary bird. Susan and I were so riveted to the action that we did not notice a couple of army ants crawl up our pant legs until we felt their poker-hot fiery stings. We must have looked like Indians on the warpath with our jumping up and down, slapping our legs, and whooping and hollering until the ants were dispatched to their happy hunting grounds. Another birding participant shared our fate and had to drop his pants so he could see to swat the ants off.

Back at Dr. Skutch's, I asked him to sign three of his books that I had lugged with me all the way from the States. John, my former tormentor, not knowing he was in the presence of one of the world's greatest living ornithologists, asked me why I brought them all that way. Of course, he was still "invisible" so I completely ignored him. Dr. Skutch graciously signed each copy with a personal note, and they hold a special place in my library to this day.

We finished our trip at the Carara Reserve on the Pacific slope. This was once the home of the Indian chief, Garabito, whom the Spanish had never seen let alone defeated. Numerous tombs within the park were solemn reminders of the once thriving indigenous population. The Reserve was famous for its Scarlet Macaws. We had to get up extra early that morning for any chance to see them because they leave their roosts at dawn to disperse and feed. Our efforts paid off handsomely as we saw several pairs emerge from their roost holes at the first rays of the sun. I added twelve new species this last day and decided to go to sleep early in preparation for a long trip back to San Jose and departure to Columbus. Eric had other plans. He wanted to explore on his own and go to the nearby town. We said okay, but be back by 10 p.m. At 10 p.m. I was in bed and Susan was waiting up. By 11 p.m. we were both waiting up. By midnight, Susan told me to go find him. I had no idea where to start. It was pitch black outside. I grabbed my flashlight and found the exit from the Reserve. *Which way, left or right?* I thought of Yogi Berra's advice, "When you come to a fork in the road, take it." I called on Hecate, the Roman goddess who determined directions for confused travelers. I went right, stumbling down a dirt road, calling Eric's name over and over. Maybe he was lost. I know I was. Maybe he was hurt. If not, he would be! I walked for an hour and then I heard a motor car in the distance, then saw a pair of headlights, then a beater car, and then our Eric. He didn't seem the least bit concerned that he was three hours past his curfew in an alien country after midnight. I was so happy to see him I could not scold him. He told me he had joined a party in the village and met a Costa Rican girl. They hung out together and he was having such a good time, he forgot about coming back. Before he knew it, it was midnight but he couldn't find a cab or beg a ride. The girl's uncle finally agreed to drop him off—for a fee, of course! I hustled him back to his mother, who was sick with worry. She was so happy to see him that she didn't scold him either. The next day we all boarded the VENT van and headed to San Jose.

As we passed through the town, we heard everyone in town who saw our van yell, "Hey, it's Ereec, Ereec!"

He had become quite an overnight celebrity. We all had a good laugh.

WORLD 1,140 • ABA 681

CHAPTER SEVEN
Malpractice Lawsuit: My First and Only

Aristotle taught that fish and eels sprang forth from sand, mud and putrefying algae, which is a silly idea. Today we know this is where lawyers come from.
—Doug Robarchek, *Charlotte Observer*

The year 1990 began with a jolt. I received a ninety-day letter stating a local law firm, on behalf of one of their clients (a recent patient of ours), was contemplating a medical malpractice suit for negligence. Since the beginning of my medical career in 1966, I only had one threat of malpractice. It was deemed frivolous and dismissed by the court before it even got started. I immediately forwarded the threat to my malpractice insurance carrier. I reviewed the medical file. This was a thirty-seven-year-old white male who recently complained of rectal bleeding. One of our doctors did a rectal exam and felt a small mass but did not know what it was. He referred him to an internal medicine specialist for a sigmoidoscopic examination. The report came back with a diagnosis of "internal hemorrhoids." We treated him with suppositories for a few weeks. He came back a month later and said he could see a little bright red blood on his toilet tissue again. He was treated again with rectal suppositories. A month later he came back and requested to see the senior doctor on staff—that was me. I did a hemoglobin test and it showed a slight anemia. Although chronic bleeding can occur over a long period of time with hemorrhoids and produce anemia, I didn't think this was his problem. I sent him for more testing of his upper and lower GI tract. These showed normal except for a small hiatal hernia. Over time these hernias can cause reflux and an erosion of the stomach and esophageal lining leading to anemia. I didn't think this was his problem either. Perplexed, I sent him to a rectal surgeon who found the problem right away. He had a tiny tumor at the tip of the anus, an extremely rare cancer especially in such a young man. It was a Stage III cancer because it had spread through the wall of the rectum. The surgeon operated on him right away and removed the affected part of the rectum. He had to wear a colostomy bag, but it was reversible. He would enjoy a long life after the tumor was removed.

The patient's lawyers took the depositions of our doctors, the internist and the surgeon as to what we'd found, what we did and why we did it. About three months later we were served papers that we, along with the internist, were being sued for $1.2 million. The allegation was that because there was a delay in diagnosis, we caused him to have a colostomy. In reality, from the time we saw him to the time of surgery, only eight months had passed. There was no way of telling what stage the cancer was at eight months before. Because it was so rare, there was very little data in the scientific literature about this type of cancer.

I sent the lawsuit papers to our malpractice insurer, and they assigned a defense attorney to represent us, Ken Blumenthal. He was a partner in a large Columbus firm only doing malpractice defense work for doctors. He had never been on the other side suing doctors, which gave me more confidence in him. He said he had approval from the insurance company to settle the case for a $1 million. If the case were not so serious, I would have laughed in his face. I told him I had reviewed the case and felt confident that we were not negligent and had not committed malpractice. My defense was simple and verified by our well-documented chart. The facts would show that as soon as we discovered the mass on the first visit, we referred him to a specialist to identify the mass. Despite the specialist's completely missing the cancer, we persisted with diagnostic tests and finally sent him to another specialist when things were not making sense. We never dropped the ball. The surgeon cut out the cancer, and I believe, we saved his life by our prudent actions. There was no way I was going to settle for even a penny. I was ready to fight. I liked Ken Blumenthal. He struck me as a tough fighter himself. Before he went to law school he was a dealer at a Las Vegas casino. He had a rough edge about him that suited my defense. I told him to go forward with the defense, and I was prepared to go to court every day until we proved our innocence.

The day before the trial, the plaintiff lowered his demand to $1 million hoping to reap a quick bonanza. They didn't know the kind of man with whom they were dealing.

I said an emphatic, "No!"

There was one hiccup. We couldn't locate our doctor who had first found the mass. He had left the state, and there was no forwarding information. This was not critical to the case because we had his notes on the chart and the "referral for rectal mass" was clearly written. However, it would have been supportive to hear his testimony. We chose a jury based on no particular courtroom theories but rather on our unscientific feeling that this juror or that juror would be objective, unbiased, and sympathetic to our side of the story. Both sides made opening statements. In Ohio, the plaintiff puts on his case first. The plaintiff calls you every name in the book—malpracticer, negligent, uncaring, and worse. The jury despises you. They seemed to be staring at me with vindictive eyes. You just have to endure it. I sat there for a week and could hardly believe what I was hearing from their experts. The prosecutor's first witness was the patient himself. Let's call him Mr. Eel. He described everything that took place in the last year. He claimed he was disabled from our malpractice and could not work. Mr. Eel was accepting welfare checks from the state. His wife did not work either. Nothing new was revealed with his testimony. His wife, who was also suing us for loss of consortium, said they hadn't had sex during his whole illness because it was too uncomfortable for him and she did not like his colostomy bag. Their testimony never hurt us or helped them. I don't think the jury was sympathetic to their story.

His first expert medical witness was the pathologist who made the microscopic diagnosis. He was chief of pathology in a Columbus hospital and a friend of the plaintiff's attorney. Their kids played baseball together. Let's call him Dr. Jerry. He freely admitted he had never seen this type of tumor before, but when asked what the doubling time was (the time it took for a tumor to double in size), he said every thirty days. That is extremely rapid for any tumor, but his answer, if allowed to be unchallenged, made their case. This implied that in the eight months between diagnosis and surgery, the tumor had time to invade the full thickness of the wall of the bowel. By invading the bowel wall, there was damage that required a colostomy bag and could shorten his life. The pathologist rendered an opinion that all of this could have been prevented by an earlier diagnosis.

The next witness was a doctor from out of town. He was a paid expert witness who made his living testifying against other doctors for a fee. In other words he was a medical prostitute. He said that our care fell beneath the standard of care for the community. He said we were negligent in not operating earlier. He quibbled over some irrelevant minor details. But he also revealed that he was not a general practitioner (as we were), but rather an internist. This turned out to be another plaintiff's misstep. Their expert did not hurt our case either.

The third witness was the surgeon who made the diagnosis and performed the operation. DiCuccio, the lead plaintiff's attorney, led her to say that we had committed malpractice by delaying the referral for so long. This was damning to have our own specialist make such a statement.

Blumenthal would take care of the surgeon and her reckless statement later. The plaintiff's attorney, a very large, blustery man, swaggered around the courtroom delighting in the drama he was creating.

The fourth witness was our physician's assistant, Ron Roberts, P.A. He had treated the patient on two occasions, continuing the treatment protocol established by our physicians. DiCuccio attempted to make it appear by his questioning that a P.A., not being a physician, was therefore not qualified to practice medicine. His motive was to try to show the jury we were delivering substandard care. Mr. Roberts comported himself extremely well and explained the licensing and duties of a P.A. in Ohio. No harm was done there.

DiCuccio's next witness was an economist who tried to tell the jury that this man's disability was worth more than a million dollars in lost wages. How could that be? He and his wife were on welfare, and he claimed he had not worked before he discovered the rectal bleeding due to a prior back injury that he had sustained on a construction job. The jury wasn't buying it. At this point, I was feeling pretty good about our case. Early on, my attorney asked me every morning whether I wanted to settle the case. He explained the money would come from the insurance company, not me, so it wouldn't cost me anything out of pocket. But where do you go to get your reputation back?

Once more I said, "No."

He never asked me again. After the first full week of testimony, DiCuccio was feeling pretty smug, and as he walked by the defense table, he whispered to me that for $500,000 he would let me walk. I laughed at him. I wasn't worried, but I could not wait to tell our side of the story.

The trial was now in its second week. I had no idea what expert witnesses Ken Blumenthal had retained for my defense. Were they competent? What would they say? I had to trust him. I batted leadoff. He wanted me to tell the story. Blumenthal called me to the stand as our first witness and reviewed my education, training, certifications, and war record. He asked me to explain all of the notes on the chart in detail to the jury. I looked at the jury as I read line by line the notes on the chart and what they meant. Ken had a big cardboard blowup copy of the notes in front of the courtroom so the jury could follow along. They could see I wasn't hiding anything. I explained what we did and why we did it. I emphasized the fact that we had immediately referred the patient to a specialist for a sigmoidoscopy to provide a direct look at the mass and biopsy if required. We leaned heavily on the results of that exam and treated him for hemorrhoids. When it became apparent that our therapy was not working, we referred him for a second opinion. That was our case. On cross-examination, DiCuccio tried smoke and mirrors to confuse me—and the jury. He was very experienced and used a lot of old courtroom tricks. At one point, he read from a very old medical book about rectal tumors and asked me if I agreed. It was all outdated information. If I disagreed with a medical book, it would appear to the jury I didn't know my medicine. So I asked him the date of publication. He gave the date, and as I guessed, it was ancient. I told the courtroom I disagreed with his textbook because it was outdated information. He then asked me a series of very specific and minutely detailed medical questions about the tests I'd ordered to make me stumble and appear unsure to the jury. This was a blunder. He was in my arena now. He didn't know what I knew and how well I knew it. Frankly, he wouldn't have known if I gave him correct answers or not. I confidently answered every question in layman's terms, so the jury could understand. He then read from a *Physician's Desk Reference* (PDR) about one of the medications we had prescribed and asked me if I agreed with the statement. I was onto his game. I took a gamble; this was an outdated reference too. I knew by the color of its binding it was an old PDR. I told him that the information he'd just read was outdated and there were new indications for the medication's use. I therefore disagreed with him. In his frustration he literally charged at me in the witness chair and yelled his next question right to my face. I had a few tricks of my own from years of giving testimony in personal injury and worker's compensation cases. Instead of answering, I turned to the judge and told him DiCuccio was intimidating me, and would he tell him to move back from me. The judge admonished him, told him to move away from the witness, and advised him in the future to ask permission to approach the witness. DiCuccio was cowed by the judge's warning and ended his barrage of questions. I could tell by their body language and facial expressions that the jury did not like his aggressive behavior toward me. After my testimony, they were looking at me more empathetically. The jury sentiment began to swing away from the plaintiff. They did not like DiCuccio, and they did not like the plaintiffs. I learned that people (in general) want to see their own doctors in a good light, and will usually give them the benefit of the doubt.

We finally got to call on our expert witnesses. Second in our lineup following me was a family doctor from Columbus. Let's call him Dr. Whelby. I had heard his name in Columbus for years but had never met him. Ken asked him the usual credentialing and experience questions. Dr. Whelby also offered that he was president of the Columbus Academy of Medicine. He was a general practitioner and practiced in Columbus for thirty-five years. He was asked if he had reviewed the patient's chart. Yes, he had. Was there anything in there that fell beneath the standard of care for a general practitioner in Columbus, Ohio? No. He said the care was fine, and there were no exceptions. He would have done the same thing himself. Dr. Whelby pointed out that the standard of care for a GP was not as high as a specialist's because of the specialist's extra training. It was important that a respected Columbus family doctor tell a Columbus jury that we met the standard of care in our own community.

Our power hitter, batting third, was a doctor from Baltimore, Maryland. Let's call him Dr. Kildaire. Neither Kildaire nor Whelby were professional witnesses. I didn't know Dr. Kildaire, but I was anxious to hear him speak about the case. Dr. Kildaire was chief of the Gastroenterology Department of Johns Hopkins Medical School and Hospitals in Baltimore, a world famous and time-honored institution. He was in his late forties and well-spoken, making an immediate favorable first impression. Blumenthal asked him if he was familiar with the type of tumor the patient had. He said yes, but it was very rare, both the location and the cell type. There were only about ten cases known according to the world's medical literature. All bowel cancers in the state of Maryland were sent to him for his review, and he kept the tumor registry for the state for all cancers. In twenty years he had only seen four tumors of this type. He was not bragging but attempting to educate the court. Ken asked him if he was familiar with *Bockus Gastroenterology*—the venerable four-volume gold standard text for gastroenterologists in the world. He was not only familiar with it, he was also one of its editors and had written the section on lower bowel malignancies.

Amazingly, Ken Blumenthal had managed to find the world's leading expert on this type of tumor. Blumenthal then asked him if he had heard the plaintiff's expert, Dr. Jerry, tell the court that the doubling time of this tumor was thirty days. Did he agree with that?

He did not agree with that because he said no one knew what the doubling time was. No one had ever studied the doubling time of this tumor. There was no data in the medical literature because there weren't enough cases to study. So here is the world's expert, Dr. Kildaire, telling the jury that Dr. Jerry flat-out made up his answer. Their expert witness's testimony was shattered, and their case for damages blew up. Blumenthal was not finished with Dr. Jerry and called him back to the stand. Ken asked him whether he was familiar with *Bockus Gastroenterology*.

"Yes, of course."

"Are you familiar with the section on GI malignancies?"

"Yes."

"Was there anything in *Bockus* with which you would disagree?"

Of course he said, "No."

Blumenthal asked him if he attended the Symposium on Gastrointestinal Diseases at The Ohio State University two months ago?

"Yes."

"Did you hear Dr. Kildaire's lecture on lower GI malignancies at that symposium?"

"Yes."

"Was there anything that Dr. Kildaire said in his lecture with which you would disagree?"

"No, there was nothing."

Finally, Blumenthal asked Dr. Jerry if he wanted to revise his answer about the doubling time of the tumor after hearing Dr. Kildaire's testimony that nobody in the world knew the answer. He stupidly held on to his lie. When DiCuccio passed my table he lowered his demand to $250,000. I guess things weren't going as well as he had planned.

Blumenthal recalled the surgeon, Dr. Deborah Mesig, who had started all of this trouble by telling the patient that we had committed malpractice. Hadn't she read our referral note that he had been examined by another specialist? Didn't we get any credit for making a second referral to her? During her testimony, he asked her if she had read any of our notes. She said she had not. Did she ever communicate to us her thoughts about the case? No, she hadn't. Then how could she make such a damning statement to the patient without trying to find out all the facts? Knowing what she knows now, did she think there was malpractice?

To her credit she said, "No."

Would she like to apologize?

"Yes."

Either as a testament to her character or to relieve her embarrassment, she did apologize. I believe this went a long way in front of the jury.

We learned that the plaintiff was a real parasite on society. We were tipped off that while on welfare and receiving disability payments, he was working a construction job and was being paid under the table. He was committing Medicaid fraud and workers' compensation fraud, both felonies and jailable offenses. We had copies of his construction job work hours. To compound his crime, Mr. Eel never paid income taxes on his earnings, a federal crime. We decided to expose his multiple frauds to the jury as evidence of his bad character. We brought him back to the stand and had him identify his work sheets during the time he had told the jury he could not work. We introduced his welfare payment records from the state. The jury was composed of all hard-working, nine-to-five, law-abiding, tax-paying citizens. Their contempt for him was obvious. Eel was just looking for another easy payday.

We were supposed to wrap up all the testimony the next day. Ken told me that DiCuccio—at the last hour—wanted to bring in a witness who was not on the original witness list. This was highly irregular but the judge allowed it. Who was this mystery witness? We had no idea. It was late Friday and the judge adjourned until Monday. I wondered all weekend whom it might be and what damage he or she could do.

Monday we found out. DiCuccio had located the doctor who originally found the mass. He was practicing in Kentucky, and they were bringing him in as a plaintiff's witness. What could he say to help them and hurt us? He was a young doctor who had not completed his residency when he came to work for me. I gave him a job when he needed one. He was smart and pleasant, but he did not get along well with one of my other doctors. They often clashed, and that was his reason for leaving. He and I, on the other hand, had a good relationship. Let's call him Dr. Young. He was called to the stand and sworn in. We made eye contact but he broke his gaze. I knew something bad was coming. DiCuccio asked him to read his notes from the initial exam. He did, and then DiCuccio used another old courtroom trick. He asked him about the "cancer." He was using the term "cancer" now instead of the original term, "mass," which was clearly written on the chart. He had Dr. Young confused, and he fell in lockstep with DiCuccio, and also began using the word "cancer" instead of "mass." We knew where this line of questioning was leading. This was damaging to our case because if we knew it was a cancer from the first visit, we should have done something corrective right away. Blumenthal and I looked at each other. Blumenthal had to turn this around and quickly. On cross-examination he asked Dr. Young to read his note verbatim describing the mass. Again, it clearly read "mass" and not "cancer." He asked him how he found the mass. Dr. Young said by digital exam.

"So, you felt it with your finger?"

"Yes."

"Did you use a proctoscope?"

"No."

"Did you use a sigmoidoscope?"

"No.

"Did you use a colonoscope?"

"No."

"Then you never actually saw it, did you?"

"No."

"Then it could have been anything, a hemorrhoid, cyst, abscess, or a benign tumor?"

Young said, "No. it wasn't any of those. It was a cancer."

Ken was on him now. "If you never used any kind of a scope, how would you know what is was, Dr. Young? Do you have an eyeball at the end of your finger?" The jury had to stifle their laughter. Ken Blumenthal had delivered the most hilarious closing line ever heard in a Columbus courtroom.

We recessed for lunch. There was nothing to do now but wait for the verdict. It only took about an hour, and we were all called back into the courtroom. DiCuccio didn't even bother to show up. Knowing he'd lost the case, he sent one of his lackeys instead. The jury had decided and was ready to deliver a verdict.

The foreman stated: "Not guilty of malpractice, no negligence, no damages, and no money award."

We were completely exonerated. Ken Blumenthal, a perfect stranger to me before the trial, became a friend after the trial. He did a magnificent defense job. When I walked out of the courtroom into the waiting area, the jury followed, and as a group, they apologized to me for my being dragged into this mess. They were very happy with their decision. They told me that very early in the trial they had developed a distrust of DiCuccio and a dislike for his clients.

There is a sequel to this story. I had been audited by the IRS every year from 1979 to 1990. I was really getting fed up with this harassment. The government never found anything out of line, just minor adjustments. Sometimes I paid them a few bucks, and sometimes I got a small credit. Partially in anger and partially in frustration, I said to my examining agent, "Why don't you go after someone who is not paying their taxes?"

She asked me if I knew of such a person. I wrote the name of the plaintiff on a piece of paper and slipped it to her.

CHAPTER EIGHT
Venezuela: I Rediscover the Brown-banded Puffbird, A Bird Absent for Fifty Years

In my Father's house are many mansions.
—John 14:2

The excitement of seeing new birds in the tropics of Costa Rica lingered through the following year and whetted our appetite to go farther afield. How about New Year's Eve in South America for 1990? I studied the various catalogues from the Big 3, VENT, WINGS, and Field Guides. VENT was running a tour to a remote part of Venezuela called Junglaven, loosely translated "jungle camp." It was located near the Colombian border on the tiny Camani River, a tributary of the larger Ventuari River, which flowed into the immense Orinoco River. This was a region of white sandy soil bridging the vast Amazon tropical rainforest to the smaller Guianan rainforest, and promised a unique set of birds. To further the allure, we would be only the second bird group to explore this region. To top it off, it was being led by a modern pioneer of neotropical birding, Steven L. Hilty, a Kansan, whose *A Guide to the Birds of Colombia* was a *tour de force* and indispensable for anyone interested in birding the northern reaches of South America.

My daughter, Dana, joined Susan and me on this adventure. I was hoping to add a view of the world outside of her academic studies. I have always believed that it is important to build knowledge, character, and judgment through first-hand experiences. We flew into Caracas, the Venezuelan capital, for a one night's stay at the five-star Tamanaco Hotel. The next morning we flew southeast to Puerto Ayacucho where we deplaned. We all filled out some forms in triplicate for some unknown reason to lay on some unknown bureaucrat's desk unread for some unknown length of time. Small, single-engine planes would take us the rest of the way. When our pilots arrived, we were asked to split up families for the flight. I realized the wisdom of this in case there were any mishaps, but I still felt a little anxiety creeping into my autonomic nervous system. I decided to split the Master gene pool. Susan and I went in one plane and Dana in the other.

I sat in the front with the pilot. I noticed he crossed himself before he started the engine. The plane sputtered a little and then took off down the runway. It lifted off with ease, and we were on our way flying over some of the most pristine, uninterrupted rain forest in the new world. I could see a spectacular range of mountains with enormous cliffs and sandstone outcroppings jutting from the forest's midst. There were flat-topped tepuis, forested islands of endemicity, in the distance. After an hour, we descended over a flat sandy belt of forest. The pilot landed on a hidden natural sandy savanna that served as the airstrip for Junglaven. We rumbled and bumped our way to a stop. *¡Gracias a Dios!*

Figure 8-1. Left to right, Steve Hilty, unknown birder, me,
daughter Dana Master, Second leader Kevin Zimmer, Elliott Tramer,
Landing strip, Junglaven.

We all disembarked, got our bearings, and immediately
started birding. The first bird was a Swallow-winged Puffbird,
one of many we would see that week. We hiked about a mile
down a newly hacked path, birding all the way. Junglaven was
a new fishing camp, roughly hewn from the forest with
several grass-thatched huts for the guests and a common
dining area. Don Vicente was the manager, a friendly and
accommodating Venezuelan. He was assisted by several
Yanomamo Indian men and a young woman cook. The
Yanomamos have a reputation for aggressive behavior but
none was displayed to us. There were about thirty-two
thousand Yanomamos remaining in their ancestral home in
Southern Venezuela and Northern Brazil. Their survival was
being threatened by incursions of mining companies. The
year we were there, the Brazilian government formally
established a Yanomamo territory of thirty-six thousand
square miles, but their borders were only weakly enforced.

We were assigned our sleeping quarters, Susan and I in
one hut and Dana in her own quarters. After the first night,

Dana joined us because she did not want to be alone at night. Howler monkeys and creepy crawly things, for a city girl weren't all that natural. We understood. We had an extra single bed, so no problem. There was a tree frog living in our commode and tarantulas in the thatch, but we got used to them. Susan is a professional model, and I wondered how she would fare the week without all of her beauty aids.

Figure 8-2. Camp at Junglaven.

On my first full day in South America, I walked the short distance to the Camani River to try out my new spotting telescope. I set up the tripod and scope on the east bank and directed it across the river to the forest on the west bank. There were lots of Swallow-winged Puffbirds flying from the forest edge to catch insects above the water. I noticed a bird of a different shape and color flying directly from the west bank over the water. I was on it with my binoculars immediately and made mental notes of its field marks. As it came closer, I saw it well in the early morning light. I watched it fly directly over me, past our camp and disappear into the forest. This should be easy to identify in Hilty's field guide: larger than a Swallow-wing, heavily built with broad head, dark band across the breast, barring on the belly, and white band across the tail. I had Hilty's book with me, hanging in a case from my belt. I thought it might be a puffbird because of its shape and size. The Brits call this identification by JIZZ or recognition by general impression, size, and shape. I couldn't find anything that looked like it on the puffbird colored plates or on any other plate. Well, I know what I saw. I began reading the text on the puffbirds. Maybe I could match what I remembered about the bird to a description in the text. Yes, there it was in the puffbird section, description to a tee, "Brown-banded Puffbird, rare." I was very excited about this find and hurried back to camp to find Steve Hilty. After all, the VENT brochure promised species that had not previously found their way onto any bird list. I confidently told Steve I had just seen a Brown-banded Puffbird. Steve looked at me quizzically. He began shaking his head no. I guess he was wondering, "Who is this guy?" Steve had never birded with me or even knew me. I brought no big birder's credentials with me. It was my first time in Venezuela, let alone South America. He asked me to describe it. I recited what I observed. He said there were no Brown-banded Puffbirds here. That species hasn't been seen in fifty years. The only reason they knew it was here, back in the day, is a preserved skin in the Caracas museum bird collection. I was grossly deflated by his answer, but I knew what I saw. I decided not to push it any further and deferred to Steve's expertise for the time being. To pour salt into my wound, he said it was probably a Swallow-wing. A Swallow-wing! That was like saying you just saw a House Sparrow. Elliott Tramer, a good birder from Toledo, had been nearby when the bird flew over, but he didn't get a good look at it, so no help there.

Over the next couple of days we explored all of the various habitats that Junglaven had to offer: forty percent *terra firme* forest, forty percent pure white sandy soil, ten percent *Várzea* forest, and ten percent river and river edge. *Terra firme* forest is the typical forest of the Amazon rainforest. It is very tall, usually more than 120 feet with a very dense upper canopy. Its rich soils produce a wide variety of tree species and tower over a dark open understory. Notable birds seen here were Rusty-breasted Nunlet, Tawny-tufted Toucanet, and an out-of-place Long-billed Woodcreeper spotted by our leader. The forest edges contained fruiting trees with a constant parade of cotingas, tanagers and honeycreepers. Mixed flocks of scavenging arboreal species were not as common as I had hoped. There were small- to medium-sized bands containing five to ten species of foraging birds moving through at a steady clip. Pick out any bird and watch it, then pick out another bird and another until they have moved on. The flocks contained antwrens, antshrikes, woodpeckers, woodcreepers, flycatchers, and tanagers, totaling seven or eight species. It was very exciting but short-lived. Sometimes you can follow them for a while by running ahead of them until they disappear into the forest. One is lucky to identify fifty percent of the species in a large mixed flock. Steve Hilty told us a story that when he first came to Colombia, his first large feeding flock held about thirty individuals moving so fast through the branches that he could not identify a single one of them.

Scrubby sandy soil areas were particularly poor in nutrients and their bird numbers were equally poor. We managed to see a Bronzy Jacamar, a flying insect specialist related to kingfishers, a Golden-spangled Piculet at the forest edge, a tiny three-and-one-half-inch woodpecker, several White-bellied Antbirds, a Black-crested Antshrike, and a Black Manakin. This manakin is a strange bird, very flycatcher-like with a long tail. It does not perform from a lek (a branch upon which male manakins call and dance to attract females for breeding) like most other manakins.

The *Várzea* is a seasonally flooded forest. This floodplain forest is rich with nutrients. The trees are heavily buttressed in its clay soil for anchorage. They often have seeds with special flotation devices that enable them to be dispersed when the river floods. An example is the rubber tree. They are an important source of food for many fish, and the fish in turn are an important means of seed dispersal. A pair of rare and very local Scarlet-shouldered Parrotlets was seen in the *Várzea* canopy. A pair of Blackish-gray Antshrikes and a pair of Black-chinned Antbirds were seen lower down at eye level.

In the early mornings and late afternoons we were skillfully and silently transported on the Ventuari tributaries by our Yanomamo boatmen. It was right out of a scene from W.H. Hudson's *Green Mansions* with impenetrable forests on either side, small creeks leading to unknown riches, and a cacophony of sound from overflying macaws and parrots against a clear blue sky. I expected Rima the bird girl to appear at any moment. These were black waters caused by the leaching of pigments and tannin from the fallen forest leaves. Visibility below water was zero. Amazingly, there were no pesky biting insects. Our boatmen quietly poled us through a tangle of lianas and low-lying branches until we were ten feet away from a family of three Agami Herons, one of the most sought after large waders in the New World. This is a member of an ancient family, the herons, egrets, and bitterns. Agamis are never seen in the open. They have the distinction of having the longest bills of any New World heron. They are a masterpiece of construction as they crouch silently with head extended, to spring on any hapless fish or small vertebrate that comes into their reach. We sat there transfixed for forty-five minutes watching them instantaneously catch and eat fish and frogs with lightning strikes of their fantastic bills. The heat of the day was soon upon us, and we were ferried back to our camp with a life bird and a lifetime memory.

Every day from the bank of our camp we saw numerous spectacled caimans, a crocodilian, and once a rare mammal, the Pink River Dolphin. I never knew there were fresh water dolphins. These were *Inea geoffrensis humboldtiana*, the Orinoco basin subspecies, one of three South American subspecies of river dolphins. Their necks and spinal cords are flexibly modified to maneuver around submerged branches, and their snouts are elongated to extract fish from hiding places. Unlike their marine cousins, they can move their heads ninety degrees in any direction because they have unfused neck vertebrae. They are the largest fresh water cetacean with lengths up to six feet. They play prominently in Amazonian folklore because they are an acceptable explanation of pregnancies in girls in small isolated river communities. The story is that at night the river dolphin turns into a handsome young man, joins with the village maiden, and returns in the morning to the water transformed back to a river dolphin. This dolphin "shape shifter" is called an *encantado*. The most amazing thing about these aquatic mammals is that they are equipped with USWS, unihemispheric slow-wave sleep. Like some birds, they can sleep as they travel long distances, dividing their brain function in half—half awake, half asleep. This adaptation allows them to evade predators and control their metabolism while traveling long distances.

Despite the black water, the crocodilians, piranhas, and other hidden predators, one person in our bird group, Gail, leaped into the water for a swim. Where there is beauty, there is a beast. She got about half way over to the other bank when we all spotted a large caiman slithering off the shore. It was summer in Venezuela—the nesting period for these crocs. The caimans are especially dangerous during this time. Gail did not see the beast swimming toward her. Was it a female defending her nest? Was it an aggressive male defending his territory? Was it a hungry teen croc looking for a snack? Or was it just a curious reptile getting a closer look at this foreign body? We were yelling and screaming to her to swim back. She turned around, but she would never outswim the caiman. Our Yanomamo launched his powerboat and within seconds was at her side, lifting her out of danger. Gail was a psychiatrist, highly educated, cerebral, intelligent and a little nutty. I wondered where her common sense was. One of the most dangerous things you could do in the Amazon was to go into black water and swim.

Two of the other participants were Richard and Patricia, parasitologists from the University of Toledo. As opposed to our psychiatrist friend, they had an over-abundance of caution and common sense. They were constantly warning the group of the parasitic dangers of eating this and drinking that. They were dropping iodine tablets into everything, cereal milk, juice, bottled water, and sodas. The one danger that did get everybody's attention was their warning about the candiru, *Vandellia cirrhosa*, the blood-sucking catfish. It is one of the smallest vertebrates in the Amazon waters and is attracted by a stream of agitated water. It rarely attacks humans, but when it does, it swims up the urethra, the opening to the bladder, and causes excruciating pain with its backward pointing barbs. At one time it was thought to follow a urine stream, but that was recently discredited by scientists.

On the fourth day of our trip, Elliott Tramer and I decided to bird a narrow trail hacked out by our Indian friends. We came upon a fruiting tree and spotted a Gray-cheeked Thrush, a North American winter visitor 2,500 miles from its home in New England and Canada. We were very pleased with ourselves finding this rare migrant. A little farther down the trail we came upon a termitarium, a huge condominium complex for termites in a tree. It was marvelous in its own right, but hold on! What was that pecking away at its exterior? *Oh my God*—I was looking at an unmistakable Brown-banded Puffbird no more than twenty feet in front of me and twelve feet off the ground; the species was not supposed to be here, and the bird hasn't been seen in fifty years. Next to it was another identical to the first. I was looking at a pair of mythical birds in one binocular view. I asked Elliott to stay with the bird, and I ran the half mile back to camp to get Steve. Breathlessly I told him I found the bird.

"What bird?"

"The Brown-banded Puffbird."

"Are you sure? The Brown-banded Puffbird?"

"Yes, not only one but a pair."

He quickly grabbed his recording gear. Like any good birder he already had his binoculars around his neck, and we tore up the trail. I was praying they would still be there when arrived. I couldn't afford another phantom sighting. We saw Elliott with his bins up watching something. As we got closer, we slowed to a walk and then to small stealthy movements so as not to scare off the prize. When Steve saw the two, he recognized them right away. The man who wrote the book had never seen these before, a lifer for Steve. This laconic laid-back man was obviously thrilled to see these birds. His expression showed it. We watched silently together for a good while.

Steve said, "Ted Parker has never seen this bird," a testimony to its rarity.

Ted Parker was one of the most accomplished neotropical birders in the world with a legendary catalog of bird calls in his memory bank. Steve took some photos for the record and turned on his recording gear. The puffbirds were making quiet murmuring vocalizations as they excavated this termite mound. They were probably preparing a nest site. After a while the birds tired and flew away into the forest. That was not the last we saw of them; we found them working away at the mound every day for a few more days.

There were no "congratulations," "atta boys," or "way to go's" from Steve. There were no high fives or handshakes for my amazing find. I didn't care. I was exonerated from "misreporting" on this mega-rarity to the world's expert. Steve used a short-wave radio to get the word out that, after half a century, the puffbird was re-discovered. I felt really good about it because others could enjoy my discovery. And they did. Over the next couple of days, single-engine planes were landing on the sandy airstrip carrying world birders to see my puffbird.

At the end of our two-week stay, we trudged our way back to the sandy airstrip to await the single engine planes that would carry us back to civilization. With little effort— sunblock and moisturizer cream—both women were aglow from the sundrenched humid jungle air and the excitement of a trip of their lifetime. I, in contrast, from dawn to dusk non-stop birding and more than a few nights of bird and animal searches looked like something the cat dragged in.

About a month later, after returning home, VENT sent us its newsletter. The article headline read, "Steve Hilty re-discovers Brown-banded Puffbird!" Again, I didn't care. In my heart and mind, I knew the real story. There was a life lesson to be learned here. Trust your instincts and do not be persuaded by others.

Five years later when Susan and I were birding in the Big Pine area of the Sierra Nevada Mountains in California, we came across a Los Angeles Audubon group. The leader had on a T-shirt that read, "I saw the Brown-banded Puffbird" and a picture of "my" bird. I stopped him to tell him the whole story. He was so pleased to meet me that he literally gave me the shirt off his back.

WORLD 1,197 • ABA 685

CHAPTER NINE
Cuba: Birding in a Communist Country

I am Fidel Castro and we have come to liberate Cuba.
—Fidel Castro

The smallest bird in the world was calling me. It was merely ninety miles offshore from the United States, and I had never seen it. It should be easy to get to, or was it? The Bee Hummingbird belongs in the Ripley's Believe it or Not Museum. At two inches long and weighing a fraction of an ounce, it can fly backward, straight up, straight down, all at thirty miles per hour and stop on a dime. It is found only in Cuba. I began making arrangements for Susan and me to go to Cuba when I ran into a lot of unexpected snags. There were no American tour groups going there because of an embargo placed on the country by our government under President Kennedy in 1960. The only way for a birder to get there was with a special permit, which allowed academic studies. There was another way that fell into the gray area of the Treasury Department rules against spending money in Cuba. I found a Canadian bird tour group that would take us to Cuba from Toronto. They would pay for everything, and we would pay them. Canada kept good relations with post-Batista, Castro Cuba. I still wasn't sure this was a safe way to go. I asked the tour company for a few references from Americans who had traveled there with them. One of their references was Phoebe Snetsinger. I knew her name. She was the most famous woman birder in the world. She had seen close to eight thousand, species of birds world-wide, more than any other human being in history. No one was even close. Besides having a prodigious world list, she was an excellent birder. She was a living legend in world birding circles. I dug out her phone number from an old ABA membership list and cold-called her. I wasn't even sure if I would reach her because she was out birding most of the year. Success—she answered the phone after a few rings.

I heard a very soft feminine voice with a mid-Western accent say "Hello."

I introduced myself and relayed the purpose of my call. She could not have been more helpful. She told me most birders go to Cuba through Canada. When they get to Cuba, they ask the Cuban immigration officer not to stamp their passports. This way they avoid uninvited questions from U.S. immigration officers on their way home. Was this breaking the rules? Not per se, as long as you verbally answer any of their questions truthfully. She told me not to spend any money there because that could be a problem. The birding was great with twenty-five endemics and the country was beautiful. If we had any trouble, we should go to the Canadian Embassy, where there was a liaison officer to the American State Department. I thanked her and wished her luck in her goal of seeing all ten thousand species in the world. She laughed at this impossibility and said good luck to me. I never got a chance to thank her in person; she died tragically in 1999 while birding in Madagascar.

I wanted to check a little more on the entry requirements and penalties for breaking the rules. I called my friend Ohio Senator Howard Metzenbaum's office. I spoke to his aide who basically told me the same thing that Phoebe had said. She also told me no one had ever been prosecuted for going in and out of Cuba without the proper paperwork. *Okay, we're going.* I made our flight plans through Detroit to meet the bird tour group in Toronto, and they would have our tickets to Havana. *Mellisuga helenae—here we come.*

Our flight from Columbus to Detroit was delayed two hours because of weather. Susan and I debated whether we should go at all because we probably would miss our connecting flight to Toronto and the tour's Havana flight. We really didn't want to fly to Cuba alone. I had a feeling of apprehension about all of this. I was a little paranoid about going into Cuba anyway. There was a slim chance we would make our connections, so we boarded the late flight to Detroit and hoped for the best. The worst case was we played tourist in Toronto for a few days and then come home. Sure enough, we missed our tour group in Toronto. Now what? Maybe we could ask James. We had James with us, James Bond, but he couldn't help us. Not the famous Sean Connery master spy, 007, but rather the shy, retiring ornithologist, James Bond. I had Bond's 1971 edition of the definitive *Birds of the West Indies* with me. Ian Fleming, the author of the James Bond series, a keen birdwatcher himself, was friends with the real James Bond, the world's expert on the birds of the Caribbean. Fleming's friend was a rather dull and unassuming man. As an inside joke, he gave his friend's name to his swashbuckling 007 hero. Fleming's original story line was that amazing things would happen to this very average man, a kind of Walter Mitty.

We decided to go to a nice hotel in Toronto, have a good dinner, and figure out our best plan. After debating the pros and cons of going in, going home, or something different altogether, we screwed up our courage and called the airline for two tickets to Havana. We landed in Havana in three and a half hours. In a minute we would be passing through the immigration booths. I was pretty nervous. I forgot how to say, "Please don't stamp our passports" in Spanish. The lines were long, and I started to perspire, I guess from the heat, at least that that was what I was telling myself. We were now standing in front of the Cuban immigration officer, and I handed him our blue U.S. passports.

The best I could do was, "Please don't pass my stampport."

The guy laughed and said in a perfect Bronx accent, "No problem, man."

We got our luggage, which was a good omen, and headed off to find our tour group, which had already been there a day. We were Americans who had just slipped into Cuba and did not have the foggiest idea where we were going. The feeling of dread was coming back. I went to the taxi line and walked up to the dispatcher.

I showed him the printed name of the Canadian tour group and said in my best third grade Spanish, "*¿Donde estan, por favor?*"

I thought the "*por favor*" would get me there. He seemed to know right away and told a taxi driver something in lightning fast Cuban Spanish. The driver put our bags in his trunk and motioned us into the back seat. He set out down the airport road. We seemed to be heading into the heart of Havana. All of my senses were on high alert. The street from the airport was lined with brightly painted 1930s period homes, all in good repair, showing off a prosperity that we learned later was all glitter and no gold—basically a movie set. He spoke a little English and I a little Spanish. Between the both of us he made himself understood. He was giving us a tour of the old city. Here is the Plaza de Armas where Castro delivers his five-hour public rants and there is something else, and blah, blah, blah. I wasn't paying any attention because I was wondering where he was taking us. He drove us into the heart of the city—run down, tawdry, blackened by soot—and stopped at what was clearly a police station. He motioned us out and drove off beyond some iron gates. We were standing there like two gringo wetbacks with unstamped passports, no luggage, and no idea where we were. I felt like a putz. What have I gotten Susan into? About fifteen minutes later he returned and motioned us back into the taxi. He told us he had gotten gas for the long ride ahead of us. We found ourselves hurtling down Highway 1 at seventy miles an hour. Where was he taking us now? Cuba is the largest island in the Caribbean. Highway 1 extends the entire length of the island, about 760 miles. The countryside was changing to a sandier scrubby rural habitat. Abandoned farm equipment was rusting in the fields. Old Eastern European cars that had no life left in them littered the countryside. This was the legacy of being an agent state of a failed USSR. After the wall came down, the USSR jettisoned its North American friends, Cuba and Jamaica. With no available parts or technicians, anything that was Russian and broken stayed Russian and broken. I began seeing signs in Spanish announcing something like, "Here is where we kicked the American imperialist asses." Billboards with Che Guevara's and Raul Castro's images were everywhere. They were hailed as heroes of the revolution! Curiously there were none of Fidel. We were in Bahia de Cochinos, the Bay of Pigs area. My mind immediately spun back to the failed April 17, 1961, invasion by a couple thousand Cuban ex-pats. We were nearing the thirtieth anniversary of the Cuban victory over the American agents. Some historians link this failure to dislodge Castro directly to the Vietnam War. These critics say that Kennedy was looking for a "patsy" communist state to fight to show the public that he was tough on communism after the Bay of Pigs debacle. He had an election coming up. Southeast Asia and Ho Chi Minh looked easy. North Vietnam and Uncle Ho turned out to be anything but easy.

The driver entered La Playa Larga beach resort and took us to the front door of a modest beachfront hotel. Doug McCrae our tour leader saw us pull in and rushed out to greet us. Amazingly, our driver had taken us eighty miles to the exact location of our tour group!

We said, *"Muchas Gracias,"* to our driver, and Doug paid him.

Within minutes we were looking at the Cuban subspecies of a Stygian Owl and downing a cold Hatuey beer.

Our room was simple but comfortable. There was only one TV channel, the Cuban State channel. Dinner was plain and nutritious. Doug caught us up on that day's activities. We were happy to know we didn't miss anything we would not see later. The next day we were to visit the bird-famous Zapata Swamp, the last site of the now presumed extinct Bachman's Warbler. Bachman's Warbler was discovered by the Rev. John Bachman (pronounced "Backman"), a Lutheran minister, naturalist, and friend of John James Audubon. Audubon would stay in Bachman's house in Charleston, South Carolina, when he visited the region. Bachman showed him a skin of the warbler he'd collected in 1832, and although Audubon had never seen the bird in the wild, he named it after his friend in 1833. Maria Martin, Bachman's sister-in-law, drew the bird, and Audubon used her drawing as a model for his own painting that he incorporated into his famous double elephant folio, *The Birds of North America*. The Zapata Swamp held exciting possibilities, for not only the warbler, but also the Zapata Sparrow, Wren, and Rail. Bachman's Warbler was a regular in the I'on Swamp in Charleston, South Carolina, until the 1950s when it crashed and burned due to habitat destruction and Cuban hurricanes.

Figure 9-1. Zapata Swamp.

The last collected bird was a male, March 21, 1941, on Deer Island Mississippi. There were many other reported sightings including an immature female photographed in Brevard County, Florida, March 30, 1977. This created a lot of excitement, but later inspection of the photo proved inconclusive. The last report of this enigmatic species in Cuba, its only wintering ground, was a report by a non-birder, a Zapata Swamp park ranger in the fall of 1988. That was only a year and a half before we got there, so there was a small ray of hope.

Figure 9-2. Bachman's Warbler specimen, Tall Timbers Museum, Florida.

The narrow trail into the Zapata Swamp quickly petered out. We found ourselves wallowing in a thick, viscous slurry of sucking mud. At one point I found myself mid-thigh in this quicksand and could not extricate myself. I couldn't go forward or backward. William Bendix's line of desperation flashed into my mind, *"What a revolting predicament this is."* The only direction for me was up. I reached up and grabbed a large overhanging branch, and lifting my two hundred pounds in a half chin-up, slipped out of my rubber

Wellington boots. I then hand-over-hand transported myself backward a few feet until I could stand on firmer ground. Susan held me around the waist as I reached forward and retrieved my Wellies from the mud. Up until this time, for all of our efforts, we had not seen or even heard one bird. I kept listening for the monotonous buzzy call of the Bachman's Warbler and the Limpkin-like call of the Zapata Rail, another mega-rarity. No luck. But hold on. We could hear in the distance, from the scrubby area at the front edge of the swamp from where we had just come, the unmistakable antiphonal dueting song of the Zapata Sparrow. These gigundous-sized sparrows form dueting pairs, male and female, like Kenny Rogers and Dolly Parton, with Kenny taking the lead and Dolly a nanosecond behind. She seemed to be saying, "Don't worry, dear. I'm right here, dear," over and over again. A couple of minutes later we saw the Zapata Wren, the only endemic wren in the Greater Antilles and the rarest wren in the world. As we scoured the surrounding areas, thirteen endemics followed the rest of the day with an amazing array of parrots, shorebirds, raptors, flycatchers, and hummingbirds.

Figure 9-3. Cuban tour leader, Dr. Arturo Kirkconnel, far right.

We spent the next morning at Los Sabalos Wildlife Refuge. There, along a ditch in an open area skirting a woodland, sitting on the tip-top of a bare branch was my most sought-after bird, the Bee Hummingbird. I almost walked by without seeing him, but he was making such a commotion I couldn't miss him. This two-inch fighter jet was fearlessly dueling with other males and chasing away any other winged creature, large or small, that had the audacity to invade his territory. He was Lord and Master over all he surveyed and that was the way it was going to stay. He was quite handsome with his fiery red iridescent throat with elongated plumes set off against his white chest and blue back. His short bill belied the stabbing power behind it. No doubt he was a force to be reckoned with. We left the little prince after a wonderful hour of observing him.

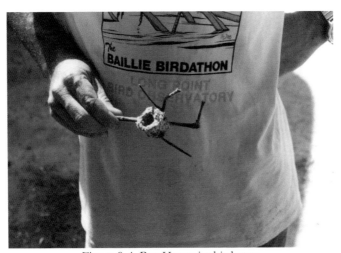

Figure 9-4. Bee Hummingbird nest.

The rest of the tour birds were just a footnote for me. We visited other habitats, Las Salinas, Santo Tomas, Guama, and Playa Guira National Park. We did manage to see twenty-two of the twenty-five endemics. Inexplicably, we missed the gnatcatcher. The Oriente Warbler and perhaps an Ivory-billed Woodpecker were living in Oriente Province, which was off limits to tourists at the time. The Cuban race of the Ivory-billed Woodpecker was presumed extinct by then, but many held out hope that it still survived in some corner of Northeastern Cuba. The last definite sighting was of a female in 1987 in the montane pines. In the early 1990s two expeditions were formed to find the bird in Cuba. Despite an intensive search, no evidence was found to prove it still existed.

Our birding finished, we headed to the old Havana Hilton, now the Habana Libre Hotel, for a wind down and some sightseeing. Passing through the city, I could not help but notice all of the early American classic cars running on the street. So this is where the old classic beauties went to heaven. There were pink and black 1951 Ford Crown Imperials, 1957 Chevy Bel Aires, and even an old Bonnie and Clyde 1932 V8 Ford, their favored getaway car. The old trollies were clanging down the main street overloaded with passengers spilling over from all sides. This was a slice of Miami from the 1950s. The *Habana Libre* was worn and tired and could use a complete makeover. Thirty-two years ago this is where Fidel set up his White House after his successful revolution. Time had taken its toll on this historic landmark. Some of the elevators didn't run and whole floors were not air conditioned. Paint was peeling and carpets were worn and stained. The moist, tropical heat in the non air-conditioned rooms was enervating. Meals were served in a huge banquet hall, cafeteria style, no waiters or waitresses here in a workers' paradise. We walked around the town but there was nothing of interest to buy. There were stores restricted to tourists with some Eastern European consumer goods. Doug had warned us not to buy anything for the locals if they asked. He also warned us not to change money on the black market. These were crimes in Cuba. Don't worry, we were not spending any money or breaking any laws here.

The night's entertainment was the floor show at the world famous Tropicana Nightclub. A bus came to the hotel to pick up our group. It was loaded with visitors from

Scandinavia, Italy, France, Mexico, and Canada gathered from other hotels. One indelible cultural impression was that every time a Mexican passenger would board the bus, he or she would say, "*Buenas noches*," to everyone before he or she took their seat. I thought this was extremely polite. We would never see this back in the States. The floor show at the Tropicana was a very sophisticated display of Cuban talent. There were singers, dancers, and, of course, the incredibly beautiful Vegas-style showgirls dressed in skimpy sequined and feathered costumes. Back in pre-revolution times the girls were nude except for the outlandish headpieces they wore. Fidel had cleaned that up with socialist moral rectitude, and the girls all wore a semblance of clothes now. They still wore the fully lit chandeliers or Carmen Miranda-style bowls of fruit on their heads. All of the lit headpieces were connected by one large very obvious electric cord that ran the length of the stage. I guess they had a hard time getting batteries.

Figure 9-5. Tropicana, Havana.

They danced to the frenetic salsa rhythms of a forty-piece live orchestra. Xavier Cugat could not have sounded better.

The music and dancing were great and they finished to a rousing standing ovation from the international crowd. After the show we headed back to the hotel. It was about ten o'clock, and the cool evening invited us to stroll the streets of Old Havana. It was charming with its ornate Catholic churches, its baroque and neoclassical architecture, and eighteenth- and nineteenth-century Spanish homes with their wrought iron balconies protecting the chastity of the women within and their red-fluted tile roofs. We were caught up in the beauty of the evening and wandered a little too far. We found ourselves walking deep into the barrio. A money changer ran up to us and asked if we wanted to change money. I shook my head no. He turned around and left as quickly as he had come. There were gangs of men hanging out on the street corners. It was now close to midnight. They eyed us; however, we passed them without any aggressive comments. I could hardly believe this. Back home as a teenager in West Philly, I would have had to fight our way out of there. There are a few advantages living in a no-nonsense, hard-on-crime country. I found a city policeman carrying a Kalashnikov and asked him directions to the hotel. He asked if we were Canadians. Receiving a positive response from us, he pointed the way.

The next morning we boarded our flight to Toronto. Our passports showed no exit stamps. We had spent no money. We had no souvenirs, bird T-shirts, Cuban cigars, or rum. We passed through immigration in Detroit with no questions and no problems. We remained dutiful, patriotic, loyal Americans with one change. We had witnessed, in person and live, the Bee Hummingbird.

WORLD 1,230 • ABA 685

CHAPTER TEN

Attu: Birding on the most remote Aleutian Island with
Inspiration for the Movie, The Big Year

Let there be cuckoos, a lark and a dove.
—Ian Grant, "Let There Be Love"

The travel poster shows a stark landscape, barren and bleak with windswept tundra. It is 4,588 miles one way from Columbus. The travel agent tells you the average temperature is thirty-nine degrees, and it rains or snows every day. Winds of thirty knots per hour with gusts up to sixty knots are always in your face. She also tells you that you will be sleeping in a room with three strange men and will be riding a one-speed bicycle every day over the tundra hillocks. Sound inviting? And, by the way, it is $4,750 for a three-week stay, not counting airfare, and it sells out every year. This is Attu, the westernmost island in the Aleutian chain. No one lives there except twenty U.S. Coast Guardsmen and your band of thirty crazed birders.

I never had any interest in birding this godforsaken place despite the allure of forty to fifty life birds. Attu was famous for its many vagrant Asian species blown off course on their way to the Siberian Arctic to breed. The island was a magnet for birders who were amassing gigantic lists of bird species seen in the U.S. Attu is in the Aleutians, and the Aleutians are in Alaska, so every bird seen there would go on their U.S. list.

199

I didn't care about that because I figured I could always see them in their native countries. I changed my mind when I read an article in *Bird Watcher's Digest* by Roger Tory Peterson, the "Father" of American birding. Peterson said it was the adventure itself that made the Attu experience great. He said it was an experience not to be missed by American birders. That article convinced me to spend my fiftieth birthday in complete discomfort.

The Attour brochures arrived, and I found myself poring over lists of exotic birds that had been seen on this tour back to its beginnings in the 1970s, none of which I had ever seen. Attour Inc. was a bird tour company formed exclusively to visit Attu, Gambel, Nome, and a few other Alaskan birding sites. Its founder, Lawrence Balch, was also a founder of the hobby group, the American Birding Association. There was a list of do's and don'ts. For example, do not wear red or bright colors; do not take more than thirty-eight pounds of gear; never take another person's bike without his or her permission; and don't bird alone. Larry had his reasons and some of them made sense. The taboo of not wearing red in the field has always rubbed me wrong. It is true that the color red signifies danger in nature. However, there are scores—if not hundreds—of bird species that are predominantly red and not dangerous. The Northern Cardinal is one. I suppose if an entire tour wore red, it would be a problem. But I don't believe that one or two participants wearing red would reduce the number of birds to view. A red bird in a rain forest can melt into the background as easily as any other. I think a lot of leaders perpetuate this myth to control their groups. There has never been a double-blind, peer-reviewed scientific experiment to prove that humans wearing red in the field scares away birds. There was an Attu Baggage Weight Schedule, listing forty-eight separate essential items and their weights totaling thirty-eight pounds and three ounces. I was getting the picture that they were really serious about this weight business. I packed the minimum amount of carefully selected clothes and gear, weighing the duffel bag after each entry until I was exactly at the limit.

There was no way I was going over thirty-eight pounds. Doing so would mean certain doom. This included my tripod, scope, bird books, and heavy boots.

A map of Attu with names like Murder Point, Infarction Creek, and West Massacre Valley got my attention. I learned that Attu was the site of a successful Japanese invasion in 1942. In 1943, American forces defeated the two-thousand-man Japanese force in a climactic *banzai* attack. This was the only land battle fought on incorporated United States soil in WWII.

All the chores were done by the participants, and a list of seventeen chores accompanied the brochure. We were to select one or we would be assigned one. Number ten: fix bicycles. No, didn't know a thing about fixing bicycles. Number sixteen: outhouse cleaner and inspector. No, not for me. Most of the chores were performed every two days, like mixing frozen juice and restocking soups, condiments, and sugar. I wanted something less frequent. There were four chores performed every five days. One of these was pot washer. Yes, I could do that, no problem. I used to do that for my mother in our New Jersey shore house. I confidently checked off "pot washer."

Getting to Attu is highly problematic. It is amazing that it happens at all. The weather is always terrible, often preventing planes from taking off or landing in the pea soup visibility. Attour has to follow a myriad number of laws, rules, regulations, and have permits and waivers for landing, occupation of government lands and God knows what else. These agencies include U.S. Fish and Wildlife, State of Alaska, Aleut treaties, U.S. Coast Guard, Reeve Aleut Airlines, University of Alaska Museum, *et al. ad infinitum.* Our commercial plane, filled with birders, hunters, and Inuit natives, left Anchorage for Kotsebue in the Arctic Circle, a 547-mile journey. Once there we were told no binoculars because we were in a military area. The Reeve Airline plane was late, and we all waited in an unheated shed for hours. It was twenty degrees, gray skies, and snowing. Larry told us that we would have to go to Attu in two shifts since the planes were overloaded. We drew straws, and I found myself in the first plane. Some of the birders who were in the second plane were bartering valuable items to get into the first flight. The flight from Kotsebue to Attu was 1,271 kilometers. We all slept, told birding stories, and played cards. I was relieved to find out that Reeve Airline was very safe, with only one accident in 1959.

We arrived at Attu without incident, making a smooth landing on the military built airstrip. Our gear was stowed onto an ATV-pulled trailer. *Wait, what is all this?* Some of the "veterans," those birders coming back to Attu year after year, had tons of baggage. What happened to the thirty-eight-pound rule? One leader even brought his motorcycle! I flashed back to my meticulously removing the extra pair of socks from my duffel so as to not go over the weight limit. I get it. It was *Animal Farm*. George Orwell's "All animals are equal, but some animals are more equal than others" was in full play.

We hiked the two miles to our living quarters, a post-WWII rehabbed cement bunker, birding all the way. There were plenty of Lapland Longspurs, birds I have seen in Ohio in March and April, but nothing else of interest. Where were all those mega-rarities promised in the brochure? This monotony of bird species would all change soon. The regulars took the same rooms they had in previous years. There were private rooms for the three married couples and another "couple" made up of a man from New Jersey and a woman from Ohio (both married to other people), who met at Attu every year for their three-week extra-nuptial tryst. I chose one of the remaining two bunk bedrooms and waited for my "cell" mates to arrive. First impressions were good, an eighty-year-old urologist from Chicago, a fifty-something gentleman from Michigan, and a gentleman in his late forties from New Jersey.

Figure 10-1. Roommates.

We drew straws for beds; I drew an upper bunk. The room was tiny with one window, a gas heater, and graffiti with names of past birders and numbers next to their names on the door and walls. The numbers were their life list totals. I checked out the rest of the place: three showers, a drying room for wet clothes and boots, a one-seater outhouse, a laundry, and a large social room. A football field away was another dilapidated building, our eating area. Connected to our sleeping area was a maintenance garage where the bicycles were fixed and stored.

Dinner was early on the first night. We all arrived in the dining room and listened to a welcome and introductory talk from Larry Balch, the tour organizer and owner. He asked us to synchronize our watches to "Balch" time, a time "King" Larry set because there were twenty-two hours of daylight and one couldn't tell what time it was anyway, and besides, no one cared. The day's activities were something like this: generators were turned on at 6 a.m. and showers were ready right away. A hot breakfast was served at 7:30 to 8:15 a.m. *Always* bring your binoculars because you never know when a good bird would turn up outside! In fact, the very next morning on the way to breakfast, I found an Oriental Greenfinch feeding on a seedy flower head, and the whole dining room emptied out. During the breakfast period, the leaders devise and announce the day's birding plans, after which the participants return to their rooms to prepare for a full day of birding. After assembling gear, the participants return to the dining room to prepare a brown bag lunch of cold cuts, peanut butter and jelly, fruit and protein bars. Following this, the parties depart with the leader of their choice. We would be in the field until 6 or 7 p.m. There is no need to leave earlier because there is no "dawn chorus." Migrants can and do arrive any time night or day. If the winds and rain are too strong, we will come in early. You just can't bird when the winds are too strong because nothing is flying. All the birds are hunkered down. Three to six parties are formed and they cover six birding areas that have a history of attracting vagrants. The farthest area, Alexai Point, is sixteen miles round trip. We were all given CBs (to hear of any bird finds) and bicycles (to race to the spot). If a bird is found, the person calls in its location on the CB and keeps a careful eye on the bird until others arrive. When a substantial number of birders arrive, then all can move in for a closer look. Photography comes last after all the clients have seen the bird to their satisfaction.

Announcements and dinner over, I walked over to check out the duty roster. There I was, pots and pans, every fifth day, but hold on! I start tonight, and I wind up doing pots and pans five times because of the twenty-one days. Everyone else had it *four* times! Well, that's the way the matzah ball crumbles. At 9 p.m. I went back to the kitchen to meet a virtual Mount Rainier of greasy pots and pans. At 2 a.m. I left a sparkling kitchen that I had scrubbed from floor to ceiling along with mounds of gleaming pots and pans and tons of spotlessly clean salad bowls and serving dishes they snuck in on me. I was beat.

This is what Hercules must have felt like after cleaning King Augeas' stables. I was thinking, *How can I do this four more times?* I fell asleep as soon as my head hit the pillow. 6 a.m. came in a flash. That morning after breakfast, they assigned the bicycles by lots. They had five new bikes, three speeds with mountain bike tires that would really bite into the tundra. The rest were the single-speed thin-tired bikes that were ages old. You needed tree trunk legs to pedal them. My luck was changing. I drew a new mountain bike. It wasn't long before my good luck dissipated. I felt a gentle tap from the wife of an older gentleman on the tour. She asked me in her gentlest voice, beseeched me, begged me to trade bikes with her husband for fear he would not be able to peddle around and keep up. I looked over at this frail old gentleman with his pleading puppy dog eyes looking back at me and promptly gave up my prize. There were many, many "Thank you's," but that was the last time they ever talked to me for the rest of the tour. Larry said more new bikes were coming. Sure, just like the thirty-eight-pound weight limit.

Our group of birders was composed of men and women from all over the United States and Canada. There were folks from all walks of life. There were doctors, a mailman, lawyers, salesmen, retired folks, academics, an engineer, housewives, and teachers—all with one goal—to see as many new birds as possible. There were some notables among the group. Sandy Komito, who held the Big Year record for the United States, headed the list. A "Big Year" is an attempt to see as many birds as possible in one calendar year. It can be in the world, a country, or a state. In 1987 Sandy recorded 721 species, a new ABA record for the U.S. and Canada. In 1998, in a friendly competition among Sandy, Al Levantin, and Greg Miller, Sandy set the new record of 745, revised later to 748. They were the subject of Mark Obamscik's book and the 2011 20th Century Fox film *The Big Year*. Sandy was bird-listing royalty, and he didn't try to hide it. He developed one of the highest ABA lists in the world. He had an edgy New York personality along with a cutting sense of humor. He was a good birder but not a great one. He was a very good photographer and often recorded his lifers on film. He was a great raconteur filled with endless bird stories. I found him to be fun and entertaining. Al Levantin was also on this trip. He was a great guy to bird with, very laid back and agreeable, a real gentleman. I buddied up with Al and a couple of other guys on our birding sorties. We tried to go with Noble Procter, a leader from a Connecticut university, who had years of birding experience and had been to Attu many times. Noble was also an expert on the botany of Attu, and had written his Ph.D. dissertation on that subject. He was a very large man with surprisingly inexhaustible energy. He was always first up those Attu mountains waiting for us huffing and puffing far behind him. If you wanted a plant identified, all you needed to do was hold it up, and Noble, through his binoculars from a hundred yards away, would name it, both common and scientific names. He also owned a great sense of humor that would often bring sunshine to the group on those slow, gray stormy days.

The level of birding expertise among the group varied widely from rank beginners to expert. Most of the regulars had life lists of more than seven hundred, which at that time was the magic number considered to be high achievement by birders. But that didn't necessarily translate into their being good birders. Mack Smith, another leader and the cook's husband, was approaching eight hundred and was number one in the world for ABA birds. I was sitting at 650. Over the next three weeks I found that a few of the big listers were not good birders. They could not even identify common birds. The abundant Lapland Longspurs kept throwing them for a loop. The longspurs baffled them on day one and continued to baffle them on day twenty-one. *Life lesson: Just because someone has a big list, does not mean they are a good birder.* Others were terrific, having that rare combination of talent, smarts, and competitiveness to find and identify birds. Noble Procter fell into that group. Many of the birders would not leave the social room until a bird they needed for their list was

announced on the CB. Sandy Komito was one of those. I
didn't respect this behavior. They might as well have been
collecting stamps, and once all the spaces were filled in, go on
to another hobby. However, the beauty of the birding hobby
is that it allows for all types of birding styles and individual
likes and dislikes. Your list is your own, and how you want to
see birds is your own prerogative.

Over the next three weeks we were inundated with
migrants. A gorgeous drake Smew, a sea duck, wowed
everyone. A Siberian Rubythroat drew admiration from its
viewers. A jet black and white Peregrine Falcon of the *pelei*
race, a race that I had never seen before, coursed over our
heads headed for some unsuspecting shorebirds. They kept
coming, the Hawfinch, the Bluethroat, the Eyebrowed
Thrush, and an incredible 41 species of shorebirds.

Figure 10-2. Pechora Pipit (photo by Sandy Komito).

Among the shorebirds, Dan Gibson, one of our leaders,
thought he recognized a Pin-tailed Snipe, never before
definitively seen on U.S. soil. Dan showed us the bird but not
the telltale hidden pin-like feathers in its tail. Those could

only be seen with the bird in the hand. The identification, therefore, was still up in the air. It needed closer inspection. That evening Dan collected it, using a fowling piece, for the University of Alaska Museum bird collection. The next morning he splayed the tail feathers and we all saw the key field mark, the pin tail feathers. The collection of the bird, which was legal under Dan's wildlife collecting permit, created a ruckus among some of the tour group, especially the older couple who had my bicycle. They were quite upset about sacrificing the snipe and complained to Larry. There is a long history that goes back centuries of collecting birds using small shot as to not tear the feather and body structures. DNA capabilities weren't as well developed in 1991 as they are now, and it did prove to be a first North American record. The skin would reside in an academic institution for further study. The high emotional pitch settled quickly as the next new bird was found.

Figure 10-3. Pin-tailed Snipe showing pin tail feathers.

My small bird-hunting party, which included Al Levantin, happened on a Common Sandpiper, a not so common sandpiper in these parts. We called in our find and location over the CB, so the rest of the group could see it. The first to arrive was one of the leaders, another Dan, the motorcycle man. He was in a foul mood that morning and tried to take his grumpiness out on us. He berated us for being too close to the bird. He said we would scare it away. In fact, we were not that close and had carefully kept watch of its whereabouts so all could see it. He then turned on Al who was wearing a dull red rain jacket and told him to leave the group and go back to change to a more suitable color. *What?* This was outrageous. Camp was four miles round trip away from where we were standing. I piped up and told him to blow it out of his anus. Who made him queen for the day? His was a most unreasonable demand. Al had already found the bird while wearing his so-called bird repellant jacket, which, per se, damaged this old bird leader myth. I reminded Motorcycle Dan we were guests paying $5,000 to be here, and he was merely paid staff. He continued to argue his point. We told him to go F himself. Al wasn't going anywhere. I then threw the trump card with my assertion that there were no scientific studies to prove his position. By then the rest of the camp arrived and the argument dissipated as we all looked with joy at our sandpiper that had just flown thousands of miles to be with us. For the rest of the tour, Dan the Motorcycle Man was a perfect gentleman, polite, and even helpful beyond what was called for. *Life lesson: Always stand up to a bully.*

Everyone was coughing and had runny noses from the damp cold. I was feeling a little queasy with an upset stomach. From the inclement weather and my toiling with my thin-wheeled bike, I was losing weight and getting dehydrated. My backside was hurting with blisters from the narrow, hard bicycle seat. I took a lot of antacids and even duct-taped a pillow to my bicycle seat. I downshifted my diet from the rich foods the cook was preparing to peanut butter and jelly. I was living on antacids. My turn was coming up for the pots and pans marathon again, and I was in no shape to pull another five-hour shift. I needed some time to feel better. I was able to trade my turn with another pots-and-pans guy's turn the next week. My left foot was aching from what I initially thought was strain from the torture bike, but when I got home, it proved to be Acute Gouty Arthritis, my first attack. I was well into the second week when I was awakened in the middle of the night with a severe stabbing pain in my abdominal right upper quadrant. I felt feverish and had to vomit. I thought it was something I ate. Nobody else was sick, so it wasn't food poisoning. I dipped into my private stash of pills and began taking Percodan® (a narcotic painkiller) and antacids, but I couldn't hold them down. The pain was getting worse, and so was the vomiting. I was getting very concerned because I thought I might have an acute surgical emergency. There were four other doctors on the tour. One was an orthopedic surgeon—no help there.

Bill Evans III, M.D., an internist from the famed Mayo Clinic was on the trip, and I asked one of my cellmates to get him. Bill kindly came down and examined me, but did not think it was an emergency. Bill Rydell, M.D., a surgeon, was also on Attu and Evans called him down to examine me. He interrupted his sound sleep to take a look at me. He did not think it was a surgical emergency either. If it got to emergency status, I would have to be evacuated from the island and sent to the mainland at a cost to me of $15,000. They were ready to radio the Coast Guard LORAN station to bring in an air ambulance. I was writhing in pain and needed a pain injection because I couldn't hold any pills down. I drew a deadline of one hour. If I were not feeling better in one hour, bring in the rescue plane. Unbelievably, after hours of the worst pain I had ever experienced, it began to abate on its own. By daylight I felt sufficiently improved to drink some water, take some pain pills and antibiotics for security, and stayed in bed until noon.

I was fretting about my pots-and-pans duties, which were the next night. I thought I would ask around to find a kind-hearted soul to pick up my chores for me. Guys I asked looked at me like the Attuvian air had addled my brain. I had no takers—not that I expected any. I had to pay someone. *Who needs money?* I did a rough psycho-sociological profile of all the tour members. This ruled out the professionals right away. There was a young Canadian in the group, early twenties. He certainly would need money. All young people do. I asked him if he would do my chores for cash. He asked me what they were.

When I told him pots and pans, he screamed, "No way! That's the hardest job in camp," and ran away from me. What is happening to our society?

There was a mailman in our group. He was a veteran and came every year. I thought five grand was a lot for him to pay. He might do it for cash. I approached him with my story that I was ill, which was true, and asked him if he would pick up my shifts for cash. He didn't run away from me. He asked me what the job was. When I replied pots and pans he said okay for $50 bucks per night. I countered with $25, and he countered at $40. We settled at $35 and shook on it. I paid him the entire $140 up front. No one in camp knew of our deal, and we kept it that way until now.

There was one resident bird that was a must see on Attu. It was a female White-tailed Eagle. It entailed an eight-hour, ten-mile round trip hike over rough terrain. This single bird was the only one of its kind in the U.S.; therefore, it had to be seen by any serious birder on Attu. The way I was feeling, I was hoping it would fly over my bunker, and I would see it that way. That never happened, and I mentally steeled myself to make the long trek to Temnac Valley to see her. There were only five hearty souls who made the journey. No bikes here because there were no trails. It was an arduous walk at a fairly brisk pace. I fell behind because of my gouty foot, which had flared up, and my overall deconditioned physical ability. I kept the line of hikers in my view at all times because being lost here was not an option. We forded a river and rappelled down a steep valley wall using an old rope. With all this effort, I thought, *she better be there.*

I caught my second wind and joined the group heading into the Temnac Valley. We stopped to survey the mountains surrounding the valley and scanned the sky hoping to spot her on the wing. Yes, a large raptor with a white tail was soaring on huge barn door wings right toward us. We couldn't miss her. Her eight-foot wingspan is the largest of any eagle in the world. This particular eagle has been on Attu for seven years. She had a mate but he had not been seen in several years. They probably came to the U.S. from Eastern Russia. We watched this majestic raptor until she flew from sight and then started back to base camp. The pace seemed a little quicker, and I fell behind again. This time, however, I lost sight contact with my group. I did have my CB if I needed it. I decided to climb to the highest point to search the valley for the group. It took me about fifteen precious minutes to climb to the summit of a large hill. There were no humans in sight. I got on the CB to send them a message. I was lost but had no CB contact because I was too far out. I stayed put, which I was taught to do as an Explorer Scout, and hoped they would recognize the fact that I was not with them. The lost party should stay in place while the search party retraces its steps. About a half-hour later, I spotted Mack Smith, our leader, coming back for me and I intercepted him about a quarter mile out. We did not reproach each other; we were both just relieved we had connected. Although there are no large carnivores on Attu, the nights drop down to freezing, killing temperatures.

The last week was just as frenetic as the first two with more vagrants arriving every day. The Aleutian Terns returned to nest on the airstrip as in previous years. A magnificent male Ruff showed off his gleaming white ruffled collar against his coal black body; looking like a Shakespearian dandy, he put on quite a show. A Eurasian Skylark performed his seductive spiraling aerobatics hoping to claim a female. A handsome drake Falcated Teal was a good find. I found an Eyebrowed Thrush, which I quickly lost in the sides of the valley's vegetation. No one else saw it and a few participants were looking at me askance with doubt in their eyes. Noble Procter hiked up that valley and found it again to help save my reputation. On the next to last day, Dan Gibson found a cuckoo at Alexai Point, a sixteen-mile round trip from headquarters. I was very tired by then, but I decided to go for it. My bike was useless, and worse, it was robbing me of my scarce energy. At the halfway point, I tossed it to the side of the road and walked the rest of the four miles to the cuckoo spot. I scoped the bird, but I could not tell if it was the Common Cuckoo or an Oriental Cuckoo. They are practically indistinguishable in the field. I reserved my identification until I discussed it with others who were more knowledgeable like Noble and Dan Gibson. I walked back to my discarded bike and walked it back to camp. The bird was still a great find and a major topic of conversation at dinner. One of my dinner mates, who had been pontificating all three weeks of how pure his life list was, how he had to see every feather tract before he would count the bird on his life list, like he was the Mother Theresa of birding, joined the conversation. He was of the opinion that the cuckoo was a Common Cuckoo. I asked him if he had seen the most important field mark, the white vent. The Oriental Cuckoo has a buffy vent. The vent is the lower flank area. He almost choked on his fried chicken.

"No. Why?"

"Because, according to your standards, you can't count it since you didn't see every feather tract."

He was hoist by his own petard. Amazingly—and to his credit—the next morning before dawn, he pedaled back to Alexai Point to see this field mark more carefully. He had to be back to break camp and make the afternoon flight out. He did all of this in record time to preserve the sanctity of his precious list that no one else gave a damn about. I wondered about this man. He was Pecksniffian about his bird list, but didn't care a whit about his wife at home as he cavorted with one of the single women on Attu. I finished the Attu part of the tour with thirty-seven lifers. I then flew to Gambel and Nome to add thirteen more new birds.

Figure 10-4. Rock Ptarmigan (photo by Sandy Komito).

Figure 10-5. Male King Eider, Gambel, Alaska (photo by Sandy Komito).

As soon as I returned home I went to see my surgeon to investigate my abdominal pain. A couple of tests showed I had an infected gallbladder and a huge stone lodged in my bile duct. My friend, Dr. Jack Perez, operated on me and said it was the worst case he had ever seen. Of course, all surgeons say that to all their patients all the time, but this time it was true. A few weeks later, Larry Balch sent us a letter announcing that the cuckoo was collected for the University of Alaska Museum and it was decidedly an Oriental Cuckoo.

There is an odd postscript to the Attu adventure. I was a member of a men's tennis league at the Olympic Tennis Club in Columbus. My partner, Joe Foley, and I had just finished a match, and we were hanging around shooting the breeze. I mentioned to him that I had been birding in Attu in the spring, fully expecting him to ask, "Where is that?" I was surprised when he said that he not only knew where it was, but that his father had served there in the United States Army in WWII. He was one of the valiant defenders against the suicidal Japanese banzai charge in 1943. He had brought home a war trophy of a camera taken from the body of a dead enemy soldier complete with seven negatives of the Japanese soldiers taken before the ultimate battle. The following week he brought them to our match and gave them to me as a present. I had them developed. The pictures were stunning, showing the now familiar scenes of Attu with—instead of birders—Imperial Japanese Army soldiers at work and play. I made several copies and sent them to the leaders of Attu as a thank you for a job well done. To the best of my knowledge they are the only photos of the Japanese combatants at leisure on Attu in existence.

WORLD 1,298 • ABA 743

CHAPTER ELEVEN

China I: An American Birding Association Tour,
My Worst Tour Ever

If I am walking with two other men, each of them will serve as my
teacher. I will pick out the good points of the one and imitate them, and
the bad points of the other and correct them in myself.
—Confucius

The 1992 China bird tour sponsored by the American Birding Association (ABA) in conjunction with the Citizen Ambassador Program was my worst tour I have ever taken bar Cameroon, which came later. The ABA promised no more than sixteen participants, which is still too many for all to get good looks at birds. Seventy people showed up with four "leaders." It was a circus. China in 1991 was just stepping into the twentieth century for tourist accommodations. Outside of Beijing and Shanghai, it was rough going. We spent two nights in Beijing. The day in between, we birded at the Great Wall, which was an early highlight, but only saw a few birds. The Chinese perpetuate the myth that the Great Wall of China is the only manmade structure in the world that can be seen from outer space with the naked eye. NASA says this is not true. It is true if you add an asterisk explaining that it can only be seen from a low orbit with high magnification lenses.

A long train ride to Manchuria in Northeast China was interesting. The Chinese passengers clambered through the windows to secure their seats. There was no way of separating first class, second class, or coach as they took whatever seats they wanted, often three to four in the same seat. It was musical chairs. The windows were open, and the soot from the coal burning engine and dust from the roads were stifling. There were as many passengers on the roof of the train and hanging from the open doors as there were inside the train.

Figure 11-1. Boarding a train, the Chinese way.

I did discover one thing that the Chinese made better than anyone else in the world—the thermos! Each pair of seats had its own giant thermos. The scalding hot water stayed piping hot for the entire eight hours, something akin to the miracle of the lights for the eight days of Chanukah. The scenery outside the chugging train had a sameness about it with miles and miles of rice paddies. We arrived in old Manchukuo and did a little birding. The children, like children all over the world, were reserved at first. Their curiosity shortly overcame their shyness toward the foreigners. Susan and I broke the ice by giving them Chiclets gum. They really liked them; they smiled broadly, and performing some very deep bows—a very un-Chinese-like thing to do in modern China—showed the vestige of Japanese WWII domination in that part of the world.

We were now deep into an emerging third world country. Any time we left the bus, we were surrounded by gawking villagers. A few approached us to practice their elementary English and of course we were willing teachers. In one village we saw an ancient woman with tiny bound feet, a sign of beauty in old Imperial China. The hunt for the Red-crowned Cranes in Jilin Provence with five buses was a complete "cluster." At one point the buses weren't moving, and we sat in desert conditions for an hour trying to figure out the problem. The word came back that there weren't any cranes. Of course there were cranes. We just had to move on and find them. Translation: the drivers wanted to quit, saying they were tired. Finally, some urging from the leader of the Chinese delegation chaperoning us pushed them on. This was an example of "saving face." The Chinese "saving face" was an obnoxious cultural game presenting great obstacles at times, which Allen Keith, our main leader, skillfully managed to play. "No cranes" meant "too tired to go." We also learned that "maybe" meant "no, never." We spent hours looking for the cranes and finally had some unsatisfying scope looks at two distant cranes on the horizon.

Figure 11-2. Searching for cranes—Qinghai Lake region.

The group comprised seventy ABA members from all over the country and—true to form—engaged in very little conversation other than about birds. The four leaders had an odd mixture of birding skills and knowledge. None of the four had ever been to China, a bad omen to begin with. Allen Keith, the head of our delegation was a capable planner and diplomatic American representative when it came to dealing with the Chinese. Francois Viulleumier was an academic from the American Museum of Natural History in New York. Having done his Ph.D. work on the Nothofagus forests of the southern hemispheres, he was not an expert field birder. However, his scientific credentials as Chairman and Curator of Ornithology at the American Museum were impeccable. He was also a great gentleman and amiable to all. He gave and received respect from everyone except one. I had never seen his style of birding before, but it showed itself to be very efficient in some circumstances. He remained in one place and let the birds come to him. Standing on a hill in Qinghai, he picked off Hume's Ground-Jay, Rufous–tailed Rock-Thrush, and White-tailed Rubythroat. This is unlike most American birders, who perambulate along looking for birds.

Paul Lehman was a young birding prodigy from the West Coast with enormous birding talents. He was part of the new breed of very sharp birders. However, he was always irritable (not a good quality for a leader). He was rude to some of the guests, including me, who were asking questions. Occasionally he would deign to speak to someone. His two egregious acts witnessed by me were a shouting match with gentle Francois in front of the entire tour group, and his refusal to show the group a Spoon-billed Sandpiper because he said there wasn't enough time before dinner. The Spooned-bill is one of the most sought after rarities in the world. Even then their numbers were declining rapidly because of loss of habitat. You cannot tell a group of fanatical birders that they cannot see a Spoon-billed Sandpiper! (Fifteen years later Susan and I finally saw one in Thailand.) The fourth "leader" was Shawneen Finnegan, the wife of Paul Lehman. She had a warm personality and was helpful to everyone. I surmised that her primary function on this tour was to be a calming influence on Paul. We also discovered that she is a terrific bird artist.

We traveled to Inner Mongolia and stayed in a large wooden icebox structure with no heat. The outside temperature was fourteen degrees Fahrenheit with a wind chill of zero. Susan and I slept in our clothes on a thin mattress over a steel frame. The pillow was made of burlap filled with uncooked rice. We covered ourselves with two army horse blankets. We shared a room with another couple and took turns going out in the frigid air to fetch water from the well for washing. The outhouse was another freezer. There were no long thoughtful pauses reading a magazine here. We saw a few birds there like Siberian Blue Robin but I swore it was not worth the effort. The food was inedible.

Figure 11-3. Sleeping quarters, Inner Mongolia.

There was no effort anywhere to cater to American tourist eating habits. I expected this; but I didn't expect that we wouldn't be able to eat most of the food because of the insects, scorpions, sea creatures, and God knows what else was in those dishes. They do serve puppy dog in some parts of China and other Asian countries. We unknowingly may have eaten them. Susan and I are both dog lovers, and that would have been unforgivable. In Qinghai Province near Tibet we were offered yak milk with yak urine—no thanks. The whole sheep's head with the eyes staring at us reminded me of comparative anatomy lab. No thanks again. Yak meat was very lean, but tough and required hours of chewing. I ate all the rice and vegetables served at every meal. Then, back at the room, I snacked on peanut butter and crackers that Susan had the foresight to bring along. I lost seven unhealthy pounds on this trip. I was desperate for American-Chinese takeout and was looking for the telephone number of Hunan Lion, our favorite Columbus Asian restaurant. *Life lesson: Always bring peanut butter and crackers, favorite snacks, and trail mix.* There was no coffee in China. Bring that, too.

Figure 11-4. Dinner, Inner Mongolia.

We flew back to Beijing for some more "birding." We had a free day, and Susan and I wanted to see Tiananmen Square, which had been prominent in world news two years before. Who could forget the student protest against the repressive Chinese regime? Thousands died. A single man stood before a moving tank and would not be moved. This image has become the revolutionary icon of freedom protests throughout the world. Our leaders asked for a show of hands for birding and those for Tiananmen Square. Sixty-eight wanted to bird and only six (Susan and I and the Armer family of four) elected the Square. I was not surprised at this vote result since the group never showed any interest in anything but birds, a sad commentary on my hobby's adherents. Some of the overheard comments were ridiculous: "There are no birds there. I'll come back another time," and the most pathetic: "I came here to bird, not sightsee." The six of us were shuttled to the Square and allowed to explore on our own without supervision.

Figure 11-5. Susan and me, Tiananmen Square.

This was the fourth largest public square in the world. Number one was also in China at Xenghai and is two and a half times larger than Tiananmen. Tiananmen was built in 1651 and is the site of battles, protests, pageants, and Mao's tomb. It was expanded by Mao to hold five hundred thousand people. It is six times larger than Red Square in Moscow, eight times larger than St. Peter's in the Vatican, fifteen times larger than Philadelphia's Rittenhouse Square and between fifty and one hundred times larger than Times Square in New York City. Mao's Mausoleum sits prominently at the apex. I mused on the thought of the Chinese honoring the greatest killer of all time, a murderer of a chilling seventy million of his own people. The Square was filled with visitors, almost all Chinese. Many police intermingled among the crowd and were conspicuous by their uniforms and weapons. There were no vendors hawking T-shirts and meretricious trinkets here. Despite its bloody history, it had an aura of quiet spirituality. It was an awesome and unforgettable experience. The other group that had opted for birding came up empty.

The next stop was Xian and the Terracotta Warrior Necropolis. Along with the Great Wall and the Summer Palace, it was designated a World Cultural Heritage Site in 1987. Birding took a backseat to this amazing third century BCE burial site. In 1974, Chinese farmers discovered the site, and further archeological exploration uncovered rows and rows of eight thousand warriors, 130 chariots, 520 horses and 150 cavalry. Evidence shows legs, arms, heads, and bodies were put together on a massive assembly line, probably the first assembly line in the world, preceding Ford by 3,300 years. The figures were about six feet tall, except for the generals, of course, who were depicted larger. The faces were made from eight different facial molds. The clay was mined right there. This army and its retainers were sent to the next world to protect China's First Emperor Qin Shi Huang. Early, some of the tomb had been looted and weapons stolen. Paint and lacquer had peeled over the centuries but most of the artifacts were intact. Our Chinese docent explained the history and cultural importance of the site. I asked him whether the warriors would ever tour the world. He looked at me skeptically and curtly responded, "No way." He asked me whether China would risk removing the fragile terracotta figures, an irreplaceable national cultural treasure, from their resting place to send them halfway around the world to foreign countries. This was an excellent point. Later in the twenty-first century, I read with great interest that twenty warriors were sent on tour to the western world and received great acclaim. Were these replicas? Was the public duped and by whom? Did the official Chinese government position change over the past two decades?

Figure 11-6. Xian terracotta warriors.

Our last stop was Shanghai and the Fengxian Marsh. Shanghai is the largest city by population in the world with more than 23 million people, although Mexico City would dispute this. It is a powerful financial center for China and the rest of Asia. It is a Special Economic Zone, and capitalism ranks high here. Even in 1991, prosperity was much in evidence with new office building construction and luxury automobiles such as Rolls Royces and Mercedes Benzes touring the streets. China itself has the world's second largest economy in GDP, but is still a full twenty-five percent behind the U.S., but in terms of per capita GDP ranks only 90 out of 183 world countries. Fengxian Marsh was remarkable in its vastness and its tidal flows allowing nutrient exchange from the Hangzhou Bay and Yangzhe River, where its reeds harbored numerous fish and bird species. We did manage a few lifers such as Vinous-breasted and Reed Parrotbills. This was the site of "Lehman's Folly" in not taking us to see the Spoon-billed Sandpiper that he and Shawneen had found. The evening ended with a joint Sino-American banquet. There were many speeches and *gan bei* toasts (dry the cup) with the Chinese vodka flowing, or overflowing for some. The speeches and toasts had much form and little substance. The next morning, we mercifully flew home.

Although the group as a whole tallied 230 species in the two weeks, I only saw 196. The number of tour participants and country logistics created too many impediments for good birding. First, the tour was weighted down by its seventy-four participants. Often the group was split into several birding parties with no way to communicate one's findings to the others. A huge miss was the Przewalski's Rosefinch, or Pink-tailed Bunting, allegedly seen by a few, which was later taxonomically split into its own family, being neither a rosefinch nor a bunting. (Twenty years later, Susan and I made a special trip back to Qinghai to see it.) The groups were too large to get good looks at anything. Peering over and through dozens of birders makes it virtually impossible to study birds. Can you imagine seventy-four people moving through a forest and not frightening the birds away? The leaders were not familiar with the Chinese avifauna, especially those tricky Phylloscopus warblers. The Brits know this genus cold. To be perfectly fair, a few of these warblers were still being studied taxonomically, and their field marks were still being worked out. China itself is vast and logistically difficult to get from one birding area to another. It often took us a thousand miles and a whole day to move our group. A side issue was that Chinese-built airplanes had very small seats for small Chinese frames, but did not fit American posteriors very well. There was not much forest left in the country since most of the land was required for food production. Even with the one child policy in effect at that time, population growth was outstripping resources at a rampant pace. The growth from the 1980s to today has seen a three-hundred-million-person increase. There was open season on hunting and trapping birds for the pot all year long. This made birds extremely skittish at the sight of humans. The mere raising of binoculars and telescopes immediately set the birds flying for cover. The streams and lakes were highly polluted, a major deterrent to supporting wildlife. There was no public health policy or environmental regulations, evident by the garbage and trash strewn throughout the countryside. There was also no proper disposal of human and animal waste. Notwithstanding those problems, there were not even the major pollution problems China is facing now. In the 1980s China was just ramping up to become the manufacturing smokestack giant it is now.

We did get to meet some ordinary Chinese people, and some could speak English. They were very curious and always very polite. Susan and I could not speak Chinese but did learn a few common phrases that we tried to use as often as we could. We had some business cards printed in both English and Chinese explaining who we were and what Health Power and The Master Plan (Susan's image consultant business) were all about.

Figure 11-7. Susan's business card, "The Master Plan."

I received some letters from people who had received the cards, inviting me to join them in business ventures. The Chinese cultural icons were the jewels of the trip, history coming alive for us. We envisioned Pu Yi the last Chinese emperor, relegated by the conquering Japanese to Manchukuo. We stood on the same ground as Chiang Kai-shek when he was taken prisoner by his own generals and forced to join the communists at the Huaqing Hot Springs outside of Xian.

The greatest benefit of this trip for me was neither the birds nor the culture. The greatest benefit was the loss of my Cold War fear of the Chinese as an adversary ready to attack the U.S. at the slightest provocation. I was a child of the 1950s with its anticommunist rhetoric and McCarthy-era scare tactics. I was a combat participant in Vietnam watching our guys getting killed with Chinese made AK47s, RPGs, and hand grenades. I bought into the domino theory of Southeast Asia falling to the commies. I soon learned there were no dominos, only pawns. China had a nuclear capability but no long-range delivery system. They are a neutralizing influence on the bellicose state of North Korea. They want their buffer states, but were not interested in physical world domination or imperialism. They are interested in economic world domination and in making money as much as possible and as fast as they can. They are not walking into the twenty-first century; they are galloping in.

WORLD 1,802 • ABA 743

CHAPTER TWELVE

Cruising for Birds:
How I turned a Failed Fiftieth Anniversary Gift for My
Parents Into a Successful Birding Tour

Life is like a bicycle; you don't fall off until you stop pedaling.
—Congressman Claude Pepper

On September 10, 1989, my parents, Gilbert and Leona, celebrated their fiftieth wedding anniversary—a rare event in today's world. What could I buy them to represent my love and respect for them and commemorate their joining together? They had enjoyed fifty years of harmony and happiness together, not without the usual matrimonial speed bumps, but always showing my sister, Julie, and me the bright side of marriage. My parents were not into material things and had everything they needed and wanted. I had already named a tennis complex in their honor. There were two scholarships named for each at Temple University where my father was Professor Emeritus. I knew they never traveled but were always looking at travel magazines and talking about exotic places. They had only traveled vicariously through brochures. They spent their lives in two places, our Philadelphia row house and our North Wildwood, New Jersey, summer house. How about a cruise? I told my parents I was buying them a luxury cruise anywhere in the world for their anniversary. They could pick it out; money was no object. They were very excited and could not contain their enthusiasm. My father was eighty, and my mother was seventy-four, and they had only been in three states in their entire lives, Pennsylvania, New Jersey, and Ohio, the last only to visit us. Of course they picked a "world cruise." They wanted to see everything in three weeks. What is a world cruise? Is it traveling the twenty-five-thousand-mile circumference of the earth? Is it stopping in every country's port? I have, on a couple of occasions heard people say they went "around the world." What did they mean? Well, it has infinite meanings. In cruising parlance it means stopping at the most popular ports on two or three continents, maybe a dozen stops in all, and spending a day or two in each.

They immediately called a local travel agent picked at random from the Yellow Pages, and were sold a twenty-one-day cruise on the Royal Cruise Line's MS *Crown Odyssey*, the top cruise liner of its time. The tour included eight days in Europe, five days crossing the Atlantic, and eight days in the Caribbean. It sounded great, so I sent the agent $25,000 and bought the travel insurance as a precaution. You know the policy that gambles with your body parts: loss of one eye and one arm, $5,000; loss of both eyes, $25,000. Well the tour wasn't great, and it never happened. A month before the departure date, my father had a heart attack and was rushed to the hospital. He was in serious condition with congestive heart failure as a severe complication. Once stabilized, he received his second cardiac bypass. There was no way he could go on the cruise. His attending physician did not know when he would be strong enough to go again. My mother tearfully thanked me for the gift, but they were not optimistic they could ever use it. *Okay, I'll find some other anniversary gift for them.* In the meantime, I filed for reimbursement from the insurance company for my $25,000. I filled out all the paperwork carefully with a letter from his doctor explaining his illness and hospitalization and waited for my check in the return mail. This was a new experience for me. After many weeks I received a letter from the insurance company. It was a flat rejection of my claim. I knew there was a mistake and called the insurance company to clear up any misunderstanding on their part. Heart attack, cardiac surgery, slam dunk! The voice on the other end of the phone said there was no mistake, and the decision was final. The voice said the insurance contract was clear and stated no refunds if the trip is cancelled by the customer for *pre-existing* health reasons. I was incredulous. I dug out the policy and pored over the document word-by-word. There was nothing in the main body of the policy about the risk of cancellation, but there in the fine print was the disclaimer about no refunds if there was a pre-existing health problem that prevented the customer from taking the cruise. Those sneaky bastards! What eighty-year-old does not have a pre-existing health condition? Who reads the fine print? This risk should be in bold print and appear prominently in the front of the contract. But this was not a stock offering highly regulated by the SEC. This was an insurance contract heavily tilted toward the company allowing them to weasel out of responsibly paying for a reasonable cancellation. I called the travel agent and innocently asked if she would refund her commission since no tour had taken place. She went off on me, and told me how much work she had put into this. It was not her fault that my parents couldn't go, and basically I was an idiot for asking. There was no way she would reimburse me. I called the cruise line office and explained the circumstances. Their answer was composed and sounded practiced and formulaic. No doubt when dealing with seniors they had many similar requests. Their answer was a polite no. They would be stuck with an empty suite, difficult to sell at such a last minute; they were sorry for my father's problem but there was nothing further to do. I was temporarily stymied, but not defeated. I would attack in another direction. True, the money was an issue but the unfairness of the situation—the fine-print bamboozle, the pre-existing nonsense, and the refusal by anyone on the other end to compromise—was charging me up for a fight. I was determined to win. My next call was to my personal and corporate attorney, Alec Wightman, a man of great integrity, a talented legal and logical thinker, and the consummate persuader. The heart of the case was $25,000 paid to the travel agent, and she kept the commission; the cruise line was paid for the suite, and they kept their money; the insurance company was paid their premium, and they kept their money; my father was still in the hospital in guarded condition, and my mother was at the hospital every day exhausted, looking over him. All the players had my $25,000, and my parents had nothing—no trip, no present, and no joy. What was wrong with that picture? Everything! I directed Alec to get my money back.

I believed the confusing language and fine print, although legal, was unfair to seniors. I called California Congressman Edward Roybal's office. He was the new Chairman of the House Select Committee on Aging and had just succeeded Congressman Claude Pepper of Florida who died in May of that year. Both Congressmen were champions of seniors' rights with different styles of politics. Pepper was fiery and bold. Roybal was quiet and conservative. I explained the problem, and he agreed to look into the whole matter. I really needed some hot "Pepper" personality here. Alec got back to me in two days and said no one was willing to budge from his or her position. I told him to send letters to all involved—agent, cruise line and insurance company—demanding payment, or lawsuit would follow, emphasizing that I had both the will and wherewithal to follow through. This got a call back from the cruise line company. The liner had just been sold to a Danish family for more than $200 million and I suppose they did not want any negative publicity. Besides, they were out nothing because they had successfully sold my parents' suite to another customer. They offered a free cruise for two of the same value to be taken within the next two years. Alec advised me to take their offer. He felt it came down to a business decision. The litigation would be long and costly. Taking the emotional element out of the equation, I agreed and accepted their offer. Susan and I took the cruise in

November 1991. After a lengthy illness my father passed away, February 22, 1992. Coincidentally, this was exactly fifteen years to the day that his mother, Sophie Master, died at age ninety-nine. My mother passed away February 22, 2002, exactly ten years after my father. Every February 22, I light three candles and stay in a bomb shelter.

Now that I had the cruise what would I do with it? A cruise summoned the images of blue-haired old ladies playing bingo and old guys hitting golf balls off the back of the boat. The confinement on one small piece of floating real estate would drive me crazy. I would probably gain ten unwanted pounds from all the food they serve around the clock. On the other hand, we were stopping at some of the great ports in Europe and the West Indies. They all contained birds, historic places and iconic works of art I had never seen before. Why not combine culture with birding? I went to work researching every stop for cultural landmarks and birds that we might find there. These were pre-internet days so I used magazine articles, field guides and personal conversations with friends to gather a dossier of information. At last we were off to Civitivecchia, the port of Rome, to board our ship for our three-week adventure.

The first sight of our liner, the *Crown Odyssey* was amazing. It was practically brand new. Built in a West German shipyard to the tune of $168 million, it sat low in the water and was 615 feet long, twice as long as the *Nabila*, the largest private yacht in the world. It housed 1,230 passengers and could do 22.5 knots. We walked through the lower deck; it was all shiny with garnet and blues reflecting from ceilings and walls with octagonal elements throughout. We were shown to our suite, one of seventy-four, on the eighth level, starboard, almost one hundred feet above the ocean surface. The suite was spacious with a king-size bed, large master bath and plenty of drawers and closets for Susan.

The coolest aspect of the suite was a mullioned sitting area with large bay windows jutting out into the sea where I could comfortably watch sea birds without leaving my room.

Figure 12-1. Viewing area.

We were up high enough so there was no noise or smell of fuel from the engine room. Susan and I explored the ship to see all of its three dining rooms, theater, show room, workout room, swimming pool, Jacuzzis, viewing area, casino, dance floor and bridge. This was a city at sea, and we did not have to pack or unpack as we traveled from one port to another. The crew gave us an obligatory safety talk, and we practiced a fire drill. The first night's dinner was fabulous, prepared by a Greek master chef and served by an all-Greek, crew. The main dining room was beautiful, and we had a comfortable table. I did think our waiter was a little too friendly with Susan, though, but passed it off for the time being. We couldn't wait to get started.

The next two days, we stayed in port and got a chance to explore Rome.

We were expected to sign out when leaving the ship and sign back in upon our return. When the ship was in port overnight, we could stay out as late as we wanted. The next day she would leave at 0800 hours, 8 a.m. If the ship was in port for the morning only, we had to be back by 1200 hours, noon. The ship would then leave promptly at 1300 hours, 1 p.m. With these deadlines in mind I would plan our day accordingly allowing enough time for sightseeing and birding. In Rome the birding was purely incidental to the sightseeing because there were no actual birding spots. But the common birds were all new to us and would be fun to see anyway. The Coliseum produced Wood Pigeon and Hooded Crow. The Circus Maximus had European Blackbird and Spanish Sparrow. Even the Trevi Fountain, where Louis Jordan and Jean Peters romanced in the 1954 film, *Three Coins in The Fountain*, produced a Eurasian Kestrel. We lucked into a Red Kite, a very uncommon bird, on the outskirts of Rome on our way back to the ship. The second night's dinner was a delicious five-course Italian meal. Our waiter was paying entirely too much attention to Susan and was beginning to really annoy me. It was true she looked irresistibly beautiful every night, but I was not going to bear twenty-one days of his unctuous charm. That night I asked the *maître d'* for a change of table and asked to meet my new waiter first. No problem. The change was great. The new guy was professional, efficient, pleasant and courteous. The rest of my trip was smooth sailing without any irritation from the wait staff.

The next morning we awoke in the Ligurian Seaport of Livorno, the gateway to Tuscany, the birthplace of three of the greatest minds that ever lived, Galileo, Michelangelo, and Leonardo da Vinci. Let's not forget Machiavelli, another son of Tuscany. A bus ride to the city of Florence revealed the golden countryside that had birthed these geniuses. What was it, the soil, the sun, the diverse genetic blend from the centuries of travelers and conquerors that gave the world these supermen? The history and the art masterpieces in Tuscany left little room for birding. Botticelli's Birth of Venus housed in the Uffizi is eternal. Florence Cathedral, The Basilica of Saint Mary of the Flower, with its polychromatic marble façade was unforgettable. The dome is the largest in the world. One of Michelangelo's four molds of his masterpiece, David, is in the Galleria dell' Academia. There were many more priceless *object d'art*, too many to see in such a short visit. Upon our return to the ship, our chef, true to form, served a complete Tuscan meal with its traditional filone, saltless bread (a five-hundred-year tradition when salt was too expensive to eat), antipasti with Tuscan prosciutto ham and salami, Florentine tomato soup, Florentine grilled steak, zucchini and peppers in virgin olive oil and fresh peccorini cheese made from sheep's milk. The last was served with fruit pickles, honey and truffles. The meal was settled with a strong aromatic espresso. What a feast!

A single Gull-billed Tern met us at the harbor. The next morning we docked in Monte Carlo, Monaco. Mediterranean Gulls, Herring Gulls and Firecrest (a tiny songbird in the conifers) met us at the pier. We headed to the Casino for a little fun and sightseeing. The Casino was featured in the 1983 James Bond film, *Never Say Never Again*. This film was the second screen version of the Bond *Thunderball* novel, both of which starred the greatest Bond of all time, Sean Connery. Kim Basinger and Barbara Carrera as Fatima Blush were not too bad either. Somehow the Casino, as grand as it is at night, during the day looked like a drab and lifeless movie set and was no fun at all. We played a little roulette and wandered off. The Principality of Monaco has harbored some of the greatest tax evaders of all time: Ringo Starr, Bono, Shirley Bassett, Gina Lollabrigida and Roger Moore. There is no personal income tax here. The great tennis star, Bjorn Borg, took residence there and opened a small tennis pro shop in which his parents worked. By doing so he protected his millions in prize money from taxation.

We took a short walk to the elite Hotel de Paris and had lunch there. We returned to the ship and turned in early.

That night we sailed to the Côte d'Azure in the South of France. We awoke in Nice, a potpourri of ethnic cultures, Moroccan, Algerian, Tunisian, Italian, Corsican and, of course, Provencal people. There were two museums we especially wanted to visit: the Musee Chagall and the Musee

Matisse. Both painters loved the soft light and the Mediterranean colors of Nice and spent a good deal of time developing their craft there. The famous Salade Nicoise was invented here, a perfect blend of sea and farm flavors. Mediterranean, Black-headed and Yellow-legged Gulls were in the harbor. Pallid Swifts and Eurasian Crag Martins were fluttering along the cliffs as we drove to St. Paul De Vence, one of the most charming towns we have ever seen. This little out-of-the way village boasts one of the world's greatest restaurants, a five-star appellation on every food critic's score card, La Columbe d'Or. It once lodged the great artists in the twenties, exchanging their art for room and board. Leger, Miro, Braque, Chagall, Calder and the legendary Picasso were among them. You can see their works decorating both the interior and exterior. The restaurant was later owned by French movie stars, Yves Montand and Simone Signoret. A spirited game of boule was being played just outside its front door. Iberian Chiffchaffs, Magpies, and Great and Crested Tits seemed to be enjoying the boule, too. We skipped the dinner on board and opted instead for the Columbe d'Or, which now also carries the Bernard Five Stars.

Figure 12-2. Susan and I, Eifel Tower.

Barcelona—or Barthelona as it was once pronounced by a lisping Spanish monarch and is still pronounced today—is one of the most populous cities in Europe. Its inhabitants speak Catalan as well as Spanish. The Catalan language, although a Western romance language, has Gothic influences in its Latin base and differs greatly from Spanish in pronunciation, grammar and vocabulary. I speak a little Spanish but was completely lost in understanding Catalan. Following its resistance to the Franco *coup d'état,* the Catalan culture was suppressed and the language was forbidden to be used throughout Spain.

From our suite we could see a diving Sandwich Tern, two Northern Gannets and six Lesser Black-backed Gulls. We disembarked into a maddening rush of traffic, the worst we had seen in Europe. Traffic was snarled at every intersection. The roads were narrowed and single laned. I was wondering how they would solve this problem in their upcoming hosting of the 1992 Olympics. Interestingly, Barcelona was the birthplace of International Olympic Committee (IOC)

Chairman, Juan Antonio Samaranch, and was selected over every other major European city to hold the XXIV Olympiad. I wondered how that had happened. The city was determined to successfully host the expected millions of tourists who would be flowing in, and poured billions into infrastructure with construction of a new outer ring of highways and major arena and sports buildings. In retrospect they pulled it off, a civil engineering miracle, but incurred a great deal of debt in doing it.

There were no birding areas per se, so we headed to the cultural centers, Parc Gaudi, Sagrada Familia and the Museu Picasso. Barcelona is famous for the renowned architectural works of Antoni Gaudi and the largest art collection of Pablo Picasso in the world. Parc Gaudi is a thirty-five-acre municipal park featuring a collection of surreal Gaudi ceramics, stained glass, wrought iron and carpentry designed to give the visitors a feeling of peace and harmony. It had the opposite effect on me. It was a jarring and whacky accumulation of walls, benches, homes, and statues with a giant salamander at its entrance.

It was a composite of Gaudi's creative ideas of Catalan nationalism, religious mysticism and ancient poetry. It looked like a giant web woven by a spider on LSD. Was he a genius and artistic saint or was he a mentally ill, drug addicted, alcoholic or a flaming exhibitionist. The world is overwhelmingly in favor of the genius status. Gaudi's *magnum opus* is the Sagrada Familia, a Roman Catholic Church begun in 1915 and never finished. It is a synthesis of Gothic and natural organic styles. It is trumpeted as the most beautiful Gothic-style church in the world, and although I have not seen every other gothic-style church in the world, I cannot imagine one more beautiful. It is truly magnificent. The use of light pouring through its stained glass windows and accentuated by the space provided by its towering height is awesome. Powerful religious symbols are everywhere. The design calls for eighteen spires representing the twelve apostles, four evangelists, the Virgin Mary, and the tallest of all for Jesus Christ. The best estimation of completion of this monumental architectural masterpiece is 2027! In Gaudi's own words, "My client is not in a hurry."

Pablo Diego Jose Francisco de La Paula Juan Nepomuceno Maria de los Remedios Cipriano de la Santisma Trinidad Ruiz y Picasso aka Picasso is the most talked about, written about, studied and influential painter of the Modern art era. Thus a trip to the Museu (Catalan spelling) Picasso was demanded. Picasso spent his teenage years in Barcelona learning his art at the city's best art academy and being nurtured by his artist father. His early deep love of the city was the impetus for building the Museu Picasso, whose construction and contents he personally directed, the only museum dedicated solely to him while he was alive. There are over 3,500 works of art here representing his artistic passage from age seven until his death at age ninety-one. He was no doubt a child prodigy and artistic savant, as evidenced by the paintings done in his earliest childhood years. Even his doodles were remarkable. The pictures, ceramics and sculptures were arranged autobiographically depicting his transformation from one art period into another: early, training, African, Modern, Blue, Analytic Cubism, and Synthetic Cubism. Some say his art evolved from one period to the next stimulated by each new woman he loved. We returned to the *Crown Odyssey* with our brains filled with images of neo-Gothic Gaudi and Cubist Picasso.

We were ending the first leg of our trip, and our birdlist was meager partly due to the abundance of famous art treasures that had to be seen, and partly because there are not that many birds in sooty concrete urban areas. The French and the Italians are infamous for shooting and trapping live birds for sport and for the pot. The "birdiest" part of the trip was just beginning. We would hit Mallorca first, finishing the European continent in Gibraltar and then on to a few of the more accessible Spanish islands, which were filled with endemic birds.

Our first island was Majorca, the largest of the Balearic Islands, ten hours due south in the Mediterranean. Coming into Palma, the capital, we were greeted by two Audouin's Gulls, a lifer, Shags, and a Black-legged Kittiwake. I negotiated a taxi ride to the Albufera wetlands northeast of Palma. There was a hide (bird blind), already filled with European, British, Spanish, Scandinavian and Dutch birders eagerly looking through their telescopes. The hide had several horizontal oblong spaces in the wooden slats through which an observer could peer through his scope without disturbing the birds. There was a large blackboard in the hide with bird sightings of that day written in chalk, all in their Latin scientific names. Each language has its own common names for the birds, so the scientific names made sense with the multicultural gang of birders in the hide. We garnered a whopping twenty-one lifers here. The most notable were Greater Flamingoss, Slender-billed Gulls, Cirl Buntings and Cetti's Warbler. Greater Flamingos are the largest of the six species of flamingos in the world. They are also the most widely distributed. I guessed the two flamingos we were watching were spillovers from the large flocks in the Carmargue, France, or from Spain. One of these giant birds lived until eighty-three in an Adelaide, Australia zoo.

Our taxi driver waited for us to take us back to Parma. On the way back we spotted an Eleanora's Falcon hunting over a field. Eleanora was a fourteenth-century ruler of Arborea in Sardinia, famous for her love of birds especially these falcons. She also promulgated a Magna Carta of her own called the Carta de Logu, which liberalized the draconian punishments for most crimes in the Middle Ages. She believed fines were better than corporal punishment. These laws lasted almost five-hundred years. Her name was appended to this Sardinian falcon in honor of her kindness to her subjects and falcons. The use of people's names for birds has been common for hundreds of years. Of the ten thousand species of birds known to science, about ten percent have eponymous names. An *eponym* is a "namegiver," something named for a person or mythical being. Eleanora's Falcon is an eponym. Many ornithologists do not like the eponymous usage but rather something more descriptive of the field marks, habits or habitat of the bird. I do like a sprinkle of eponyms on a bird list. A little digging would reveal the rich historical connections of people to birds. Of late the word, *patronym*, has crept into the birding lexicon as a substitute for eponym. At this point in the development of the English language, patronym is used incorrectly. It has nothing to do with birds and does not appear in the Oxford English Dictionary or the Merriam Webster Dictionary. I suppose over the years, through usage, it will be accepted as a synonym for eponym. The word *patronymic* actually refers to a family name derived from that of the father or a paternal ancestor usually by the addition of a prefix such as Mac of MacDonald, or suffix such as son of Donaldson, both meaning son of Donald.

Majorcan pearls are world famous, and as we had no souvenirs yet, this would be our first purchase. Our driver took us to the pearl factory where these simulated natural pearls have been made for more than one hundred years. The whole process of making these pearls takes a couple of weeks. They start with glass balls and dip them in a mixture of adhesive paste of oil and fish scales or mother-of-pearl called hemage. They polish and remove imperfections and then repeat the process about thirty times. To ensure durability they subject the pearls to gasses or solutions to make them impervious to discoloration, chipping and peeling. They are a lot less expensive than natural pearls, but only an expert eye can tell the difference.

The next night and following day our ship headed southwest off the southern coast of Spain to Gibraltar. I spotted a total of five Cory's Shearwaters from my suite along the way. The next morning we awoke at the "Rock," the Rock of Gibraltar. To many this icon represents stability, indomitability, and timelessness. To world birders it represents a chance to find the Barbary Partridge, the national bird of Gibraltar, a rare game bird only found here and North Africa. We headed to the Mediterranean Steps and climbed the shrubby terraced hillside until we at last flushed one and then another until we saw a total of ten. Most of them just scurried away in front of us. A few flew short distances and were quickly lost in the dense vegetation. We added numerous Black Redstarts, Sardinian Warblers, a flock of Serins, and a single Blue Rock Thrush. A Red-headed Bunting, far out of place here, showed itself for a minute. They are found in Central Asia and India. This is a frequently kept cage bird because of its beauty, and I imagined it was an escapee. Back at the wharf we found a Northern Wheatear walking amongst the cargo containers. Gibraltar is only two and six tenths square miles so there was really no other place to go once we finished the birding. Because it so small and densely populated by its thirty-thousand people, they pour cement into the sea as "land reclamation" to allow for more building. Although it is located at the southernmost tip of Spain, it is a British overseas territory and the Gibraltarians want it that way as evidenced by two separate referendum votes in favor of British citizenship. We boarded the *Crown Odyssey* and were on our way to Cadiz in the southwest coast of Spain.

We landed in the port of Cadiz and were greeted by Common Black-headed Gulls, Sandwich Terns, Caspian Tern, Little Grebes and four Mallards, a duck common in Ohio. Along the mud banks were Common-Ringed Plovers, European Oystercatchers, Whimbrels, Common Sandpipers and a Eurasian Curlew. A short ride took us to Jerez. As we explored the Alcazar, a Moorish fortress from the eleventh century, we spotted a Eurasian Kestrel and two Black Kites floating above. Further inland we explored parts of Seville, stopping for lunch and, being in the Sherry capital of the world enjoyed a glass, the best in the world. Outside Pontius Pilate's house we saw Blackcap, Willow Warbler, Pied Flycatcher and Coal Tit. We stopped at the America's Park, part of the Parque Maria Luisa, and typical of city parks it was inhabited by common birds, Eurasian Blackbird, European Robin and the magnificently beautiful pure white Rock Pigeons (not albinos) that frequented the square. They were a gift from the Philippines in 1929 for the Spanish-American Exposition and are found nowhere else in Spain.

Figure 12-3. Pure white Rock Pigeons. America's Park, Seville

That evening the ship's chef prepared a fabulous Andalusian feast representative of the countryside's cuisine complete with gazpacho, fish dredged in flour without egg and fried in virgin olive oil from Seville, *bocas de la islas* crab, and for desert, *amarguillos*, almond macaroons. The stomach was settled with a selection of after dinner Sherries, from the light Manzanilla to the heavier Amontillado. They were true Sherries from the Spanish "Sherry Triangle" made only from palomino grapes, properly aged and fifteen and a half percent alcohol by volume.

The night was not over. Cadiz is in the heart of flamenco. To add fire to our spicy meal, a troupe of flamenco dancers and musicians were brought on board. For an hour and a half we sat mesmerized with their soulful and passionate performance. The flamenco music and dance is hundreds of years old influenced by Gitano (Romani) traditional folksongs and dances with Moorish, Christian, and Jewish influences. Although there are some individual improvisations allowed usually on the spur of the moment, it is a set of formal and complex repeating forms that have been done thousands of times over for many centuries. All flamenco has *cante,* singing; *toque,* guitar playing; *baile,* dancing; and *palmas,* handclapping. The musical notes are more percussive and less sustained than classical guitar music. It expresses sad and bitter feelings, performed most often by older more mature performers who have lived the life. There are many subtle interval and tonal changes. The women adopt arrogant and irreverent poses with backs arched dramatically and arms held up and close to their olive-toned faces and tightly pulled back jet-black hair. Our women dancers wore fiery red dresses with flared bottoms; the only man wore black satin and a traditional perfectly round, wide-brimmed black *cordobés* hat. The music expressed urgency and intensity. Castanets were used that night but are not always. The guitars are similar to classical guitars with six strings but thinner and have less internal bracing. They are made of cypress or sycamore with rosewood on the sides and backs for more volume. The player must send his music above the sound of the clapping and nailed shoes striking on hardwood floors. It is also equipped with a *golpeador,* tap plate, to protect the guitar from the rhythmical *golpes,* finger tapping. The techniques, playing postures and strumming patterns are complex and passed down from musician to musician rather than written down. Following their main performance and two encores, we could hardly sleep that night.

Once the ship left Gibraltar and headed west we were officially in the Atlantic Ocean, leaving the Mediterranean behind. We were headed 540 miles to Madeira, once a Portuguese possession, now autonomous, famous for its wine of the same name and the endemic Trocaz Pigeon. There is a 1956 salacious tune about Madeira wine by the Limelighters, "Have Some Madeira, M'Dear," that runs through my head at the strangest times. This is a twenty-million-year-old volcanic island that has never been connected to the African or European continents. The flora and fauna have been left to their own devices until the last four-hundred years when settlers arrived to destroy the natural wonders of the island. The Trocaz pigeon hangs on and in fact is doing better since the Madeira government recognized its value and has taken steps to protect it. It is no longer on the "Threatened" list of endangered birds. *En route* I spotted a flock of 111 Manx Shearwaters from my stateroom. We made port in the capital city of Funchal. We hired a car for the day and made our way to Bancoes for the Trocaz Pigeon stopping along the way to look for migrants and resident birds. We were rewarded by a gorgeous Mistle Thrush in a meadow pass, Pallid and Plain Swifts against the cliffs, a flock of Linnets, and a regional endemic subspecies of Blackcap, *Sylvia atricapilla heineken*. Gray Wagtails and Chaffinches, another endemic subspecies, *Fringilla coelebs maderensis*, were numerous at every level. At the summit we watched our target bird, the Trocaz Pigeon, for more than an hour, in a flock of thirty circling below us and six to eight more flying in singles and pairs. *Veni, vidi, vici* came to mind as our plan successfully produced this highly sought after and rare endemic species. On the way back to Funchal we took a thrill ride down the mountainside using the Madeira toboggans. These are wicker baskets on wooden rails pulled by *carreiros,* two men dressed in white with straw hats. These sledges can reach speeds of forty-eight kilometers per hour, and the only brakes are the rubber-soled shoes of the *carreiros.* We rode all the way down to the city. When we reached Funchal we made a stop at the children's playground behind the bus station, a known location for the lowly Spanish Sparrow, a close cousin of our House Sparrows, raiders of our feeders back home in Worthington. Just like home we saw two picking through the debris around the bus stalls.

We were two hours SSW after leaving Madeira, when I saw the birds of the trip! There were three Cream-colored

Coursers, desert shorebirds, flying parallel to our ship and faster, much faster. We were more than a hundred miles off shore. From where were they coming? Just south of us in the Canary Islands where they breed? Where were they going? To their wintering grounds in North Africa? Morocco, perhaps? Their exact migration routes have never been tracked. A half hour later I spotted a lone Dunlin, another shorebird, crossing our bow. I had seen loads of Dunlin in the new world, but they were all *Caladris alpina pacifica*. This guy had to be the Northern European subspecies, *Caladris alpine alpina*, on its way to its North African breeding grounds. From my viewing distance I could not determine any plumage differences so my subspecies call was based solely on geographical location.

On our twelfth day of the trip we were heading to the Canary Islands, our last port-of-call, before the five day Atlantic crossing. The trip was going extremely well, too well. I expected a visit from the goddess Discord, the grand disrupter of the best-laid plans, the ultimate party pooper. And then she struck on November 21. Our routine was to be first off the boat, beat the crowd, go directly to the waiting taxis, go over a route and time frames with a driver, and negotiate a half or full day fee depending when the ship would leave. This worked fine until Tenerife. I wanted to drive to the southern opposite end of the island to Punta de la Rasca, a British and American enclave. Here we had the best chance of finding Berthelot's Pipit. The drive would take an hour. Birding the Point would take another hour. I wanted to return via the mountains looking for the Blue Chaffinch, Canary Islands Chaffinch, Island Canary and Chat. That would take a third hour. A return route down the mountain would get us back to Tenerife and the ship in another hour, four hours in all. The ship wants the passengers back no later than noon and then ready for a 1 p.m. departure. It was imperative that we were back on time before the Atlantic crossing because the next port was all the way down to the southernmost island in the Caribbean Lesser Antilles,

Barbados. I explained in detail to the driver, using a map and Spanglish, what we wanted to accomplish. He said he understood, and we took off. We made it to the Point in an hour flat. *So far so good.* There we found a bonanza of bird life, Eurasian Thick-Knee, four Eurasian Spoonbills, Lesser Whitethroat, Blue Rock Thrush, Spectacled Warbler and European Goldfinch. We searched for a full hour and finally spotted a lone Berthelot's Pipit. Mission accomplished, we jumped into our taxi and told the driver to head into the mountains. Susan sensed that we were farther away from the ship than we had first thought and advised that we should return by the route we had taken in getting here. No, I overruled her and headed into the mountains. An hour later we had not even returned a quarter of the way. The road was very winding with many hairpin turns and switchbacks. This did not allow for speed. The traffic was heavy and to boot there were many slower cars in front of us impeding our progress. I told the driver to step on it and pass these slowpokes. He did not. The narrow single lane road did not allow for good visibility let alone passing. It was 11:30 a.m., and we were nowhere near Tenerife. I still held the belief that if we did not stop to bird, we could make it back to the ship by 12:30 p.m. *Not so fast.* Discord had other plans for us. It started to rain, hard, I mean pour buckets. The taxi's high-speed windshield wipers were not keeping up with the torrent of water cascading down on our vehicle. Visibility fell to zero. We could not see the car in front, and I am sure we were invisible to the car in back. The driver pulled over to let the worst abate. Susan and I thought at this point we would never get back to the ship in time, but we still had a small outside chance. We took stock of our resources: both passports, yes! Cash, yes! And a Platinum American Express card! No worries. We could purchase anything we needed. If we missed the departure, we would fly home and have the liner ship us our belongings. At 12:40 p.m., the rain stopped.

I was yelling to the driver, "*¡Mas rapido! ¡Mas rapido!*"

At last we could see Tenerife. All three of us were sweating profusely. We still had a shot. But Discord was not finished. The city traffic was in gridlock, and we were hitting every red light. I couldn't think of the Spanish to tell the driver to drive on the sidewalk. We could finally see the docks in the distance. At 1p.m. we could see our ship, but it was the last ship docked all the way at the far end. We hit the docks, and I swear the driver was going fifty miles per hour on the heavily trafficked wharf. People were jumping out of the way. Damn, I could see the gangplank going up. We'd missed it by seconds! The ship was slowly moving away from the dock. I was picturing an end to our cruise and a long flight back to the States. I jumped out of the still-moving taxi and sprinted to the ship, yelling something unintelligible at the top of my lungs and waving my arms. I thought I saw the ship stop and return to the dock. Yes, it did, and a small emergency gangplank was let down. The taxi followed me close behind. Susan jumped out, and I threw a fistful of greenbacks through the driver's open window. Hearts racing and out of breath, we tried to walk calmly up the gangplank as if nothing happened.

A very, very unhappy British purser with a grim look of dismay said, "Next time would you please be a little more prompt."

The last time anyone in our family had completed an Atlantic crossing was in 1945 when Susan's mother Mary Fickel (nee Rosendahl) joined another four-hundred Australian war brides on the *H.M.S. Queen Mary*. Before that, around 1905, my nineteen-year-old maternal grandfather, Joseph Majeski, made the trip from Poland and landed in the port of Chester, Pennsylvania. Before him, my paternal great grandfather, Jacob Rosenzweig and daughter, Charna (Sophie) Rosenzweig, my grandmother arrived in the late 1890s from Russia. Preceding them and first arrivals in our family was my paternal grandfather, David Master, from Russia in the mid-1890s, who probably came through Ellis Island. Those crossings took weeks in uncomfortable quarters fighting *mal de mer* the whole way. In contrast, Susan and I were in the lap of luxury going twice as far in a quarter of the time.

On the next day, November 22, no sea birds were seen in four hours of watching. We started enjoying the conveniences the ship had to offer, sunning on the main deck with Olympic–sized pool, first-run movies in the theater, top-flight entertainment at night, spa and workout facilities, Bingo, dancing and a casino. There were private and Captain's parties, themed dinners, formal dress night, and trivia contests with cash prizes.

The boat was loaded with elderly, but there were a few couples our age. We naturally migrated to each other. There was a couple in their forties from Canada whom we thought were nice. We had dinner with them one night and attended a couple of parties with them. Our conversations were about family, travel, and our hobbies and work, no politics or religion. One afternoon, Tom, the husband, and I were at the pool just relaxing, having a cool drink and talking sports. I closed my eyes for a quick nap when I heard him say, "Hitler was right."

I opened my eyes, turned in his direction and said, "What do you mean?"

He responded, "Kill all the Jews." I wondered why and where did this come from? It had to have slithered out from the gutters of his warped mind.

I got up from my lounge chair and said to him, "We can never be friends," and left him there befuddled that another forty-year-old white man did not share his sick views. He had no clue that my father was Jewish and that my uncle Vince Majeski was in the front lines of the Normandy invasion protecting America, the world and our way of life from Nazi tyranny. Anti-Semitism is alive and well in the most out-of-the-way places. It rears its ugly head when least expected. We all must stand up to it publicly. It has no place in our American life or in any decent person's mind. We avoided this Canadian trash for the remainder of the trip. This incident provoked long conversations between Susan and me, and later when we returned home among our friends. The crucial question is how far would we go to protect Jews? African-Americans? Other minorities? Would we go as far as to give our lives?

On our second day on the open sea I saw a petrel of the Soft-plumaged complex. Splitting of this taxon into Fea's, Zino's and Cape Verde had not been worked out yet. I reasoned geographical location might help for later more specific identification. I called the bridge, and they readily gave me the nautical location: 851 miles southwest of Tenerife; 0840 hours; Latitude 24 degrees, 24 minutes, north; longitude 71 degrees, 106 minutes, west; course, 251 degrees southwest at 22 knots. An hour later I spotted a small passerine flying around the upper stateroom decks, eating crumbs from the passengers' breakfasts which had fallen to the deck. This was most interesting and with my Zeiss 10 x 40 binoculars it proved to be a Chiffchaff, a European songbird, presumably but not certainly a Canary Islands Chiffchaff. It made a few unsuccessful attempts to launch itself into the air to free itself of the ship, but the wind currents were too strong for the little guy, and it was hurled back to the deck. I found this bird on three successive days, sometimes looking for hours on all the decks. It continued to make unsuccessful flight attempts off the boat. I had read of ship-assisted transport of birds coming long distances to North America. The origin of alien species in the Americas is always problematic. The Cattle Egrets of Africa, postulated to have arrived in the New World on banana boats, are presumed to be in this category. We were two days out of Barbados. I was hoping this waif would make the whole crossing alive to be North America's first record of this species. It would go into the record books with an asterisk as a ship-assisted bird but nevertheless a first continental record. The last two days I searched the ship carefully but found no signs of it. It either had died on board or perished in the North Atlantic gales.

I had lots of non-birding time because the sea was empty.
I thought I would try my luck at Bingo. After all, this was a
child's game, right? Wrong. The auditorium was jammed with
hundreds of blue-haired old ladies all with three, four and
even ten bingo cards in front of them. A number was called
out and flashed on a screen, and within nanoseconds these
gals had their spots covered. The caller was wasting no time
and number after number was called in rapid succession. *Oh
my God*—I was way behind every octogenarian in the place.
They were cleaning up on me, and I was running out of cash.
This was professional Bingo played by professional gamblers.
They had earned their chops at Knights of Columbus Friday
night Bingo tournaments and made their bones at St. Maria
Goretti's South Philadelphia Saturday night charity
fundraisers. These women were not to be messed with. After
two days of not winning one time, I decided to turn my
bruised ego to the casino. This was more my style. I was a
veteran of the Las Vegas high-roller community. Not a whale
but a medium-sized shark. Craps was my game, and I had a
good system, not infallible, but I won more times than not. I
walked into the small empty casino. I guess everybody was at
the Bingo tournament or taking naps. Where is the craps
table? There was none. There was a roulette table and a few
one-armed bandits. Gambling is still gambling. Successful
gambling depends on money management and discipline. Of
course luck helps, and playing the best odds is a must. I
played large bets on red/black and four squares thereby
increasing my odds of winning. Occasionally I would place a
small wager on one number, thirty-five black. I was winning
most of the small bets, and then *wham!* I hit a thirty-to-one
single-number bet. Here was the luck. In less than an hour I
had won $5,000. I left the table with the croupier asking me,
begging me, to stay and play more. Here is where money
management and discipline comes in. I walked away from the
tables. I gave Susan a dollar chip to play one of the one-
armed bandits. It was the last machine on our way out. *Bam!*
She hit a jackpot of $1,000. I took her and the cash and

headed to the onboard jewelry shop. She picked out a sixteen-carat aquamarine and diamond ring as a souvenir from the cruise.

Two days out from Madeira the bird traffic completely disappeared. On days two, three and four I scanned the ocean surface and skies for any sign of bird or mammal life. It was devoid of any sign of life. This came as a big surprise to me. We were a small cork floating in a watery abyss. I expected to see at least a few sea birds somewhere. I had been on approximately forty pelagic seabird voyages and always came up with something, but they were usually seen over deep sea trenches with nutrients upwelling from the ocean floor, usually no more than 50-miles offshore. This was different. The Atlantic is vast, deep, and salty. It is 41.1 million square miles and takes up twenty percent of the earth's surface. The average depth of the Atlantic Ocean is about two and a half miles. It is the saltiest of the oceans. Not much can live out here in these extreme conditions. A major exception to this inhospitable desert is the Sargasso Sea, which is a moving spiraling current of water in the Atlantic filled with nutrients. It is made up of Sargassum seaweed, a major food for American and European eels and other vertebrates. Incidentally, this sea's western boundary near North Carolina is the feeding grounds for the once thought extinct endangered Bermuda Petrel. The southern boundary of this sea is Bermuda. We had not reached it yet.

On the fifth and last day of the crossing and ninety miles from Barbados I began seeing birds again. A Leach's Storm-Petrel was nighthawking low over the waves. Closer to Bridgetown I found a Brown Noddy and a few Parasitic and Pomarine Jaegers. These last two species eat lemmings in their far-north, top-of-the-world breeding grounds, but once on migration they turn to kleptoparasitism as they aggressively chase gulls and terns until they regurgitate their food for the jaegers to steal. At the time of my sightings, ornithologists had not yet worked out their migration routes.

The seabird texts at that time made no mention of their being in the Lesser Antilles in November.

We were now in the Caribbean Sea which is part of the Atlantic Ocean, occupying roughly the watery space to the south and west of the Greater and Lesser Antilles (together once called the West Indies). We disembarked in Bridgetown, Barbados' capital, and hired a taxi to take us straight away to Graeme Hall Swamp, the site of the first North American record of Grey Heron. To our dismay it was flooded following a week of torrential rains. We could not explore it. But we were not shut out. We found our first hummingbirds of the trip, strictly New World species, "Dr. Boo-boo," aka the Green-throated Carib, and the Crested Antillean Hummingbird. A wintering Northern Waterthrush popped into view, bobbing his tail rapidly and walking slowly, confidently picking up bugs from the ground. Red-necked Pigeons and the Barbados race of the Yellow Warbler were nice finds. Cattle Egrets were abundant, and a Green Heron squawked its presence before it flew into view, maybe an Ohio visitor like us. On the way back to the ship a trio of Gray Kingbirds was seen on a wire. Back at the Bridgetown Harbor I noticed there were no gulls. I wondered who the jaegers were harassing in their place.

The next morning we awoke with the island of Martinique in view. We saw more jaegers, six Parasitic and one Pomarine. There were several Royal Terns and a Herring Gull for the jaegers to mug. We hired a car for the morning and traveled up the mountainside. There were lots of hummers especially Purple-throated Caribs in the upper elevations. Carib Grackles were numerous. A good find was a Caribbean Martin at Presque Isle de Caravelle. An out of place Orangequit, a bird from Jamaica, was a real oddity. Perhaps it was an escaped cage bird. A Gray Kingbird was observed calling, "Peepeewee." Our taxi driver somehow translated this to, "If it's in your mouth you don't own it until you swallow it in your stomach," a bit of colloquial wisdom worth remembering. The Lesser Antillean Pewee, Scaly—breasted Thrasher and Streaked Saltator were all lifers.

The final day of birding was in St. Thomas, American Virgin Islands. Seventy miles from Charlotte Amalie harbor I was seeing more jaegers, five parasitic, one pomarine and a lone Audubon's Shearwater. We birded the morning and picked up a Pearly-eyed Thrasher, Antillean Mango and a single migrant Greater Yellowlegs. That afternoon we played the role of another cruise ship tourist and shopped for a few souvenirs in the town. I bought a small gold ingot on a chain when gold was for $35 an ounce and sold it years later when gold leaped to $1,700 per ounce. We arrived in Puerto Rico the next morning but had no time to bird because we had to hurriedly get to the airport to return home. One memorable scene was an elderly frail woman in dark glasses, bundled up in a wheelchair being whisked through the huge mass of disembarking people by a member of the ship's crew. Susan recognized her. She was actually in her forties, had been at the disco every night partying to the wee hours of the morning. There was not a damn thing wrong with her. Her subterfuge worked, and she was out boarding a bus to the airport before anyone else.

Our final tally was: 18 cities, 12 ports, 12 countries; 133 total species, 84 lifers.

WORLD 1,392 • ABA 743

CHAPTER THIRTEEN
Kidnapped in Brazil:
An Ornithological Expedition Goes Bad

Brazil, where hearts were entertaining June.
—From "Brazil," song by Ari Barroso (1939),
the official FIFA song of the world soccer championship, 2014

In the 1990s, National Audubon—in the guise of Audubon Ohio—barged its way into Ohio, unasked, unnecessary, and unwanted. The only good thing that came from this brief foray was my meeting Frank Gill, Ph.D., at one of the fundraisers. He was serving as chief scientist for their organization at the time. I liked him right away, super-intelligent, a wealth of bird knowledge, and open to friendly discussion. We communicated over the next couple of years, and even began planning a bird trip together to see the Siberian Tit, a chickadee in Alaska, my last regularly occurring nesting bird in America. He was a world expert on chickadees. Unfortunately our plans were interrupted by a family social event of mine and I still have not recorded that bird in America.

One morning in May, 2003, I received a call from Frank. After a few pleasantries, he invited me on a scientific expedition to the Brazilian Amazon. Under the auspices of Field Guides, a noted bird tour company, and led by Bret Whitney, the world's expert on Brazilian birds, a group of eminent ornithologists and a few of their guests interested in

South American birds were going to be traveling by boat to record vocalizations and collect bird specimens for the purpose of better understanding the evolution of birds in that region. There was one opening, and I would fill that slot as Frank's guest. Of course it was not free—the invitees would be underwriting the cost of the expedition. Wow, was I excited about this opportunity. This, for me, would be "citizen science" at its best, with the best experts in the largely unexplored vast Amazonian rain forest.

Bret Whitney was on a mission to prove that the eruption of the Andes about twenty million years ago had collected huge amounts of water from the Pacific Ocean that, when dumped on the Andes as rainwater, created four new south-to-north rivers flowing through the Amazon basin and ultimately into the Amazon River. He postulated that the evolutionary result of this massive geological formation established rivers too wide for existing resident bird populations to cross, preventing the mixing of their genes, and thereby evolving new bird species on either side of these large rivers. His methodology to prove his hypothesis would be to travel by boat, stopping every one hundred kilometers to record vocalizations and collect a bird on one side of the river, then record and collect its counterpart—currently presumed to be the same species—on the direct opposite side of the river. The vocalizations would be reduced to sonograms for computerized study. Sonograms are visual representations of a bird's vocalization, scratch marks on a computer screen. Many birders have very well-educated ears for recognizing bird species when heard in the field. Bret Whitney is one of them, maybe the best. But the human hearing apparatus has its physical limitations especially with high- and low-pitch ranges and discriminating duration between individual sounds, sometimes only nanoseconds. Sonograms allow a leisurely look at the vocal expressions of an individual bird. The collected bird skins, preserved and refrigerated on board, would be taken to the National Amazonian Research Institute in Manaus, Brazil, for DNA study. Sonograms and DNA, together with the bird's life history, anatomy, and physiology, will allow science to recognize a new species. However, there is always a degree of subjectivity involved in taxonomy. Bret uses a 97.5% degree of certainty before he calls a bird a new species. Some other researchers use less.

For his laboratory, Bret chose the Madeira River, which begins in the foothills of the Bolivian Andes and descends for eight-hundred kilometers north through the expansive Amazonian rain forest to Manaus on the Amazon River. The Madeira is the largest and widest of the south-to-north rivers and theoretically creates the best barrier to avian gene flow. It is largely unexplored ornithologically at least in modern times. The Rio Roosevelt runs parallel to it, and was the site of a most fascinating adventure involving our twenty-sixth President, Theodore Roosevelt, in the earliest part of the twentieth century. This account in *The River of Doubt* is a must read for anyone interested in American history, natural history, or just plain exciting true life adventure stories.

All the participants met in Manaus at the Manaus Tropical Hotel for an introductory briefing by Bret, and to formally meet each other. Co-leading the expedition was Mario Cohn-Haft, Curator of Birds of the National Amazonian Research Institute, a young American ornithologist living in Brazil with his Brazilian wife. He is an expert on the genus, *Hemitriccus,* flycatchers with the common name, Tody-Tyrants, a little known group of tropical insect eaters. Mario was affable and easy mannered but seemed serious about his work. Of paramount importance, he held a collecting permit from the Brazilian government, which enabled our group to legally collect wild bird specimens by shooting them with "dust shot." The pellets are about the size of millet grains fired from a .22 long rifle. This method prevents undue damage to the feathers and body of the collected specimen and has been used for centuries by ornithologists like John James Audubon. I found out later that this was much harder than it looked. There was little discussion about this tool used to study birds as everyone present was given abundant forewarning about our sacrificing birds for scientific study. The time to speak out was long gone. It was implied by your presence that you had no serious objections to this method. Collecting birds by shooting them became highly controversial as new and more "humane" scientific tools for identification became available. I don't believe Watson and Crick, the discoverers of the DNA double helix, ever saw this coming. Today, almost all serious field ornithologists have abandoned this method.

The guests assembled that evening for a cocktail mixer. It was a disparate group from mostly the East and Midwest with one thing in common—birds. Dr. Frank Gill, my host inviter, was there with his wife, Sally Conyne, both excellent birders and fun travel companions. Bill Buskirk, Ph.D., an ornithologist and former professor of Bret's at Earlham College in Indiana lent a great deal to the scientific studies and lectures on board the ship. A May/December couple from Vermont were clients of Bret's on previous tours. Dr. David B. Donsker, a pathologist from New Hampshire, was also a client of Bret's. David was a good birder, a master of trivia and had a steel-trap mind. Jack Siler, a computer whiz at the Wharton School, University of Pennsylvania, and his wife, Sue, were talented birders. Jack Siler's website, *birdingonthe.net*, was a favorite of mine and still is. At the time, it was by far the best website for birding information. He also had amassed a giant personal list of world and South American lifers. Dan and Barbara Williams from Rockford, Illinois, were part of the group. Dan, an attorney, was a former president and early organizer of the hobby group, the American Birding Association. He is also the ABA's legal counsel. Barbara and Sally Conyne are sisters. Dan and Frank are brothers-in-law. The Williamses were also avid birders and fun to be with. Larry Hood, a former Illinois Fish and Wildlife officer, was a blast to travel with. He had loads of hilarious and interesting stories about birds, his job, and life in general that he told in a back-woodsy accent. His easy "good old boy" manner belied a very high level of sophistication and expertise in birding. I knew him from a previous bird tour in Northeast Brazil with Bret a year earlier. Rounding out the group was an octogenarian couple, Al and Nancy Boggess. They turned out to be the most interesting and accomplished people, and in one way, the most important members of the group. Nancy loved birding and Al, a non-birder, loved Nancy.

The next morning we flew to Porto Velho (Clear Water) and boarded the *Harpy Eagle*, our floating hotel for the next seventeen days. Everyone was upbeat, and there was a high level of expectancy in the air. I was especially ebullient about my prospects. We were going to *terra incognita* with the "Captain Kirk" of the bird world, taking us to "boldly go where no man had gone before." The chance of discovering new species and seeing mega-rarities was a birder's dream.

We were with the number one discoverer of new species in the last decade. Bret Whitney was famous for discovering new species by hearing them first. He had recorded one new species a year, every year from 1990 to 2003. There were fifty-seven new species described during that time period in the whole world, and Bret contributed thirteen of those. I had seen Bret in action a couple of years earlier when I joined his tour in Northeast Brazil. Our co-leader, and Bret's partner in the Field Guide bird tour company, was John Rowlett, no lightweight himself when it came to recognizing calls emanating from the rainforest; however, John would be the first to admit he was not in Bret's class.

I was so impressed with Bret's skills that I wrote a limerick in his honor when we were in Jequie, a locality at which he had previously discovered a new bird:

There once was a birder in Jequie
Who recorded a bird he had seen
His fame was supported
When he reported
A spinetail the world calls whitney
The end to this story is set
But a trick of fate could have upset
If Bret had stayed and sent his aide
This spinetail would now be rowlett

He had collected so much field material that he could never sort it all out in his lifetime. He was passionate and driven in his pursuit of knowledge. For Bret, there was no finish line! I felt I was on the Apollo 11 space shuttle headed for the first walk on the moon.

Porto Velho was the capital of the Brazilian state of Rondonia, the southernmost state of the country bordering Bolivia on its southern edge. It was named after Candido Rondon, famous in Brazil as a champion of Indian rights, cartographer, engineer, and holding the highest military rank that can be achieved in Brazil, that of Marshal. He is known to American historians as the man who saved the Madeira River Roosevelt expedition from ruin and thereby certainly saved Teddy Roosevelt's life.

The *Harpy Eagle* was a sixty-foot, seaworthy clipper with three decks and all modern conveniences. There were three outboard motor boats available for land excursions. The cabins were spacious with private baths and comfortable bunk beds. The galley was ably staffed with cook, Areta, preparing delicious native dishes. The Madeira River is smooth and swift, and no one suffered motion sickness. The captain, Leo, and first mate, Antonio, were first-class sailors and knew their business. The order of the day was stopping at pre-selected spots every one hundred kilometers or so, boarding the outboards after a full breakfast and exploring the area looking and listening for bird species that Bret had designated for study. After the morning exploration, we returned to the *Harpy* and ate lunch. A siesta followed in the heat of the day. We returned to the outboards for an afternoon of further exploration, returning to the boat by 6 p.m. for showers and cocktail hour. Caipirinhas, the national cocktail of Brazil, a delicious alcoholic beverage made from Cachaça, fruit, and sugar, flowed freely. The Caipirinhas packed a wallop with its cachaça at thirty-eight percent to forty-eight percent alcohol by volume, and as one might expect the conversations were loud and lively. Dinners were always delicious, nutritious, and varied. Bird lists were done after dinner with everyone chiming in with their sightings. The list was followed by a lecture by Bret or Mario on subjects pertinent to the day's activities. These talks were extremely informative, covering history (both general Brazilian and ornithological), bio-geography, taxonomy, and the like. There was always a question and answer period. One evening Mario gave a mock defense of his Ph.D. dissertation on speciation of Hemitriccus Flycatchers, expertly fielding the questions fired at him from the ornithologists in the crowd. He received a standing ovation for his brilliant presentation. I kept a daily journal of these lectures, which I referred to often in writing this chapter.

As fortune would have it, on the very first day I spied a hummingbird sky-high in the canopy along the Rio Caracol, a tributary of the Madeira. It did not look like any bird I had seen in the field guide, so I called Bret and Mario to identify it, but they did not hear me. No one else seemed interested as I yelled "hummer" repeatedly. Finally Mario came to me for a look at what I was so excited about. He put his binoculars on the hummingbird, but no look of recognition came across his face.

He said, "I'll have to collect this bird. It could be a first record for Rondonia or even Brazil."

At first, the bird was too high for an accurate shot. As it came closer, Mario fired the rifle and brought the bird down to the ground. It fell somewhere in a plot of thick weeds, and we spent the next half hour treading lightly and meticulously separating grass stems to look for this tiny creature. Both Bret and Mario examined the bird, and no identification was forthcoming because neither of these field-experienced ornithologists had ever seen one like it before.

Bret's prodigious memory bank finally produced the following conjecture: "It might be a Bolivian thornbill species known only by two specimens collected by Hellmayr in the early 1880s. It might be a first Brazilian record. More research has to done."

The specimen was duly tagged with date, locality, habitat, and my name and Mario's appended to it.

Every day brought new birds and new surprises; however, no more birds were collected until the sixth day when a putative Chestnut-tailed Antbird, *Myrmeciza [hemimelaena] sp. nov.*, was recruited on the east bank of the Madeira in Amazonas state. Three days later another similar bird was heard and seen on the north bank of the tributary, Rio Mani. After numerous failed attempts to collect this later bird, Mario finally gave up.

The group of sixteen was getting along surprisingly well in the beginning, but it wasn't long until the friendly veneer of a couple of folks wore away and their true natures were displayed. This is to be expected on group tours. Some people cannot adapt to situations outside the comfort of their usual everyday surroundings. They get surly, critical, grumpy, whiny, and taciturn. Their brains become static, and they stop processing their emotions and external experiences in their normal way. They are uncomfortable in their new surroundings with new people and a new set of rules to follow. Toward the end of the first week, I could tell who the good birders were and who the weak and non-birders were, who had good energy and who was giving a bad vibe. The Vermont couple seemed a little off kilter, but I did not pay any attention to them. The wife looked and talked like an aging hippy, a good-looking woman thirty years ago. The whole time I was there, I only had one brief conversation with the husband. He was not in good health and did not come on every walk, choosing to sleep a lot instead.

During one search, Bret stopped in a clearing facing the forest. He heard something different that needed investigation. Our large group had stopped on the narrow trail, single file. I did not have a view of Bret because he was preparing his recording equipment to capture the call if the bird called again. I quietly took three steps forward to get a better view. About the time of the second step, I felt someone gripping my arm trying to yank me back. No notice, no warning. I wrenched my arm free and took the third step only to feel a hand on me again, pulling me back. I tore my arm loose and said to Mrs. Vermont in a stern tone, with a serious look and pointing my index finger at her face, "Never do that again." I had been on many a bird tour and experienced lots of crazy people, but this was a first. Back in West Philly this would have earned the aggressor a slug in the mouth. The bird never showed itself, and we headed back to the boat. On the way back, she turned to me and said she would like a word. "Okay, fine. What do you have to say?" She said she apologized for "invading my space," and then looked at me expectantly. I said I accepted her apology and began to catch up to the group. I was willing to forget the whole thing.

She then asked, like we were two kids not getting along in the sandbox, "Aren't you going to apologize, too?"

"For what?"

"For shouting at me."

"I didn't shout at you, and I am not going to apologize. I was the victim here. You were the aggressor. Let's leave it at that."

She then denied she had grabbed me and recounted her fabricated version of what had transpired. Of course, she was the angel, and I was the bully. Strangely it was beginning to sound like a husband-wife spat. I ended it all by turning away and catching up to the others. Well, it was not over. Back on the boat, Mario asked to have a word with me, and I knew it was about the incident. I explained what had happened, and he asked me to apologize anyway to keep harmony on the boat. I thought about it for a while, and decided I was in a no-win situation unless I offered her an apology. I had to take the higher ground. If not, I would "pay hell" the rest of the trip, be branded a bully, probably get into an altercation with her elderly husband as he came to defend her honor, and wind up having a miserable time. I waited until she was in the company of a few others and made my public apology. I avoided her like the plague after that.

There must have been a full moon that night because disorder ruled. The next morning we were headed for the town of Manicoré and a trip into the forest to see Kawall's Parrot. This large Amazon parrot was rediscovered in 1996 after a hundred year's absence. It can be found only in Brazil. Our transportation was late, and we did not get to Manicoré until about 8 a.m. That is a somewhat late start for birding. Most birds have finished their early morning feeding, the dawn chorus is over, and the heat of the rising sun comes early in the tropics. A school bus took us deep into the forest on a well-trafficked road. I was wondering who would be using this road out in the middle of nowhere. I would soon find out. The bus stopped, and we all got off following Bret down a forest trail for about a half hour. He was familiar with this area having scouted it the year before. And sure enough we could soon hear a ruckus made by these large parrots as twenty-to twenty-five Kawall's came into view, feeding, flying freely from fruit tree to fruit tree, and paying no attention to us at all. We watched them go through their antics for about fifteen minutes and then as a group fly away. Satisfied with seeing our target species, we headed back to the bus to drive to another area for more birding. Something unexpected was awaiting us at our bus, two men, one in the uniform of a FUNAI official (Bureau of Indian Affairs) and the other an Indian, thirty-ish, in jeans, shirt, and a pistol in his waistband. Most of his left ear was glaringly missing, like it had been chewed off. Neither was smiling. Bret came forward to introduce himself. No pleasantries were exchanged. This struck me as indicating trouble because Brazilians are extremely polite. Bret speaks Brazilian Portuguese like a native, and I could see a heated discussion underway. There was no smiling or laughter. Body language was very tense. The Indian affairs guy would talk, and then Bret would talk. The Indian would talk, and then Bret would talk. The discussion went on for an hour as we stood in the blazing noonday equatorial sun. Bret finally came to our group to explain what was going on. The men said we were trespassing, and they were going to confiscate all of our equipment—binoculars, spotting scopes, recorders, cameras, and our vehicle. They claimed their land was a duly constituted Indigenous Territory established legally by the Brazilian government as their homeland. They were fining us two thousand Reais apiece, about $900, and we could leave upon payment. If we didn't pay what they demanded, we would be held in the Indian village and our equipment would be sent up river to Manaus until we coughed up the money. Bret actually laughed in their faces at this outrageous demand. He can speak in the vernacular and knows all the nuances of the language. He knew this was sheer banditry, extortion, and kidnapping. He turned to our group to explain what was happening. We asked Bret to continue to negotiate. The Indian, Chief of the Munduruk tribe as it turned out, was attempting to pull off a heist, and the Indian Affairs guy was in on it. The chief told us to get back into the bus, and he took us to his village. We sat on the ground and rocks while Bret continued negotiations. Bret argued that they were not recognized as an Indigenous Territory by the Brazilian government because he had checked before he came, and therefore, the trespassing charge was bogus. They were actually calling it a more serious charge of "invasion of the homeland." He continued his defense arguing that there were no fences marking their boundaries, no trespassing signs, and no way for a tourist to know they were out of bounds. We were tourists. We were not there to disturb their forest or collect their wildlife, only to observe nature. He discovered through this discussion that a primate new to science, the dwarf marmoset, had been discovered on their lands a few years ago. Scandinavian scientists came in and collected some specimens without Indian permission. They were still sulking from this and promised to heap retribution on the next interlopers. Part of this extortion was linked to this event as a revenge factor. Nevertheless, Bret protested, we were innocent of all and any wrongdoing. To paraphrase Dr. John, "I was in the right place but at the wrong time." As settlement for any perceived harm done Bret offered to pay them $30 per person. This was twice the amount of the going rate he would pay to enter any legal Indigenous Territory. The chief then returned the laugh in Bret's face. By this time, we were surrounded by the chief's henchmen, menacing us with their weapons—machetes, a handgun, a shotgun, and bows and arrows. The chief's woman, whom we dubbed the "princess," was urging him on to get the money from "the rich Americans." She was constantly in his ear to rob us of our money.

Recognizing that their bullying tactics were not working, the Indian Affairs official put Bret in his car and drove him to the Bureau's office in Manicoré. Bret kept his cool and told us he would be back soon. This whole time Mario was conspicuously absent. He remained silent and had slinked out of sight. He did not lift one finger or utter one word to assist Bret or our group. We sat huddled in the hot sun for five hours with no comforts, food or water. After a couple of hours two of our women got up and walked toward the bush to relieve themselves. The guards jumped up to intercept them, fearing an escape attempt. Their husbands jumped up to their rescue. Guns were drawn until we made it known they only wanted to urinate. This was a powder keg ready to explode with fatal consequences. The guards put their guns away, and the husbands escorted their wives behind the trees, a catastrophe averted. Word was spreading to the nearby town that the Munduruk were holding a group of Americans hostage. A newsman from the local paper in Manicoré showed up on his motorbike to the Indian village. He asked us what was going on, and we told him in our best "Portuspanglish" that we were being held against our will.

Not hiding his revulsion at what he was witnessing, he shouted to the guards, "What are you doing? These are tourists. Let them go!"

He began to record us for the evening news. About this time, Bret arrived back, wan and weary, but unharmed. He flashed us a tired but reassuring smile. We listened raptly and hopefully as our leader recounted the details of his captivity. He said they had taken him to their office, sat him under bright hot lights, something they must have seen in an old American B-movie, and tried to sweat him out. They clumsily faked a call to the Bureau's office in Manaus explaining the situation and their two thousand Reais solution to a non-existent official on the other end of the fake phone call. They told Bret that their bosses were all for their plan. Bret held firm. They threatened to burn down our boat. Bret didn't budge. None of this was working for the kidnappers. Their strategy was weak and was failing. Bret was holding up magnificently, and then he delivered a master stroke, a spark of genius, a game changer. He counter-attacked and mounted his offensive. He singled out the crooked government official and told him we had two eighty-year-olds in our group. They both had severe heart problems. The hot sun, lack of food, water, medicine, and all the stress could kill them. If that happened, the official and the chief would be charged with murder! Brazil still had the death penalty. The official paled. The chief wavered. The "princess" fell silent. All of a sudden, their little caper had dire consequences for them. They were not in this game for a murder charge. They immediately settled for the $30 and drove Bret back to the village. The battle of wills was over, Bret, the clear victor. The newsman wanted a statement, and Bret said something simple and nonsensical like a college football coach addressing the media after a win. The chief handed Bret a T-shirt touting tourism in the area, a ridiculous gesture after this nightmarish event. If we were not so weary from the whole anxiety-filled day, we would have died laughing at this buffoonery. We loaded back onto the bus and high-tailed it back to Manicoré where the local police were waiting.

They asked us if we wanted to press charges for kidnapping, and we replied, "No."

We just wanted to get back to our boat, have supper, and get a good night's sleep. The police were last seen racing in the direction of the Indian village to get their share. This birding is a dangerous hobby.

Who were the Boggesses, the octogenarians whom Bret successfully used as a subterfuge to spring us from our hostage predicament? Al and Nancy were both Ph.D. astrophysicists of world renown in the field of cosmology. Al looked like Ronald Reagan, a handsome man with dark brown, neatly combed hair, parted to one side, showing not a single gray strand. Before retirement he worked for NASA as manager of the famed Hubble Project. Al told me that following the Hubble flight, the first photographs from outer space were slightly blurred. In his mind this was a major failure, a potential loss of billions of dollars to the United States and a disgrace to our space program. He figured that the lens was not manufactured precisely to NASA's original specifications. He and Nancy had a plan to fix it. A second smaller lens would be manufactured that would make the necessary corrections when affixed to the original lens. The Pentagon, on the other hand wanted a complete re-do of the lens. Nancy and Al argued at length for their plan, which would cost the country far less money and could be done more quickly. The Pentagon finally agreed. NASA sent out the RFPs and, taking no chances this time, selected not one, but three different companies to make the new lens. NASA was right to be cautious the second time around. As it turned out, one manufacturer never finished, a second manufacturer ground a lens to the wrong specifications, but the third company produced a quality lens. A manned space flight fixed the problem, and Hubble began sending clear sharp images of deep outer space back home.

Nancy, a diminutive sprite, was also in her early eighties. She was accorded singular praise from the greatest theoretical physicist of our time, Stephen Hawking, for having made the most important astrophysical discovery of the twentieth century. What was this most extraordinary discovery? Working for NASA, her team of scientists discovered that the static, such as seen on the early TV screens, was in fact electromagnetic waves coming from outer space. She saw that they were composed of different wavelengths of the light spectrum, each traveling at different speeds, but over time the waves were increasing speed. This was the first substantial evidence that the universe was expanding and not static as once believed. Her measurements of background radiation from the "Big Bang" confirmed theories of the origin of the universe.

Once back on the *Harpy,* Bret asked that we all assemble in the dining room. He introduced a friend of his who lived in Manicoré and had heard about our misadventure. Through Bret's translation, he said we bore witness to what the locals live with every day—murderous and thieving Munduruks. His father and his father's best friend, both rubber tappers, were attacked by men of this tribe, and his father's best friend was killed by the Munduruks. His father narrowly escaped death himself. That night, before turning in, I wrote a full account of the day's experience in my journal while it was fresh in my mind.

The remaining days were very exciting in terms of finding new birds; however, the excitement seemed less palpable than it deserved because of our recent harrowing experience. Occasionally a canoe would pull up to our boat and sell Areta fresh fish for our dinner. The word somehow got around that I was a physician despite my reticence to tell the group or the crew. One evening the captain came to me in a weakened state with a five-day resistant form of dysentery. Cipro® knocked it out in twenty-four hours. After that success, I could have opened an office there. The whole crew came to see me with one malady or another, all minor. The next day the captain brought me an elderly man who had paddled quite a distance to our boat from a nearby village. He was complaining of chest pain. I had to take this seriously because of his age and his efforts to reach me. I took him to my cabin with the captain as translator. I had no tools of my trade with which to work and only a meager supply of self-meds. I felt like a physician from the Dark Ages. I felt his head, no fever; looked into his mouth and nose with a flashlight, negative; palpated his neck, negative; listened to his chest with ear to rib cage, negative; heart rate regular, no murmurs; lungs clear; pulse strong. He did show some expansion of his rib cage often seen in chronic obstructive lung disease. I palpated his abdomen and checked his extremities, both negative. The guy was in better health than I was. I didn't exactly know what was wrong with him but esophagitis/gastritis was high on my list. I gave him my whole personal supply of antacids and some daily vitamins and sent him on his way amidst his copious *obregados*. I was praying I didn't miss a heart attack.

Something was bothering me about Mario's not speaking out during the kidnapping. After all, he was a close friend of Bret's, he spoke Portuguese like a native, and he was the co-leader of our expedition. Toward the end of the trip, I took Mario aside and asked him why. He replied that he tried to blend in and not make trouble because he was afraid to lose his job at the Institute since he was not a Brazilian citizen. Positions like his were almost impossible to get in Brazil for aliens. If he were fired, he would be deported. Self-survival is a basic instinct.

We continued to follow our plan of stopping every one hundred kilometers to record and collect. Final count of our total specimens collected for the seventeen days tallied a paltry (mercifully) eighteen individual birds. We did manage a lot more recordings. Compared to the collectors of the past in this area (Klages, more than 23,000 specimens from 1918 to 1923, all in the Carnegie Museum; Emily Snethelage, 1929,

119 specimens in twenty days; and the grand champions, the Olallas brothers, exceeding 30,000 specimens in the 1930s), ours was a puny effort.

The following are bird species we saw that need more taxonomic investigation:
• Two forms of Least Nighthawk with different calls, the nominate subspecies *pusillus* and another undescribed form found near Borba
• Two forms of Band-tailed Nighthawk with different calls, a "chuck cherwonker" and a "triller"
• Thornbill Hummingbird collected the first day
• Bar-breasted Piculet, two forms, one heard on the west bank of Rio Aripuana and another form found in *terre firma* forest at Borba, the type locality.
• Chestnut-winged Foliage-gleaner, seen at Porto Velho Parke Natural, according to Peters could be a new species
• Rufous-rumped Foliage-gleaner, seen at Porto Velho Parke Natural
• Plain Brown Woodcreeper could be split into six species
• Long-tailed Woodcreeper south of the Amazon could be split from species north of the Amazon
• Wedge-billed Woodcreeper will be split into five species
• Straight-billed Woodcreeper on the W. Madeira will be split
• Curve-billed Scythebill on the W. Madeira
• Tupana Scythebill, *Campylorhamphus gyldenstolpei*, 2013
• Tapajos Scythebill, *Campylorhamphus cardosi*, 2013
• Castelnau's Antshrike"birds" seen on blackwater island at Parana Da Eva near Manaus
• White-shouldered Antshrike, *punctuliger ssp.*
• Saturnine/Dusky-throated Antshrike seen on W. Madeira
• Sclater's Antwren, fast song type
• Long-winged Antwren, ssp. *transitiva* may not be a good subspecies
• Gray Antwren expected on the W. Madeira but seen on the E. Madeira

• *Herpsilochmus sp. nov.* 1 from the W. Madeira and *Herpsilochmus sp. nov.* 2 collected on the E. Madeira
• Warbling-Antbird (4), Peruvian, Bolivian, E. Madeira and Spix's types
• Black-faced Antbirds collected W. and E. Madeira
• Spot-winged Antbird, *ssp. rufifacies*, a split?
• Chestnut-tailed Antbird collected E. Madeira
• Spot-backed Antbird collected W. Madeira
• Scale-backed Antbirds, W. and E. Madeira
• Rusty-belted Tapaculo heard on the E. Madeira
• Slender-footed Tyrannulet, seen and heard on W. Madeira, different song than E. Madeira
• Snethelage's Tody-Tyrant, 4 types by song, type 1, *ssp. pallens* and type 2, collected W. upper Madeira. Types 3 or 4, *ssp. snethelage?*
• White-eyed Tody-Tyrant, W. Madeira
• New undescribed Tody-Tyrant collected the first day in Rondonia
• New undescribed (2) Tody-Tyrants seen and recorded Rio Marmelos, tributary of E. Madeira
• Yellow-margined Flycatcher, seen W. Madeira, will be new species
• Yellow-breasted Flycatcher, *ssp. subsimilis* or *ssp. nov. borbae?*
• Greater Schiffornis, *Varzea* forms seen and heard multiple times

The following are the rarities we saw:
• Dark form Hook-billed Kite
• Cryptic Forest-Falcon, first described by Bret as a new species 2002
• Buckley's Forest-Falcon initially found by me
• Madeira Parakeet, Madeira subspecies of Painted Parakeet
• Bald Parrot, first record for the Western Madeira, newly described 2002 and endemic to Brazil
• Sick's Swift
• 200+! displaying Sand-colored Nighthawks on a sandbar

- Fiery-billed Awlbill
- Black-spotted Bare-eye at an ant swarm
- Pale-faced Antbird, "Skutch's Antbird," a newly described species, 2002, the rarest find of the expedition. Prior to this sighting only five birders had seen this species. The bird was quietly standing in the open allowing a long examination by our group.
- Sharp-tailed Grass-Tyrant, first Amazonian record, collected
- White-winged Becard, black color form
- Guianan Flycatcher heard. First record for Rondonia. Second record this far south
- White-shouldered Tanager, a pair, rare south of the Amazon River

The following is a list of the collected species:
- Least Nighthawk
- Thornbill sp.
- Cinereous-breasted Spinetail
- Curve-billed Scythebill
- *Herpsilochmus sp.*, (1) E. Madeira and (1) W. Madeira
- Rusty-backed Antwren
- Chestnut-tailed? Antbird
- Spot-backed? Antbird
- Snethelage's Tody Tyrant type 1
- Snethelage's Tody-Tyrant type 2
- White-eyed Tody-Tyrant
- Tody-Tyrant sp. nov.
- Spotted Tody-Flycatcher
- Euler's Flycatcher
- Sharp-tailed Grass-Tyrant
- Tooth-billed Wren
- Scaly-breasted Wren

The following are the species discovered on our expedition, which led directly or contributed indirectly to their description as a new species to science with the dates of publication:

• Western Puffbird, *Nystalus obamai*, from Striolated Puffbird, Whitney et al., 2013

• Predicted Antwren, *Herpsilochmus praedictus, from Herpsilochmus sp nov.* 1, Cohn-Haft et al., 2013

• Aripuana Antwren, *Herpsilochmus stotzi*, from *Herpsilochmus sp. nov.* 2, Whitney and Cohn-Haft et al., 2013

• Spix's Warbling-Antbird from Warbling-Antbird 1, *Hypocnemis cantator*

• Manicoré Warbling-Antbird, *Hypocnemis rondoni* from *Hypocnemis [cantator] sp. nov.* 2, Whitney and Cohn-Haft et al., 2013

• Chico's Tyrannulet, *Zimmerius chicomendesi*, 2012

• Sucunduri Flycatcher, *Tolmomyias sucunduri*, 2013

• Inambari Woodcreeper, *Lepidocolaptes fatimalimae*, 2013

• Spot-winged Antshrike subspecies, *perusiana*, is newly described, 2013.

WORLD 5,484 • ABA 767

CHAPTER FOURTEEN
Health Power Goes Public: My Largest Business Deal

*Sweat equity is the most valuable equity there is. Know your business
and industry better than anyone else in the world.
Love what you do or don't do it.*
—Mark Cuban

By 1993, Health Power (HP) and the MEDCenters were
stable and profitable. Our earlier regulatory issues were
behind us. My next step was to take HP to a higher level, to
more cities with more providers using our successful
managed care model. A few years earlier, I believed I had an
opportunity to expand our company to large cities like
Chicago and Detroit. A former friend and colleague of mine
had met the Rev. Jessie Jackson. Rev. Jackson was open to
speaking to me about a position with HP to help spur this
development. Of course I knew who he was. As a guest of
the Ohio delegation, I had heard him speak at the 1984
Democratic National Convention in San Francisco. I had
witnessed first hand his powerful and persuasive style of
speaking. There were many cities that had large Medicaid
populations who were being medically under-served in the
old expensive fee-for-service system. Rev. Jackson had entrée
to all their community leaders, religious and government. Our
managed care network model would bring affordable and
quality care to these millions of patients. In "corporate
speak," it was a "big idea."

Rev. Jackson with Jessie Jr., Dr. Elliott Feldman, a. HP board member, Dr. Ben Cohen (who was introducing Rev. Jackson) and I met at the Philadelphia Four Seasons Hotel. We had a productive meeting, businesslike and friendly. I outlined what I thought Rev. Jackson, as a vice president employed by HP, could do for us. He was amenable to my suggestions, and we agreed to memorialize our understanding in a formal contract that our attorneys would draw up for his signature. Cohen and his partner would get a finder's fee for their introduction. The employment contract was prepared by the law firm of Baker and Hostetler and sent to Jackson. I thought that HP, with this new association, was going to write a new chapter in the annals of American health care. This relationship was not to happen. Unbeknown to Jackson, just before he signed, I received a call from Cohen. He straight out told me that he would prevent the signing unless he and his boss, a developer in Columbus, would get fifty percent of the HP stock. I was shocked and embarrassed for Cohen, now an ex-friend, for his unbridled greed, lack of business sophistication, and failure to know my character and the extent of my resolve. Without hesitation I refused his offer and countered with a small amount of stock, less than any of our investors had purchased. What Cohen stupidly failed to realize was the advanced degree of development of HP with its HMO licenses, Certificate of Authority to do business in fifteen counties, solid corporate structure, hundreds of contracts in place with its health care providers and a strong financial statement with a steady stream of profits. These took years of hard work and millions of dollars to develop. I wasn't about to give him half of this prize for the signature of Jesse Jackson and an uncertain outcome of what he might bring. Cohen told me no deal, and we never talked about it again. I closed the conversation by telling him that we would compare financial statements in ten years and see who had done better. When I look back, I know I did the right thing because later Jackson engendered negative press and lost much of his moral authority.

I needed millions to take HP to the next level. In a few years our computer system had become obsolete. I had to replace it. We also needed to expand our program in Ohio. Cleveland, with its unmanaged 250,000 Medicaid recipients, was waiting for us, as well as Youngstown and Akron. I planned to make acquisitions of smaller managed care companies. Most importantly, HP needed a deep reserve to buffer us against the political vagaries of the ever-changing Ohio administrators and lawmakers as they cycled through the state capital from election to election. These folks were knee-jerk reactors to any negative press or pressure from the fee-for-service camp. They could and did change, in the past, the financial requirements and rules for managed care companies without notice. I had raised $4 million to start HP. I would need a lot more than that to move HP forward. How and where would I get that much money?

My close friend, Fred Mayerson of Cincinnati, had taken the Chi Chi's restaurant chain from a single location to a nationwide chain in a couple of years. He did it by selling a piece of the company to the public and using the proceeds to expand. This was an appealing idea, and I studied his and other models. He used a banking consultant from Medina, Ohio, J. Jeffrey Brausch, to help him take his company public. Jeff had a long and reputable history of finding financing for companies with mergers, acquisitions, and "going public." I called him, introduced myself as a friend of Fred's, and told him I was interested in exploring the possibility of taking HP public. We talked in general terms about health care and the managed care industry. We talked specifically about HP, its history, plans for the future, finances, administration, marketing, and successes in Ohio. At the end of our conversation he said he would come to Columbus to take a look at everything and give me his opinion as to whether HP was a candidate for a public offering. I was sure that we were, but I wanted an expert's opinion.

Jeff came down the next week and spent the better part of the week looking at everything and everyone with an "electron microscope." He talked to regulators, doctors, employees, vendors, and our competition. He pored over the financial records. After his intensive scrutiny, he gave me his opinion. Yes, HP was a good candidate for a public offering. For year end 1993 we were heading for $40 million in revenues with ten percent taken to the bottom line in profit. We were in good standing with our regulators, network of physicians, hospitals, and our patients. We had no debt. We had $4 million in liquid reserves. He estimated that we could sell twenty percent of our 4 million shares outstanding for $9 to $10 a share depending on market conditions, and we were eligible to be listed on NASDAQ (National Association Dealers Automated Quotations), the largest of the American stock exchanges.

There were plenty of negatives in going public. We would add two more regulators to our already weighty list, the SEC and the Ohio Division of Securities. We needed recent audited statements from the previous two years with clean opinions. Timely quarterly and yearly reporting to the regulators would carry a lot more liability for the officers and directors. In fact, the Sarbanes-Oxley law, enacted several years later, carried stiff criminal penalties for what were deemed fraudulent statements. We would increase our liability by the number of new shareholders the sale would create. Minority shareholders had rights. All of our reports and our personal lives would be inspected under a bright light by investors, regulators, competitors, employees, and the press.

The positives were few but compelling. We would gain the cash we needed to grow and protect our company. All of our early investors' stock would be freely tradable on NASDAQ after a six-month lock-up period. They would then realize a return on their investment of anywhere from two hundred to three thousand percent, depending on the price at which they had bought their original stock. My 1.3 million shares would be worth around $13 million a return of 130 to 1 on my investment. The SEC rules for buying and selling were different for the officers and directors but not onerous. The positives greatly outweighed the negatives, and I gave the green light to go to the next step.

Our next step was to prepare the financial statements and legal requirements for the offering. Jeff made inquiries to six name-brand banking firms on Wall Street to see if any would be interested in meeting with us and hearing our story. All said yes and appointments were set up for early fall. We were to make presentations to the most prestigious underwriters in America like Merrill Lynch, Morgan Stanley, and J.P. Morgan to name a few. We were to meet these company's decision makers when it came to IPOs (Initial Public Offerings). We began preparing our script. Jeff would make the introductions and hand it off to me. He knew all of these Vice Presidents personally and had worked with them in the past on various deals. He had earned their trust. I would tell our history. And, as founder, I would explain my vision for our future. Our president, Mr. Arnold, would talk the numbers. I was excited about our prospects as were all of our officers and directors. Outside of these people, we were not talking about it. The old adage, "Loose lips sink ships," held here.

Close to our meeting dates we did a dry run with Jeff on the expected format of the meetings, including possible questions and answers. I could tell the history without a hitch because I had lived every moment for the past ten years. I could not curb my enthusiasm and passion for HP. I knew the technical lingo, and I had a clear vision of HP's future. I knew all of our numbers from day one in 1984. I was one of the few doctors around who could read a balance sheet and a P&L statement and knew what every line meant. Tom, who had been with me for three years, also knew the numbers inside out. I was feeling very confident and could not wait to hit the "Big Apple" and tell our story. In preparation for our meetings, I got a fresh haircut and shaved my moustache, which I had worn since Nam.

The day finally arrived when we boarded our flight to New York City. I was dressed in a conservative dark suit, pinstriped tie, white pima cotton buttoned-down shirt, black above-the-knee hose, and black highly polished Ferragamo wing-tip shoes. I called this my banker's uniform. We stayed at an old but still-distinguished mid-town hotel. I was having trouble sleeping from excitement, and it didn't help that my room was next to the elevator shaft. It was one big wind tunnel, and I was afraid I would not be fresh for our first appointment at 8 a.m. I called down to the desk to have my room changed. After some piddling resistance, the desk clerk finally moved me, and I slept well the rest of the night. Jeff, Tom, and I enjoyed a hot breakfast in the morning. We were ready for game time.

Our first meeting would set the tone for the next two days. All of these banking houses had sumptuous entry ways with comfortable leather-bound chairs in their waiting rooms, expensive art on their walls, private dining rooms for their officers, and well-appointed large corner offices with great views of Manhattan for their VPs. The first meeting was with Piper Jaffrey. I was surprised to see a thirty-five-ish VP sitting behind the desk. He knew Jeff and welcomed us warmly to his kingdom. After some preliminary chit-chat, we settled into our script, and some pertinent questions followed. I thought it went great—with friendly reception, solid presentation with no glitches, followed by meaningful dialogue. They obviously wanted to make a good impression, as did we. The following meetings went pretty much the same way. All of the VPs were young. The IPO world was being run by young men my son's age. They were all knowledgeable about the health care industry. They would all get back to us.

For the rest of the week we all waited with optimism. Finally, Jeff called me. He said they all loved our story and future prospects, but… The big "but" was we were too small for them. It would take just as much time and energy for them to take a larger company to the market place as it would to take a small company like HP. The profits for them in a larger deal would be proportionately higher, but... This second "but" was much more encouraging. They all thought we could go public and urged us to take our company to a smaller banking house, a regional house, or a boutique firm who did these smaller deals all the time. To the large banking houses, we were not even a "mini." We were a "micro." Jeff recommended a regional firm called Roney & Company.

The next week Jeff, Tom, and I found ourselves sitting in front of Bill Roney, managing partner of Roney & Company, an old and honored Midwestern regional banking firm located in the heart of Detroit, Michigan. He liked our story and our future prospects. He relied heavily on Jeff's due diligence investigation of HP and his glowing recommendation. There were two more hurdles before Roney would accept us as a client: a grilling session with Roney's health care expert and Roney board approval. I sensed that Roney was eagerly looking for new products to sell. We had all the characteristics of a great fit for them: the right size with a ten-million-dollar offering, a local company in their own regional backyard, and a growing revenue top line with bottom profit line. Besides we were not a start-up, but rather, beginning our tenth year in business, a proven winner.

Another meeting was set with Roney, me, Tom, Roney's health care expert, and Dan French, Roney's man to negotiate the final deal between HP and Roney. There were loads of agreements and fees to be ironed out if the deal were to go forward. Before the meeting, which Jeff would not attend, Jeff sat with me to have a private conversation. He told me this was basically the last hurdle because the Roney board would rubber stamp Bill Roney's decision. The expert would try to appear smarter than me and attempt to fluster me, all a test of my knowledge of the industry and aplomb under fire. Jeff said, "Be the expert in the room!" I was extremely confident of my expertise in health care systems, and nobody understood managed care better than me. *Let the games begin!*

The chess game began with formal introductions and the exchanging of business cards—a ritual important in the business world. I began the meeting with an explanation of the state of the Medicaid market in Ohio, emphasizing HP's growth and complete dominant penetration into that market. For the next twenty minutes I talked about how we had overcome various obstacles, our financial strength, and my vision for HP's future. I expected a barrage of counter-arguments to my view of health care in the future. Instead, their expert only made a few statements regarding his vision of the industry, which was completely in line with my own. I did politely correct one or two of his facts to show who was *the* expert in the room, to which he gave no rebuttal.

We were heading into mid-December, 1993, and we had not heard from the Roney board on their decision. Susan, Eric (my step-son) and I had a birding trip planned to Madagascar, off the east coast of Africa in the Indian Ocean, and the home of some of the strangest birds in the world. We had to leave before we heard their decision. I asked Tom to fax me their decision in one word, "Yes'" or "No." The second day after we'd arrived in Madagascar, I received the fax. I scanned quickly down the paper and saw that big fat "Yes." *Hooray!* That was it, just as I was hoping. The airline had lost my luggage *again*, but the fax machine had worked. The bird tour went splendidly and I couldn't wait to get home to start preparing for the "Road Show." This would be the opportunity to tell all the Roney stockbrokers about my company.

January, 1994, was spent finishing all of our documents for filing with the SEC and the other regulatory agencies. I went over every word of our prospectus before I signed off on it. The prospectus is a straight-forward, no-puff piece. It has to be truthful and verifiable. All the potential liabilities to investing in our company must be listed in the early pages, and some even require multiple listings and bold print. February brought me face-to-face with Dan French, Roney's best negotiator. His reputation preceded him—very polished with a little bit of "street kid" in him. We had to agree on the fee structure for Roney and the opening price at which our stock would be sold. Dan was pushing me for $9 to $10 a share, and I was pushing him back for $12. I was also asking that a number of early investors, including a few charities to whom I had earlier gifted stock, could sell their shares along with HP's on the opening day. Some of these investors had waited patiently for a return on their investment for nine years, and I wanted them to see some money on day one. Underwriters are averse to this policy because it could send a negative message to the public and dampen sales. In other words, if the company is so great, why would any of their shareholders sell their stock? Dan agreed to my request as long as no insiders (i.e., officers and directors) would sell and would agree to a six-month lock-up provision. This meant they could not sell their shares before six months after the initial sale to the public. This would send a better message. Determining the actual share price was a different kettle of fish and somewhat subjective. When evaluating a company, the appraiser takes into account many criteria: comparison with similar companies of similar size, industry, geographical region, revenues, profitability, etc. Dan had us pegged at a $40 million valuation, while Jeff had us at $44 million. HP would sell twenty percent of its shares. Using Dan's $10 per share, the eight hundred thousand shares the public would buy would amount to only $8 million for HP. The lower-priced stock would be easier to sell by the Roney brokers, driving more commissions. At $13 a share, HP would garner an additional $2.4 million, a substantial difference. When there is money on the table, take it. Once money is left on the table, you can never recover it. I fought hard for the $13 share price but Dan would not budge. We settled at $12 a share, which would put close to $10 million in our treasury. It would also more than double to triple the early investors' returns.

The Road Show was next. This is when the spokespeople of the company go to the banking house's brokerage offices and tell the company's story. The story is short, clear, concise, and told in a manner to stir excitement among the sales force. Roney had ten retail outlets located in Michigan, Indiana, and Illinois. We would barnstorm over several days, visiting their best brokers. Behind the scenes, Roney was lining up other independent brokerage houses to sell our stock, in our case fourteen companies called the "book." Roney would be the lead underwriter, and would be assisted by the "book." Roney agreed to sell all of the eight hundred thousand shares on an all-or-nothing basis.

We had professionally prepared a high-quality, twenty-minute Power Point Presentation and allowed for a question and answer period. Through mock sessions, with the guidance of Jeff and Dan, Tom and I honed our answers. February in the Midwest is frigid and snowy. The weather forecast predicted snowstorms for the week we were scheduled to be on the road. On top of that, I developed a bad case of laryngitis two days before liftoff. There is no cure for viral laryngitis. We could not cancel because we had hundreds of brokers lined up. I just sucked it up, and with the help of tea with honey and lemon and warm moist towels, I improved to the point I could talk above a whisper. I donned my banker's uniform, and we all hit the road. The Road Show was basically a repeat of our New York presentation last December. We had great reception, and the air was electric. My gravelly bass voice had power to it. There were no glitches. Tom and I enjoyed the experience immensely. Jeff and Dan also thought it went extremely well. The selling shares were fully allocated to all the Roney people and the "book." All of our registration papers had been filed and approved. March 3, 1994, was our opening day on NASDAQ, and I could hardly wait.

The morning of March 3, I went downtown to the office of one of my stockbrokers, Brad Kastan. He gave me a corner of his office and a computer screen. The markets open at 9:30 a.m. Very shortly after the opening, the action began. It opened at $12 as agreed to but quickly jumped to $12.50

Aha! I was right all along about its valuation. The Bloomberg News announced that Health Power, symbol HPWR, was its pick as the stock to watch along with a company called Cisco—*never heard of it.* The stock popped again to $13 and by the end of the day was at $14 a share with heavy volume. We were all high–fiving in the office. I felt exhilarated. I called Jeff, Dan, and Tom, and congratulations were passed all around. The next day the stock traded in the $14 range and did so for a couple of months.

Now, we needed to get down to serious business to achieve the financial numbers we had promised. The first quarter and every subsequent quarter that year set records in revenues, profits and EPS (earnings per share). By the end of 1994, we had $20 million in our treasury. We bought a new computer system for $600,000 to run the company's information. Tom and his staff chose it after a long, intensive search. True to form, as so many of these computer systems fail, ours never worked properly to give us timely and accurate information. The company we bought it from, although recommended as the best in the managed care industry, could never get it fully operational. We wound up throwing it in the trash heap—a clear waste of a lot of money.

I sent my best and most trusted employee, my step-son Eric, to Cleveland. Within one year he had built Health Power of Cleveland into a functioning and profitable entity with thousands of patients and hundreds of contracts with providers including the prestigious Cleveland Clinic. His was a remarkable accomplishment. My next goal was to find an acquisition to fit our growth plans. We had the money, stock, and reputation to attract another company in our industry.

The acquisition of CompManagement (CM) sort of "materialized" out of nowhere. Tom had just been visited by Bob Bossart, the president of a company which provided third party administrative (TPA) services to private enterprises like HP. Their services included monitoring the quality of health care provided to employees, checking health care bills for unbundling, overcharges, fraud, excessive hospital length of stays, and checking the workplace for health hazards. CM monitored the length of absence of employees who were injured on the job, and ferreted out fraud when employees did not return after an acceptable time period. Their charges were reasonable and affordable. Tom liked Bossart and wanted me to meet him to hear about this new form of service. I too immediately liked Bossart, a great people person with a great new idea. CM's cost-cutting services were necessary in an industry plagued with fraud. By rooting out health care fraud and improving efficiency and safety in the workplace, why wouldn't every business and the state of Ohio want CM? I asked to meet with the other principals, Dick Kurth and John Wagner, both impressive young men with great people skills and pioneers in a new field. Not only did I want their services for HP, I wanted to acquire CompManagement. Theirs was a company with great potential for growth and profits and they were a perfect fit with HP in terms of containing health care costs. On a subsequent meeting with Bossart, I broached the subject of joining forces to grow our combined businesses. HP had the three crucial ingredients to be successful: a great idea, great leadership, and the money to accomplish its goals. CM had two of the three. They were strapped for cash as one look at their balance sheet showed. One look at HP's balance sheet with its $20 million in liquid assets glowing in the dark told them they needed us. We were both in the same business of quality cost control. We all liked each other and could work together. The synergies were there. HP set about making an offer.

I asked Jeff Brausch to evaluate CM. After his usual thorough investigation, he thought CM was worth $2 million. Their revenues were about $1 million for the year, but there were no profits because the three principals paid themselves all the remaining cash at the end of every year. This is not uncommon in a closely held small, private company. They had no liquid assets. I made them an offer of $2 million in

HP stock, which was selling in the $14 a share range back then. I expected a counter offer of about $3 million, maybe $4 million. I must admit I was stunned when they countered with a hefty $10 million price tag. We both knew that was excessive and to me somewhat outrageous. I thought they were testing my level of desire to buy their little jewel. Why not ask for the moon? I countered at $4 million and expected them to accept. Instead they replied at $8 million. Over the next few weeks it became obvious they would not budge on their price. They would not give up their autonomy for anything less than the $8 million and, left on their own would grow organically. Then *deus ex machina!* I heard privately from a friend in the Voinovich administration, an unimpeachable source, that the state of Ohio was going to privatize the services of the Office of Worker's Compensation! Everything would be "turfed out" to private companies to manage, for substantial fees, the broken system that the state was now badly mismanaging. I thought this was a great move for the taxpayers of Ohio but even greater for CM. This would amount to an amazing windfall for companies like CM with their good systems, large customer base, great reputation, and corporate structure already in place. I could foresee many start-ups joining the feeding frenzy, but we would be far ahead of these smaller competitors. Every non-self-insured business in Ohio would be compelled to join, and that meant millions in profits to these new Managed Care Organizations (MCOs) with CM leading the pack. Quick "back of the envelope" arithmetic showed me $8 million would then be more than a fair price for the purchase of CM. Although there would be a sixteen percent dilution to our share price, this would soon be recovered in one to two years. I agreed to their price despite disagreement from Jeff and Tom. The HP board approved it, and CM received $7.4 million in stock and $600,000 in cash. This acquisition became the second most important event in HP's history as we will later see. Number one remains going public.

My judgment proved correct. The entire area of worker's injuries was indeed privatized in 1996. CM's revenues grew from $1 million the year before our acquisition to $40 million in 2000. It was enjoying ten percent bottom line profits EBITDA (Earnings Before Interest, Taxes, and Amortization) every year. It quickly became both the largest TPA (Third Party Administrator) and the largest MCO in the state of Ohio.

CHAPTER FIFTEEN
Vireo masteri, *A New Bird to Science:*
The Discovery and Naming of a New Bird in Colombia

"On the basis of field observations and two specimens from
two localities in the Choco biological region of western
Colombia, we hereby describe *Vireo masteri, sp. nov.,*" begins
the opening statement of *A distinctive new species of vireo
(Passeriformes: Vireonidae) from the Western Andes of Colombia,
IBIS 138: 610–619 by* Paul G. W. Salaman and F. Gary Stiles

In 1989 I wanted to purchase a vanity license plate with a bird
name for my new sports utility vehicle. When I arrived at a
birding event, people would know I was a devout birder. In
Ohio, at the time, you could request a special plate with up to
five characters. I chose "EAGLE," since the Harpy Eagle was
my totem bird. The Ohio Department of Motor Vehicles
informed me that "EAGLE" was taken. They told me to
send them a list of ten names, and they would choose one. I
sent them that list with a randomly chosen ten bird names
like "RAIL," "VIREO," "CRANE." A few weeks later I
received two plates with "VIREO" stamped across them. The
convict who made them was probably thinking, *What the hell
does that mean? Vireo* actually comes from the Latin, *virens,*
meaning a small, green bird. I was very happy with their
choice; the beauty of the name *vireo* is that only birders would
know what it means. Non-birders wouldn't have a clue. It

certainly engendered a lot of conversation from curious people in parking lots. They would ask me, "What is that 'Viray-o'"?

On August 25, 1991, a small bird flew into a mist net set up by a team of ornithologists in western Nariño located in southwest Colombia. The site, about 1,500 meters (five thousand feet) in altitude, was in a narrow strip of intact, very wet forest along the Rio Nambi, a habitat described as Choco. Choco extends from southern Panama down through Colombia and Ecuador. It ranges from mangroves and moist rainforests to dry tropical forests. It is the area of the highest biodiversity in South America, but because of deforestation for agriculture, sadly only five to ten percent remains. The Choco is home to 2,250 animal species and 9,000 plant species with twenty-five percent of these found only in the Choco. Alto de Pisones is the home of twenty-four endemic birds, and Rio Nambi, thirty-nine.

Ornithologist Paul Salaman extracted the bird from the net but could not identify it. It was not one of the hundreds of Colombian species he had seen, and with which he was familiar. The bird was held in captivity overnight for further study, but unfortunately it died during the night. Salaman prepared a study skin, which was partly destroyed by ants. The remains were taken to Bogota. Somehow the specimen was lost. The bird was small, a little more than four inches, lightweight at 11.4 grams, and greenish in color with a broad, wide yellowish wing bar. It had a distinctive facial pattern with a long white stripe above its eye. It reminded Salaman of the Yellow-winged Vireo of Costa Rica and western Panama but was much smaller and had that striking eye line. Photos and notes of this bird were circulated as a probable undescribed form of vireo at the Neotropical Ornithological Conference at Quito in November, 1991.

In early June, 1992, another ornithologist, Gary Stiles, working independently in Alto de Pisones was repeatedly seeing a small canopy bird he could not identify. The site was an extremely wet cloud forest ridge on the west slope of the

Western Andes in Risaralda. Observations were made from 1,450 meters to 1,600 meters. Study of the specimen and correspondence with Salaman established that the Rio Nambi and the Alto de Pisones birds were probably the same species. Stiles collected a specimen, and the Salaman specimen was finally relocated in a collection at Bogota. Although the two specimens were collected three hundred miles apart, confirmation was made that they were indeed the same species. Later, yearly from 1992 to 1995, each scientist returned to their original sites of discovery and made more than one hundred observations and numerous recordings of the bird's calls and songs. There was not a shadow of a doubt that it was a new bird to science.

Vireo masteri, Choco Vireo, Colombia

Figure 15-1. First photo of *Vireo masteri* by discoverer, Paul Salaman.

Here is where I became involved. I read an article in *BirdLife International* magazine, "World Birdwatch," about the discovery of a new bird to science. The discoverers were willing to sell the naming rights of the new species in exchange for funds to preserve both the Rio Nambi and the

Alto de Pisones areas. These areas were under intense pressures of habitat destruction. A highway had already been built in the Alto de Pisones area, and the Rio Nambi site was being destroyed by timbering and agricultural incursions. They needed more than $100,000 to establish and maintain an endowment fund for the site's protection. I was intrigued by the idea to become involved with saving a new species from vanishing forever from our planet. This was also a golden opportunity to honor the memory of my wonderful father, Dr. Gilbert Master, who instilled in me the passion to love and protect birds.

I sent my personal Health Power stock to BirdLife International, and it was sold on the open market to gain the funds needed. I was the only donor to come forward. The Rio Nambi Community National Reserve was established with my funds and became the first reserve in South America in which the local community owns, administers, and manages a protected area. This Reserve protects 7,500 acres of pristine rainforest and at the same time provides an income for the local people. Not only was Rio Nambi the first of its kind, but it also served as a prototype for the seventeen reserves that followed in Colombia.

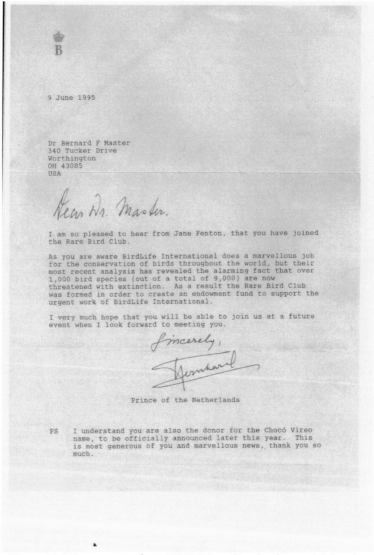

Figure 15-2. Letter to me from HRH Prince Bernhard upon joining the Rare Bird Club.

The naming rights of a living thing new to science belong solely to the discoverer. In the vireo's case, this belonged to Paul Salaman. He basically sold and assigned his rights to me.

Anatomically, the bird was in the genus *Vireo*, a genus well described and of long standing. The genus name cannot be changed except when there is overwhelming evidence to the contrary. My naming rights pertain to the specific epithet, the second word that follows the genus name. I chose my family name, Master, Latinized to the possessive case, *masteri*, meaning "of Master." So the species scientific name became *Vireo masteri* or Vireo of Master. Salaman gave it the common name, Choco Vireo, for obvious reasons, and the AOU (American Ornithological Union) accepted both.

The scientific paper, "A New Species of Vireo," describing *Vireo masteri* was submitted to the ornithological journal *IBIS* in July, 1995 and published in 1996. Publication allows the world to read the description of the new species and invites comments, corrections, or objections. Hearing no valid objections, the species joined the pantheon of ten thousand previously known described bird species in the world. The discovery was announced to the general public in *World Birdwatch*, December, 1996.

Over the next fifteen years I made three attempts to see *Vireo masteri*, but every trip had to be aborted because of rebel activity in the area. I was not going to risk being kidnapped (or worse) to see my bird. In 2009, my friend, Forrest Rowland, informed me that he was going to Colombia to scout for some upcoming tours. He said he would be in the Choco habitat and would search for the vireo. I re-read the original paper in *IBIS* to find any helpful clues to help Forrest in his search for *V. masteri*. There was one recurrent fact that the researchers reported every time they located the bird: The vireo was always in the company of, or nearby, the Gold-ringed Tanager and Purple-mantled Tanager.

On December 24, 2009, I received the following e-mail message from Forrest:

> *Details:*
> *The first afternoon at El Carmen, birding the cow trail (rarely used) up to Octavio Montes' farm, we*

encountered several mixed flocks. Bangsia, Crested Ant-Tanager, all the good stuff present that we had hoped for. We gained the ridge and called in Gold-ringed Tanagers, did a little further exploration of the 3 other trails leading off from Octavio's farmhouse, none of which have ever been birded. At 1520 we were back at the main trail junction, top of the ridge, when Gold-ringed Tanager, Dusky Bush-Tanager, Purplish-mantled Tanager, Glistening Green Tanager, and the rest of the "usual" flock birds for the region started vocalizing and moving in front us. Buffy Tuftedcheek, Fulvous-dotted Treerunner, and all the furnariid constituents of a BIG flock were present, so we started scanning through all the small tyrannulets and flycatchers, etc. Trevor Ellory commented that there was an odd bird that looked kind of like White-banded Tyrannulet, but wasn't, in the top of a huge tree in front of us, above eye-level, and about 20m distant. I took one look at it and said, "F$%& me! That's THE BIRD!!! Get on this get on this get on this..." We watched it forage for about 40 seconds, while Matt got the recorder ready for to try and get a cut. the bird was silent, so I ripped one verse of its song. It came DOWN out of the crown of the tree to just about 40 feet distant and sang back to us for about 20 seconds. Through the excitement and commotion Matt was able to get two full verses of song recorded from the bird, in response to my playback. But that's more than sufficient. All 5 of us saw the bird very well and all had the same impression - How the HELL can that thing be called a Vireo? It looks more like a Phylloscopus warbler! The song is so elegant, whistled, and clean, that it SOUNDS like a warbler. It has a Philadelphia Vireo cuteness to it, but really more along the lines of something like a Plain Leaf-Warbler, with Big, broad, creamy, wingbars and dusky flanks. We were all freaking out.

None of us could believe it. The day was incredible Bernie. We bagged EVERY SINGLE bird we looked for - Black Solitaire (seen once at the site before), Crested Ant-Tanager (seen once at the site before) both Bangsias, White-headed Wrens, and then, to top it off, we accomplished the unthinkable that Paul Salaman and Robert Giles thought only a distant hope. The feeling is still there. It's was one of the most satisfying unique experiences I've had. Hopefully, I can refind it for you. There is plenty of habitat and the flocks are great, fairly slow, and easy to pick through. You have a solid chance. We just need the weather to cooperate.
Merry Christmas B

It is hard to relate how excited I was about Forrest's message. Did he really have the vireo? His location was about three hundred miles from any known Choco habitat. Forrest does not make mistakes on identification. He is careful and conservative in his calls. The best part of his message was that *V. masteri* was in a new and safe locale. There was no rebel activity in El Carmen. I arrived in Bogota on New Year's Eve, 2009, and spent that night in a small hotel in El Carmen dreaming about the next day. Would it still be there? Would the weather hold up? New Year's day, Forrest led me to a site below the ridge where he'd first found them. I peered into the mist but saw nothing. I finally heard some tinkling sounds drifting down from the highest part of the trees. I saw a tiny figure moving through the leaves; then I saw it clearly, a small olive sprite with two wing bars and a white eye line. After fifteen years I was watching three Choco Vireos singing and playing high in the canopy mist. I watched them for two hours; I could not pull myself away. I managed to get a few distant photos of my namesake birds, the newest members of the world's bird fraternity. I became one of the few humans who had ever laid eyes on these living creatures.

The discovery and naming of a new species creates quite a stir in the birding world. I received a call from Christoph Imboden, CEO of BirdLife International (BLI) in Cambridge, England. He was planning a visit to the U.S. and wanted to meet me. He came to Columbus and we spent hours together talking about world bird conservation and the role of BLI as the world's leader in this effort. We even got a chance to bird together as I took him to some of the hot birding spots in Central Ohio like Green Lawn Cemetery. We got along very well, and at the end of his visit he invited me to become the at-large council member of BLI. I deemed it a great honor to be asked to be a "Governor" of the "United Nations" of world bird conservation, and I accepted with great pleasure. There would be two meetings a year in Cambridge. I would join two other Americans among the nine council members. The chairman, Howard Brokaw, from Delaware, was a legendary American philanthropist for bird conservation causes. The other American was Gerry Bertrand, former CEO of Massachusetts Audubon, a professional bird conservator and next in line to be Chairman of BLI.

During the next five years, I diligently attended every meeting. While on council we devised and promulgated the concept of Important Bird Areas (IBAs) for the Americas, designating areas of special importance for bird migration and breeding for government protection. We gave this idea to the American Bird Conservancy, our American partner at the time in 1995, and they ran with it, creating five hundred IBAs in the U.S. Later the National Audubon Society began a second IBA program when it became the American partner of BLI. Back home in Columbus, Green Lawn Cemetery and the Whittier Peninsula received this designation. I was asked to speak at the opening ceremony at Green Lawn. This was a rare opportunity to see a germ of an idea, of which I had been part of since its inception, become a reality years later in my own town. We also came up with BLI's slogan, "The global Partnership for nature and people," and a new logo.

BLI's finances were not in the best shape. I forced the resignation of its treasurer, and BLI brought in Tasso Leventis, a financial wizard already serving on council, to turn things around, and he did straightaway. Michael Rands, a capable and creative administrator, succeeded Imboden. Gerry Bertrand, already a council member, succeeded Brokaw as chairman. There was a new look and new energy at BLI. We enjoyed five years of continued successes in the conservation world. When my second term was over, I joined the board of BLI's American partner, The American Bird Conservancy (ABC), headed up by its visionary founders, George and Rita Fenwick. My old BLI friend, Howard Brokaw, was serving as ABC's chairman. I served six years there. In my opinion, ABC is the most important and best run conservancy that has the sole purpose to protect birds in the Americas.

International nonprofit NGOs (Non-Government Organizations), unlike American nonprofits, have no reserves. They spend every penny they receive on projects, which is admirable but risky, and so they depend on a steady stream of donations. BLI cements commitments for annual long-term giving from organizations like The Royal Society for the Protection of Birds (RSPB), their major sustainer, and individual large donors called "patrons." I joined the patron group along with HRH Prince Bernhard, HRH Prince Philip, and Crown Princess Masako of Japan, pretty lofty company. By selling my shares of HP stock periodically, I could donate a sizeable chunk of cash every year to various charities. One year, I underwrote the introductory video produced by my daughter Dana for the BLI Malaysian Conference.

Following the announcement of the discovery and naming of *Vireo masteri*, I was informed I would be fêted at a gathering of the Rare Bird Club (RBC) at the Grand Duke of Luxembourg's palace. HRH Prince Bernhard of the Netherlands, honorary president of the RBC, would present me with a painting of my namesake bird by the noted European bird artist, David Quinn. Prince Bernhard, himself a legendary leader in the environmental movement, would include his personal commendation for my role in world bird conservation. This was all so exhilarating for me and Susan; I could hardly stand the anticipation. The RBC agreed to my seeing the painting ahead of time. I would have it shipped to the hotel and hand-carry it to the ceremony. The painting was a lovely oil depicting a pair of Choco Vireos in their natural canopy habitat. They were lifelike, accurately shown with their greenish bodies, broad yellow wing bars, and long white eye stripe. I felt like I could reach out and touch them. David Quinn's signature appears quietly in the lower right corner.

We arrived in the Grand Duchy of Luxembourg on the day of the ceremony. We checked into our hotel, and immediately looked for the painting. No painting! Checking with the front desk and concierge produced no good news. It had not arrived. A feeling of uneasiness spread to a sense of panic as the hour to the ceremony drew closer. It had to be at customs. I called customs and hoped for an English-speaking agent. I reached the Belgian customs office and talked to a very doleful official. I explained that I was waiting for the painting and asked if it was there. At first he was not very helpful. I changed my tack and told him it was for the Grand Duke of Luxembourg, and it was urgently needed within two hours. He immediately changed his attitude and said it was there. It had been held up in customs because they did not know its proposed use—personal or sale. I told him it was a present for the Duke, and he said he would release it and send it over. Forty-five minutes later there was a knock on my hotel door. The customs official delivered the painting himself.

Figure 15-3. Susan and me at the Grand Duke of Luxembourg's palace.

Susan and I were picked up at our hotel in a chauffeured Mercedes limousine. After a short drive we reached the gigantic wrought iron palace gates. The palace guard let us in and we followed a long and ornately landscaped driveway. The livery dropped us off directly at the palace's marble steps. There we were met by an assistant secretary to the Grand Duke and escorted up the marble steps to a large ante-room richly decorated with eighteenth-century paintings and period furniture. Jane Fenton, secretary to BLI was there waiting for us. As Americans we were not used to meeting royalty. Jane, a British subject, had lots of experience and told us the protocol. A Grand Duke is one rung below a Prince and two rungs below a King on the royal ladder. A slight nod would be fine. Americans were not expected to bow. It wasn't long before a man in his forties came bounding down a set of marble steps leading from the second floor. As Jane was introducing him to me, I gave him a small nod dictated by my perception that he was the Grand Duke. And then I heard the rest of the introduction—that he was actually the secretary to the Grand Duke. I tried to cover my nod with some fidgeting and prayed my little faux pas was imperceptible. He escorted us up to the second floor into a large hallway. I could see ahead a distinguished and handsome older man of medium height and build and next to him, an elegant, beautiful woman in the reception line. The man wore a formal military uniform; the Grand Duchess wore a blue haute couture gown with a triple strand of pearls. They made a stunning appearance in their formal attire. At this point, there was no mistaking who was the Grand Duke of the Grand Duchy. Many of the guests had already arrived, had passed through the receiving line, and were waiting for us. The Grand Duke made some small talk after I shook his hand; he thanked me for my contribution. The Grand Duchess shook my hand and welcomed me. They both spoke flawless British English. Everyone looked splendid in his or her formal attire. HRH Prince Bernhard was last in line. He gave me a sincere warm greeting and thanked me for my donation.

Susan looked elegant in her Christian Dior dress, and I was feeling pretty spiffy in my Armani tuxedo and antique Tiffany cufflinks. Champagne was poured and tasty hors d'oeuvres were passed around. There were about twenty RBC members in the room. We were the only Americans. A formal seven-course dinner followed accompanied by three separate flights of remarkable wines. After dinner, The Grand Duke made some welcoming remarks and HRH Prince Bernhard talked about the declining state of bird habitats in the world. He was in his eighties and sharp as a tack. His sentiments were clear and well delivered. He spoke beautiful American English without a hint of his German ancestry. He presented a painting of a new member's favorite endangered bird to the new member, a ritual that went back to the RBC's inception. Following polite applause, the Prince then spoke about *Vireo masteri*, my donation, and the establishment of the Rio Nambi Community National Reserve. He talked about the importance of sustainable conservation, and enlisting native peoples to protect the Reserves thereby mutually benefitting both. He then turned to me and praised my contribution of helping to build the Community Reserve, the first of its kind in South America. The presentation of David Quinn's beautiful painting of *V. masteri* received many approving "oohs and aahs" from the other guests.

Figure 15-4. HRH Prince Bernhard presenting painting of *Vireo masteri* to me at the Grand Duke of Luxemburg's palace.

This was an especially memorable and gratifying moment in my life. Toward the end of the evening, the Grand Duke came over and asked how long we were staying. I told him two more days. He asked if I would like to do a little birding the next day. I said, "Yes, of course." He responded that he would send his Royal Naturalist to pick us up in the morning to spend a day birding. When I told Susan of his magnanimous offer, she was speechless. Royal Naturalist! Were we cast back to the eighteenth century?

The next morning his man picked us up as promised, and we headed out to the countryside crossing into Belgium. He asked me if there were any particular birds I wanted to see.

Yes, the Black Woodpecker and the Black Grouse. I knew they were Middle Country species. It wasn't long before I was looking at a glossy black woodpecker perched on the trunk of a burned out tree in the Ardennes Forest. A short drive later he spied a chunky game bird in a hedge row along a cultivated Belgian field. The Black Grouse joined my life list. Mission accomplished, we headed for lunch.

Lunch was at a small converted Belgian farmhouse. Typical Middle Country foods with beef stew, sausages, country bread and wild boar pâté, soft cheese, potatoes with carrots, leeks, endive, white asparagus, and even hamburgers with fries were on the menu. They had local beers ready to wash it down. Once they saw they had American customers, they turned their music off and played the "Macarena." I hated the "Macarena" and lived in a "Macarena"-free zone at home. I asked them to put the light classical music back on.

On the way back to our hotel, I saw a cemetery with perfectly straight row after row of crosses radiating out from a large central marble tomb. The grass was meticulously clipped to the same exact height throughout. We stopped to look at this memorial site. A richly carved marble sarcophagus was in the center of an extravagantly grand marble tomb. It was Roman in architecture with ornately carved marble columns and bronze statues, Latin inscriptions etched in the walls, and a ceiling painted like the Sistine Chapel. It was fit for a Caesar. It was the final resting place of General George Patton, "Old Blood and Guts," the legendary hero of the Battle of the Bulge in World War II. His final wish was to be buried with his men, and there he lies, in state, in Luxembourg among his five thousand American heroes.

Figure 15-5. General George Patton's tombstone, Luxembourg.

Figure 15-6. Ceiling of General George Patton's Tomb, Luxembourg.

Susan and I joined the Rare Bird Club (RBC), a group of three hundred bird conservators, mostly Dutch and Brits, traveling the world together to see rare endangered birds and lend financial help to reduce their existential threats. At that time there were 1,111 endangered bird species in the world.

We were given the privilege to choose one, and a painting of the bird (done by an artist of our choice) would be presented to us at an RBC meeting. The rather hefty initiation fee goes directly on the "ground" to conserve our chosen bird. We would then be forever linked to that bird. All of the endangered species, the names of their conservators, and their paintings are published in a BLI book. I chose the Nukupuu, a Hawaiian honeycreeper, only found on one slope of Haleakalā on the island of Maui, Hawaii. I had seen it together with Doug Pratt, bird tour leader, artist and author of *The Birds of Hawaii and the Tropical Pacific*. I chose him to paint my bird. Today it hangs in my house—beautifully frozen forever eating insects from its favorite koa tree. Susan chose the Dwarf Jay that we saw with bird leader and author, Steve Howell, in southeast Mexico. She also chose Pratt to paint it. Pratt painted the jay eating insects from its favorite bromeliad in the eastern Sierra Madre Mountains. It is keeping company side-by-side with my honeycreeper.

Figure 15-7. Dwarf Jay by Douglas Pratt.

Figure 15-8. Nukupuu by Douglas Pratt.

There were about twenty Americans in the club, including Roger Tory Peterson, who in my mind is the Father of American Birdwatching, and James Clements, the creator of the *Clements World Bird Checklist*, a system of bird classification used by the American Birding Association (ABA) and most American birders. I brought in several new club members Jeff

Brausch, my banking consultant; his wife, Sandie; and the Beurets, a couple from California whom we had traveled with on several bird tours. As a club we traveled to the Seychelles Islands, Bermuda, and Jordan to see rare birds and meet local conservationists under the official auspices of their governments.

In Jordan we met with Queen Noor, née Lisa Hallaby, the wife of King Hussein and the daughter of JFK's FAA Director, Najeeb Hallaby. Queen Noor is a Princeton graduate and a lovely and intelligent woman. We had dinner at the palace with her and traveled the country under the King's aegis, looking for rare birds and enjoying the many sights of antiquity. She and her daughter, both casual in jeans and T-shirts, joined us at the Dana Reserve to find the Sinai Rosefinch. They flew in by helicopter, and the pilot mistakenly landed in front of the hide (bird blind), with us in it, scaring all the birds away. We all had a good laugh about her birding skills, and she took the kidding good-naturedly. She also lent us the royal yacht to go snorkeling in the Red Sea.

In the Seychelles, aboard a dive boat, we visited the World Heritage Site, Aldabra, a small atoll in the Indian Ocean. Humans are not allowed entry. However, BLI supports a scientist on the island who does turtle and bird counts. In the morning we went ashore, met our man, and saw the rare Aldabra endemics, Aldabra Drongo, Fody, flightless White-throated Rails, and radiant Souimanga Sunbirds. At one point, Susan and I stood on a strip of gleaming pure white sand with our binoculars fixated on a large flock of Crab-Plovers idling in the lagoon only 150 feet from us. Crab-Plovers are a hard-to-find species anywhere in the world. They belong to *Dromadidae*, a monotypic family, which means they are the only representative of their family. Monotypic families comprise 46 of the 230 world families known at this writing.

Red-footed Boobies flew close to me to inspect this new visitor to their island. What a thrill to know that I was standing on a strip of beach where no other human had ever stood before.

Figure 15-9. Me standing on virgin beach on Aldabra Atoll with curious Red-footed Boobies.

With ornithologist Robin Skerritt, the foremost expert on Seychelles birds, we saw the first Seychelles record of European Bee-eater. Earlier I had seen the country's first record of Leach's Storm-Petrel, rare anywhere in the Indian Ocean. I told Robin about it, but without other observers or a photo, it became just an interesting but unverified sighting. I understood that and was okay with it. Robin had just submitted for publication his manuscript of the first edition of his field guide to the birds of the Seychelles, but the bee-eater was not in it. He would have to add an account of this species when he got home to Mahe before it was sent to press.

Figure 15-10. Male Abbot's Sunbird, Cosmoledo Island.

In the afternoon we snorkeled among sea turtles and exotic fish until a curious shark approached. *Oh my goodness!* It was a tiger shark. Tiger sharks are man-eating denizens of the deep. Tiger sharks, along with Bull and Great Whites, are notorious for attacking humans. We quickly swam back to our boat and stayed put for the rest of the afternoon. On our trip back to Mahe, we stopped at Assumption Island and saw and photographed an Abbot's Sunbird. It is the world's rarest sunbird.

Bermuda is the home of the Bermuda Petrel and the birthplace of *The Wonderful Wizard of Oz*. In 1900, L. Frank Baum, staying in Bermuda, penned the classic. Some have interpreted it as an allegory for the Gold Standard. The Bermuda Petrel or Cahow, named for the eerie sound of its call, was thought to be extinct for three hundred years. In 1951, a single Cahow carcass was found at the base of a Bermuda lighthouse. The Cahow existed, but where and how many? The hunt was on. Eighteen breeding pairs were found on a rocky isle in Castle Harbour by American ornithologist Robert Cushman Murphy and Bermudan naturalist Louis L. Mowbrie. They were accompanied by a teenage boy, David

Wingate. Wingate devoted his life to protecting the Cahow, which became the national bird of Bermuda. He built concrete burrows to keep out rats and wooden baffles to keep out other larger nesting birds such as shearwaters. All the birds were moved to Nonsuch Island, a short boat ride from the main island, where these structures served as safe nesting places. His work is now being assisted by warden Jeremy Madeiros. There is no finish line for these two as they work tirelessly night and day to protect this species! As of 2005, there were more than 250 Bermuda Petrels because of their efforts. Their small numbers include them in the BLI category of "Critically Endangered," which denotes the highest probability of extinction in our lifetime.

We were escorted to Nonsuch Island one evening by Jeremy Madeiros to see the Cahow colony that he and David had so painstakingly curated over many years.

This was a rare privilege because the island was off limits to everyone else. We saw the birds in their concrete burrows. Jeremy showed us the two-toned pink and black feet unique to this seabird. Two of the young were walking near their burrows exercising their wings and strengthening their flight muscles. The young are reared by both parents by taking turns flying five hundred miles one way to the Sargasso Sea to hunt krill and then returning, taking five to seven days for the round-trip feeding flight. The parent arrives at the burrow, belly full, and disgorges its catch directly into the open mouth of its young; the other parent immediately sets out to sea for another krill run.

The next night we returned to Nonsuch Island because Jeremy suspected that one of the young birds was ready to leave the island and begin its first perilous sea journey. In the dim light of the moon, Susan and I saw a young Cahow standing on a rock repeatedly flapping its wings. After two hours—and into in the wee hours of the morning—we were honored and privileged to witness the maiden voyage of one of the rarest birds in the world, an odyssey that would take five years to complete before it returned to its Nonsuch home. The young Cahow took flight into the Atlantic and in seconds was lost to our view in the shroud of the sea mist. We were stunned. We knew immediately how lucky we had been. We were one of the few humans to ever witness this miracle of nature. Our elation was mixed with dread as we pictured this youngster, alone, beset by squalls and full-blown hurricanes, hunted by winged and swimming predators, relying only on its instincts to find food and return home safely. The future of this entire species, with its depleted population hanging on by a thread, theoretically was at stake and relying on this one bird.

We spent a day birding with David Wingate who proved to be a good all-around birder. There is a small list of nesting birds on Bermuda, and David knew where to find them all. The president of the Bermuda Audubon Association, Andrew Dobson, joined us. He is an avid birder, strong conservationist, and not a bad tennis player—as I found out after two sets on a Bermuda grass court. Bermuda is only seven hundred miles off the coast of North Carolina. Over the course of many centuries, migrants and lost birds from America and Europe have found their way to the island. Many exotic birds like the Northern Cardinal and the Yellow-crowned Night-Heron were imported by well-meaning Bermudans and now thrive there. Native birds like White-tailed Tropicbirds and Great Shearwaters abound. There is also a subspecies of Common Tern found only there that I was lucky to see. The Bermuda trip ended with a State dinner at the home of the governor of Bermuda, Sir John Vereker, an appointee of Queen Elizabeth II. A native palm tree was planted in honor of the RBC, and everyone present added a spade full of dirt.

The RBC had many special events. We were invited to London's Museum of Natural History for a luncheon to raise funds for the conservation of birds. Prince Bernhard was in attendance. After lunch he spoke about the killing of albatross by entangling and drowning in long line fishing nets, a practice he wished the world would abolish. Prince Charles is also in favor of eradicating this method. I was invited along with Michael Rands, CEO of BLI, to accompany Prince Bernhard for a special private viewing of the museum's bird room. After donning white museum gloves, the curator showed us two of the museum's prize possessions. We were treated to one of the ultra-rare original John James Audubon *Double Elephant Folio*, called such because of its enormous size. I was left to my leisure as I viewed all 435 pages of bird paintings in this mega book rarity. The watercolor and aquatint-painted lithographs were as fresh and lively as the day they were when printed. Of the original 200 sets printed by Havell in 1838, this was one of the surviving 119 sets. It was worth a cool $11.5 million at that time. Following our inspection of the Folio, the Curator brought us his second treasure, the log book from the HMS Bounty and accompanying notes from the ship's naturalist. I was in awe as I perused the handwritten entries of Lt. Bligh on his first voyage to Tahiti in 1778 to obtain breadfruit for the Caribbean slaves. The ill-fated voyage is known to all as the *Mutiny on The Bounty*.

As I look back on my journey, from birding with my father in Cape May as a young boy, would I have ever guessed it would have led to my standing with the Prince of the Netherlands, both Bernards, enjoying the wonders of the bird world? Was that nameless, faceless clerk at the Ohio Bureau of Motor Vehicles, who assigned me the license plate VIREO, some prescient diviner of my future?

WORLD 6429 • ABA 776

CHAPTER SIXTEEN
Trouble in New Guinea: Three Dangerous Encounters

It is not learned until it is in the muscle.
—Papua New Guinea proverb

Papua New Guinea (PNG) is the rape capital of the world, and the predators don't discriminate; they are equal opportunity violators. They attack men, women, and children without prejudice. Gang rape is particularly popular. After a rape, the predators frequently kill their victims. PNG is a poor country barely emerging from its stone-age culture. It has great natural resources, but the export money does not trickle down to the village level. The average pay is $1.25 per day. PNG is a lawless country run by a bunch of "Big Men," the headmen from each village. What they say goes. AIDS is rampant. There are still traces of headhunting and cannibalism. The natives spend their time raising subsistence crops, hunting, and committing "payback" killings. It's the Old Testament version of an "eye for an eye." Some of these feuds extend back hundreds of years. Women have no rights at all and are fourth in the social hierarchy after men, male children, and pigs. (I did not make that up). New Guinea has been described as the second most dangerous place in the world. I know you are asking yourselves, *So why go there?*

For birders it offers the most fantastic bird family in the world, the Birds of Paradise (BOPs). Of the forty-one BOPs known in the world, most live on the island of New Guinea, with two in the Moluccas and four in Australia. The BOP family is about twenty-four million years old. Most are luminescent and beautiful, but shy and difficult to find. They are closely related to crows, but couldn't look and act any more opposite. New Guineans collect their brightly colored and oddly shaped feathers for ceremonial dances. They remove the legs and feet first when they kill them. Sixteenth-century European explorers brought these birds back home. They were imagined to be mythical phoenixes, and because they lacked feet and legs, were thought to be sent to earth from the gods in paradise. They were given the name *apoda,* which means "no feet," and called Birds of Paradise.

Because New Guinea is the second largest island in the world, with razor-sharp rugged mountains and impassable valleys—many unexplored—its biogeography is complex and not well understood. Alfred Russell Wallace, the co-discoverer of evolution, and the man who spent years in this region unraveling its biological mysteries. He divided the region with a line running north to south in Indonesia, called "Wallace's Line." The fauna west of the line is largely Southeast Asian, east of the line, Australasian. New Guinea is in the eastern section.

For "culture vultures," anthropology nuts, and adrenaline seekers, the island is a treasure trove. It boasts 848 languages, the most languages in the world, many of which are inexplicably unrelated linguistically. Each parcel of land is owned by a particular village. The headman must be paid a fee (money or pigs) before one crosses. Trespassers will shortly become surrounded by angry spear-wielding natives, who have no problem killing people. Ceremonial dances are long and trance-like. Costumes and masks are elaborate. Old masks, death poles, and penis shields are a prize for collectors of South Pacific artifacts. It was this thirst for rare island artifacts that led to the murder of the twenty-three-year-old son of Governor Nelson Rockefeller, Michael, by the Asmat tribe, November, 1961, in West Papua. His murder was a revenge killing. As is the custom in some tribes, Michael was eaten. Natives believe that by eating a man, his power and strength will transfer to the tribe. The only vestige of his ill-fated visit was his metal belt buckle. Cannibalism still exists in some parts of the island. Eating the brains of an enemy or dead relative is the source of "Koru" or "Running Amok," a prion disease related to Kreutzfeldt–Jakob Disease.

It was July, 1997. After a Qantas flight from Sydney, Australia, Susan and I arrived at the capital, Port Moresby. We were shuttled to the Gateway Hotel where we met our VENT tour group members and leader, David Bishop. David was a former policeman in London and lived in Australia and New Guinea after his marriage to an Australian woman. He came to birding late but through experience and diligent study became an expert of the birds in that region. He was a large man with a booming voice. He had an easy laugh and an outgoing personality. After we settled in our rooms, Susan and I decided to take a stroll around the hotel grounds. Having never been in the region before, we ticked an easy eleven lifers in an hour. We headed back to our hotel to get ready for dinner. When we tried to enter the hotel, we were blocked by a crowd of about a dozen native men. We had no pre-conceived notions about these islanders. This was our first encounter with New Guineans, and it made a very bad first impression. They simply would not move out of our way as we tried to excuse ourselves to gain the front door. Having enough of this aggressive and rude behavior, I reached back to my West Philly roots and pushed my way through the human blockade yelling, "Out of the way. Out of the way." Confused by this atypical behavior from a white Westerner, they moved out of our way. Susan was close behind me.

After dinner, I related this event to David, and he seemed very concerned. He paused in thought for quite a while and then told me his hair-raising story. Two years before, he was leading a private bird tour with the renowned world birder, the great Phoebe Snetsinger. She was famous in the birding world on two counts. She was the first birder to see more than eight thousand species in the world, and she was a woman. She was always well prepared for every trip, studying the bird species she hoped to encounter. She kept detailed field notes about genera, species, and subspecies because she knew that genetics were fluid and taxonomy could change. With more study, a subspecies could be elevated to species status and a species could be elevated to a new genus or even higher to a new family. This was the same Phoebe Snetsinger who had given me advice on birding in Cuba six years earlier. David and Phoebe had set out their first day to bird a nearby Port Moresby wetland. After several hours of birding, they found on their return a log blocking the road. This was curious because it had not been there a few hours ago. David got out of the vehicle to investigate, and two native men who had been hiding in the bushes confronted him. They both had very large bush knives and threatened to kill him. He thought it was a robbery. They tied up David and Phoebe and drove them to a hut hidden in the forest. They drank some kind of homemade brew and proceeded to get stinking drunk. They sexually attacked Phoebe multiple times. David, bound with rope, felt helpless because he could not come to her assistance. He spoke Melanesian fluently, also pidgin, and some tribal tongues, and heard them say they would kill them both in the morning. The two monsters fell asleep in a drunken stupor. David worked feverishly to loosen his bonds and wrest his hands free. He finally did, untied Phoebe, and they slipped out of their torture chamber and began running for their lives. They had no idea where they were or in what direction to go. Their luck changed when, after four hours, they found a well-used road and followed it to a farmhouse. By this time, dawn was breaking. The owner, awakened by their pleas for help, brought them inside to safety, notified the police, and delivered them back to their hotel.

David felt a profound sense of guilt and shame following this nightmarish incident. But it was not his fault and it could have happened to anyone. That was what I was fearful about. This was the first time I had heard this macabre tale. It was alarming, and I was afraid for Susan's safety. I told David we would not go near that place no matter how many great birds were there. He assured me he would avoid that wetland, in fact he planned to never return. This story put me on high alert for our security for the rest of the two-week trip. I kept the story from Susan until we were safely on the plane on our return flight home.

Exploring Varirata National Park for four days, we found berrypeckers, gerygones, monarchs, fruit doves, and the incomparable Raggiana Bird of Paradise, all new to us. We had to have a T-shirt with the amazing Raggiana emblazoned across the front.

A few miles east of Varirata National Park runs the Kokoda trail, which connects north PNG to south PNG. This area was of special importance to Susan's family. It was the scene of some of the fiercest fighting in World War II. The Australian forces, later aided by the Americans, outfought a superior number of Japanese and thereby saved their homeland from invasion. The Northern Territory of Australia was already evacuated because of the expected Japanese invasion. Because of fanatical bravery of the Aussie men, the occupation of Australia never took place. Also fighting with the ANZACs in New Guinea in 1942, was Susan's father, American soldier Fred Fickel. On R&R in Melbourne, he met the beautiful sheila, Mary Rosendahl. Later they married, and Fred brought his war bride home to Columbus, Ohio. Nine years later my wife Susan and her twin sister Sandy were born.

The birds were spectacular, but it was here that we ran into our most dangerous situation. Outside the park we arrived at a site known as a regular spot for the Blue BOP, considered by some to be the loveliest bird in the world. No shrinking violet, it is almost a foot in length. Its violet blue and maroon feathers subtly blend together above its wiry tail feathers. It is scarce and very hard to find even in its own backyard—a real prize for a world birder. The site was a steep hill with a wide footpath. My guess is it was approximately a twenty-five-degree inclination, hard walking at seven-thousand feet. We arrived around noon, pretty late and pretty hot to be birding, but we had limited time. The next day we were flying to Kiunga. The hike didn't offer much in the way of scenery, so for fun, David challenged Susan to a footrace to the top of the hill. This was a monumental error in judgment by our leader. Susan was extremely fit (she could do level ten— the highest level on the stair master—for one hour). That is considered Olympic athlete fit. Bets were made, and David was the narrow favorite. The betting was split right down the middle with the women betting on Susan, and the men, except me, on David. I was betting big kina on Susan. At that time, there were eight kina to the dollar so it was like monopoly money. The race was on. Susan took the early lead, and David, despite his long strides, could never catch her. Susan demolished him by several steps and was the clear victor. I won about sixteen kina or two bucks. It was all in good fun, and David was a good loser. The women gave her high fives all around, and we continued to bird.

The frivolity ended when we spied a pickup truck with seven or eight men dressed in miner's clothing pull into the base of the hill. The men piled out from the back laughing and talking loudly. They were already stinking drunk and continued to drink, becoming even more boisterous. The drunker they became, the more belligerent they became. They spotted us half way up the hill and started cat-calling to us in their native tongue. We had no idea what they were saying, but my guess was they were not inquiring about our health. I asked David for direction. He told me not to pay any attention to them. They would soon go away. They became drunker, louder, and more aggressive. It was around 1 p.m., so we continued to climb the hill looking for our target, the Blue BOP. Around 3 p.m. we finally found a male high in a tree hiding amongst the dense branches. At first we had trouble seeing the whole bird to our satisfaction, but gradually the bird came into full view for everyone. It was worth the long hunt. His radiant violet blue and cinnamon brown feathers caught by the sun were exquisite. Soon the sun was going down, and David told us we had to go. We had a long drive, and he did not want to go back in the dark. We had to leave a Blue BOP still preening in the sun—*unheard of.* The bird never paid the slightest attention to its admirers. Now we shifted our attention to the bottom of the hill. David's prediction that the natives would tire and leave was wrong—I was hoping not *dead* wrong. They did not go away, and we would have to walk down that long hill and walk by them or through them to get to the safety of our van. We had to leave, and we had to face them.

David approached me, and out of earshot of the others flat out told me, "Be prepared to kill someone!"

There was no subtle mincing of words.

"What! Kill someone? You have got to be shitting me!"

This was a bird tour. I quickly reflected on my first day's conversation with David about poor Phoebe's horrible encounter with the rapists. My adrenalin was pumping now. I was in fight-or-flight mode. I quickly assessed our fighting power. It was terrible against these odds. Our group consisted of only two experienced fighters, David and me. The rest of the group included older women, a retired pediatrician, and a man with severe Parkinson's disease. There was Tim, a younger man, whom we could probably count on. We had no weapons. The only advantage we had was that the men at the bottom of the hill were drunk.

I called to Susan and quietly told her to wrap her binoculars around her fist. "Plant it in the head of anybody who comes near you."

I held my tripod in one hand and a large branch I found on the side of the road in the other. I didn't know how effective my weapons would be against bush knives, but I had to try. David was very cool under pressure. His training as a London bobby and stint as an Australian peacekeeper gave him a steadiness when confronted with danger. He was the ideal leader under these circumstances. He explained to the group that we were going to walk down the hill slowly but deliberately, right past the group of natives. He suggested that we make no eye contact, because in PNG culture that is an aggressive signal. I strategically arranged the order of march. David and I, a wall of six footers and two hundred pounders, were in front; the women and our Parkinson's man walked in twos behind; and the pediatrician and the young man brought up the rear. The natives were sitting on the ground at the base of the hill waiting for us. They were quiet now and were just looking up at us. New Guineans possess a countenance that is scary at best and terrifying at worst. They have deep-set eyes, pronounced foreheads, and large broad noses with flared nostrils. Their out-of-proportion, over-sized heads sit on short, dark brown, powerfully built bodies. In the bush they paint themselves, wear bones in their noses and ears, and carry spears or bush knives. Even the kindest and sweetest of them looks menacing. They are basically unsocialized by Western standards and follow their own mores, sense of justice, and rules of behavior. One must keep in mind that only a few decades ago, one hundred thousand people were discovered living in the Tari Valley, completely unknown to the outside world.

As we approached, I felt my pulse quicken and breathing rate increase. All of my senses were sharpened. The natives were rigid and tense, their eyes transfixed on us. I can't imagine what they were thinking. Here were a bunch of white Westerners with strange ornaments hanging from their necks. *A tasty looking group?* I guess we looked frightened even though we were doing our best to hide it. We made a sharp right turn at the bottom of the hill and made a beeline to the sanctuary of our van. *No van!* David peeled off and approached the group. We kept walking. We could hear David speaking calmly in Melanesian or pidgin. We were straining our eyes, searching and praying for our missing van. We could hear laughter coming from the native group. I snuck a look back, and David was sitting on the ground entertaining the group. Body language was relaxed and all were smiling or laughing. Our van came into view, and we breathed a collective sigh of relief. We jumped inside and locked our windows. David soon followed and assured us all was well. The driver had gotten scared at the approach of the drunken miners and had zoomed off. His conscience had gotten the best of him; however, and he'd decided to return and pick us up—or what might be left of us.

The next day we flew to the township of Kiunga on the border of West Papua (then called Irian Jaya), containing one of the three largest remaining undisturbed lowland forests in the world. In the next five days we found a dazzling assortment of fairy wrens, robins, imperial pigeons, whistlers, honeyeaters, lories, parrots, and both Greater and Magnificent BOPs. We were the first bird tour to see the White-bellied Pitohui in the field. The pitohuis are the only birds in the world that are poisonous. The natives won't touch them, let alone eat them. Their skin exudes a powerful alkaloid cardio- and neurotoxin, batrachotoxin, just a bunch of benzene rings that can kill you. There are no known antidotes for this toxin. Ornithologists wear gloves when handling them. They get their toxin from eating beetles in the genus *Choresine*. Fourteen thousand miles away in the New World and in a completely different class of animals, poison dart frogs get their poison the same way by ingesting venomous arthropods like ants and centipedes. This is an example of convergent evolution. Pitohuis and poison dart frogs are brightly colored, warning predators to stay away. This is called *aposematism*. Some less toxic birds and frogs mimic their more poisonous cousins for protection, called *Mullerian mimicry*.

With our close-call behind us, we settled in to a few days of some relaxed birding near the town of Tabubil. On the fifth day, while birding on a dusty road outside of town we saw a large group of young men coming toward us, maybe a dozen in all. Once they reached our group, they stopped to find out what we were doing on their turf. David told them we were looking for birds and enjoying their beautiful countryside. He asked where they were going. They said they were heading to the town council to register a complaint. *Okay so far.* Then David spotted a shotgun in one of their cases. All guns are outlawed in PNG. There are heavy criminal penalties for having them. David, a former policeman, acted instinctively and warned the carrier not to remove his gun. He threatened the man that if he did, he would "make monkey meat out of him." The gang became restless and agitated. David further escalated the scene by calling them *raskols*, a pejorative in PNG synonymous with street gang. The gang looked to their leader, anxiously waiting for a command to charge us. We sensed the imminent danger and ran back to the van. The door was locked, and the driver was asleep! The gang seemed to deliberate on what their next move was going to be. We banged on the door to wake our sleeping driver and rushed inside, the gang closed in behind us. We locked all of our windows, and the men pelted our vehicle with rocks and sticks. They banged on our windows with fists and clubs. It was all very unnerving.

We yelled to our bewildered driver, "Move! Drive!"

The van driver hightailed it down the road as fast as that old jalopy could go and left the gang in a cloud of dust waving their fists and clubs and calling after us. I believe to this day that David's aggressive policeman behavior caused them to overreact in that manner.

We had two more days in this region, and I was getting sick and tired of these run-ins. Were we seeing everything through the post-traumatic tinted glasses of our leader who had been attacked and nearly killed just two years before, or were these natives really aggressive to foreigners? I chose the latter and decided not to psychologically analyze David, the natives, or myself for that matter. I was looking forward to the end of the trip. The birds were great but not worth all of this. I was doubly anxious because Susan was with me. I promised myself never to bring her to any of these dangerous countries again. We would never see Iran, Iraq, Afghanistan, Somalia, Sudan, Nigeria, Chad, North Korea, DRC, countries with rebel fighting, or countries with incurable viruses like Ebola and their ilk.

On the fourteenth day we flew to Tari in the southern Highlands, the home of the Huli people. When we landed at the Tari airport, there was quite a throng that was welcoming a local hero. The men were face-painted in yellow, coifed with hair from some unknown beast, ornamented with kona shells, and sported nose and ear bones. The women covered their breasts with store-bought bras and wore grass skirts. No one wore shoes. They performed their welcoming sing-sing and danced in line. The object of their adulation was one of the other disembarking passengers, a member of the PNG congress representing this region. The crowd wildly applauded him as he stepped off the plane. What a sight he was in his traditional costume. He wore a colorful shirt, khaki skirt, and a kona shell necklace. He had a bone in his nose and carried a handsome leather briefcase. Susan and I remarked at this incongruity. Picture taking was frowned upon by PNGers since it is considered direct eye contact. We were aware of these customs, and after what we had been through, did not want to test breaking them.

We stayed at the luxurious Ambua Lodge, heralded as one of the most beautiful forest lodges in the world. We agreed with the five-star rating. It was set on an expansive alpine meadow surrounded by montane forests. Our cabin was beautifully appointed with comfortable rustic furniture facing the Doma Mountains. Lorikeets and fairy wrens flitted outside of our veranda. Here I found the New Guinea Harpy Eagle, one of the three harpies in the world. Eventually I saw them all, New Guinea, Philippine, and American. The lodge headquarters was beautifully constructed from native woods. The mahogany bar held top-shelf brands of liquor, whiskeys, cordials, vodka, rums, and premium wines. The lodge was the central hub of a spoke-like radiation of birding trails loaded with exotic species such as parrotfinches, ifritas, grassbirds, fantails, whistlers, honeyeaters, and so many more—enough to satisfy the taste of the most discriminating world birder.

Stopping at a Huli village one afternoon, we were treated to a sing-sing. For a small sum, we were permitted to take photos. Chanting traditional songs, Huli men only in full regalia, performed their ceremonial dances. The Huli people were very gracious and invited us to join their line dance, which we did. Out of the corner of my eye I spotted a woman, bare breasted, suckling some animal form, not a human baby. I approached to see what she was breastfeeding. It was a piglet! Dumbfounded, I managed to ask her how she selected that particular pig. She answered that it was the prettiest. Beauty is in the eye of the beholder.

Figure 16-1. Susan with Huli men.

It was in Tari that Susan and I saw the bravest display of personal courage and integrity of a birder that we have ever had the honor of witnessing. Searching for the rare and elusive Chestnut Forest-Rail, David heard one walking in an extremely dense portion of forest. The trees and thorny bushes made going into the forest nearly impossible. Our native guide had to hack his way with a bush knife to try to get close enough to the spot for just a glimpse of this forest ghost. The overhanging branches were so low that we had to hunch down and practically crawl to the spot. One of our group members, David Lavietes from North Carolina had severe Parkinson's disease, an inflammatory degenerative brain disease. He also had a deep love of birds. His disease had degenerated to the stage in which he walked with a festinating gait—hurried, stiff, short steps. Despite this severe limitation, and with the help of his wonderful wife and David our guide, he saw practically every bird that any of us saw on the tour. I was in constant amazement of his will to keep up with the group and his drive to see all the birds. Well, I thought this time was going to be different. It was nearly impossible for us with two healthy legs to enter this impenetrable forest. We fought our way in. Unbelievably, there he was behind us, crawling on his hands and knees. We came to a wet boggy area with logs to use as a walkway. We could barely balance ourselves crossing this barrier, and many of us fell off into the muck. I thought this would be where his journey ended. Not so. This did not stop David L.—he slowly and painfully crawled over the logs. His trousers were torn, and he was sweating profusely. I think the forest-rail was as much in awe of him as we were of it. It stopped to stare at him, thereby giving us all amazing looks at this rare denizen of the deep New Guinea forest. David L. was elated, and the tiniest smile broke across his frozen face. I could see in that small space of time, and by his magnificent effort, that there was no finish line for this man.

On our second night at Ambua, we were awakened with a bullhorn and spotlights at 2 a.m. Alarmed, we jumped out of bed, dressed, and waited for someone to tell us what was going on. David came by and said there had been a break-in through the fence and to stay in the room. We locked our door and stayed awake the rest of the night, eyes and ears alert. In the morning before breakfast, David came by and said we could walk to the lodge but not alone because there could still be trespassers on the grounds. Even though we saw an amazing fourteen species of BOPs at Ambua, and a colossal three hundred new birds for the trip, it was all anticlimactic. Birders talk about "earning" their birds. I felt like I'd "earned" these birds but under severe stress. On our last day we flew back to Port Moresby and visited the National Museum and Art Gallery to view the finest collection of "Primitive Art" in the world. In a collector's shop we bought a couple of masks and a storyboard depicting a Harpy Eagle saving a child from a crocodile. These are hanging in our home. On the plane ride home I finally told Susan about Phoebe's and David's horrible ordeal two years ago. At first she was shocked, but then took it in stride. I vowed never to return.

WORLD 3,797 • ABA 758

CHAPTER SEVENTEEN
Search for the Ivory-billed Woodpecker:
I Join the Official Arkansas Search Team

All truth passes through three stages: First it is ridiculed. Second, it is
violently opposed. Third, it is accepted as self-evident.
—Arthur Schopenhauer

The following is a reprint of the book review I wrote for the
Columbus Dispatch, published June 9, 2005, regarding, *The Grail*
Bird, Hot on the Trail of the Ivory-billed Woodpecker by Tim
Gallagher:

> *This is the story of the rarest bird in the world, the*
> *Ivory-billed Woodpecker (IBW). It is so rare that it*
> *was declared extinct by* almost *every bird expert. The*
> *last official sighting in the U.S. was 1944... until*
> *now.*
>
> *This bird was living undetected for the last 60*
> *years, not in darkest Africa or deepest Amazon but*
> *near Little Rock, Arkansas. How could the largest*
> *woodpecker in North America live under the radar*
> *screen of every birdwatcher this long? Its habitat is not*
> *a Metropark for a Sunday afternoon bird walk.*
> *Treacherous dark water currents, quicksand,*
> *cottonmouths, and monsoon-like rains await an IBW*
> *chaser.*

For years rumors of IBWs have drifted up to such venerable institutions as LSU and Cornell Lab of Ornithology from local guides and backwoods hunters but were largely discounted. These reporters were considered unreliable, kooks, liars or stringers. A stringer in birding parlance is a person who in his zeal to see a rare bird twists his sighting of a common bird into a rarer bird and fervently believes his self-deception. There is even skepticism among academics toward reports emanating from their own colleagues. Because of this attitude some topnotch professionals have suppressed their observations of IBWs for fear of ruining their reputations or their entire careers.

Tim Gallagher, magazine editor of Cornell Lab and a fervent ghost-chaser, a person who spends all his spare time searching for so called "extinct" birds, was undaunted by the prospects of forbidden swamps and forbidding experts. His obsession with the IBW began in the 1970's with a Life magazine article about John Dennis's sightings of the species in the Big Thicket of east Texas. This is no ordinary backyard bird. This is a bird venerated by Thomas Jefferson and admired by Teddy Roosevelt, painted and praised by Audubon and Roger Tory Peterson. It is called the Lord God Bird *because when people see it they say "Lord God, Look at that Bird." The author's exhaustive research of primary sources and personal communications gives us a meticulous reconstruction of the modern history of the IBW. Gallagher drags us along with his ghost-chasing buddies through the muck of the Louisiana bayous as he follows every lead of IBW sightings. He tells us chances of seeing the IBW are not as good as winning the lottery. Is it chance that the last great expedition to see this species was launched in 1935 by Dr. Arthur A. Allen, founder of the Cornell Lab? Is Gallagher the avatar of Allen? In Arkansas there is a fresh report of a sighting by Gene Sparling, a savvy backwoodsman. Gallagher rushes us to Bayou de View, a long thread of swamp forest, unlikely in its smallness to hold an IBW, but it is here that we finally see our ghost. Incredibly we fail to get any pictures for the scientific community necessary to confirm the sighting!*

Back at Cornell Lab, Gallagher relates his find to his boss, John Fitzpatrick. A seasoned scientist, Fitzpatrick subjects Gallagher to a grueling 90 minute inquisition on every minute detail of the sighting. At last convinced, Fitzpatrick places all the considerable resources of Cornell Lab behind an expedition to refind and photograph the bird, once and for all confirming its existence. The pace quickens as a SWAT team of the birders with the best ears, eyes and birding instincts are assembled—a Delta Force of birders.

The rest is history. A small article on April 29, 2005 in the Columbus Dispatch *on page 8, announced its rediscovery. It made headlines in the* New York Times. *Millions of people rejoiced.*

The Grail Bird *is a story of failed conservation and its redemption. Gallagher wrote this book to raise awareness of the continued need to conserve a valuable American treasure, southern bottomland forest and its jewel, the IBW. Lately a spate of books about the IBW has appeared.* The Grail Bird *is arguably the best of those but categorically stands alone as the only one whose author has actually seen the* Lord God Bird.

Dr. Bernard Master is Vice Chairman of the Board of The Nature Conservancy, Ohio Chapter.

After I wrote this book review, I became more interested in the day-to-day search and the searchers in Arkansas. John Fitzpatrick, CEO of the famed Cornell University Laboratory of Ornithology, headed up the team. He was accompanied by

Tim Barksdale, documentary videographer; Martjan Lammertink, a Dutch expert on large woodpeckers and author of the woodpecker section in *Birds of the World;* Gene Sparling, expert tracker and hunter; Tim Gallagher, author; Andy Farnsworth, noted field birder; and a host of other expert birders and scientists. The search, conducted in secret, lest the area be overrun by rabid birders, lasted for fourteen months. When the public announcement of the IBW's existence was made, I called Rich Shank, CEO of the Ohio Chapter of The Nature Conservancy. I had worked with him as a volunteer board member for TNC for ten years and thought it was a slam dunk that I would be invited to join the search team for a few days. Rich Shank got back to me and informed me I could join the search, but there was a catch. It was a seven-figure catch. Rich told me that for a measly $1 million, I would be permitted to search with the team for three days. For a paltry $100,000, I could spend one day with the team; no refunds if you did not see the bird. I decided this was one species that would escape my life list. I sulked for a couple of days, rejecting their outrageous proposal, but then I got another call from Rich. He said that because of my long history with TNC and my work and donations, I could join the team with no strings attached.

"No strings attached?" I repeated.

"Right. No strings attached."

That night I set to work familiarizing myself with the Ivory-billed's appearance in the field and flight patterns from texts on the internet. I studied the 1935 Arthur A. Allen film with audio of the Ivory-billed and memorized the sound of its multiple "kint" calls. I reviewed David Luneau's three-second video of a flying IBW. I was prepared for success.

The next day, May 22, 2005, I was waiting in Little Rock, Arkansas, with my bags and binoculars. I will never forget this date because it would have been the sixtieth birthday of my beloved sister, Julie, who was taken from us two years earlier with ovarian cancer. Harriet Shue, the secretary of the

Arkansas TNC picked me up and drove me to a motel in the tiny town of Brinkley.

Figure 17-1. Welcome sign to Brinkley, Arkansas.

She was my gracious hostess for the next five days. That night we headed over to Gene's Restaurant, the local watering hole for the search team, to have dinner and meet everyone. They were a very congenial group and were delighted to relate their search stories to a new listener. There had been an uninvited birder seen in the swamp the day before, but he never saw anything. I was the first invited guest to join the team. Gene Sparling said he would pick me up at the motel very early in the morning and would take me into Bayou de View. This was where David Luneau had seen the IBW. This was getting really exciting.

Figure 17-2. Gene's Restaurant, Brinkley, Arkansas.

The next morning at dawn, Gene picked me up in his SUV with canoe strapped on top. We had some coffee at a local early morning convenience store and in a half hour I was sitting in the tandem canoe paddling into the Bayou with Gene. It was just as Tim Gallagher had described in his book, the one I reviewed for the *Columbus Dispatch*. Within minutes, I was lost. The tupelos and mangroves all looked the same. But Gene knew exactly where he was. He had been there hundreds, maybe thousands, of times in his life.

Figure 17-3. Entering Bayou de View.

Bayou de View is the quintessential habitat for the IBW, primary hardwood bottomland forest with lots of dead and burned-over trees. These dead trees were the substrate for the beetle larvae, the main food of the IBW. The scientific name for the IBW is *Campephilus principalis* which translates to "fond of caterpillars," derived from a combination of Greek and Latin etymology. The grub of the beetle family, Cerambycidae, is its favorite food. In Classical Greek mythology, the man Cerambus was changed into a beetle to fly above a flood sent by Zeus to punish the wicked. I could envision in the not too distant future a high-tech Cerambus drone delivering the photographic proof in a matter of days if not hours that the IBW exists.

Gene showed me where Tim Gallagher had first seen his bird and where David Luneau had videoed his flying bird. We paddled all day, swapping stories and jokes, and the time passed quickly. I thoroughly enjoyed myself, even though we didn't get a whiff of the IBW. We saw a pair of handsome Prothonotary Warblers and quite a few cottonmouths.

We headed back to Gene's for supper and to hear what the others had discovered that day. No luck for them either. I turned in early for a big next day with Tim Barksdale, who would take me back to Bayou de View to walk some of the forest edges looking and listening.

Tim was a professional videographer of some note. The rules of the search team were that all cameras and sound equipment must be turned on and ready to capture any split-second encounter of the Ivory-billed. Tim was ready, and so was I.

We walked for a few hours and paddled for a few hours, talking about his video projects and my world birding, a great day but no IBW. We headed back to Gene's, and found a big surprise was waiting for us. Ed Bradley of *60 Minutes* and his film crew were there at our dinner table. I heard his cameraman tell our group, that while looking from their helicopter for a site to film, he saw an IBW flying over the train trestle site in Bayou de View. This was what I was waiting for, a report—how reliable, a report, I did not know, but it certainly meant a stakeout for the next day.

The next morning I borrowed a folding chair, packed a sandwich, and told Harriet Shue we were going for a big sit. The following is the report I sent to John Fitzpatrick of Cornell Lab of my big sit:

> *Following a report of an IBW sighting by a 60 Minutes newsman on 5/23/05 around 3:30 p.m. flying north of the trestle, I staked out the site by sitting quietly at the west end of the trestle with a 270 degree view of N, S & E on May 24, 2005 from 8:00 a.m. to 12:30 p.m. & 2:00 p.m. to 6:30 p.m.*
>
> *At 3:10 p.m. I heard a bird call with which I was not familiar. It sounded like "Kint...kint...kint...kint...kint" - 5 calls & then nothing. Each sound lasted about a second & each space between lasted about a second, with clear tone, slightly nasal, and each part of the "song" on the same note and key. There were no introductory or finishing series of notes or chattering. It came from mid-canopy from the big woods and was clearly and easily heard. It was strong and unidirectional as if coming from a stationary bird. I estimated it was emanating from about 125 - 135 meters away in the big woods southwest of the trestle. I could look down a side channel directly in front of me created by sparsely growing tupelos. The big woods were 100 meters away and, as far as I could tell, only held a couple of bald cypress with lots of tupelos, but I couldn't tell the condition of these trees. I did not know the names of any of the other trees. Other species calling at the same time as the mystery bird were American Crows coming from the same area but higher in the canopy. The crows, I judged 2 individuals, were calling repeatedly and for a couple of minutes after I heard the mystery call. Prothonotary Warblers and Carolina Wrens*

were calling at the same time as the subject bird. There were no White-breasted Nuthatches, Blue Jays, or Northern Flickers calling at the time. I stood up and scanned the trees in front but saw no birds. I turned to Martjan Lammertink who was sitting about 15' behind and slightly to the left of me and asked if he heard that call. He asked "What call?" I said that "Kint, kint, kint, kint, kint call" repeating what I just heard and pointing to the direction I heard it from. He said "no, only the crows." "It was under the crows," I said. Rather incredulously I asked again, "you didn't hear that call?" He said "no." I saw that he had been running his video with audio camera, and I asked him to play it back. Surely it would have caught that vocalization. He said it had run out of juice about 10 minutes before. Harriet Shue, AR TNC staff, had been sitting next to my right when the subject bird called, and I asked her if she heard the call. She said "yes" but couldn't repeat the sound when asked. She is not a birder. I then walked down to the middle of the trestle scanning the trees to the southwest reviewing rather excitedly what I just heard, repeating the tones aloud. I remembered the "tin horn" description from the books I had read on the subject and asked myself was it "tinny," which I thought it was somewhat. I scanned the trees again and glimpsed a crow flying east among the trees, high up. I decided at this point, 3:17 p.m., to call a member of the search team because I thought that an IBW was still in the woods, and I did not want to miss a golden opportunity. I also walked back to the west end of the trestle to be less visible in case the IBW would fly over. I called Gene Sparling and told him all of the proceeding. I urged him to send someone down to look for it. He said he would call Lammertink and ask him what he thought. He would also call Tim Barksdale and ask him to come down with a canoe.

Lammertink had not moved from his seat. I guess he was unimpressed. I then remembered there was an original Tanner recording which was copied by some. I walked back to Lammertink and asked him if he had a copy of the vocalization. He had to walk acros the trestle to get it, but he did; and I listened thru earphones. The 1ˢᵗ vocalization on the cd, a long series of "kint" calls started high pitched and "tinny" and then dropped down into the frequency similar to the calls I had heard earlier although its spacing was much closer between "cents." than my bird. The call I heard was even, strong, well-spaced with approximately one second between each call and each "Kint" lasted about one second, and seemed "relaxed." I pictured an IBW perched on the trunk of a tree and casually giving his signature call.

I sat back down hoping for a repeat vocalization or a sighting. I continued to scan the woods to the southwest of the trestle with no further evidence of an IBW. Some 20 minutes later I began hearing White-breasted Nuthatches calling back and forth from either side of the trestle much closer than the original mystery call. The nuthatch vocalizations were much more rapid, long series of "yanks," nasal not "tinny," with 15 - 20 "yanks" in the series with millisecond pauses between each "yank."

The call was distinctive and unique. I had never heard that call before. It was not part of my bird vocalization lexicon. I have been birding over 50 years, intensively since 1989. I have no prior experience with IBW's. I have seen 6,000 species of birds in the world, 769 species in the ABA region and almost 1,600 species in North America. I grew up in Pennsylvania and New Jersey and live in Ohio. I am familiar with all vocalizations of species living in those states. My hearing, especially in mid-tones is excellent. I served one 3 year term on the Ohio Rare

Bird Committee and know the problems a single observer report presents.

I wrote these notes the evening of the occurrence and typed them 2 days later. I used no references.

Sincerely,
Bernard F. Master, D.O.

Figure 17-4. Site of my encounter with IBW, Bayou de View.

I had already told John what I had heard when he and Ed Bradley and their crew appeared at the trestle after I had called in my report. They were looking for the bird scoop of the century, hoping to capture the first clear image of the mysterious Ivory-billed on film. Lammertink and Barkley donned hip waders and went to the spot where I'd heard the bird. They spent an hour investigating the area looking for any sign, but I had heard the bird a good hour before. Too much time had elapsed before they'd begun their search.

Figure 17-5. *60 Minutes* crew, Ed Bradley (distant left), John Fitzpatrick, (distant right), trestle, Bayou de View.

The bird had "flown the coop" with my fifteen minutes of fame and *60 Minutes'* bird scoop of the century. I sent John my report to memorialize the encounter because I believed it was more valid than a mere glimpse of a flying bird. Experienced birders depend on their ears first to identify and alert them to the presence of a bird.

The following is John's reply:

> *Dear Bernie—Thank you very much for this detailed account. It is indeed an interesting event, and we'll definitely place it into the "master log" of what— for lack of any better term—must be called "possible encounters." I do not for a moment discount the possibility that you heard an IBW. By the same token, as I know you are aware, I cannot make any statement about the probability of this being true. Such is the nature of single-observer cases, especially for heard-only encounters. In my own experience within*

the region, the only likely species that this might have been other than the woodpecker is White-breasted Nuthatch, which I have heard giving quite deliberately spaced notes that, more than once, have "made my head turn." But I remain, as I must, agnostic about what you heard.

It was really great to see you out there, and I look forward to meeting with you again—perhaps, next time, under a roost hole!

Best wishes, and with deepest thanks for your sincere interest in and support of this project.

Fitz
John Fitzpatrick
Director, Cornell Laboratory of Ornithology

Following the announcement of the IBW's rediscovery, there was quite a furor over the scientific validity of such an announcement. Of the few but outspoken naysayers, led by Jerome Jackson, professor at Florida Gulf Coast University, the main and often harsh criticism was that there simply was not enough evidence to make that pronouncement. There was no bird in hand, no active nest, no foolproof re-sightings, and no skin to examine. All of these were valid arguments. Review of the Luneau video produced varied conclusions. A few of the opponents said the video was that of a Pileated Woodpecker, fairly common in those woods. One examiner said the broad, white wing stripe on the video's bird was produced by albinism in a Pileated Woodpecker.

After spending five days with the research team, I learned of the rigorous treatment of all the evidence leading to the joint announcement of the IBW's re-discovery. The facts were overwhelmingly convincing. David Luneau's video was a strong piece of evidence despite the three-second grainy image. When David, a trained academic, first eyeballed the bird, he knew what he had. My review of the video showed a non-Pileated Woodpecker, presumably an Ivory-billed. But the clincher, and the strongest evidence to date, was the intense FBI-like study of that video. The examiners measured the wing chord of the flying bird compared to the length of the wing chord of a flying pileated. They measured the wing chords of museum specimens of IBWs and pileateds. They measured the wing chords of IBWs and pileateds perched in photos. The wing chord extends from the wrist to the end of longest primary feather. All of the measurements of the ivory-billeds were longer than all of the measurements of all the pileateds. There were no crossovers in any of the three settings. As a physician, I know anatomy does not change. A runt you say. No way. Runts cannot survive in that harsh environment. To me this was unassailable evidence that the Luneau video showed an IBW. How about the fact that after years of searching another IBW has not been seen? Cornell fed this problem to a mathematician and his computer. What are the chances of finding a single bird in more than one million acres of swampland, with ten searchers searching every day for ten hours a day for three months? The answer came back, "approaching infinity."

The fact that three agencies of excellent repute: The Nature Conservancy, the U.S. Fish and Wildlife Service, and the Cornell University Laboratory of Ornithology all courageously risked their reputations, spoke volumes to me about their degree of certainty. It is easy to snipe at them from afar because there was no bird in hand to examine by everyone. That would be the highest standard to prove with one hundred percent certainty that the bird existed, but not necessary. Absence of evidence is not evidence of absence. The evidence *en toto*, rigorously examined, meets a standard that is acceptable to most scientists except the most skeptical. I can see their point of view, but theirs does not change mine. My personal encounter that day at Bayou de View, hearing the IBW, seals it for me. I have learned to trust my ear and my inner voice. The IBW is the only "heard" bird on my American bird Life List and it will stay there. The line was drawn in the sand with The Nature Conservancy, the U.S.

Fish and Wildlife Service, and the Cornell University Laboratory of Ornithology on one side, and Jerome Jackson and a few others on the other side. I am still standing firmly with the former.

The following is a proof sheet prepared for *Birdwatcher's Digest*, 1995, to show the differences between the Ivory-billed Woodpecker and the Pileated Woodpecker with permission of the artist, Julie Zickefoose.

Figure 17-6. Pileated Woodpecker.

Figure 17-7. Ivory-billed Woodpecker.

The original is 22 x 30," a full sheet watercolor. Julie writes:

> *It was a lot of work. But fun to do. The flight sequences were especially challenging. I had great reference on the flying pileated, virtually nothing on the ivory-bill, but I tried to imagine what the verbal descriptions of its flight style would translate to in life.*
>
> *Best,*
> *Julie*

WORLD 3,788 • ABA 757

CHAPTER EIGHTEEN
The Sale of Health Power, Inc.: Converting Stock into Cash

Life handed him a lemon,
As Life sometimes will do.
His friends looked on in pity,
Assuming he was through.
They came upon him later,
Reclining in the shade
In calm contentment, drinking
A glass of lemonade.
——Dale Carnegie

George Voinovich became Ohio's sixty-fifth governor in 1991. During his first term, payments to health care plans managing the state's Medicaid health needs remained at about a two percent increase per year, which was less than the inflation rate. All the plans managed to eke out a two to four percent profit under this rate scale. During his second term, however, there was a radical change in the rate structure and his administration's attitude. He savaged the Medicaid rate by seventeen percent without warning and without convincible evidence that it was warranted. The rate was traditionally drawn from the prior year's rate plus an inflation factor, and adjusted for age and gender. This allowed the rate formula to float, depending on how many expensive young and elderly a plan had enrolled. No one in Voinovich's administration could explain the Draconian rate cut. No amount of coaxing, pleading, reasoning, demanding, or pure mathematics could change his mind. What was once a thriving industry in the state with seventeen plans had shriveled to only five plans with parts of the state completely uncovered with health care for the poor. Did the fat-cutting and fraud-eliminating efficiencies by the plans lead to their own demise? Did the government, after inviting private enterprise to solve their health care budget woes, then chase out most of the plans once it was fixed? Government agencies always preferred to work with fewer plans, which was much easier than working with several plans. I suspected there was a little of all of those ideas involved in the reasons for slashing the payments. I found out later, from a Voinovich insider, what his real motive was. Voinovich had his own agenda for his second term. He had his eye on a Senate seat. His plan was to go after the revenues of the Medicaid managed care plans with a meat cleaver. No one should make money from Medicaid anyway. This savings would result in a large surfeit in the state's budget. He would then return this to the state's taxpayers with much ballyhoo as a "rollback" of their state's income tax, one of the highest in the United States. He would then run for the Senate, extolling his state tax cut. However, his plan was derailed when the Ohio Supreme Court ruled that the state's educational system was dispensed to minorities and rural school districts in an unconstitutional way. That money, clawed from the Medicaid managed care companies, never found its way to the taxpayers. The Medicaid managed care industry never recovered, and the school system was never fixed. Voinovich did manage to serve two Senate terms without his scheme, both quietly and largely ineffectively.

I had to make a decision. Our CompManagement (CM) side of the business was growing well and was profitable. It felt as if the HMO business, our original business, was under attack by Voinovich. Should I slash our budgets with layoffs, reduce payments to providers, freeze salaries, and cut out benefits to staff and patients? This would cause great stress on our staff, providers, and patients. Would that cause more harm than good? Would it turn out to be a futile effort to save the biggest provider of health care to Ohio's Medicaid recipients? The stock price would fall, but it would fall anyway. Maybe we would fail, but we had to try. The life of the company was paramount. Working with my CFO, Mr. Arnold, and my CEO, Mr. Benedict, and looking at the skimpiest budgets, I believed that with hard work and a little bit of luck we had a chance to survive and get through this next three-and-a-half-year cycle until a new administration was elected and raised the rates. It would take us two years to do it.

I set up compulsory weekly meetings with all of our management personnel—vice presidents, directors, and managers. I assigned specific cost-cutting and revenue-producing projects to individuals and teams. Everyone had an assignment and would report weekly on his or her progress. A big chart at the front of the room would measure everyone's progress or lack thereof. Remarkably, the staff reacted with great loyalty and welcomed the challenge. A few people sought employment elsewhere, but my key people stayed. Surprisingly, some of my middle echelon managers showed a lot of talent, creativity, and energy—more than I thought they possessed. We looked at every contract and every profit center to see where we could save or make money. We needed to find $2 million in the next two years. We also strengthened the barrier between the HMO and the CM workers' injuries sides of the business—legally, financially, and accounting-wise. There was absolutely no seepage between the two halves. I didn't want the government or the creditors reaching into CM to help themselves to our profits. In the back of my mind there was always a suspicion that the Voinovich administration would eventually try to devastate the workers' injuries managed care industry in the same fashion as they did the HMOs, by slashing their rates.

I attended every weekly meeting for two years with fresh ideas and a super sleuth's commitment to rooting out waste. We were succeeding, but only slowly. The first year we cut out $1.5 million from our budget but still fell beneath the state's mandated liquid reserve requirements for HMOs. This failure invited in the regulators to approve or disapprove all of our financial transactions. This made it nearly impossible to work forward. We continued to work toward our goal. We were ahead of our budget time lines and I fervently believed we could make it. Besides, in the second year, the state gave us a 1.5 percent increase. Everything helped. Toward the end of that second year, I saw we would fall short by $200,000. Without a large cash injection, the HMO would have to undergo liquidation. I could not risk any more investor money or my own during this time period under the Voinovich administration. I must admit, this was the lowest point of my business career. I was only used to success, and the wonderful feelings that would accompany my achievements. I did not recognize the negative thoughts that were filling my brain. My biggest disappointment—involving deceit from my most trusted employees—was yet to come. During a casual conversation with the CFO after one of these weekly meetings (toward the end of the two years), he casually mentioned to me there were two contracts that combined to be worth about $100,000 annually. These contracts had never been reviewed. One was with the Red Cross for public service announcements; the other was with a TV station for advertising. They had been operating for the past two years without ever being brought forward for examination in the light of our weekly meetings. There was my $200,000 shortfall! Why in the world were they now just coming to light? Mr. Benedict said that Mr. Arnold had asked him not to say anything about them. Some digging revealed to me that Mr. Arnold was on the Central Ohio Red Cross Board of Trustees. What was his motive? There was ego involved. My CFO told me that the TV station contract that my CEO had committed our company to had been executed through a salesman friend of his. There were boondoggle golfing weekends to Arizona involved. I suspected there was corruption involved. I could hardly believe what Mr. Arnold was telling me. They both saw me and their staff struggling to save the HMO. They both had sat through the 112 weekly staff meetings, watching us wrack our brains and drive our staff to relentlessly search for answers. It was agonizingly painful for me to watch this happen, but apparently not for them. I deemed the failure to mention these two contracts to be lies by omission. The gravity of their actions was compounded by the dire financial condition of our HMO division. This called for immediate action to rid the company of Mr. Arnold and Mr. Benedict, our parasites.

That afternoon I called our legal counselor, Alec Wightman, to tell him what had occurred, and that I had decided to fire both men. His always cautious advice brought up their ages and suggested a compensation package. My first reaction was no benefits for either. More thought changed my mind on Mr. Benedict, my CFO. I would keep him. I needed someone to supervise the closing down of the HMO. He knew where all the dollars were, and after all, he was only doing the CEO's bidding, as wrong as it was. Mr. Arnold, on the other hand, was history. During his five-year tenure he had made some huge mistakes, among them his purchase of a $600,000 software package and his choice of a new COO, neither of which ever worked. I had overlooked these errors because of my personal relationship and shared journey through the public markets with him. That was gone now, shattered, never to be repaired. He was fired on Friday of that week with Alec Wightman in attendance. He gave no protest. I gave him a modest compensation package. He soon found employment elsewhere in another HMO.

The HP HMO did have some valuable assets. The Certificate of Authority to do business in the State of Ohio, which was very costly in terms of acquisition time and money but was required to operate in Ohio, was worthless. No company cared to do business with the Voinovich cadre in this hostile environment. Under normal situations, that could be worth a half million dollars. Our fifty-five thousand members were still valuable, though, worth anywhere from $100 to $300 per member, depending on the region and age/gender ratios. I personally called every remaining HMO CEO, once competitors, to see if they wanted to buy this asset. They all eagerly agreed and prices were set. I submitted a plan to the regulators to sell the membership to the remaining four plans. The state would benefit because the membership would remain in the less expensive managed care plans. The new owners would benefit from increased membership, and HP would benefit by the cash already earmarked for our creditors. The regulators approved the plans with the exception of the Ohio Department of Human Services regarding the sale of our Cincinnati HMO. For some indecipherable reason, they blocked it. We had no choice but to abandon those Cincinnati members back to the fee-for-service system, losing all of that potential revenue from a sale. Within days the ODHS changed its mind. It now asked us to perform an orderly transition of all the patients to the remaining managed care company in Cincinnati. It was too late. The patients were already back on the old welfare health system. Nobody benefitted from ODHS's hare-brained decision. True to form, when a plan was in trouble, like two chickens—one healthy and the other sick—government would kill the healthy chicken, make chicken soup, and feed it to the sick chicken.

After thirteen operating years, the HP HMO was liquidated in an orderly fashion. Our creditors were paid off at about fifty cents on the dollar. HPWR was delisted from the NASDAQ exchange. I had mixed emotions about the end of the HMOs, a concept that I had brought to Ohio in 1983, and whose influence and heritage continues to this day. Our company was the first HMO contracting with the State of Ohio to manage the health care of Medicaid patients in Columbus and Cincinnati and the second in Dayton. We finished with a network of fifty-five thousand patients, five thousand physicians, and fifty-five hospitals, as well as dominant market share in the State of Ohio. Over the life of the HMO business, we enjoyed a half-billion dollars in revenues. We introduced many firsts for our patients: free transportation; free over-the-counter medications; and easy access to high-quality health care providers. We took the muss and fuss out of medicine. But it is difficult to be first in a fledgling industry. I remembered seeing a sign in a country store out west, "Pioneers always get arrows in their back."

After the closing of the HMO division, we switched our energies to our CompManagement division, the largest managed care organization for workers' injuries in the state with eighty-eight thousand employers as clients. That old warning about government inviting in private enterprise to solve their problems and then once solved, treating them disdainfully, remained in the back of my mind and kept haunting me. I was very distrustful of state government and decided to secretly find a buyer for the entire company, HPI. I was sick and tired of the politics, wrangling for rates, the competitive wars, and untrustworthy employees. I decided to sell the company while we were on top. I began some talks with a Columbus insurance company and received a lowball offer of $14 million, which probably could have been stretched to $18 million. I thought it was inadequate. We were looking forward to $40 million in revenues and at least ten percent profit by fiscal year end 2000. The management team was superb, and we enjoyed a great reputation with the state and our client base. I quietly brought in my old friend, Jeff Brausch, to evaluate our company. He arrived at a $32 million valuation or $8 a share. I secretly set about getting a buyer. My first call was to Dan French in Detroit, once with our underwriters, Roney & Company, who now had his own venture capital company. We conferenced with Brausch and decided a quasi-auction would bring in the highest price. Under confidentiality agreements, Dan contacted several companies that should have an interest. By mid-2000 we received three bids. I investigated all three not only for price but also for corporate culture, leadership, trustworthiness, and financial history, and selected a company headquartered in Greenwich, Connecticut. They were listed on the American Stock Exchange, and all their information was public. After their due diligence, we agreed on a $30 million purchase price, all cash at the closing. You can't beat cash. Cash was, is, and always will be king.

With the closing of HP HMO there would be a deleterious financial effect on my MEDCenters. Without the added revenues from the HP capitation checks, the revenues to my MEDCenters would tumble. I began selling off my personally owned MEDCenters in Columbus and Cincinnati, both practices and buildings. It took me six years to accomplish all the sales at favorable terms. One Cincinnati group had already bought my practice but was dallying on purchasing the building. Although the group was paying a fair rent, I really wanted out of the real estate business. Bill Loving, my very capable real estate agent, had trouble getting a purchase contract from the renter. They were a nonprofit and run by a charitable board. Their board simply could not make a final decision to sign the contract. This went on for months. In frustration, I finally called Bill and asked him to call his best friend, have him dress up as a businessman in a suit and tie, tote a briefcase, and walk him through the MEDCenter during business hours. At the end of the sales tour his friend was to exclaim in a loud voice for all the employees to hear, "I'll buy it." The next day I had my signed contract from the group's board. My last MEDCenter was sold in 2005 after I detected a massive embezzlement by my most trusted employee, my manager of six years.

Buyer and seller set about preparing all the legal documents, audited statements, opinion letters, and federal and state authorities' written approvals. Fees were agreed upon. There were a myriad of agencies to inform and from which to extract approvals. The paperwork, e-mails, and telephone calls were voluminous. Everything was set for a November, 2000, closing. In the words of that great philosopher, As the well-known saying goes, "It's not over till the fat lady sings." A call from Joe Boeckman, one of our corporate attorneys, was startling and most disturbing. The buyer wanted to adjust the purchase price down by $4 million. Boeckman, himself, on behalf of the HPI management group, Bossart, Wagner and Kurth, had gone behind my back, and without my knowledge, negotiated their new employment contracts with the prospective buyer. The buyer wanted to subtract the value of these contracts from his purchase price. When there was blood in the water, the sharks came out to feed. What was I not getting here? Management was part of our company, and we were selling the *whole* company. The buyer deemed our management such an essential part of the deal that he wanted to cement them to the sale. Management wanted, to what amounted to, a "no-cut" contract. I could see the buyer's point of view, but why should that cost our shareholders another $1 per share? I could also understand management's position, but why should the shareholders cough up the money for management's security? I admonished Boeckman for his surreptitious behavior, which was antithetical to the interests of our shareholders. I thought his actions were unprofessional. I immediately called Bossart and found out his side of the story. He had negotiated their management contracts in good faith with the buyer and did not know the buyer would subtract the purchase price from the sale price. He thought I knew about it because he was using our corporate attorneys. In any event, they were standing firm on their new contracts regardless of the outcome. I explained to him that since their management group as a whole owned sixteen percent of HP stock, any diminution of the stock value would also hurt the group proportionately. They were "robbing Peter to pay Paul." Bossart was not budging. I talked to Wightman about the situation and the role Boeckman had played, but I received no helpful comments or results. I guess they were hoping for some new clients after the sale. I talked to Bossart several times over the next three weeks and sensed some give in his position to move the sale along. I had to make a Solomonian decision. I took stock of my assets. I was not in a weak position. I, therefore, drew a line in the sand, a fifty percent or $2 million rollback in the management contract price, which amounted to a $0.50 increase in the shareholder stock price or no sale. This would give them some security and the shareholders a fairer price. I admit it was not perfect, but it could satisfy all parties. If they would not take my offer, they would continue to work for me, but under much less enlightened governance. I could stand firm. I had controlling interest in the company. No one could outvote me. The management group could leave, but we had non-compete agreements. We could replace them. They could leave and wait out their non-compete timelines, but where would that get them? At least a year behind the competition and a start-up company in an already saturated industry. Bossart and "the boys" took the deal, and we continued to the closing, now set in early December 2000.

The "fat lady" had not sung yet, and another phone call from our attorneys in early December delayed the closing aria. Wightman informed me the outside HP Board members were not going to vote for the sale. *What?* These were all carefully hand-picked friends and associates, all shareholders themselves. In the past thirteen years there was never a hint of discontent or dissension. Once we decided on a board policy, we followed in unison until we met our goals. It had always been that way. My policy was, "Get on board or get off." Wightman told me the group of dissidents was being led by Mr. Tanlan, the elder statesman of the group, an original board member and my go-to guy to deliver the message to the other board members as to the direction I thought we should go. He always led the vote. He was my Majority Leader. He was a respected and charitable businessman in the Columbus community. 1 admired him greatly. Apparently it was not mutual. The board's collective "beef," led by Tanlan, was they were not being paid enough for their board participation. The non-employee board (outside) members received a $10,000 per-year stipend and $500 for every board and committee meeting attended, more than adequate for a company our size. They were also awarded a small amount of common stock at the end of every year. Not satisfied, they were demanding a raise to $30,000 a year, retroactive for three years, or they would vote against the sale. Some called this a "beef." I called it what it was—extortion. I remembered some years back when Schottenstein Stores, a public corporation, wanted to take its company private, they issued a stock buy-back at a certain price. All the shareholders tendered their shares back to the company except Tanlan. He had a significant minority position and forced the Schottenstein Company to pay him more money than anyone else. I knew of this story but never thought he would try that with me. I now know a tiger never changes his stripes.

My first call was to Dr. Crystal Kirkendahl, an educator in Washington, D.C. I had heard her speak several years earlier at a Martin Luther King, Jr. award ceremony in 1995, at which I was the honoree. She was a brilliant orator and delivered her message of equal education under the law to all children to her rapt audience. I had to have her on my board, and she accepted. Over the few years, we became fast friends. I asked her what was going on. She sheepishly said that Tanlan had talked everyone into his position without anyone really thinking it through. Easy money, I guess. She said she would vote for the sale and was sorry she had caused me any problem. My next call was to one of my oldest friends and colleagues, Dr. Elliott Feldman, an original board member and a large shareholder. He too said he had gotten caught up in the moment and would certainly cast his vote for the sale. He was sorry for any discontent he might have caused. The third call was to another friend and colleague, Dr. Burt Schear, an original board member and owner of three key practices in the HP network in Dayton. He had just finished a lengthy and expensive court battle with his brothers over a family business. He wanted no more rancor or attorney fees. He was also a large shareholder. Yes, he would vote for the sale. My last call was to Bob Garek, the co-founder with his wife, Marge, of the Marburn Academy, a school for learning disabled children. He was an original board member and a close confidant of mine. He was embarrassed to get the call and immediately told me he would vote for the sale. I never called Tanlan.

The day before the board voted, I called each member again to check on their reliability. Everyone was firmly on the "aye" side of the vote. The day of the special board meeting arrived. The sale of the company was put to the vote. I moved for an open voice vote, and the motion was seconded by Dr. Feldman. An open voice vote exposes everyone's vote publicly—no dissembling there. Tanlan did not know of the lobbying I had done to change the votes to a yes. The poor man did not know what hit him.

All yeses were recorded, and when the vote got to him, instead of a "no" he said hesitantly, "I abstain."

The corporate attorneys immediately asked for a time-out and took Tanlan outside the meeting room.

When he came back he said, "I change my vote to 'yes,'" which made it unanimous.

I had painted him into a corner, and he was confused, rare for a man of his wisdom and abilities. The attorneys told him that an abstention had to be explained in a public document to the SEC. How could he possibly explain his abstention? He did not squeeze enough money out of the company to buy his vote?

It was a long struggle, but the shareholders finally received nearly $7 a share net of all fees and expenses. Many shareholders had sold back in 1994 for high premiums, $12 at the opening, and $14 to more than $17.50 a share months later. Many, including me, had bought more at lows of $1 to $3 when things were going sour. I wanted the closing to take place on January 2, 2001, to save myself from paying income taxes on the sale until the following year, 2002. The buyer wanted the closing December 31, 2000, to enjoy whatever tax deductions they would reap in the same year. I agreed to a

New Year's Eve day closing, December 31, 2000. I had learned from many a deal that when there was money on the table, take it.

In anticipation of a November closing, I had scheduled a birding trip with Susan to South Africa. Now it was a month later, and I would not be in the country for the closing. I gave wiring instructions to the transfer agent to wire the money to my Columbus bank when the deal closed. I asked my long-time personal assistant, Sandie Lloyd, to telegram me in Cape Town when the money hit my account. The closing took place in the morning. When the telegram arrived, Susan and I drank a bottle of Moet & Chandon, 1967, in the elegant Victorian dining room of the Alphaen Plantation on the edge of Cape Town to celebrate the sale of HP and welcome in the New Year, 2001, and the third millennium. I swear I could hear Kate Smith singing "America the Beautiful" in the background. The fat lady had finally sung.

CHAPTER NINETEEN
Health Tips for Bird Tours

Be careful about reading health books. You may die of a misprint.
—Mark Twain

I always take the following with me on my bird tours:

• Surgical kit: All sterile and disposable—#15 blade and handle, needle holder, suture, forceps, surgical gloves and bandages. These should be carried by everyone who knows how to use them. Fortunately I have never had to use this kit; however, in Papua New Guinea I wish I had it when one member of our tour group slipped in the dark and lacerated her elbow. We were out in the middle of nowhere. I brought the skin edges together by "butterflying" with duct tape (another use for duct tape) and covered it with a thin layer of NEOSPORIN® Ointment and some Band-Aids®. Weeks later she wrote me from home thanking me. Her family doc said it was the best job he had ever seen, and it healed great.
•   Vial of 2% Lidocaine® for local anesthetic for health care professionals
• (4) Disposable 2.5cc syringes
• (2) 22 gauge disposable needles
• (2) 25 gauge disposable needles
•   I carry my own sterile needles and syringes for personal use in case I need an injection. This avoids HIV and Hepatitis

B- and C-contaminated needles and syringes. These diseases are rampant in underdeveloped countries. Many health care facilities in poor countries re-use needles, syringes and yes, bandages, too.

- EpiPen® emergency adrenaline injection for anaphylactic reactions.
- Small bottle of StingEze® for local application to bee stings, jellyfish stings and painful sunburn. It gives immediate relief.
- Tweezers
- Alcohol cotton swabs
- Assorted Band-Aids®
- 3-inch Ace bandage

Medications:

- Small tube of eye ointment with antibiotics and steroid for infections and allergies
- NEOSPORIN® Ointment for small skin wounds and minor infections
- Steroid cream for rashes and itches
- Antifungal cream for fungal rashes from humidity and heat
- Cipro® 500 mg for traveler's diarrhea and any suspected gram negative infections. Cipro is great for knocking out Giardia and other protozoan infections. I begin it right away when I feel any GI upset. The benefits greatly outweigh the risks. Why wait and spoil a three-week trip? I do not recommend taking Cipro prophylactically.
- Keflex® 500 mg 4 x a day for gram-positive infections like Staph and Strep.
- Tamiflu® when travelling in Asia especially China. Early usage will diminish the symptoms and shorten the duration of the various Influenza virus infections.
- Prednisone®, 10 mg tablet for anti-inflammation. I use it on a decreasing daily dosage regimen starting at 40mg for five to seven days. I use it judiciously for serious reactions only

because of potential harmful side effects. Again, weigh the risk-reward ratio.

• Laxative. Constipation may occur due to dehydration, change in food habits, water, time change, etc.

• Dramamine® tablets, 12.5 mg, every four to six hours for motion sickness. It makes me too drowsy, so I break it a 25 mg in half. My formula to prevent sea sickness for pelagic trips, and everyone has their own method, is to not eat breakfast and take a Dramamine® tablet 12.5mg, an hour before embarkation. I wait until my stomach feels steady then I can have a snack or lunch. Furthermore I remain on deck in the fresh air, not in an enclosed space, and gaze at the horizon, the only fixed point seen from the boat.

• OTC cold tablets like Claritin-D®.

• Painkillers, Ibuprofen 200 mg tabs, two every four hours or three every six hours for pain or hydrocodone, one or two every four to six hours for severe pain barring any contraindications.

• Inhaler for wheezing and/or difficulty breathing caused by dust, allergies, pollution, URIs, and bronchitis because it occurs in places like China.

• Imodium® for severe dehydrating diarrhea. This with Cipro® conquers the most serious cases.

• Rehydration powder—this is a balance of sugar and electrolytes like sodium and potassium. Mix with clean water and use liberally. Dry skin, dry tongue and failure to perspire are warning signs for dehydration. The normal kidneys put out at least 50 cc of urine every hour. That's about 1.7 fluid ounces or 0.2 cup every hour. That's one cup of urine every five hours. Make sure you are urinating. Your urine should be straw color and clear, not dark or cloudy. Without the manufactured version of the rehydration powder, use six teaspoons of sugar, half a teaspoon of table salt and one liter (about a quart) of clean water and drink often. I had to use this last formula for a dehydrated child with diarrhea in Venezuela. The parents had paddled a whole day to see me when they heard there was an American doctor in the region.

I heard word that it worked, fortunately. Add bananas and rice to the diet. In the States I also use applesauce and skim milk.

• Antacid tablets like TUMS®.

• Anti-malaria prophylaxis—I use Lariam®. I have never had some of the side effects reported by some patients, and they can be severe. There are alternatives like Doxycycline® that work equally well with much less chance of severe side effects. Severe sunburn is a problem with Doxy. Check the CDC recommendations for the country in which you will be traveling. You must start the Lariam® a week before you go; take one tablet per week while there, and continue one week after you return home.

Regarding vaccines, check with the CDC for the required immunizations for the country you are visiting and keep up to date. The diseases you might encounter in other countries are potential killers. As of this writing there are no vaccines to protect against malaria, Ebola virus, Chickengunya fever, Hantu virus. Trypanosomiasis (Sleeping Disease transmitted by the Tse-Tse fly), River Blindness transmitted by the Simulium fly, flukes, dengue fever and a multitude of other killers. With these, an ounce of prevention is worth a ton of cure.

Use DEET® for protection against the most dangerous animal in the world, the mosquito. Keep arms and legs covered especially at dusk when the mosquitoes are most active. Button that top button. Use Permethrin®-imbedded clothing, but be aware this chemical can have serious neurological side effects. (On a side note: Mosquitoes do not carry the AIDS virus.) DEET® will also help remove leeches.

Drink bottled water and other bottled drinks only, like beer and Coke. Make sure the bottle caps are original, sealed and not replaced. Have them bring the unopened bottle to the table so you can open it yourself and see it was not tampered with. Be careful bathing in still water, a breeding ground for flukes.

Everything you eat should be well cooked especially pork, which carries Trichina, and eggs and chicken which could have Salmonella. Leafy vegetables, when not washed, can harbor E. coli which causes Traveler's Diarrhea. You are always at risk for Staph food poisoning and E. coli diarrheal infections because some food handlers simply don't wash their hands. There is no 100% foolproof way to prevent these infections except to eat at restaurants that have good reputations. When you sample foods from street vendors, which is very romantic, you invite gastrointestinal trouble. I avoid those opportunities. The cleanest restaurants and safest eating, besides your own cooking, are restaurants catering to the Muslim community. They prepare their meats following the orthodox *halal* Islamic dietary prescriptions. They slaughter their animals for cooking in a ritually humane manner. They provide wash basins with soap. Look for the universal color of the Muslim religion, green, on the outside of the establishment, which denotes a Muslim-owned restaurant and *halal* food.

Bring iodine tablets to purify water if pure water is not available. This actually happened to me in Madagascar. If you suspect contaminated water, drop one iodine tablet in the solution and wait a half hour before drinking. This applies to not only water but also all non-bottled and unsealed beverages like juice and milk.

Wear sunscreen.

If you have a cold, sinus infection or some nasal congestion and are going to fly, take a decongestant and a painkiller an hour before you fly. This will prevent the pain from a blocked Eustachian tube, which can be horrific. Even mild congestion can lead to a ruptured eardrum in an airplane.

Take Melatonin when you return home to help return you to your normal sleep cycle. It takes one day per every time zone you cross to return to your regular biorhythms. Each time zone is about a 1,000 miles.

CHAPTER TWENTY
How to Choose a Bird Tour:
My Top Choices

You know it is time to go home when you start looking like your
passport photo.
—Unknown

For those of you who have never been on an organized bird tour, this is for you. The selection of a tour is dependent on time of year, distance, birds one wants to see, political unrest, safety, dollar value, weather, altitude, choice of country, one's health and physical limitations. Once you have gone through that algorithm, choose the best leader. Bird tour companies that have been in business a long time usually have excellent bird leaders. That is how they stay in business so long. But young companies can be outstanding, too. Word of mouth from past participants usually provides the most helpful information. Over the past twenty-five years, I have traveled with many bird tour groups and have experienced many bird tour leaders. Obviously, I have not birded with them all. I have heard rave reviews about several tour companies and leaders whom I have not birded with. I have also heard about some bad companies and leaders. Opinions vary and different people like or dislike different tour groups and leaders for different reasons. I believe the quality of a tour begins with the quality of the ownership of the company. Strong ethical, and caring owners produce great tours and great bird leaders. Attributes of a great Tier I bird tour leader: Know your territory, including habitats, weather conditions, seasonal bird population changes, and trouble spots to avoid. One must be able to identify every bird in your territory. Know where to find them in multiple sites and how to get there. Know the calls. Have the recorded calls and ability to record and play back. Use the recorded calls judiciously. Know when to quit on a bird. Have a spotting telescope for your participants. Don't waste participants' time with your own photography. Make an attempt to have everyone see the bird, but don't waste an inordinate amount of time trying to show a bird to someone who can't see. Have great communication skills; provide friendly, open, detailed instructions for proper dress and footwear for that day, eating arrangements, target birds for that day, times of departure, and meals. Don't show your annoyance at stupid or repetitive questions. You are a professional, so handle it. Share your rules of birding with your clients before you start out, such as no loud talking or extraneous noises. Change the order of the line on narrow trails periodically so everyone gets a chance to be up front with the leader. Rotate the seating arrangement in the transport vehicles. Instruct how to share the trip scope so everyone gets a chance for a look. Don't be afraid to move a scope hog off the scope. Feel free to point out names of flora, fauna, topography, and historical interests. Know some facts about the bird you are looking at. Do not chastise or confront a participant in front of the group. Know how to show a bird to a client. Always start with the most important: name, direction, and distance. Move to more detailed instructions like landmarks, and how high or how low. Use the hands of a clock as reference and how far in from the periphery of a tree or bush to pinpoint the location. Don't be afraid to quietly point in the bird's direction. For a flying bird, use directions, left, right, or straight away or coming straight to the group. Describe how high above the tree line or other fixed point by using the binocular's field of vision as a reference point like, "one field above the red barn." Use a laser beam or mirror to show a bird that's in a confusing tangle or leafy tree if the ambient light and distance to the bird allows. Take a quick look at the members of your group to see which direction their heads are facing. You can easily spot the birder who doesn't have a clue what you are pointing out.

Be prepared to change plans when outside influences like potential danger or acts of nature dictate change. Never jeopardize the safety of a client. When summarizing the day's trip list, do it rapidly, and save long discussions for afterward. Birding is always first, photography second. Insist that your drivers gas up the vehicles and eat breakfast before the birding day starts. Tier I bird tour leaders always conduct great tours.

The following are Tier I bird tour leaders (listed alphabetically) in my opinion:

• **Ken Behrens**, Tropical Birding—Enthusiastic, great birding skills, energetic, considerate of clients' needs.

• **Christian Boix**, Africa Geographic—Energetic, very experienced in Africa, very considerate to clients, great birding skills, and fun to be with.

• **Paul Holt**, WINGS—A man of great character and a tremendous person to be around. Great birder, knows those tricky Phylloscopus warblers. Shorebird expert. Very considerate of his clients' needs.

• **Steve Howell**, WINGS—Amazing wealth of bird knowledge, articulate and good thinker, seabird expert, gull expert, birds of Mexico expert, banding expert, all-around expert, fun to be with. He is also a good illustrator. Sometimes gets a little salty. Feed him chocolate.

• **Ben King**, retired Kingbird tours—A wealth of experience in Asian birding, has seen more birds in Asia than anyone else, inexhaustible energy, an abundant supply of birding stories, and fun to be with. A health guru.

- **Phil Maher**, Australia—A former tracker, very organized, knows Australian birds cold. He has the only franchise to show the Plains-Wanderer.
- **Susan Myers**, WINGS and independent—A great young talent and like a fine wine, improving with age. Good decision maker, knows her territory well. She wrote the book on Borneo birds.
- **Noble Procter**—Attu leader, not leading anymore, but a treasure.
- **Forrest Rowland**, Rock Jumpers—The best birder I have ever birded with. Has it all together, identification skills by sight and sound, talent, personality, sense of humor, and energy.
- **Bret Whitney**—An amazing wealth of knowledge about Neotropical birds, the foremost expert on Brazilian birds, fun to be with. He has discovered birds new to science. Knows all the bird sounds. A great leader.
- **Dennis Yong**, WINGS and independent—A real character, chain-smoking, flip-flop wearing Sino-Malaysian birder. Very organized and speaks several languages fluently.

- **Responsibilities of a tour participant: Do unto others as you would have them do unto you.**

BEST IN CLASS

The following are the best in class, in my opinion:

• **Best all-around field birder:** Forrest Rowland everywhere, Jon Dunn in the U.S., Richard Crossley wherever, Paul Holt.

• **Best in Ohio:** Jim McCormac

• **Most talented:** Forrest Rowland

• **Best organized:** Judy Davis

• **Best bird artist:** Julie Zickefoose

• **Most fun:** Forrest Rowland, Christian Boix, Steve Howell

• **Wittiest:** Steve Howell

• **Most energetic:** Ben King, Christian Boix

• **Most intellectual:** Robert Ridgely

• **Best writer:** Steve Howell

• **Best dollar value:** Ben King

CHAPTER TWENTY-ONE
Things You Will Never Read in a Bird Book:
Practical Birding Tips

In order to see birds, it is necessary to become part of the silence.
—Robert Lynd

- When birding is slow, look and listen for chickadees. They are flock formers.
- "Carolina Wrens just don't say, 'Tea kettle, tea kettle,' anymore." —Marlene Woo Lun
- Even the most expert birder can miss a bird ID.
- Everyone cannot identify every bird every time.
- "On its wintering grounds, Least Flycatchers at rest will raise their tails slightly upward and then downward. The downward motion will ratchet down like a screen door on a spring until it comes to rest." —Steve Howell.
- A few IDs differentiating Cooper's Hawks from Sharp-shinned Hawks in the field cannot be made with one hundred percent certainty. They are "tweeners." The same goes for Greater and Lesser Yellowlegs.
- Blackbird flocks' flight patterns: Red-winged Blackbird flocks fly like an accordion-expanding and shrinking. They also show dark patterns (males) against light patterns (females). Starling flocks fly in unison. Common Grackle flocks show a combination of long tails (males) and short tails (females).

- "Snow Buntings hate snow." —Milt Trautman.
- The two most beautiful bird songs that birders rarely hear are Winter Wren and Blue-gray Gnatcatcher.
- Don't waste your time "spishing" in Asia, Australia or Europe. It does not work.
- Song Sparrows always come to "spishing."
- Vireos and flycatchers do not have flight notes.
- Do not contradict someone when they report a bird sighting that is not likely. He or she will hate you forever. Just nod your head and move on. One thing is for certain—you cannot see or hear exactly the same thing that another person sees or hears.
- Be willing to agree to disagree on bird IDs.
- You will learn something about birds you never knew every time you go birding if you carefully observe.
- After puberty it is very difficult but not impossible to learn bird songs.
- Use your car as a bird blind.
- Look at every bird you see through your bins, especially birds in flight. Practice makes perfect.
- Before you bird, adjust and clean your lenses for clarity.
- Never leave a "hotspot."
- When looking for a bird in a dense area, pre-adjust your bins' focal length for the distance where you think the bird might appear. Also focus on openings or sight lines where you think the bird might cross. This saves valuable seconds to clearly see the bird. It will also gain you lifers.
- Keep your bins close to your eyes so you can raise them quickly to see the bird.
- You have an average of three seconds to see and identify a bird.
- When searching for fruit eaters like parrots, look for fruiting trees.
- When searching for hummingbirds, look for flowers.
- Birds have great fidelity to a particular location and will return faithfully but don't count on it.

- Wear a harness strap on your binoculars to distribute the weight across your shoulders and reduce the weight on your cervical spine.
- "Birding is best in the morning, but you can't be everywhere every morning." —Dr. Tim Fitzpatrick
- Do not wear camouflage outside of the U.S. That is what rebels and militia wear. You might end up on the wrong end of a bullet.
- Winter is the best time for beginners to learn birds in Eastern North America. There are small numbers, but no leaves and no confusing fall plumages.

CHAPTER TWENTY-TWO
My Quest for All the Bird Families of the World:
Short Stories in Rwanda, Cameroon, the Arabian Peninsula, Argentina, and China

One more labor lies in store boundless, laden with danger, great and long, and I must brave it out from start to finish.
—Homer, *The Odyssey (Book 7, L. 236)*

RWANDA

Christian Boix, while working for the bird tour company Tropical Birding, enticed me to join him birding in Rwanda. Christian, a Catalan, living in South Africa for the past ten years is an expert on African birds. There was still a huge hole in my African bird list in 2008, having only visited Kenya, Madagascar, and South Africa.

Rwanda—isn't that the place where everyone is killing everyone else? Why would I want to go there?

Christian explained that it was quite safe now under the new President Kagame, an American trained military man. The country is located in central Africa in the Albertine Rift, chock full of rare endemics and rich with fancy birds like turacos, batises, and wattle-eyes. They had exotic names like Ruwenzori–this and Ruwenzori–that. Besides, there were mountain gorillas and chimpanzees.

There was one little hitch in the beginning of the tour. Christian was lacking a document that he needed to enter the country. It was a new requirement that he did not know about. Without this little piece of paper, the Rwandan officials were ready to fly him back to South Africa. He had the presence of mind to call Emanuel, his Rwandan ground agent, who immediately called the Minister of Tourism, waking him up. The unhappy minister called the immigration officials, and Christian was allowed to proceed without further delay. The ground agent in that one stroke had earned his pay. Christian and I covered the length and breadth of that small republic in ten days. There were no signs of hostility amongst the Hutus and Tutsis. The Holocaust was over. There were signs of unity posted throughout the country, "We are one" and "Never again." It was a peaceful, verdant country with a bustling economy. They welcomed tourism and wanted trade with the West. They had zero tolerance for corruption of any kind. Why would you not want to go there?

Christian and I were joined by fellow ABA board member, Paul Bristow. In ten days we covered the whole of Rwanda from Nyungwe Forest to Akagera National Park and saw many of the Albertine Rift endemics including the rare Red-collared Mountain-Babbler.

Figure 22-1. Shoebill—In Uganda, seen from Rwanda.

On the next to last day, Paul spotted what appeared to be a motionless dot across the river from where we were birding. He trained a spotting scope on the dot, and what an amazing surprise! It was a Shoebill, a rare and unique bird found mostly in South Sudan with less than fifty individuals in Rwanda, a truly lucky find. It is the size of a heron but it has this unexpectedly exaggerated deformed bill, the shape of a large wooden Dutch shoe. For the record, I took a distant but identifiable photo (Figure 22-1) of this creature through the telescope using a small hand-held compact camera. This method is called *digiscoping*. The Shoebill or *Balaeniceps rex* is the only member of the Shoebill family, and a new family for me.

On my last night I took a room at the Hotel Rwanda *(Hotel des Mille Collines)* the very hotel from the book and 2004 movie of the same name. I reflected on our lucky sighting for a while. This saved me a trip to Uganda where most birders have to go to see this species. But mostly I thought of the thousand terrified victims jammed into a few rooms years earlier that manager Rusesabagina (Don Cheadle) saved from the slaughter that was taking place all around them outside.

Figure 22-2. Hotel Rwanda, Mille Collines, birding companion, Paul (far left) Kigali.

There was one incident that scarred my otherwise marvelous trip to Rwanda. On our last night our ground agent, Emanuel, took us to dinner at the finest restaurant in Kigali. He was a patriot and a businessman. He wanted to talk about his country and how to increase tourism from the United States. I gave him several ideas, which I learned later he followed up on. I asked him to recommend a trustworthy shop in Kigali where I could purchase some genuine antique African artifacts for my collection (masks, carvings, and unusual art works). I wanted to avoid the usual made-for-the-tourist-trade junk. He understood. He said he would pick us up in the morning, a couple of hours before our plane left, and drive me to one particular shop he vouched for. The next morning his driver took us into downtown Kigali to a large shop with an attractive outer appearance. We entered and met the owner, who showed me around.

My first question to shopkeepers everywhere is always, "Do you take American Express?"

AMEX is a traveler's best insurance against shopkeeper shenanigans, deceit, fraud, and non-performance. AMEX will back its cardholders to the maximum. Yes, he took American Express.

"Do you ship?"

This is important because you cannot always hand carry your purchases home.

"Yes."

"How do you ship?"

He shipped by airfreight, which is faster than sea but much more expensive, charging by the pound.

"Do you know how to ship?"

The proper way to ship valuables is to crate them in a wooden carrier. This protects the contents from breakage by rough or even normal handling.

"Will you insure the contents?"

"Yes."

Having received satisfactory responses from the shop owner, I went about choosing the best he had, a Songhai village spirit carving, three feet tall and more than one hundred years old, decorated with monkey hide, brass, Guineafowl feathers, and paint; an ornately carved king's chair; a circumcision ceremonial mask; and a war shield—all from the Democratic Republic of the Congo. Congo artifacts are becoming more difficult to find, and their prices are rising because no one goes there anymore except missionaries and a few other do-gooders. I also purchased some beautifully woven decorative baskets for the house and four ceramic gorillas for my grandchildren. We negotiated a price, and I gave him my AMEX card number. As I left the shop, I told him not to forget to insure everything. He assured me he would.

Three days after I returned home, I received the first half of my shipment from Rwanda. It was crudely wrapped in newspaper and tied with cord and tape. An old cardboard television box, dented on every side, covered the outside. The gorilla figurines were smashed into hundreds of pieces; the finials of the king's chair were broken off; the mask and shield were intact. The village spirit had not yet arrived, but I was filled with apprehension as to what its condition would be. I waited until it arrived before I made any insurance claims. The next day it arrived, wrapped the same way in newspaper, cardboard, and rope. The base was smashed, and there were large cracks running horizontally through it. I was mortified and angry. Thanks to AMEX, my investment was protected. I called the air freight carrier to report the damage and make a claim. The carrier reported that the sender had not insured it, and the carrier was not accepting any liability. My next move was to email the vendor in Kigali and tell him of the condition of the goods received, and admonish him for the poor shipping method and the lack of insurance. I was sending back the damaged goods C.O.D., and he could deal with it. I was canceling the AMEX charges only for the damaged pieces, which were the most expensive ones. I attached photos of the damaged goods. I called AMEX to cancel the charges, and to my surprise there were no charges.

The vendor never processed my AMEX card. AMEX explained that the vendor was not on the AMEX list of approved clients. *What's going on here?* For security, I cancelled my card. A return email from Kigali said that he refused to accept any return shipment and demanded full payment. I told him by return e-mail that I would pay for the damaged goods at twenty cents on the dollar and the others at full price or he would receive everything back C.O.D. Which choice did he have? I was completely in the driver's seat now. I had the merchandise, had withheld the payment, and was ten thousand miles away. He insisted on full payment. I told him the goods were on their way back to Kigali.

"No, no, no. Don't send them back. I will take the first choice."

I wired the agreed upon sum to the shop's account and thought that was the end of it.

Exactly seventeen days later, I received an email from the shop owner again demanding full payment. I had already sent the agreed amount to his bank. I called my bank to make sure the wire had been sent, and it had. I fired back a reply that there would be no more money, and I considered the matter closed. A return email accused me, the rich American, of taking advantage of the poor African. This appeal fell on deaf ears. The shop owner followed with a threat that he would put an ad in my hometown newspaper telling the community what a crook I was. I did not answer. He followed with another email that he would report me to Interpol and to the consulate. I did not reply. The next threat got my attention. He said he knew where I lived, and that he had an American visa. He was coming to America. I had to take this threat seriously for the sake of my family and staff. There were all kinds of West African rabble living in the U.S., and maybe, just maybe, he would send one of his cronies on a collection mission. I increased my house security. I already had a concealed carry weapon license. I was hyper-alert anyway, post Vietnam. My two best friends, Smith and Wesson were ready, and they were backed by a seven shot Remington single-barrel shotgun. I called the FBI to officially record the threat. The person who answered the phone told me that it did not warrant FBI involvement. I called a fellow ABA board member who had lived in Africa with the State Department for twelve years for advice. He told me to call the State Department, Rwanda desk, and they would assist me. I called and never received a reply.

I was going about this all wrong. I was acting like a doctor from Worthington. I changed my thinking. I put on my old West Philly hat. I emailed Emanuel, my ground agent in Kigali, and explained what I had been up against for the last month. I knew he was connected by the way he had sprung Christian earlier into Rwanda. I told Emanuel that his recommended shopkeeper had disrespected him and me and was ruining his reputation and business. He asked for all the messages from the vendor. Emanuel's reply was that these were typical West African "mafia" extortion tactics. He asked if I wanted him to take care of it.

"Yes, by all means."

"Do you care how?"

"No. As you see fit."

I never received another threat from Kigali.

After I returned home from Rwanda I began wondering how many bird families had I seen. A perusal of my digitally based records showed the Shoebill to be my 225th family out of an existing 228. I use the Clements systematics because I report my totals to ABA, a requirement for reporting. There are other systems in use around the world equally good or better, but all ABA reports use Clements. Chasing the three remaining families would be fun and a lofty goal. At that time no American had seen them all. What were the three remaining families, and where were they? The most interesting and perhaps the most difficult to find was the rockfowl, or Picathartes. There are two species in this family, Gray-necked and White-necked Rockfowl. They are in West-central and West Africa, respectively. The second family is the Sheathbills, a family of garbage eaters that pick through the fish scraps that seals and penguins leave behind in their colonies. There are two species in this family, Snowy and Black-faced Sheathbills. The Snowies are found only in the southernmost parts of South America, Chile, Argentina, and Antarctica. The third family is the Hypocolius, an enigmatic species of a monotypic family in India and the Arabian Peninsula. By doing two trips a year, I would accomplish my goal in eighteen months.

I chose to go after the Picathartes first. This would be the most physically demanding trip with long hikes in equatorial Africa. I wanted to do the toughest trip first while I was relatively healthy. My Rwanda guide, Christian Boix, was leading a trip to Cameroon and the Gray-necked Rockfowl was a target bird. *Perfect.* There would be one five-mile hike over relatively level ground. We would sleep in lean-tos for three nights in a national park and make daily attempts to see the rockfowl at a known nesting site. The whole trip, including a pre-trip to Gabon, would be thirty days. This was a very long time for me to be birding. Past experiences have shown me to disconnect by three weeks. I start thinking about home, Susan, my family, the Buckeyes, a movie, tennis, and a nice dinner out. There would be five or six other guests, but I figured if they were going for the same bird, they must be pretty fanatic and experienced birders. The more experienced eyes the better. In the last few years I stopped doing group tours because of all the nonsense that I had experienced in the past with most of these groups. Birding attracts a disparate group of people from all walks of life, professions and personalities. Birders have varying degrees of mental stability and physical fitness, and levels of birding skills. Some participants are high maintenance for the leader and the group and detract from the pleasure of the birding experience. A few are great fun and interesting to be with. When thrown together for two or three weeks, it makes for an interesting pot.

The night before I was to fly to Cameroon, I received a phone call from the owner of the tour company I had contracted with. He told me there was civil strife in Cameroon. Public transportation workers were striking for more pay, and violence had broken out in Yaoundé, the capital. In fact, he had a tour stranded there because they had come under fire driving to the airport. I told him I had cleared my calendar for the rest of the month, had my passport and visa, and was fully packed and ready to go. I also had paid him a substantial amount of money. He said there was no way he could let the tour proceed, and there was no telling when the violence would end. I fully understood and accepted his decision. *How about another African country?* I could easily change the flight plans and obtain a visa when I arrived in the new country. I figured the cost would be about the same. He thought that would work and asked me where I wanted to go. Ethiopia had always appealed to me as a birding and cultural destination. No problem. He had a tour guide in South Africa as we spoke and he could have him in Ethiopia the next day. We would work out the difference when I returned. *Great, let's do it.* The rockfowl would have to wait.

When I returned from a fabulous trip in Ethiopia, I received a bill from the tour company for $12,000 for what it claimed was the difference in the two trips—Ethiopia and Cameroon. I had already paid the company $17,000 for the first Cameroon trip that had been cancelled. The two countries, both poor, are practically identical in expenses for food and lodging, car and driver, ground agent, tour guide and Tropical Birding's overhead and profit. There must have been some accounting error. In fact, since I had spent fewer days on the tour in Ethiopia than I had planned to spend in Cameroon, I had expected a refund of a $1,000 to $2,000. I emailed back that I suspected there was an error in the computation. They wrote back that there was no error. Simply put, that trip to Ethiopia was going to cost me the outrageous sum of $29,000 plus airfare. I told them no way was I going to pay that amount. I could practically buy the whole country for that amount of money. This email was followed by a near hysterical phone call from the owner, who demanded the money and was fairly shouting at me over the phone. He ludicrously told me he could not get my money back from the various hotels and ground agent who had been pre-paid. *So what?* It was not the client's responsibility to get his own refunds from the tour vendors. He yelled some more and called me "morally corrupt." I hung up on him. When he called back he said something had cut us off. I reflexively dragged out that old Strother Martin line from the Paul Newman classic, *Cool Hand Luke* that I loved so much: "What we have here is a failure to communicate."

I told him that only one person can talk to me that way and that she wasn't here right now. I asked him to talk to me in a business-like tone or not at all. He settled down for a while. I reminded him of his own contract that stated that if the tour company cancelled the tour for any reason, the client would be held harmless for the money, and all sums would be returned. This was standard language for all bird tour contracts at the time. He seemed to have forgotten his own contract. He insisted that I was not an attorney. I reminded him I was an American and could read English. I did not need to be an attorney to make sense of the contract's straight-forward language. After all, it had been written by him. How could he argue that it was not straightforward? He continued to harangue me for the egregious sum, and I continued to refuse to pay a cent more. Finally, to settle the disagreement, I offered a solution. Take the actual cost of the Ethiopian trip and add his customary percentage of overhead and profit, which I believe he had earned, and subtract it from the money I had already paid him for the cancelled Cameroon trip. Refund me the difference. If the Ethiopian trip cost more than the Cameroon trip, I would pay him the difference. If that were not fair and acceptable to him, we could argue it out in another and higher venue. He agreed, and a couple of days later I received a small check from him. In his anger, he blackballed me from any more birding tours with his company. I wore this as a badge of honor.

In the meantime, another family, the Pink-tailed Bunting or Przewalski's Rosefinch popped up as the 229th world bird family. Neither a Bunting nor a Rosefinch, scientists assigned it to its own family, the Urocynchramidae, quite a mouthful but no worse than Przewalski. It had been patiently waiting since 1918 for its own designation. It was formally published in Clements 6th edition and announced to the general public in November, 2008. I just appended it to the end of my bucket list of families that I needed to see. I realized this was only the first of many new families to be described in the future since bio-science was advancing its technology in genetics and biochemistry at a rapid pace. It was inevitable that many changes in ornithology were on their way.

CAMEROON

I signed up for the March, 2010, Cameroon tour and Gabon pre-tour with the company that had banned me. I guess they forgot about their blackball because I found myself standing in the immigration line in the Libreville, Gabon, airport with Christian Boix waiting for me outside. What should have been a routine five-minute immigration inspection turned into a forty-five-minute debacle. First, they "lost" my luggage. A dollar to a porter readily produced it hidden away in a dark room off to the side of the baggage area. This delay put me last in the immigration line, which seemed to take forever to shrink. There were no fans or air conditioner in the overcrowded hot and humid reception room. The smell of body odor and old sweat permeated the air. It was midnight, and the temperature was still in the high nineties. When I finally reached the immigration officer, a large scowling man with the personality of an un-tipped waiter, my ordeal was just beginning. He was going to show the rest of the onlooking airport passengers, taxi drivers, and immigration staff how to handle an American. He started in rapid French asking me a volley of questions. I replied in English that I did not speak French. He continued his barrage of questions in French. I replied in French that I did not speak French. I could actually understand a little bit, enough to hear him berate me for coming to a French-speaking country without knowledge of the language. He asked me where my interpreter was. Christian, who speaks French, was waiting just outside but was not allowed in the arriving passenger area. I was really getting agitated now; my clothes were soaked from perspiration from this sauna and most uncomfortable welcome. I showed him my paperwork, visa and passport. He asked me where my letter of invitation was, a necessary item for entry to Gabon. He knew quite well that I had already delivered it to the Gabon immigration office because no visa would be issued without it, and I had a valid visa. He started going through my bags, item by item. All of a sudden he switched to perfect English.

"What is this? What is this for? What is this?"

I calmly answered all of his questions. I was not going to give him any reason to prolong his affront. I was the last person standing in the reception area. Everyone had cleared out. He continued with his questions. I could not stand it anymore. I finally went off on him.

"Look here, pal, all of my paperwork is in order! Let me pass!"

He was taken aback at my outburst, but he realized the show was over. There was no reason to continue this mockery. As he looked away from me, he waved his hand toward the exit as if shooing a small annoying insect out the door. A nervous Christian was waiting for me. We drove to a nearby hotel in a run-down district of Libreville but close to the river from where we were departing the next morning. After four hours of a mosquito-ridden, face-slapping sleepless night we headed downriver to a fishing camp for the next five days.

The camp was comfortable. My cabin had the basic creature comforts, commode, shower, and fan. The heat and humidity were oppressive. The birds were very low density, with walks barely producing one bird per hour. I did manage to see seventeen lifers and take a couple of good photos, Reichenbach's Sunbird, an uncommon species, among them.

Figure 22-3. Reichenbach's Sunbird, Gabon.

The much sought-after endemic Black Bee-eater eluded us. Because of the heat and humidity we limited our birding to early mornings and late afternoons. We had two outstanding mammal sightings—a forest elephant expertly swimming across the river, and a banteng, the African wild buffalo related to the Cape buffalo. Now off to Cameroon.

During the boat ride back to Libreville, I asked Christian what was the real reason his boss had badgered me for the extra Cameroon money. Christian freely admitted that the original ground agent had stolen all the advance money, and the owner had tried in vain to force me to make him whole. Now who was "morally corrupt?" Cleary he had projected his character flaw onto me.

A flight into the airport at Yaoundé, capital of Cameroon, produced more heat and humidity. The rains in West-central Africa had not yet arrived, and everywhere was suffering from a prolonged drought. The crops were failing. The meager electrical resources were being tested to their limits by the excessive use of electricity and air conditioning in the big cities, Yaoundé, Douala, and Garoua. No such overload in the countryside, though. They didn't get electricity to begin with. The country has many hydroelectric dams, but the energy produced is sold to neighboring countries for added revenues for the kleptocrat leaders. The 40 million inhabitants benefit little from the sale. The birds and animals were stressed from the heat and lack of water and food. When it is dry, there are fewer insects, which cuts down on the food supply for insectivores. The birds kept their mouths open and panted to increase heat removal from their bodies. I was facing three weeks of this. I began wondering if the rockfowl would be in its usual place, or if it had moved on because of the drought, and this trip would be a total waste of time and money.

My compatriots on this tour were all experienced birders. A Brit from London was especially good at identifying the few shorebirds we encountered. A lawyer from Washington, D.C. was a board member of the American Birding Association, a position I formerly held for six years. A Frenchman from Paris, a man whom I was prepared to dislike, turned out to be a great birding companion. He knew all about wines, gourmet cooking, and of all things, the NBA (National Basketball Association). He helped me with my untrained pronunciation of some French words, like my favorite salad, *Salade Niçoise.* A preacher from Texas was also a good traveling companion. A devout Christian, he tread lightly on that subject to the relief of most of us.

The days became hotter and hotter with no relief in sight; not a wisp of a cloud hung in the merciless, clear sky. Most of our sleeping quarters lacked air conditioning. The birding was tough with searing sun and suffocating humidity. I recorded daily ambient temperatures from 108 F to 114 F on my Casio watch. The ground temperature had to be much hotter. It was hotter than Vietnam. Once at a tennis tournament in Columbus, the outside temperature was 95 degrees

Fahrenheit, but the ground temperature was 134! There was no shade in Cameroon, because many of the shade trees had died or wilted. The river beds were bone dry. The rocks were so hot that it was impossible to rest your behind on them because they would burn right through your jeans. Standing in those dry river beds without rest or relief made me think of the Styx, the River to Hell. One eight-hour walk for the Quail-Plover without success almost did me in. I was getting sick from the heat, and water from my canteen and added electrolytes were not helping. Logistics were difficult, with long drives to birding areas. The drivers thought that running the air conditioners would waste gasoline, a proven fallacy. The metal vehicle was transformed into a metal oven. In the van I was pouring water onto my head and letting it drip onto my neck, and body to cool myself. All the windows were kept open, and we drove on the deeply pockmarked roads at thirty-five miles per hour with all sorts of debris rushing through the open windows. At one point a grain of sand came through my window with such velocity that it lodged in the white of my eye. No sort of simple attempts to remove it such as lower lid wiping the upper lid, or splashing water in my eye were working. With every blink, the pain was becoming more unbearable. Finally at a rest stop, with "necessity as the mother of invention," I brainstormed a first-aid process that worked and worked quickly. I needed an eye-cup. I saw that the plastic cap on my water bottle was the same circumference as my eye socket. I poured fresh water into the cap and placed it over my afflicted eye, moved my eye in all directions and *voila*, the pain was gone and the grain of sand was resting harmlessly in the cap.

After one particularly long and dusty ride we arrived at our destination, the Ngaondaba Ranch, only to find that our reserved rooms had been taken by another group. The other group who had kicked us out—and I am not making this up—was the Cameroon Department of Tourism led by the minister himself. Their conference was to develop ideas to promote tourism. We were forced to stay a two-hour drive away from this park, which meant 4 a.m. starts every morning and a two-hour drive back in the dark every night for the next three days. I was wearing out. I was not enjoying the birding because I felt so sick. We were not even halfway through the tour; Korup National Park and its Gray-necked Rockfowl was over a week away. I had to tough it out until I saw the rockfowl, and then I could leave.

At the trip halfway point, while staying at Benoue, there was a blackout. All power failed. This meant no refrigeration for cold drinks or food, and no air conditioning or fans. The intense heat and humidity continued with a vengeance. After a long, unproductive walk on a dry river bed, I felt dizzy and nauseated. I left the group and returned to my hot box. I tried to lie outside the cabin, hoping a breeze might help cool me. I had stopped perspiring, and my skin felt hot and dry. I was retching now and had to do something fast. The sky was spinning. I was beginning a heat stroke. I took an aspirin. Was there something else going on within me I was missing? I took a Cipro just in case. There was a tub in the bathroom. I filled it with cold water and lay in it for the rest of the night. I felt my core body temperature coming down. I forced myself to drink water in between vomiting. I was determined to beat this. By morning I felt better, but skipped the morning meal and, of course, skipped the bird walk. I got some warm Cokes from the kitchen and drank them for sugar and electrolytes and rested all day. By evening I felt better, well enough to eat an egg and some bread. I missed five lifers that day but did not care. The next morning we were out of there, and I stayed in recovery mode for that travel day.

That evening we hauled into a small hostel five miles from Korup National Park and the Rockfowl. I was still in a weakened condition from the heat stroke, but I was steeling myself mentally for the five-mile hike ahead of me the next day. Our driver came to me because he had heard I was a doctor. He had a high fever and chills and didn't think he could make the drive in the morning. He had contracted malaria years ago, and my diagnosis was most likely a relapse of the disease. I had some chloroquine-primaquine tablets in my pharmaceutical arsenal and gave him a couple that night and repeated them in the morning. I thought, *no driver, no rockfowl.* His fever broke, and he recovered by morning. The five-mile trip, over what had to be the worst road in Cameroon, took more than two hours. The potholes were cavernous—the largest I have ever seen. Whole families could have lived in them! We arrived at our jump-off site, a long hanging bridge over the Mana River, at 7 a.m. and waited for the porters.

We had hired five porters, all locals, to carry our food and supplies including live chickens, seven tents, and our personal belongings. Christian had learned, while still in South Africa, that a policeman had beaten a local villager. In retribution, villagers had rampaged through Korup, destroying our campsite and lean-tos. In their fury they burned everything to the ground.

The porters did not show up by 10 a.m. and Christian made a command decision to start out for the campsite without them. He had been there in past years and thought he remembered the way through the forest. The porters would catch up with us later, we hoped. The temperature was already over ninety degrees. I took my time and steadily fell behind. Christian kept doubling back to check on me. About an hour into the trek, I caught up to the group. They were all standing and sitting in a clearing. Christian was lost, and he was waiting for the sound of the porters so they could show us the way, but they were nowhere near. He started back to find the porters and after about an hour came back with them in tow. We started out again but this time at the porter's pace, which was too fast for me, and I slowly slipped back. The path was clear and straight with no forks, and I moved along at a comfortable pace. Every so often, I would see Christian's face peering at me through the forest checking on me. After five hours I made it to the clearing, and as I entered the Rengo campsite stopped short at a most bizarre sight. My group was sitting calmly on rocks and stumps. But they were covered with something from head to toe. I could not believe what I was seeing. They were covered with thousands of African bees. These were the real life pure African bees that we see killing people in National Geographic footage. The bees were lapping the salty sweat off of my comrades. The group waved me in and told me not to worry because the bees were not stinging. I walked in and found a rock. I was overheated and exhausted. I was immediately covered by a swarm drinking my perspiration. It was an eerie scene, out of a sci-fi movie, humans feeding insects with their body fluids. Everything was peaceful for a few minutes until one of our group starting swatting at a bee or two. I heard a faint hum explode into a deafening roar, a crescendo of anger, as the bees began to vibrate as one. On a signal known only to the bee world, the whole hive started attacking us. Pandemonium filled the camp as birders chased by swarms of bees fled to all parts of the camp, yelping and swatting as they ran. I had spied a stream at the entrance to the campsite when I'd first arrived, and I headed for that as fast as I could.

Figure 22-4. Stream, Korup National Park.

My adrenaline was pumping my weary legs as fast as they would carry me. I could have outrun Usain Bolt. I jumped in with all my clothes on and stayed under water for as long as I could hold my breath. When I peeked my head out, I could see a few bees still looking for me, so I ducked down again. When I thought it was safe, I raised my head slowly and I could see five others, heads only, all looking at each other. It was a ridiculous sight, and we all laughed out loud—I guess partly from sheer nervousness and partly from relief. The bees disappeared when the sun went down.

Figure 22-5. Rengo camp, Korup National Park.

Incredibly, after all of this chaos, Christian announced we were going to try to find the rockfowl. It was getting dark, and we were all tired, yet he insisted we go. It was about a mile hike, part trail and part cross country.

He said, "Bernie, you can't go."

"Why not?"

"You are too tired and you will hold us back. We have to get to its cave before dark."

Well, I knew it was all true, but I had to try. I told him I would follow if he gave me one of the porters to help show the way if I fell back. He did not like the idea and told me he took no responsibility for my safety. The group started at a torrid pace, almost a trot. I saw how stupid my decision was. I was plain tuckered. I needed food and rest. After a hundred steps, I turned back to camp. I was resolved to go early the next morning. The porters set up my tent and prepared a tasty hot dinner for me. I took a nap and waited for the group's return. They got back to camp around 8 p.m. without a sighting. I was only partly relieved by their news. I did not want to miss the sighting, but I was disappointed that it was not in its usual nest cave. Had it moved on because of the lack of rain? I told Christian I wanted to try the next morning for it. I asked the group if anyone else wanted to go with me. Frenchy said yes at first and then abruptly changed his mind. Christian said I was on my own because they planned to search for other birds in the morning. I did not care about the other birds until I saw the rockfowl. He said okay but that I would have to get up at 4:30 a.m., have breakfast, and set off by five. It usually takes an hour, but he said it would take me an hour and a half. His words did not discourage me. I went to bed early and had a great night's sleep. My Casio wrist alarm woke me at 4:30 a.m., and breakfast was already being prepared for me. Everyone else except Christian was still fast asleep. As a good leader, he had gotten up to give me last-minute instructions to increase my chances of seeing the bird. He gave me a porter, Stephen, to show me the way. We were off by five as planned with flashlights to illuminate the trail. It took me an hour and a half to negotiate the muddy track with its tangled roots and fallen tree trunks. I also had to ford a small river. I arrived at the cave at 6:30 a.m. and entered the front of the cave quietly. Daylight was forming, and I could see the outline of the cave's interior. It was about eighty feet deep, twenty-five feet high, and twenty-five feet wide, surrounded on two and a half sides by cave walls. In the dim light of dawn I could make out a large mud and stick nest on the back wall about five feet off the ground. It looked fresh. I sat silently against one side of the cave in order to watch the opening. Stephen sat behind me. He was very restless and kept moving around. At one point, he got up to relieve himself in the cave.

Oh my God, I will never see this bird with Stephen making this ruckus.

I gave him the universal sign of silence with my forefinger across my mouth accompanied by a very stern look to signal him to be quiet. We both sat motionless for one hour and fifteen minutes waiting for even a glimpse of our quarry. And then I heard a rustle in the leaves in front of the entrance. It was full daylight by now, and I could see the form of a small dinosaur, long necked, about a foot high, hopping in the leaves. It half leaped and half flew to the top of the low wall at the front of the cave. Now that it was in full view, my heart raced. The Picathartes, a male Gray-necked Rockfowl, was standing right in front of me, all of it, a reward for all my travails. A feeling of sublime pleasure ran through my whole body. All the fatigue left me. He then hopped out of view. I knew where he was heading. There was a small second entrance to the cave closer to his nest over my right shoulder. I pivoted my body and raised my camera, aiming for the spot at which I was sure he would appear. Within seconds he showed himself again, exactly where I thought he would be. I steadied my camera for a shot. Stephen moved suddenly and startled it—it was off in an instant. I waited another hour hoping for his return. I never saw him again. As it turned out, no one else did either. I turned to Stephen who had a broad smile on his face. I gestured thumbs up, and he gestured thumbs up back.

He said quietly to me, "Lifer," not a question but a statement.

"Was this a new bird for you, Stephen?"

He nodded yes. We shared a moment, both men—an American from ten thousand miles away and an African who lived ten miles down the road—having just seen this amazing living creature together for the first time.

Figure 22-6. Stephen, side entrance to cave of Picathartes, Korup National Park.

We took our time going back, relishing the experience we had just shared. The morning sun was starting to get hot, but it was an easy walk back in a beautiful forest. All of a sudden, Stephen, leading the way, abruptly stopped. Frozen still, he slowly turned only his head to me and pointed his hand ever so furtively ahead and slightly to the right. I saw the objects of his concern—a family of forest elephants upwind from us, only one hundred feet away, grazing young leaves from the trees. Neither of us moved a muscle. I was instructed by African rangers in the past that if confronted by elephants, do not try to outrun them. You cannot. Look for a tall tree to climb or at least find a thick tree to hide behind. If no trees are available, bend over, put your head between your legs, and kiss your butt goodbye. We both stood motionless for about fifteen minutes while the elephants, three females—a mother and two youngsters—oblivious to us, fed. All of a sudden, the wind direction changed. The large female's trunk went up to taste the air, and then all hell broke loose. The three started running, knocking down trees—big trees—and trumpeting loudly the whole time. The earth was shaking. I had staked out my tree in that fifteen minutes of silence and was heading for it when Stephen called me to come back. The elephants were running in the opposite direction. We remained quietly where we stood for the next ten minutes until Stephen sensed it was safe to move on. When I returned to camp, the group was there, anxiously awaiting my report. I walked in slack-necked, eyes cast down, and tried to appear disappointed.

"Well. Did you see it? Did you see it?"

I paused for effect, lifted my head, and exclaimed, "Yes, I saw it!"

"How well did you see it?"

"I saw it so well that even Stephen can count it."

I related the whole course of events, and I expect they had a mixed reaction like I did the night before—happy it was still there and therefore possible to see, but sad they had not been there to enjoy it with me. In cases like this, some are always skeptical of other's reports of sighting rare birds, especially if they had missed it themselves. But in this case, good old Stephen was there to back up my story.

The Frenchman said, "I knew I should have gone with you."

The next three mornings and two nights, the group returned to the cave with no luck. I spent my time birding in the park, swimming in the creek, taking photos, and cat-napping. The night before we left Korup, I told Christian I wanted to leave early to beat the heat. Frenchy, overhearing my request, wanted to go with me. The rest of group wanted to try for the rockfowl a sixth time. The next morning right after breakfast, Frenchy, Stephen, and I hit the five-mile trail to return to our jump-off point. There was a guard house there we could use to get out of the sun, and with a little bit of luck, our driver and van would be waiting for us. We ambled back in the cool of the morning, birding the whole way, talking about fine wines, great food, and professional basketball. The French star, Pal Gasol from the Lakers, was Frenchy's favorite player. The superstar Buckeye, LeBron James from Akron, was mine.

I made that once five-hour trip in only three hours and felt great. My luck was holding. Our driver was there, fully recovered from his bout with malaria, and he cheerfully took us back to the hostel. We arrived about noon, took a cold shower, and had a great lunch. I took a long nap in the heat of the day with a fan blowing cool air on me and awoke completely refreshed. The group straggled in about 6 p.m. completely exhausted and with no rockfowl sighting to show for all their efforts. I was the only one in the group to see this near mythical being, but I never mentioned my sighting of the rockfowl to them again.

The final leg of our tour was the long trek up Mount Cameroon, the second highest mountain in Africa at 13,255 feet. Mount Cameroon was an active volcano with its last explosion as recently as 2000. It was part of the Cameroon Line, a series of active volcanoes extending from the Gulf of Guinea in the west all the way up to Lake Chad in the north, about seven hundred miles. It was a favorite destination for climbers, and the summit could be reached in four and a half hours by experienced climbers. We only had to get to six thousand feet to a base camp, and then explore to eight thousand feet to find the endemic birds there. The Mount Cameroon Speirops and the Mount Cameroon Francolin were our target species. There were several endemic subspecies like Mountain Saw-Wing and Mountain Robin-Chat that also would be worthwhile to see.

A taxi dropped us off at the base of the mountain, but it was a two-mile hike across open farmland to begin the ascent. I started out with the group, but it was already about 9 a.m., and the broiling African sun was high in the sky. There was no cloud cover or shade trees in the denuded landscape, and I soon felt the effects of the heat. I became very dizzy, and my blood sugar was dropping. I stopped and called to Christian. I told him that I had to quit and asked him for some Cameroon money since I was going back to the road to hail a taxi and return to the hotel. He gave me cab fare, and I headed back. A few minutes later, a series of clouds moved in from the Gulf, and a light breeze began to blow. I ate a protein bar I always carry for emergencies. I felt revived. I had never quit a trip before. Maybe, under these new conditions, I could make the base camp at six thousand feet. According to my Casio altimeter, I was starting at two thousand feet. I turned around and headed back to the trailhead. The cloud cover held as I walked the two miles to begin my climb. My group was nowhere in sight. My heart sank when I finally saw the beginning of the trail. At first it looked straight up, an impossible climb. A more realistic assessment was about a twenty- to twenty-five-degree incline, but covered with rocks and huge boulders. Hikers were streaming past me as I pondered conquering this obstacle. *Should I really quit this time?* No, there was only one way to do this, *poco a poco*, little by little. I would take ten steps at a time and then rest. I did not care how long it would take. I was determined to reach the base camp. I was in the forest now and could use the trees for cover, and the boulders for rest. The protein bar kicked in, and I felt some strength returning. Climbers were passing me like I was standing still. I *was* standing still. I had to put my plan into action and get going, one step at a time for ten steps, again and again. Four hours later I saw my group; they looked surprised—more like stupefied—as they watched me walk into the basecamp. They all appreciated my effort because they knew how sick I had been. Words of praise were passed to me. Preacher said he could now see why I had been so successful in my career.

The basecamp was a shithole, plain and simple, and not fit for human habitation. There was trash and garbage and human waste all over. There was no sanitation of any sort. The sleeping quarters were dark unlit barracks with rats and vermin sharing the space. There was no way I was sleeping in those conditions. I moved my bedroll out into the fresh air, malaria be damned, and set up my own living quarters.

Figure 22-7. Mount Cameroon basecamp, 6,000 feet.

Early the next morning before breakfast, we continued the ascent, birding all the way to eight thousand feet. First the Speirops came into view, then the Saw-Wing, Little Oliveback, Mountain Cameroon Bulbul, and one by one the rest of the target subspecies. Christian then dropped a small bomb. He informed us the Mount Cameroon Francolin was another ten miles away on the other side of the mountain, another five thousand feet straight up, and then down for an unknown distance.

"Any takers?"

By the group's dead silence I took it to mean that this would be one species lacking from the trip list. By my careful count I had seen all of the Mount Cameroon endemic species and subspecies. I announced to the group that I was heading back to basecamp and breakfast. No one followed. Our porters made me a good hot breakfast. I decided to pack my things and start back to the hotel. I was finished here. I had seen all the birds and did not want to spend another night in this crap hole. As I was packing, the group returned. I told Christian that I was returning to the hotel in Douala. I was thinking of a hot shower, clean sheets, CNN, an air-conditioned room, and room service. The rest of the men were probably thinking the same thing because they all said they were coming with me. Christian put up a feeble argument that we had one more night here, and we might see something good. Nobody was buying it, and this "mini mutiny" continued. He reluctantly joined the group. I was the first one down the mountain because it was much easier to go down than up. The hotel room was exactly as I had envisioned, a great reward for all of my hard work.

On our last day, we did some birding around Douala and added a few species at the Limbe Botanical Gardens including the lifer Western Bluebill. We all toured the Limbe Rehabilitation Center—except the Washington attorney, who for some unknown reason, refused. The center was expecting us. I had sent a message to the Rehab Center while in the States that I would visit and would like a tour. It had been the recipient of a small grant from the Columbus Zoo, of which I was a board member, to nurse back to health eight hundred African Gray Parrots rescued from Nigerian smugglers at the Yaoundé airport. These poor birds had been stuffed into individual toilet rolls to escape detection. The parrots were in deplorable condition, and only three hundred survived. The Limbe workers were all dedicated women volunteers from the U.S. and Europe who had pledged one month of their lives and $3,000 of their own money to work there. They paid to work there! I thought this was an extraordinarily selfless show of commitment and love of birds and the environment.

I paid a heavy toll for the experience of seeing the Picathartes. Cameroon was by far my most physically taxing and mentally demanding bird tour. The effects of Cameroon stayed with me a long time afterward. When I returned home, I suffered from intense itching of my legs, so much so that I would scratch the skin from my legs while I slept, leaving blood on the sheets. I thought it was from the dry Columbus air, so I added a commercial-sized humidifier to my home HVAC. It helped a little, but I decided to see my dermatologist in case I was misdiagnosing myself. She thought it was eczema and prescribed some creams and mild soaps that helped but not altogether. I also had crusting of my eyelids, which persisted for weeks. I visited my ophthalmologist, and she too diagnosed eczema and prescribed a steroid ointment that helped for a while. The crusting and itching stayed with me intermittently for three years. The symptoms were annoying, but I continued the ointments and soaps with some relief. The worst was yet to come.

One morning in November, 2013, while lying in bed, I felt a small mass in my chest wall just under my right breast. It was well circumscribed, hard, and non-tender—about the size of a grain of rice. *What the hell is this?* I had never noticed it before. My beloved sister had died prematurely in 2003 from ovarian cancer. As a doctor, I knew that males in the family of women who had the genetic mutant for ovarian cancer were six times more at risk than the normal population for developing male breast cancer. I freaked out and immediately called my surgeon. I also called my sister's family to see if there was any recollection of the doctors talking about a mutant gene or if there had been any genetic testing. No one knew of any such diagnosis, and the females in the family had not been tested. Either my sister had not been tested for the mutant gene or the results were negative.

I saw my surgeon the next day. He said it was not cancer, but he did not know what it was.

"How about an X-ray and an ultrasound?"

"How about right now?"

The mammogram showed a mass, but the radiologist could not identify it. The ultrasound showed a mass, but again the radiologist was stumped. A biopsy was done, and the pathologist was stymied. He said it looked like some kind of parasite that had encysted itself in my rib muscle, but he had never seen anything like it before. I was getting very anxious. I had always put the pathologists at our hospital on a pedestal, thinking they were the smartest guys on the medical staff. If he didn't know what it was, I was in big trouble. He sent the pathology slides to the CDC in Washington on a Friday. I had all weekend to read my medical books about tropical diseases and worry. The answer came back Monday afternoon, *Onchocerciasis* or River Blindness. I vaguely remembered this disease from somewhere in medical school. This was a common disease of West Africa causing permanent blindness in four percent of those afflicted. It was the result of a bite of a Simularium blackfly injecting microfilaria parasites into the victim's body. The adult worm makes its way through the muscles of the body and finally rests in the eye tissues of the patient. It is curable and not contagious. Its chief symptoms are intense itching and crusting of the eyes! I made an appointment with an infectious disease specialist, an old timer who told me I was the only case in the U.S. and the first case he had ever treated. He had to go to the books and the medical literature to find the latest treatment. He called me that night and we discussed his suggested treatment—a "five-hundred-pound bomb" to kill any parasite lurking in my body and a month's dosing of an antibiotic to kill a bacterium that always accompanies the worm. I started the medications that evening and by the next day, my energy level soared and my symptoms disappeared. I had been carrying this Cameroonian hitchhiker for three years in my muscle without my knowledge.

Having River Blindness was bad enough, but that was curable. A far worse sequela was my inability to thermoregulate my body temperature. The heat stroke had burned up my internal thermostat, and I could no longer stand any kind of heat. I stopped playing tennis on hot days and do not go to the beach anymore. I cannot even walk in the heat without getting sick.

WORLD 7309 • ABA 785

ARGENTINA AND THE SNOWY SHEATHBILL

The Gray-necked Rockfowl was number 226 on my world family list. I had three more families to see to complete the family list, the Sheathbills, the Hypocolius, and the newly designated Pink-tailed Bunting. After the rigors of Cameroon, I wanted an easy comfortable trip. I also wanted to take Susan along and make it a couple's vacation. I signed on for the VENT Southern Argentina tour in late November, a good month to leave cold and rainy Ohio. Patagonia in Southern Argentina is the best place to see the Snowy Sheathbill just before it leaves for Antarctica to breed. They can be found hanging around penguin colonies and patrolling seal and sea lion herds always on the hunt for food.

They are garbage eaters, relishing offal, human and animal waste, stillborn seals, afterbirth and other disgusting fare. Their diet belies their outward beauty. They are large and showy snow-white birds. Their white forms should stand out against the brown mammal colonies. Well, this hunt should be a cinch.

We joined our group in Buenos Aires, the very European-like capital of Argentina. The city reminded me of Rome and why not? There had been three major immigrations of Italians to Buenos Aires in the last hundred years: the 1890s, post-World War I, and post-World War II. The cuisine rich in pasta and bread, the ornate architecture, and the musical lilt of the Spanish language spoken there were all evidence of Italian influences. One can also hear the Brazilian Portuguese influences on the language with its double "Ls" turning into that soft fuzzy "zh" and the "Ys" reversed to "Js". The mixture of Italian, Spanish, and Indian heritages make a very handsome race of people.

Our group consisted of an older Brit, a lawyer, her friend from New Jersey, and an older woman from California. Our leader was Judy Davis, leading her last tour as a professional.

I let Judy know I was there to see the Sheathbill. She did not think that would pose a problem because she saw them every year on every tour. I liked the sound of that. This is a hobby involving chance and unexpected outcomes. I was cautiously hopeful. The Southern Argentinian bird list is small and manageable, making it relatively easy for the group to see most of the birds.

Figure 22-8. Gilded Hummingbird.

The job of the leader becomes easier, too. She must keep everyone on schedule, take us to the right habitats, and point out birds. She deals with the transportation, housing, and meal logistics. Judy Davis did all that well. She gave great instructions, and well ahead of time. I find most people like to know what they are doing before they do it. She was a female Ronald Reagan, the "Great Communicator." There were no hitches as we birded our way south from Buenos Aires to Tierra del Fuego in Patagonia. There were no Snowy Sheathbills either. Talking to some park rangers, I discovered that the Sheathbills move south early to their breeding range in the sub-Antarctic islands and continental Antarctica. Had I missed them? Was this going to be a wasted trip? We had recorded a respectable list of more than two hundred species and photographed some beautiful scenery, but I *had* to see that Snowy.

Figure 22-9. Andean Condor.

Figure 22-10. Magellanic Oystercatcher.

The history of Patagonia is intertwined with Darwin's voyage on the *Beagle*, a pivotal chapter of his life and his development of the theory of evolution. The penguin and pinniped colonies we inspected were also interesting, but I was getting anxious that I would miss my target bird.

We reached the Peninsula Valdes, a World Heritage Site. It was remarkable for its conservation of southern sea lions, southern fur seals, elephant seals, guanacos, and forty thousand Magellanic Penguin nests.

Figure 22-11. Magellanic Penguins, Peninsula Valdes.

Golfo Nuevo and Golfo San Jose hold a large population of southern right whale mothers and calves. Orcas opportunistically swim on the periphery but never get a chance at the babies. The mothers are too alert and powerful. Our group watched a mother right whale feeding her calf, regulating its volume of milk and rate of feeding by wisely timing her gentle rolls from her side to her back.

Figure 22-12. Right Whales, mother nursing calf, Golfo Nuevo.

I had one last chance for the Snowy. On our last day and at our last seal colony, I was walking from one side of the parking lot to the other looking down to the beach filled with seals and sea lions looking for a puff of white. The gale-force icy winds were punishing us as we searched in vain for the Sheathbill. I was about to give up and return to the van when all of a sudden I was startled to see a white pigeon flying low over the lot heading directly for me. *Wait a minute; there are no pigeons here.* I shouted to the group, "Here it is! Here it is!" and managed to snap a few shots as it veered away from me to be lost forever in the seascape.

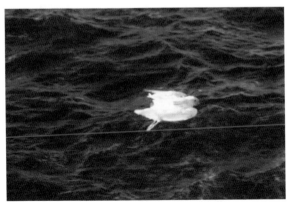

Figure 22-13. Snowy Sheathbill.

We never saw another one. I mused that it had to be the last Sheathbill in Argentina. I felt both triumph and relief. I'd tucked number 227 away at the twelfth hour and had a photo to boot! Two more to go! The remainder of the trip was magical. The Moreno Glacier was a gorgeous combination of ice whites and blues. However, its receding mass was a disturbing reminder of climate change.

Figure 22-14. Moreno Glacier.

We followed Darwin's 1833 course through the Bay of Darwin, picking out the landmarks named for him and his shipmates, among them Mont Fitz Roy and Cordillera Darwin.

Figure 22-15. Darwin's Bay.

Waved Albatrosses and Chilean Skuas cruised the open sea. Austral Negritos, Wilson's Phalaropes, Magellanic Oystercatchers and Kelp Gulls dotted the sandy shores.

Figure 22-16. Austral Negrito.

A single enigmatic Magellanic Plover, itself possibly a third member of the Sheathbill family, showed up at Lake Argentino. The tour ended with capturing a rare Rufous-bellied Seedsnipe on video following a long, steep climb up the Martial Glacier in Ushuaia. This seedsnipe was my fourth and last seedsnipe on my world list.

THE ARABIAN PENINSULA & THE HYPOCOLIOUS

I had never heard of the Hypocolius and I doubt most birders have. It sounds like an anatomical segment of bowel. In reality it is a beautiful thrush-sized bird with gray satiny plumage, very secretive and hard to find. There are plenty of them in certain parts of the world, but they are scattered in the wrong places. In today's dangerous world, who would travel to Iraq, Iran, Afghanistan, Pakistan, or northwest India to see one? Well, maybe a "crazed twitcher," someone who goes anywhere anytime to see birds. Their breeding grounds are in Arabia. With all the bad press of Arab extremism and anti-Western sentiment, I had to think long and hard before venturing into Arab lands. Dubai and Oman had known breeding sites and they were considered safe. I talked to my birding buddy, Forrest Rowland, with whom I had birded throughout northern South America for years. I remembered he had lived in Saudi Arabia for eight years while his father, a geologist, had worked there for an oil company. He said that, as far as he knew, they were safe countries, had many good birds, and he would love to go back. He even spoke Arabic. He was also the best birder I had ever birded with. Then the choice was easy, Oman and United Arab Emirates it was.

In October, 2010, I flew into Dubai, the most populous city in the UAE. I looked for the immigration line to get a visa for entry. I asked an immigration officer where to get this visa. He asked if I was an American. How did he guess? When I nodded in the affirmative, he stamped my passport and ushered me into his country. This was the easiest entry I'd ever experienced in the one hundred or so countries I had visited. There were no armed guards, police or military visible either. Forrest and his friend Cyrus were waiting for me. Both darkly handsome, swarthy, and sporting beards, they looked like native princes. We traveled throughout Dubai City and beyond for five days. I was astounded by the ostentatious display of wealth. The skyline was long and magnificent with one skyscraper taller than the next. There were cranes everywhere erecting even more buildings. There were so many cranes, the guys joked that the national bird of the Emirates *was* the crane. The crown jewel of Dubai was the newly built Burj Khalifa, the tallest building in the world standing at 2,722 feet including its tower. It took three photos with my Canon 400mm lens to include its whole length.

Many of the buildings had extensions cantilevered out from their top floors for tennis courts, swimming pools, and recreation areas. There were twelve-lane highways to nowhere. The streets were exceptionally well lit with a series of closely grouped streetlamps. From our fast moving van, they appeared painted in gilt. Concrete shopping centers and concrete playgrounds were numerous. I guess the Arabs had not heard of those fall-safe rubber playground surfaces. McDonalds, KFC, and Pizza Hut were well represented. There were also many major brand knock-offs like Burger Prince, McDingels, and Pizza House. But something was amiss. There were no green spaces. The Sultan of Dubai, with all of his fortune, did not allow for any green spaces. The people on the streets and in the shops were ninety percent non-Arabs. Poor Filipinos, Pakistanis, and Bangladeshis do the work for the Arabs. Women were absent. Arabia is one of the top three countries in the world where Diabetes is epidemic. This is partly genetic but aggravated by inactive lifestyle and high-caloric and high-carbohydrate diets. There were no Arab joggers. I saw a few cyclists. Women are never seen in health spas, workout rooms, or even walking for exercise because of the proscription against showing the female form in public. There were some Westerners on the street—probably teachers and businessmen. High salaries—often $75,000 a year—attracted English teachers, but the job required an extended stay. Workers had to surrender their passports to ensure their staying for years.

Figure 22-17. Dubai City.

There was no obvious uniformed or armed constabulary. Maybe they were in plain clothes. These nations deal very severely with their criminals. There are no Muslim terrorist activities in these countries. Muslim extremists that defy the Arab establishment are dealt with swiftly and terminally, by beheading or stoning after torture. Water boarding would be a treat. They readily give up their co-conspirators. Their families are also shunned and dealt with harshly. Following the precepts of Sharia law, there are no real defense attorneys or Western-type trials. On the other hand, there are no prolonged trials, attorney grandstanding, not-guilty verdicts, years on death row or multiple appeals. Those are considered not humanitarian. Nobody messes with Arab oil money or tourism. I was told there is a double standard of Muslim adherence to Sharia law in these countries. Alcohol and Eastern European women are used behind closed doors.

We birded the few wetlands and forests that remained in that concrete jungle. The beaches were a good source of gulls, terns, and shorebirds. Jouanin's Petrels, Persian Shearwaters, and Socotra Cormorants—all lifers—were seen from the shore with patient sea watching. Raptors were numerous riding the currents created by the tall buildings and thermals reflected from the white sandy soil. We recorded nine raptor species including a Shikra, rare in the Emirates, at Mushrif National Park. The Dubai Pivot Fields were loaded with shorebirds. There was one spot that was known as a wintering spot for the Hypocolius, but in two days of searching we came up empty-handed. Forrest said to never fear because there was a much more reliable spot in Oman. An out-of-place Common Chaffinch, rare in the Emirates, showed up at Ain El Faydah.

The food in the open air restaurants was nutritious and inexpensive. The eating establishments were clean with washing stands available everywhere. A complete meal with a huge fresh salad, big bowl of lentil soup, large plate of Basmati rice, and a main dish of chicken, beef, lamb, or tofu was only $5. We never walked away hungry. We completely avoided the $35 hotel cheeseburger. The meats were always prepared by *halal* standards. After several days of eating Arabic food, we had a hankering for Mickey Ds. We stopped at the downtown Dubai McDonalds and walked into a crowded restaurant. Friendly Filipino countermen took our orders. Arab families were enjoying the same Happy Meals complete with the toys that American families were enjoying. The women, covered head to toe, did not let their burkas get in the way of enjoying their fries. They just slipped them up and under their veils. I discovered that a Big Mac is a Big Mac all over the world.

We came to the Emirates/Oman border and crossed over with no red tape. The Emirati immigration officer asked

Forrest, who looked the most Arabic, a few questions in Arabic, and Forrest was "busted." He had told me before the trip he spoke Arabic. He didn't speak a lick of Arabic and couldn't understand it either. He just sat there mute with not even a flicker of Arabic language recognition on his face. It was like when you checked off "bilingual" on your job application, "English and Japanese," and your HR interviewer was Japanese. Cyrus, of Persian descent, didn't have a clue either. The extent of my Arabic was *salaam*. The officer politely switched to English. The young Arab wanted to talk awhile to some young Americans, and they humored him by talking about nothing in particular. He passed us through to Oman with a smile. A few hundred yards later at the Omani gate, the Omani immigration officer said our passports did not contain the Emirates stamp of exit. During all of that camaraderie the young Emirati failed to exit stamp our passports. We had to go miles ahead to a turn around, explain to the new Omani officer that we were attempting to go back to Emirates for our exit stamp. He had to talk to our first guy by phone, and we finally got through. We found another turn around and headed back to the Emirates gate. A new guard stamped our documents, and then we went forward to the Omani gate where we had to pay $50 each to enter Oman. After this ring around the rosy and an extra hour and a half, we headed to our rooms in the ancient capital city of Muscat. Our ground agent rented us three rooms in her apartment building and provided breakfast. Our landlady was unique. She looked like she wore a permanent Halloween clown costume with her garish makeup, frizzy bright red hair, and hilariously loud colored print dresses. She was obviously educated and cultured, but eccentric would be an understatement. She had photographs of her beautiful actress daughter who had starred in *The Hunger Games*. Cyrus photographed our oddball landlady and used it to prank us every day, pretending to show us pictures of rare birds. I fell for it every day providing entertainment for Cyrus and Forrest during those long desert rides. Once we paid her, she asked for more later, saying there were extra expenses, a shameless custom I had run into before in Jordan. We used her apartment as a base of operation for three days as we birded the city environs and beyond. Forrest had once birded this area extensively when he was a teenager more than a decade ago. He was in disbelief and saddened how it had changed with excessive development and loss of wetlands and green spaces. The best bird for me was a chance sighting of a Little Curlew spied from the Muscat Bridge, a rare bird that had managed to escape me over my six decades of birding. A stop along the Northern shores of the Sea of Oman revealed a breathtaking display of wintering shorebirds and gulls, stretching as far as the eye could see. More than a million birds occupied fifteen miles of shoreline, making up the largest collection I had ever seen. We identified thirteen species of shorebirds and nine species of gulls. Of special interest were hundreds of Crab-Plovers and uncountable thousands of Black-tailed Godwits.

Figure 22-18. Gulls and terns, Sea of Oman.

We birded our way south along the Salalah Highway to the Muntasar Oasis. The Oasis was only a five-acre green dot in thousands of square miles of desert white, but it was the most reliable location for the Hypocolius. On our way to Muntasar, we stopped to examine a frankincense forest. Oman was cultivating frankincense as a commercial product for export. It comes from the sap of the tree, is gummy, and has a mildly sweet pleasant aroma. My trivia question to the guys, which Cyrus nailed, was the following: What were the other two gifts to the baby Jesus from the Three Wise Men?

Figure 22-19. Commercial frankincense forest, Oman.

Oman was not as developed as the Emirates. The landscape was flatter and contained longer stretches of desert. Large herds of freely roaming one-humped camels appeared on the horizon like scenes from *Lawrence of Arabia*. For fun, we began counting the herds but stopped somewhere around one hundred.

Figure 22-20. Omanis with camels, Salalah Highway.

A Greater Hoopoe-Lark put on a fabulous leaping courting display complete with song as he was trying his best to attract a wife.

Figure 22-21. Displaying Greater Hoopoe-Lark, Oman.

Thermals supported many hundreds of raptors, sixteen different species in all, with Steppe Eagles predominating.

Oman was remarkably free of roadside litter. Dump trucks filled with trash and garbage lined up in single orderly file for miles patiently waiting their turn to jettison their cargo into the city landfill. The drivers used the wait time to palaver with their mates. Everybody smoked. Near the city of Salalah in the Jabal Qama Mountain Range in the Dhofar Region, we passed by the putative burial tomb of the biblical Job. His burial site is also claimed by Turkey and Lebanon.

Continuing on the Salalah highway, we finally arrived at the Muntasar Oasis and Qitbit Hotel in the early evening and immediately scouted for the Hypocolius. All was quiet so we decided to try early the next morning. We stayed in the small comfortable Qitbit hotel right on the oasis grounds. The next morning at daybreak I bounded out of bed, gathered the guys before breakfast, and headed straight to the oasis tree line. I had a really good feeling about finding it. I heard some soft melodic phrases coming from a copse of trees at the edge of the oasis. I followed the sound, and within minutes I was looking at a male and two female Hypocolius. Photos followed, and we all watched them for a while.

Figure 22-22. Hypocolius, Muntasar Oasis, Oman.

They did look like large waxwings, gray, smooth, and sleek. I suppose they got tired of watching us, and flew across the oasis and out of sight. Later that afternoon we refound them and watched their behavior some more. We returned in the evening, but they were gone, roosting in another location. The next morning we found them again. This was family number 228, my penultimate family, with only one more to go.

WORLD 7,490 • ABA 787

CHINA 2012 & PRZEWALSKI'S ROSEFINCH

For almost 130 years, the Przewalski's Rosefinch (pronounced Sheh-vahl-skees), variously known as Przewalski's Rosefinch, Pink-tailed Rosefinch, Pink-tailed Bunting, or just plain P-finch, had been lumped into the same family with all the other Asian rosefinches. It certainly looked and sounded like one. Examination of the anatomy of the bird showed it had a tenth primary feather unknown in any of the other rosefinches and buntings. This finding became extremely important in its final classification. There were some other outward differences like a thinner bill and a long, graduated pink tail that got some ornithologists thinking that this species belonged in a family of its own, but it was that tenth primary, unknown in related families that spurred more investigation. Little was known of its natural life history, mating, nesting, and vocalizations. The odd specimens in museum drawers were not giving of their DNA back then. The bird tour leader Ben King, a specialist in Asian birds, was one of those interested in the species, and reported his field information to Jeff Groth at the American Museum of Natural History in New York. Groth, using new molecular identification methods, closely analyzed the DNA from the toe skin of one of the museum's specimens and proved the P-finch was unlike any rosefinch or bunting and stood alone in the bird bush of evolution. In fact it was as old or older in evolution than the finches. Clements accepted this fact in 2007, and the ABA rubber-stamped it in 2008. It was recorded on my 2002 ABA China tour, but I didn't remember seeing it. Perhaps only Paul Lehman saw it and put it on the trip list. Anyway, I had to go back to see it to claim, without any doubt, all of the world's bird families.

Ben King, my go-to guy for Asian bird tours, was retired from leading. I sent a message to Susan Myers, another one of my favorite tour guides and an expert on Asian birds, asking her to lead Susan and me to the P-finch in Western China. We agreed to meet in September in Qinghai Province.

I had two requirements, a comfortable four-wheel drive vehicle for those long drives up into the high elevations and an English speaking Chinese guide to answer my many questions about Chinese history and culture. No problem. I knew the high elevations that my P-finch frequented were going to be a problem—but never would have guessed how much of a problem.

Neither our driver nor our Chinese guide spoke English, nor did they understand it. Susan Myers, who was fluent in several Asian languages, did not speak Chinese. My Susan and I are language impaired and did not have a clue. The first few restaurants chosen by our Chinese guide were stink holes. They were indescribably filthy with a week of grease on the unwashed tables and mounds of chewed chicken bones on the floors. There were no hand washing facilities and no toilets, and I knew it would be Cipro time soon. I noticed our driver, whom I called "Driver," never ate with us. Was this some kind of Chinese custom or driver protocol, not eating with your clients? Before we sat down for the next meal I followed Driver and saw him going into another restaurant, decorated with green paint on the outside. I asked him about it through sign language. He pointed to his Muslim cap and motioned the sign for eating along with the Chinese words, *chi chi*. Oh; he was a Weigar, a Muslim, one of the fifty-six Chinese minorities. Weigars make up about ten percent of the Chinese population and are much disliked by the Han Chinese. At our next meal, we all followed Driver to his restaurant choice. It had the Muslim green paint on the outside. The restaurant was very clean, had washbasins and toilets, and the food was fresh and delicious. We only ate in Weigar restaurants from that day forward.

I am convinced that the absence of hand washing by the Chinese, their utter lack of personal hygiene, and their complete disregard for public health in their polluted streams, air, and soil are the major source of the world's flu epidemics. All of the mass viral epidemics of the last twenty years, Swine

Flu, Bird Flu, SARS, and God knows what else, have emanated from China.

Industrial pollution goes unregulated. Instead of regulating the outpouring of soot from their smokestacks, they wear masks. All of that particulate matter is blown to the four corners of the earth. If you have friends complaining about the EPA, ask them to live in China for a month. They overcrowd their workplaces in poorly ventilated and unhealthy conditions. Their fish, whatever is left of them, are poisoned with chemicals like heavy metals. There are no tangible signs of a public health system to effectively and safely dispose of human waste, a source of contamination and reinfection of their people. Animal waste and infected animals are recirculating through their agricultural system because they feed these sick animals to healthy animals and use their dead contaminated bodies for fertilizer. Their child labor practices, which subject youth to long hours in hazardous working conditions, affect the health of future generations.

Altitude illness still remains a medical mystery. It can affect anyone, even the most experienced climbers, at any time over eight thousand feet. It is a genetic trait, and there is no test for it. Training and physical fitness does not lower one's risk. Previous bouts of altitude illness (AMS, Acute Mountain Sickness) are not a predictor for future bouts or severity. Most of the symptoms are mild in AMS such as nausea, headache, shortness of breath, and vertigo. However, a small group of people get serious neurological complications like stroke from cerebral edema. Pulmonary edema (HAPE, High Altitude Pulmonary Edema), a serious life-threatening condition, can also occur in a few cases and demands immediate escape to lower elevations. Angina and heart attacks can occur in a small percentage of people from the low atmospheric oxygen tension. Once in Chile, at eighteen thousand feet, I experienced an angina attack, my first ever, a warning sign that I had a potential coronary problem. Bloating is an annoying and common problem as the gut gasses double in volume from the low atmospheric pressure, and impede the diaphragm from freely moving up and down, adding to the symptoms of shortness of breath. Increased UV light, cold, and lack of humidity complicate everything. I brought along four small canisters of oxygen in anticipation of the thin air, but the Chinese airline officials had confiscated them. They simply had never seen them before and did not want to take a chance that they might combust on the airplane. We started our journey from Xining at eight thousand feet for three days hoping to acclimatize.

Acetazolamide, an ion exchange diuretic, is recommended by some to prevent altitude illness, but past experiences have shown it does not help me and only leads to more frequent urination and a nasty metallic taste in my mouth. On September 9, we ascended to 12,500 feet to reach the Menyuan Preserve, Qinghai Provence, the home of Przewalski's Rosefinch. Our Chinese guide, who spoke no English, of course, kept gesturing to various sites to stop for the bird. We knew he was wrong by descriptions we had read in trip reports. He was pointing to bare open spaces while we were looking for a stretch of low growing trees. When we hit a stand of stunted trees, we began walking and listening.

I heard a faint bunting-like song and spotted a small flock of what looked like finches. They had long tails, were streaked, had small thin bills but not a speck of pink was showing anywhere.

I called to Susan, our guide. "Are these the Przewalski's?"

"Yes," she answered after looking through her bins.

"Are you sure?"

"Yes, they are females and young males."

Finally we saw an adult male, with the expected pink underparts and tail. This guy was the real deal, and I could make a positive identification. I snapped a couple of photos of the flock, but the adult male escaped my camera lens. Jubilation! My last family!

Figure 22-23. Przewalski's Rosefinch, immature male or female, Menyuan Preserve, Qinghai.

We gave high fives all around and lingered for a long while to savor the moment. The Gangshika Snow Peak with the sun corruscating off its ice and snow covered peak radiated its beauty behind us, a broad expanse of emerald mountain grassland in front of us. The P-finches moved on, and we left that memorable spot for our van. I thanked Susan Myers for her expert guidance.

Figure 22-24. Gangshika Snow Peak, Qinghai.

Figure 22-25. Qinghai grasslands.

My immediate quest was over, but we still had ten more days of birding. Over the next few days we climbed steadily to over fifteen thousand feet. We saw snowfinches and accentors but the breathing got harder, and Susan and I both developed a bronchitic cough. Even at that lofty elevation, there was dust and dirt in the air from all of the road construction. We both became nauseated and headachy. Ibuprofen took care of my headache, but Susan's became steadily worse, increasing into an excruciating unremitting pain, pounding her temples on every heartbeat. I became alarmed, very alarmed. I began monitoring her vital signs. I reached into my pharmaceutical bag and gave her hydrocodone around the clock. I also started steroids to reduce any cerebral edema. Both of our dry hacking coughs interrupted what little sleep we were getting. We were both taking bronchodilators. Our room was on the third floor, and there were no elevators or porters to help with our bags. Every step was a major effort. The Chinese hotel beds were as hard as plywood. No amount of complaining to the manager would change it. They were so stingy with everything—denying us extra towels, soap, and toilet paper. I found myself sneaking into other rooms, stealing the mattresses to pile onto our own beds. We were sick, exhausted, and having no fun. We had already seen our target bird. *What is the sense of continuing this madness?* I made a command decision and asked Susan Myers into our room. We had to go down to lower elevations, and go now! We were both sick, and my Susan was seriously ill. Myers understood and said we would leave immediately but—and it was a big but. We first had to go up to cross the mountain pass for two days before we could go down. We had to chance it. We left immediately and started our long drive across the mountain pass. That next night was the most miserable of my birding experience. We were still at about fifteen thousand feet but a day closer to our descent. Susan's condition was unchanged, and I was vomiting. We were both awake all night. I kept checking her pulse, respiratory rate, alertness, and holding my ear to her chest to listen for any telltale sounds of crepitation, the dreaded sign of early pulmonary edema. There were none. Thank heaven she held steady, and the next day we sped down to eight thousand feet and recovery. The cost to me for the P-finch was almost irreparable.

It wasn't until a year after my return that I saw it in the ABA lists. I was one of three Americans to see all of the world's bird families! I checked the list on *Surfbird* and there were a couple of Europeans who had also seen them all. A few months later, I discovered in *Birding* magazine that I was actually the first American, having accomplished it a year before the others. I enjoyed that distinction for almost two years. In August, 2014, the ABA released its new lists. There were a whopping five new families described, four of them in New Guinea. A quick check of my computerized records revealed I had seen those four on my previous New Guinea trips. I just pulled them out of escrow, and they counted toward my new 233 total. Sometimes one has to go back to go forward. At this writing, another American has surfaced with 233 also. The fifth new family, the Spotted Wren-Babbler is in Bhutan. It is waiting for me.

Clements now recognizes 10,400 species of birds in the world, divided into 234 families. Approximately twelve percent of these, including ninety-one in the United States, are endangered or threatened with extinction in this century. My goal remains to join the thousands of impassioned and committed conservationists in the world to save as many of these species as possible. I want to see and enjoy as many as I can during the remainder of my life and create a lasting conservation legacy for all of our children and the unborn future generations. We must continue to work without tiring, without doubt, and without frustration. We must not quit.

There is no finish line.

WORLD 7,800 • ABA 791

ACKNOWLEDGEMENTS

The writing of *No Finish Line* took about a year with the usual breaks, writer's block and flurries of cerebral activity. It involved careful reflection on the influences on my life, both subtle and powerful.

My parents, Gilbert and Leona, placed no obstacles in front of me but instead created a wonderful childhood filled with fun, small adventures and guideposts for living. The acquisition of knowledge for knowledge's sake was high on the list. Self-reliance, owning your actions, and "facing the music" for your errors were all Master family requirements.

My parents provided me with the means to obtain a college and medical degree. I acknowledge the crucial role medical school, President Tom Rowland, pediatrician Dr. Tom Santucci Sr., and otorhinolaryngologist Dr. Harry Stein played in my acceptance to medical school.

During the growth of the MEDCenters and Health Power, I acknowledge the role of my most important employee, Sheryl Cardwell of Columbus, whose unfailing loyalty, expertise, devotion, and watchful eye contributed greatly to my success.

I acknowledge the birding expertise of neotropical bird leader, Forrest Rowland, African bird specialist, Christian Boix, and Asian bird experts Ben King and Susan Myers. I went on many birding trips with these guides, and their professionalism and bird knowledge gained me thousands of new birds to my world list.

My capable and loyal, longtime assistant Sandie Lloyd helped me with the technological aspects of producing this book. Sandie also served as a sounding board for my ideas and writing style. My wife, Susan, provided a feminine reader's point of view and injected her soft and easy manner into many of my stories. She was invaluable in providing her opinions about the many ideas I wanted to convey.

The process of publishing this book took four months from the actual finish of the manuscript. I acknowledge the input from my personal editor, Christine Buchendahl. Christine produced a professional edit with many corrections of my misuse of commas and quotation marks. She gave me supportive comments along the way. She pointed out my predilection for the use of the British spelling of certain words and corrected my spelling Anglophilia. When finished, I presented a polished autobiography to my publisher, Karen Scarpulla, of Little White Dog Press.

I extend a big thank you to my valued friend, Bill Thompson III, co-owner, editor, and publisher of *Birdwatcher's Digest* for graciously writing his generous foreword.

With a few exceptions, I took all of the photos in this book. I want to thank Sandy Komito for his gift to me in 1991 of the Alaskan bird pictures. I acknowledge the gift of copies of the fantastic drawings illustrating the differences between the Ivory-billed Woodpecker and the Pileated Woodpecker by world-famous artist and friend Julie Zickefoose.

I acknowledge and thank my publisher, Karen Scarpulla, and her entire team for professionally and diligently pursuing a finished product for the public to enjoy. Karen gave me invaluable insight into the process of publishing, constant personal and literary support, and innovative suggestions without tampering with my writing style or ideas. There is no finish line for Karen.

I thank all of the many bird tour leaders and birders who

helped me find, identify and enjoy my 7,800 world bird species.

Finally, and surprisingly to some, I thank all of the fraudsters, con men, and manipulators that early success brought to me when I was a young doctor and businessman *before* I hit my peak earning years. By the time I was forty, I had learned how to say "no" and ask decision makers to say "yes."

INDEX: BIRDS

H

I

J

INDEX: PEOPLE & PLACES

B

C

Made in the USA
Lexington, KY
14 May 2015